LEISURE SERVICES WITH THE ELDERLY

LEISURE SERVICES WITH THE ELDERLY

JOSEPH D. TEAFF, Ed.D.

Professor, Department of Recreation,
Southern Illinois University at Carbondale,
Carbondale, Illinois

With **51** illustrations

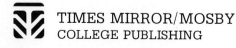 TIMES MIRROR/MOSBY
COLLEGE PUBLISHING

ST. LOUIS • SANTA CLARA • TORONTO   1985

Editor: Nancy K. Roberson
Editorial assistant: Kathy M. Sedovic
Editing supervisor: Judi Wolken
Manuscript editor: April Nauman
Design: Jeanne Bush
Production: Linda R. Stalnaker, Margaret B. Bridenbaugh

Library of Congress Cataloging in Publication Data

Teaff, Joseph D.
  Leisure services with the elderly.
  Includes bibliographies and index.
    1. Aged—Recreation—Study and teaching—United
States. 2. Aged—Services for—United States.
3. Gerontology. I. Title.
GV184.T4   1985   790.1'926   84-9867
ISBN 0-8016-4893-9

AC/VH/VH 9 8 7 6 5 4 3 2 1   05/A/615

I wish to dedicate this book to my parents
Joseph F. Teaff (1905-1970) and **Corinne Sphire Teaff**
who taught me very early in life that older persons should be valued
not just for what they have done but for what they are.

Preface

Students of leisure services, as well as students of gerontology, require a background in leisure services with the elderly because *leisure is an integral part of the life-style of the elderly.* Educating individuals to provide leisure services with the elderly is expected to become more important because of the growing size of the elderly population, the availability of leisure settings and services, and both the current and potential job markets for trained leisure service personnel. The purpose of this book is to introduce students to the emerging and exciting area of leisure services with the elderly.

This book is designed as a textbook for undergraduate- and undergraduate/graduate-level courses in leisure services with the elderly, but it will also serve as a resource for graduate students and leisure service providers. The information is presented in a concise form easily read by the average undergraduate student. The use of current literature and research studies, case histories, and illustrations makes this text interesting and enjoyable.

This text has several features that other texts in the area of leisure and aging do not have. Current literature related to gerontological theory, research, and practice is integrated in a comprehensive, concise, and organized format easily understood by the average undergraduate student. Procedures for developing leisure services in a variety of community and institutional settings or in specific program areas are presented, thus providing students with concrete, specific information about programming. Future leisure services and the elderly are discussed to alert students to anticipated changes in the elderly population and leisure services. Extensive references and suggested readings at the end of chapters assist the instructor in lecture development and students in reading assignments and term papers. Finally, students are alerted to job opportunities in community and institutional leisure service settings. The book further benefits from my 17-year history of involvement with the elderly as an educator (Columbia University, Texas Woman's University, and Southern Illinois University at Carbondale), researcher (Philadelphia Geriatric Center), and service provider (Duke University Information and Counseling Service for Older Persons, North Texas Area Agency on Aging Advisory Council, Park and Recreation Board member advisor to Denton, Texas, Senior Center), and advisory council chairman for SPAN (Service Program for Aging Needs, Denton, Texas).

PEDAGOGICAL FEATURES

The philosophical orientation of this text is grounded in the basic principles that aging is a natural life cycle process and that leisure services are absolutely vital if there is to be enjoyment in life throughout the life cycle. The book reflects this philosophical orientation in its organization. Part One introduces the student to aging and leisure through an examination of background, physiological, psychological, and social characteristics of the elderly, followed by a chapter on social theories of aging, and closing with a chapter examining the research on leisure and the aged and concluding with a theoretical framework with particular application to leisure services. Part Two examines leisure service settings that form a continuum from community to institution (voluntary associations and volunteerism, senior centers, planned community housing, and institutions), with each chapter highlighting procedures for developing leisure services in each setting of the continuum. Part Three addresses the subject of special leisure services in four domains: sensory-motor (exercise), affective (creative arts), cognitive (education), and environmental (outdoor recreation); each chapter focuses on step-by-step procedures for delivering special leisure services for the domain under consideration. Part Four orients the student to the projected characteristics of the future elderly and future leisure services for the elderly.

This book employs a variety of pedagogical aids to facilitate its use by students and teachers. *Chapter outlines and introductions* in each chapter provide overviews of the main topics to be presented. *Figures, tables, and illustrations* are important in each chapter; these visual materials are keyed to the content of the chapter. The *summaries* at the end of each chapter capsulize the chapter's major contents. *References and suggested readings* after each chapter are listings of references cited in the chapter and recommended readings from books and the periodical literature. Six *appendixes* of practical interest contain lists of state agencies on aging, state arts agencies, national organizations pertaining to the elderly, periodicals on aging, and programmatic resources (books and periodicals, films and slide presentations, and phonograph records) and a summary of the Older Americans Act of 1978. A *subject index* is included to facilitate location of information in the body of the text.

ACKNOWLEDG-MENTS

This textbook, while appearing to be the work of one person, is in actuality the work of many persons. I owe a great debt to a number of professors and colleagues from the University of North Carolina at Chapel Hill (H. Douglas Sessoms, Thomas Stein, and Mary E. Fortune), Columbia University (Elliott M. Avedon, Richard Kraus, Ruth Bennett, Comilda Weinstock), and the Philadelphia Geriatric Center (M. Powell Lawton and Morton Kleban), who helped to shape through word and example my teaching, research, and service skills in leisure services and gerontology.

My colleagues at Southern Illinois University at Carbondale were a constant source of support. Current and former faculty from the Department of Recreation kindly allowed me to have some weekly writing days unencumbered by departmental responsibilities: William Abernathy, John Allen, Leonard Cleary, Regina Glover, Walter Kinney, Jean Loveland, Douglas McEwen, and Owen Smith. Special thanks must go to William E. O'Brien, the former chairman of the Department of Recreation, for his very special interest, and to Donald Beggs, dean of the College of Education, who very generously acted as my advisor from the very beginning of this undertaking.

Reviewers are an absolutely essential component of any successful writing venture. I was very fortunate to have very fine teacher-scholars to review the manuscript: Robert M. Beland, Ph.D., University of Florida; Barbara D. Sanchez, M.A., T.R.S., North Texas State University; Shirley J. Kammeyer, Ph.D., California State University at Sacramento; Ann Gowans, M.S., formerly of the University of Missouri at Columbia; Andrew Weiner, Ed.D., University of Kentucky; and Carol Cooper, Ed.D., University of Northern Iowa. In addition, chapter-by-chapter reviews were done by two classes of upper division undergraduates enrolled in my course on leisure and aging at Southern Illinois University at Carbondale. Earlier chapters were reviewed by Maureen Barrett, Randy Bettis, Laura Dyer, Laura Fickel, Monica Lee, Mary Beth Logue, Michael Nolan, Joseph Stafford, Patricia Stang, Cynthia Terao, and Bridget Truitt. Later chapters were reviewed by Curt Baer, Sondra Cocking, Colleen Lesniak, Roni Jankowski, Jeanine Janos, Yvonne Menke, Marla Minsky, Richard Murphy, Susan Stapleton, Rhonda Ubben, Barbara Weisbruch, Tammie Widloski, and Brenda Yusko. These students provided invaluable insights concerning substantive and stylistic issues as the manuscript was being written.

I was also fortunate to benefit from the expertise of outstanding graduate assistants and typists. Graduate assistants Sue Bulmer and Nancy Kaufman spent hours researching reference materials and providing expertise based on their years of experience as providers of leisure services with the elderly. Typists Mary Falaster and Loretta Koch were very conscientious in their attention to detail and provided reviewers with clean copy to make their jobs easier.

The staff of Times Mirror/Mosby College Publishing skillfully guided this complex publishing task with expertise and enthusiasm. Special thanks go to my editor, Nancy Roberson, who provided the efficient organization essential to a project of this magnitude. I wish to acknowledge in a special way the work of Kathy Sedovic, editorial assistant to Nancy Roberson, whose attention to detail and good humor saw me through some difficult times, and the fine work of April Nauman and Judi Wolken, manuscript editors, who contributed immeasurably to the readability of this text. Finally, thanks to all the behind-the-scenes production staff.

I am deeply grateful for the loving support and encouragement of my wife, Evelyn, and our two children, Kevin and Karen. What a delight they are.

Joseph D. Teaff

Contents

**PART FOUR
The future
elderly and
leisure services**

PART ONE
Introduction to aging and leisure

Quality leisure services with the elderly very much depend on the quality of the personnel providing these services. Leisure service providers have been criticized for their lack of understanding of aging and the relationship between leisure and aging. Chapter 1 examines characteristics of the elderly through an overview of the background, physiological, psychological, and social characteristics of older persons. Chapter 2 is an overview of some of the more significant social theories of aging that have emerged in recent years. Chapter 3 reviews conceptualizations of leisure, leisure through the life cycle, and leisure and the elderly. These three chapters serve as the foundation on which following chapters are built. Considerable effort has been made to condense this information into a readable and concise form, yet to document it fully with references and resources for additional reading.

Characteristics of the elderly

Demographic characteristics
Population growth
Life expectancy
Sex ratio
Marital status
Living arrangements
Place of residence
Racial and ethnic composition

Physiological characteristics
Brain and nervous system
Heart and circulatory system
Lungs and pulmonary system
Digestive system
Excretory system
Skeletal system
Muscular system
Endocrine system
Skin

Psychological characteristics
Sensory processes
Psychomotor performance
Mental functioning
Psychological disorders

Social characteristics
Education
Economic status
Health status
Political status
Religion
Family

Summary

The elderly are becoming a larger and more influential element in American society. The decreasing birthrate in the 1960s coupled with increasing life expectancy are resulting in a demographic shift toward a greater percentage of elderly in the total population. The number of elderly with economic and political resources is growing; government officials are becoming more sensitive to their voting strength and political influence. Colleges and universities are creating educational programs tailored to the interests and needs of older persons. Researchers in specialties such as medicine, physiology, psychology, sociology, and other disciplines are increasingly focusing their research attention on old age. Thus government, organizations, and professions have moved from little or no interest to a very active interest in the elderly.

Despite growing interest in and knowledge of the elderly, older persons are still the subject of myths (erroneous generalizations) and stereotypes (oversimplifications). Although problems with health and income may become more pronounced as persons age, the elderly are still a diverse group because of varied life conditions and are likely to become more diverse in the future. To focus on the frail elderly, those in nursing homes, and the impoverished is a serious misperception—the elderly possess many widely differing characteristics. The elderly are not a homogeneous group despite similarities of age.

The study of the characteristics of the elderly may not immediately remove all myths and stereotypes, but it may counteract, with evidence, the more harmful ones. Palmore (1977) developed a short quiz of 25 true or false questions to determine the amount of factual information that differing segments of society possessed and to attack some of the common myths and stereotypes. The quiz included statements such as:

1. The majority of older persons have incomes below the poverty level.
2. The majority of older persons are socially isolated and lonely.

TABLE 1-1   **The total aging population in the United States**

Year	Number of persons age 65 and over (thousands)	Percentage of total population	Percentage of increase from preceding decade
1900	3,099	4.1	—
1910	3,986	4.3	28.6
1920	4,929	4.7	23.7
1930	6,705	5.4	36.0
1940	9,031	6.8	34.7
1950	12,397	8.2	37.3
1960	16,675	9.2	34.5
1970	20,087	9.8	20.4
1980	25,544	11.3	27.1
Projections:			
1990	29,824	12.2	16.7
2000	31,822	12.2	6.7
2010	34,837	12.7	9.5
2020	45,102	15.5	29.5

From U.S. Bureau of the Census: Census of population, 1970, detailed characteristics, Final Report PC(1)-D1, Washington, D.C., 1973, U.S. Government Printing Office; and U.S. Bureau of the Census: Statistical abstracts of the United States, Washington, D.C., 1981, U.S Government Printing Office.

TABLE 1-2   **Life expectancy at birth: 1920 to 1975**

Year	Total	Male	Female
1920	54.1	53.6	54.6
1930	59.7	58.1	61.6
1950	68.2	65.6	71.1
1955	69.6	66.7	72.8
1960	69.7	66.6	73.1
1965	70.2	66.8	73.7
1970	70.9	67.1	74.8
1971	71.1	67.4	75.0
1972	71.1	67.4	75.1
1973	71.3	67.6	75.3
1974	71.9	68.2	75.9
1975	72.5	68.7	76.5

From U.S. Bureau of the Census: Statistical abstracts of the United States, Washington, D.C., 1977, U.S. Government Printing Office.

3. Intelligence declines with age.
4. Older workers are not as good as younger workers.
5. The ability to learn declines with age.
6. Rates of mental illness increase with age.
7. Most older persons are set in their ways and are unable to change.
8. Most older persons have no capacity for or interest in sexual behavior.

It is hoped that this chapter can help remove some of the myths and stereotypes surrounding the elderly. However, there are many gaps in our knowledge about the elderly and the aging process, and even some of our current thinking may eventually be contradicted by newer evidence. This chapter is an examination of the characteristics of the elderly. It is divided into sections describing the demographic, physiological, psychological, and social aspects of the elderly and the implications of these aspects for leisure services with them.

DEMOGRAPHIC CHARACTERISTICS

The following are some demographic characteristics of the elderly in the United States, based on 1980 census data when available. It must be remembered that the elderly are not a homogeneous group whose diversity can be truly captured in a series of profiles.

Population growth

Using 65 or older as the operational definition of an older person, it is evident that the number and percentage of older persons in the United States have increased dramatically during the twentieth century. Table 1-1 indicates that there were slightly more than 3 million persons over 65 in 1900 and more than 25 million in 1980, rising from 4.1 percent of the population to 11.3 percent (U.S. Bureau of the Census, 1973a, 1981). It is projected that by the year 2000 there will be in excess of 30 million persons older than 65 in the United States and that they will comprise more than 12 percent of the population (U.S. Bureau of the Census, 1973a, p. 3; 1976b, p. 3).

The composition of the aged population has also changed. For example, in 1930 29 percent of the aged were 75 years of age or older, but in 1975 the 75 or older age group was 38 percent of the aged (Harris, 1978), indicating that the aged population is aging. These differences are due to the changes in birthrate, mortality, and life expectancy; the factor responsible for the greatest growth is life expectancy.

Life expectancy

The increased population growth has been accompanied by increased life expectancy. In 1900 life expectancy in the United States was about 49 years; by 1981 this had risen to almost 74 years (U.S. Bureau of the Census, 1983).

Women have experienced a greater increase in life expectancy than men. Table 1-2 shows that in 1920 the life expectancy for women in the United States was 54.6 years and 53.6 years for men, but by 1975 the life expectancy for women had increased to more than 76 years, compared to almost 69 years for men (U.S. Bureau of the Census, 1977).

Sex ratio

There is a change in the sex ratio during the later years of life, since the average woman lives longer than the average man. Table 1-3 indicates that in 1975 for the age group 65 years and over the ratio was 69.3 males for every 100 females; for the age group 75 years and over, the sex ratio was 58.4 males for every 100 females (Siegel, 1976, p. 13). This disparity means that the friendship and companionship of men their own age are increasingly denied to women.

TABLE 1-3   **Sex ratios (males per 100 females)**

Age range	1900	1930	1960	1970	1975
All ages	104.4	102.5	97.8	95.8	95.3
Under 15 years	102.1	102.8	103.4	103.9	104.1
15 to 24 years	98.3	98.1	101.4	102.2	102.2
25 to 44 years	109.1	101.7	96.9	96.9	97.3
45 to 54 years	113.9	109.4	97.2	93.3	93.6
55 to 64 years	106.5	108.3	93.7	89.7	89.6
75 to 84 years	NA	NA	77.4	65.9	61.5
85 years and over	NA	NA	63.8	53.2	48.5
65 years and over	102.0	100.4	82.6	72.0	69.3
75 years and over	96.3	91.8	75.0	63.3	58.4

From Siegel, J.: Demographic aspects of aging and the older population in the United States, Current Population Reports: Special Studies, Series P-23, U.S. Bureau of the Census Pub. No. 59, Washington, D.C., 1976, U.S. Government Printing Office.
NA, not available.

TABLE 1-4   **Living arrangements of persons 65 and over by sex**

	Male	Female
In families	79.8	56.1
Head of family	76.1	8.5
Wife	—	35.0
Other relative	3.7	12.7
Living alone	14.8	37.3
Living with unrelated individuals	1.2	1.2
In an institution	4.2	5.3

From U.S. Bureau of the Census: Demographic aspects of aging and the older population in the United States, Current Population Reports, Series P-23, Pub. No. 59, Washington, D.C., 1976, U.S. Government Printing Office.

Southern Illinoisan Staff Photo by Jerry Lower

What are the implications for leisure services in a female-dominated older population with more unmarried women living in their own homes and constituting an increasingly greater percentage of the more sparsely populated rural states?

Marital status

Most older males are married (about 79 percent), and most older females are widowed; only 39 percent of older women are married (Harris, 1978). The percentage of older persons that are married decreases with age—a result of the differences in life expectancy of males and females. For example, after age 75 and older 69 percent of men and only 22 percent of women are married (Harris, 1978). As a result of sex differences in widowhood, older women are more likely than older men to live alone.

Living arrangements

The sex differences in marital status are reflected in the living arrangements of older men and women. Table 1-4 presents data showing that 79.8 percent of older men and 56.1 percent of older women live with families; 14.8 percent of older men live alone, whereas 37.3 percent of older women live alone; and only about 4 percent of older persons live in institutions (U.S. Bureau of the Census, 1976a, p. 48). Most older persons (70 percent) live independently in homes they own rather than rent (Carp, 1976).

Place of residence

There are considerable variations in the concentration of older Americans by state. In 1980 there were seven states with more than 1 million people 65 and older: California (2.4 million), New York (2.2 million), Florida (1.7 million), Pennsylvania (1.5 million), Texas (1.4 million), Illinois (1.3 million), and Ohio (1.2 million) (U.S. Bureau of the Census, 1983), although the percentage of elderly in the population of each state is not exceptional. States with the highest percentage of older people are Florida (17.3 percent), Arkansas (13.6 percent), Rhode Island (13.4 percent), Iowa (13.3 percent), Missouri (13.2 percent), South Dakota (13.2 percent), and Nebraska (13.1 percent) (U.S. Bureau of the Census, 1981).

Older Americans are more likely to live in metropolitan areas, and just more than half live outside the central city. Black and Hispanic elderly are more likely than older whites to occupy the central city (U.S. Bureau of Census, 1983).

Racial and ethnic composition

In 1982 about 12 percent of whites, 8 percent of blacks, 6 percent of Asians and Pacific Islanders, 5 percent of American Indians, and 5 percent of Hispanics were 65 years of age and older. During the last decade (1970 to 1980), the elderly white population grew by about 25 percent; the elderly black population grew by about 33 percent. The black population grew faster than the white population as a result of higher fertility levels and gains in life expectancy (U.S. Bureau of the Census, 1983).

PHYSIOLOGICAL CHARACTER-ISTICS

Physiological changes often accompany the aging process. These changes are usually most noticeable and most feared because they are indications of decline. However, it must be emphasized that declines are often gradual and often do not significantly affect functioning. It must also be emphasized that many of the physiological declines are not inevitable but may be turned around by a life-style that includes good nutrition, exercise, and other good health practices.

Brain and nervous system

Brain and nervous system changes often occur with increasing age. The loss of brain cells results in diminished brain size and weight. With advancing age there is also the loss of cells from the nerves that convey messages to and from the brain. This loss of nerve cells means that messages travel at a slower rate, resulting in a slower response rate in older individuals (Bromley, 1974; Shock, 1974; Solomon, Shock, and Aughenbaugh, 1970; Weg, 1976; Woodruff, 1975).

Physical damage to the brain or physical impairment of brain function can result in organic brain syndrome. The most notable change with this type of disorder occurs in orientation and memory; individuals become disoriented as to time and place or are unable to remember names or recent events. For many individuals this disorder is mild, requiring only adjustments in life-style to allow them to continue leading independent lives, but for others the disorder is so severe that they have to be hospitalized or institutionalized. A more complete description of organic brain syndrome appears on pp. 14-16.

Heart and circulatory system

The heart pumps oxygenated blood and other nutrients through the body's system of arteries and veins. Reduced heart output, reduced elasticity of the large arteries (hardening of the arteries), and general deterioration of blood vessels can interrupt blood flow to the heart and brain, leading to high blood pressure and increased risk of stroke. Exercise in conjunction with a proper program of nutrition and a health-conscious life-style can bring about increased blood flow, lower blood pressure, an improved cardiovascular system, and a reduction in the risk of heart attack (Harris and Frankel, 1977).

Lungs and pulmonary system

Lung tissue absorbs oxygen that is carried through the bloodstream to various parts of the body. With increasing age the lung capacity becomes smaller and the lung tissue more scarred, thus reducing the expansion capacity of the lungs and the ability of the lung tissue to absorb oxygen. The decrease in oxygen can cause a lack of strength and endurance, sleepiness, confusion, and poor motor coordination. Exercise can greatly improve the body's cardiovascular and pulmonary systems by making the body more efficient in transporting oxygen. A study by Sidney and Shepherd (1977) revealed that vigorous exercise four to five times per week for 30 minutes per session is generally sufficient to raise the aerobic capacity (the ability of the body to use oxygen) by 33 percent in aged men and by 20 percent in aged women.

Digestive system

The digestive system may not function as well as that of a younger person. Problems in digestion may be incorrectly attributed to the aging process, whereas in reality there may be other causes. Missing teeth or loose or poorly fitting dentures may not allow the older person to chew foods well enough for the action of saliva and gastric juices necessary for digestion. Poorly chewed foods can lead to gastrointestinal complaints such as constipation (Osborn, 1970).

Excretory system

Waste materials pass from the kidneys and bladder in the form of urine and from the intestines and rectum in the form of feces. Efficient kidney functioning may decline by as much as 50 percent in individuals over 80 years old and can show the greatest decline with increasing age of any organ in the body (Heron and Chown, 1967). Peristalsis (muscle movement) in the alimentary canal also diminishes with age and thus causes constipation in many older persons. Constipation can also be caused by improper diet and lack of exercise (Shock, 1961, 1962, 1974).

Skeletal system

Bones provide support, protection for vital organs, and leverage for muscles that provide mobility. With increasing age there is often a decrease in bone mass, resulting in bones becoming weak and brittle, more prone to break, and less likely to heal quickly. Calcification, or hardening, can occur around the joints, restricting or causing painful movement. The layer of cartilage between joints may become thin and splinter or fragment. The decrease in synovial fluid used for joint lubrication may cause dryness and eventual joint crumbling. Teeth, a bone structure affected by increasing age, may be discolored, damaged, or lost, thus interfering not only with digestion but also with social interaction. Comfortable dentures that fit well, look natural, and are free of "denture odor" will improve food intake and enhance social interaction.

Muscular system

Muscles are of two types: involuntary (smooth) and voluntary (striated). Involuntary muscles perform functions such as controlling breathing, propelling food along the intestines, and dilating the eye. The voluntary muscles are found in the arms, legs, and other parts of the body. Muscle elasticity, mass, stamina, power, strength, and ability to quickly respond decline after age 30. However, these changes may be due to atrophy, since most individuals over age 30 no longer exercise regularly. Research has shown that there is less decline in muscle function and mass in those who remain active than in those who become sedentary (Bromley, 1974; Shanck, 1976; Shock, 1961, 1962, 1974).

Endocrine system

The endocrine system is a network of glands that release substances called hormones directly into the bloodstream. Hormones regulate growth, development, and reproduction, as well as the balance of salt and water and the level of sugar. It has been found that in general these glands are less coordinated with increasing age, resulting in the altering of normal metabolic processes. For example, the blood sugar level has to be considerably higher in an older person before the pancreas will release insulin (Bromley, 1974; Finch, 1976; Weg, 1975).

Skin

The skin, or integument, serves as a barrier against germs, protects tissues, and helps to regulate body temperature. One of the most serious changes with increasing age is the loss of the skin's ability to regulate body temperature. There is a reduction in the number of sweat glands, resulting in an inability to sweat freely, which can lead to heat exhaustion. The outer skin or epidermis becomes thinner, and the subcutaneous fatty layers (under the skin) lose their fatty tissues. Combined with a decline in the circulatory system, this can make the aged susceptible to the cold (Bromley, 1974; Rossman, 1976). The loss of the fatty layer can also increase the probability of an older person getting decubitus ulcers (bedsores)—a result of lying in one position in a bed for an extended period with the resultant pressure reducing the blood supply to the soft tissues and skin in the affected area.

PSYCHOLOGICAL CHARACTERISTICS

Through the life span sensory and cognitive functioning are in a state of constant change, requiring continual adjustment and compensation. One of the themes of life span development psychology is the necessity for continual adaptation—the need for learning new skills and reorienting personal expectations with each successive life stage. The process of adaptation may not always be successful and may result in psychological disorders reflecting stresses and the vulnerability to organic disorders. To examine the psychological characteristics of older persons, an examination of the sensory processes, psychomotor performance, mental functioning, and psychological disorders is needed.

Sensory processes

The senses gather information about the external world and pass this information in an organized way to the brain. The threshold, or amount of stimulation a sensory organ must experience before sensory information is passed to the brain, often rises as a function of age. Thus the stimulus intensity must be increased if a response is to be evoked. For example, some older persons may require a considerable amount of sound to reach the required auditory threshold for hearing. With the complete failure of a sensory organ no amount of stimulus can evoke a response (Birren and Schaie, 1977; Botwinick, 1978).

VISION. Vision generally diminishes with advancing age. Accuracy for near and far objects often decreases, resulting in the need for glasses or large-print books for reading. Adequate adaptation to darkness is not as good as in young persons; extra care must be taken in night driving. As a result of the gradual yellowing of the lens and filtering of the violet, blue, and green colors of the spectrum, color discrimination may change. Thus the older person's environment should contain more yellow, orange, and red and less of the darker colors (violet, blue, and green). The amount of light entering the eye of the average 60-year-old person is about one third as much as that in the average 20-year-old. Because of the reduction in the average diameter of the pupil, levels of environmental illumination need to be increased for older persons (Atchley, 1980, p. 42). Cataracts, the clouding of the lens that produces diffusion of light and heightened sensitivity to glare, occur in about 25 percent of persons over 70 (Botwinick, 1978, p. 144) and may be treated by replacing the lens with a contact lens. Vision impairments decrease the orientation of older persons to their environment, curtail activities of daily living, and lessen mobility.

HEARING. As individuals age, the ability to hear diminishes, often because of atrophy of nerve tissues and calcification of bones in the inner ear, as well as disease and accidents. Hearing loss can make it difficult for older persons to hear high-pitched sounds, resulting in a preference for music with low-pitched sounds such as organ music (because of its rich, lower tones). Communication with older persons is not always enhanced by raising the volume of one's voice, since increasing the volume often increases the pitch. Hearing problems can be reduced by having a properly fitted hearing aid, removing distracting background noises and environmental factors that distract or cause sound to reverberate, and employing face-to-face interaction and simple verbal communication (Botwinick, 1978; Burnside, 1976; Corso, 1977; Ernst and Shore, 1975; Ruben, 1971).

Diminished hearing can have an impact on a variety of daily activities. Problems in social interaction may be created when an individual with a hearing loss does not respond or responds incorrectly to a question. Hearing loss may also lessen an individual's awareness of certain dangers (e.g., he or she might not hear a fire alarm).

TASTE. Recent evidence (Engen, 1977) has challenged the generally accepted belief (Bischof, 1976; Burnside, 1976; Ernst and Shore, 1975; Herr, 1976) that the ability to taste declines with increasing age. It has been speculated that the loss of the ability to taste is the result of a pathological condition or because of a factor such as smoking (Botwinick, 1978).

SMELL. The loss of the ability to smell is not universal with increasing age but may simply be, as taste, the result of some pathological condition or factors such as smoking or air pollution (Engen, 1977). The continuation of the capacity to smell makes important contributions to an older person's ability to recognize dangers (e.g., smoke from a house fire) or to enjoy simple pleasures, (e.g., smelling the fragrance of a flower).

TOUCH. The ability to feel sensations on the skin declines with increasing age (Burnside, 1976; Ernst and Shore, 1975; Kenshalo, 1977), resulting in a decline in the body's ability to inform the older person of changes in temperature, of pain, and of skin pressure. Consequences of this are that inadequate home heating or cuts and bruises may go unnoticed. However, an advantage is that individuals may not be aware of the pain of a chronic condition such as arthritis. This loss of sensitivity usually starts in the body's lower half and spreads upward and is more severe in the lower extremities.

Psychomotor performance

Psychomotor performance is a learned response made by the voluntary muscles that involves taking information from the senses, evaluating it, giving it meaning (perception), incorporating and integrating it with other ideas in the mind, deciding what response is appropriate or necessary, sending the message to the correct voluntary muscle, and activating the muscle's response. Factors that influence psychomotor performance are reaction time, speed, and accuracy.

REACTION TIME. Reaction time is the period of time between the presentation of a stimulus and the execution of a measurable response. In general reaction time increases with advancing age, being very slight for simple motor performance and greater for more complex motor performance (Bischof, 1976). From research it appears that the differences between young adults and the aged occur during information processing (the aged taking longer to decide which response is appropriate) and not in the perceptual or responsive components (Botwinick, 1973). The effects of a slowing in reaction time can be reduced through exercise that contributes to cardiovascular functioning and that provides mental stimulation to prevent the atrophy of neuron cells (Botwinick, 1973; Botwinick and Thompson, 1968; Spirduso, 1975). Practice can also reduce the effects of the slowing of reaction time (Botwinick, 1973).

SPEED AND ACCURACY. Speed and accuracy of motor performance decline as an individual grows older. For simple motor performance there is less of a decline in speed than for complex motor performance. Accuracy of movement for a complex motor performance can be compensated for by allowing the older person more time for more difficult tasks (Welford, 1959). When unlimited time is available, older persons do almost as well as younger persons; when time is limited, older persons increase their errors because the trial-and-error method of solving a complex problem must be used. (The trial-and-error method is effective only if a large number of trials can be made; with the older person's decrease in speed, the number of trials necessary to solve the complex problem cannot be accomplished.) An implication of these findings is that age has little effect on the capacity of older adults to function in basic daily activities as long as speed is not important.

Mental functioning

The term *mental functioning* refers to the processing of information between the perception of a stimulus by the senses and the activation of the response. The three areas of mental functioning to be examined here are intelligence, learning, and memory.

INTELLIGENCE. Research is currently challenging the traditional assumption that intelligence declines in later life. Schaie and his colleagues (Baltes and Schaie, 1974; Nesselroade, Schaie, and Baltes, 1972; Schaie, 1974, 1975) suggest that intelligence itself does not decline with age, but that the information and skills of older persons become obsolete. For example, most intelligence tests such as the Wechsler Adult Intelligence Scale (WAIS) measure achievement in terms of knowledge of current information being emphasized by the present educational system. Older persons are usually further removed from formal education experiences than younger persons. Perhaps the most significant factor may be the impact of the older person's environment—one that often interferes with optimum behavior and the maintenance and acquisition of knowledge (Schaie, 1974, 1975).

LEARNING. Learning is the acquisition of knowledge or a skill (Craik, 1977) and is usually measured through an improved response or performance. Research has shown that older persons can learn, although they often perform at lower levels than younger adults. A number of factors such as pacing, environmental conditions, and type of tasks have been identified as conducive to good performance. Pacing, or the amount of time an individual has to perceive a signal and make a response, has been examined in a number of studies (Canestrari, 1963, 1966; Hulicka, Sterns, and Grossman, 1967; Kinsbourne and Berryhill, 1972), and it was generally found that the slower the pacing, the better the learning performance. Learning performance of the aged has increased when the environment is supportive (Ross, 1968) and the tasks are familiar, meaningful, and not too abstract (Canestrari, 1966; Kausler and Lair, 1966; Zaretsky and Halberstam, 1968).

MEMORY. Whereas learning is the acquisition of knowledge or a skill, memory is the retention and ability to retrieve the knowledge or skill (Craik, 1977). Studies indicate that both *short-term memory* (recall from several seconds to several weeks) and *long-term* memory (recall of events from the distant past) decline with increasing age (Bahrick, Bahrick, and Wittlinger, 1975; Warrington and Silberstein, 1970; Watkins, 1974). Well-educated, mentally active people do not exhibit the same decline (Botwinick, 1973).

Psychological disorders

The term *psychological disorder* refers to a decline in functioning in areas such as perception, memory, and emotional response. Pfeiffer (1977) claims that about 15 percent of the aged have psychological disorders. This section will look at the two major classifications of disorders: functional and organic.

FUNCTIONAL DISORDERS. Functional disorders have no apparent physical or organic cause, and may be divided into two groups: neuroses and psychoses. Neuroses do not greatly distort an individual's perception of reality and do not result in a great amount of personality disorganization but may impair thinking and judgment. Depression, a neurotic disorder, is the most common of the functional disorders among older persons (Butler and Lewis, 1982). It is characterized by physical symptoms (e.g., sleeplessness, loss of appetite, and fatigue) and psychological symptoms (e.g., withdrawal, sadness, and difficulty in making decisions). Psychoses involve a severe loss of contact with reality and personality disintegration characterized by diminished impulse control, delusions, and hallucinations. An example of a common psychotic disorder is schizophrenia, often called paraphrenia or senile schizophrenia in the aged (Butler and Lewis, 1982).

ORGANIC DISORDERS. Organic disorders, or organic brain syndromes, are caused by physical impairment of the brain's functioning or by actual physical damage to the brain. These disorders generally produce an impairment in memory, speech, and orientation to the environment, as well as depression, anxiety, euphoria, hyperactivity, and other symptoms. There are two major types of organic disorders.

Reversible organic brain syndrome. *Reversible organic brain syndrome* is

Thea Lorin Breite

Physiological and psychological changes, although not inevitable with aging, may require leisure service personnel to adjust and adapt certain activities. What physiological and psychological changes may require adjustments and adaptations of the above outdoor recreation opportunity?

a temporary impairment that may be caused by a number of factors—congestive heart failure, metabolic malfunctioning, malnutrition, alcohol and drug abuse, head injuries, and other traumas of a physical, psychological, and social nature (Butler and Lewis, 1982). Complete functioning can be restored if there is careful diagnosis and treatment and elderly patients are not regarded as "only senile" (Butler, 1975).

Irreversible organic brain syndrome. *Irreversible organic brain syndrome,* commonly called chronic organic brain syndrome, results in gradual mental deterioration and is caused by cerebral arteriosclerosis or brain deterioration. Individuals affected may manifest a number of behavioral changes—wandering from their places of residence, poor personal care, sleeplessness, agitation, and delerium. The prevalence of chronic organic brain syndrome tends to increase with age. Researchers such as Shanas and Maddox (1976) have reported that at age 80 about 20 percent of the population have this disorder, whereas at age 65 only about 2 percent are affected. Wershow (1977) suggests that as many as 50 percent of nursing home residents may have some degree of chronic organic brain disorder, making it the most disabling and costly condition facing the elderly.

SOCIAL CHARAC-TERISTICS

Physiological and psychological changes that occur when individuals age have an impact on society, and that society has an impact on the older person. The interaction between individual and society determines how the older person will fit into society and what expectations that society has about its older members. This section is concerned with some of the social characteristics of older persons.

Education

As a general rule, it may be stated that the older a person is in the United States today, the less formal education a person has. This educational gap, however, has been narrowing, and it is projected that between 1980 and 1990 the percentage of high school graduates 65 years of age or older will increase from 37.9 percent to 49.4 percent (Table 1-5) (U.S. Bureau of the Census, 1973b). Certain stereotypes about the elderly—that they are more conservative, rigid, and less politically active—may simply reflect the current level of educational attainment. As a larger proportion of the older population attains higher levels of education, the future elderly may be more liberal, politically active, and of higher economic status.

Economic status

The economic status of the average older person in the United States has improved in recent years. Poverty is less common among older persons now because of increased social security benefits, Supplemental Security Income

TABLE 1-5   **Educational attainment**

Year	Percent high school graduates, 65+	Percent high school graduates, 25-64	65+ as percent of 25-64
1957-59	19.8	46.1	43
1969-70	28.2	60.4	46.7
1980	37.9	71.6	52.9
1990	49.4	79.7	62

From U.S. Bureau of the Census: Some demographic aspects of aging in the United States, Current Population Reports, Series P-23, Pub. No. 43, Washington, D.C., 1973, U.S. Government Printing Office.

(guaranteeing older Americans a certain income per month), Medicare, social services such as transportation and public housing, property tax relief, and private pensions becoming more common and more adequate. However, older persons are still one of the most economically deprived groups in the United States. Of those 65 years of age or older in 1981, 15.3 percent were below the poverty level, while 13.9 percent of people under 65 were so classified. If the "near poor" (money income below 125 percent of poverty level) are included, the poverty rate of the elderly is closer to 30 percent (U.S. Bureau of the Census, 1983). Poverty varies among subgroups of the older population, with poverty being particularly high among blacks, the Spanish speaking, and older women not living with families (U.S. Bureau of the Census, 1977a).

Economic status has an important influence on the older person's quality of life. Low income in old age often means inadequate housing and clothing, poor nutrition, lack of recreation, and neglect of medical and health needs.

Health status

Health is a very difficult and complex term to define and yet it is basic to any discussion of the experience and process of aging. The World Health Organization has defined health as "a state of complete physical, mental and social well-being and not merely the absence of disease or infirmity" (World Health Organization, 1946). Implicit in this definition is the notion of well-being and satisfaction, which are subjective terms, yet basic to any discussion of the aging experience, since health, particularly *self-rated* health, is the most important determinant of satisfaction among the aged (Palmore and Luikart, 1972). In fact, it may be more important than measures of objective health in relation to future longevity (Maddox and Douglass, 1974). However, "physical, mental, and social well-being" is hard to measure, so health is usually defined as the absence of *conditions* that cause disease or infirmity.

Conditions causing disease or infirmity may be classified as *acute* or *chronic*. Acute conditions are illnesses (e.g., the flu or a cold) or injuries (e.g., a cut) that are temporary. Acute conditions tend to decline with age, but when they do occur in an older person their impact can often be more severe and can result in more days of bed disability and restricted activity than in a younger person (Wilder, 1974). Chronic conditions are illnesses or impairments that are long term or *relatively permanent*. Chronic conditions significantly increase with age; for example, in the age group 45 to 65 about 72 percent have one or more chronic illnesses, with this figure increasing to 86 percent for the age group 65 or older (Harris, 1978). In the United States the chronic conditions that most frequently affect older persons are arthritis (38 percent), hearing impairments (29 percent), visual impairments (20 percent), high blood pressure (20 percent), and heart conditions (20 percent) (Harris, 1978).

Disability, or the inability to carry out the activities of daily living, affects only a small portion of older persons. Although 86 percent of older persons have chronic conditions, 54 percent are not limited in any way, and only 14 percent are severely limited (Atchley, 1980). Thus most older persons do not suffer serious illness or disability. Higher prevalence of disability is associated with low income and little education and being nonwhite and male (Wilder, 1974).

Political status

The political sphere is of tremendous importance to older persons, as it is to almost every segment of society. This section examines political views, political participation, and age-based organizations.

POLITICAL VIEWS. A common assumption about the political views of older persons is that individuals become more politically conservative with advancing age. From available evidence this assumption does not appear to be true; in fact, most elderly demonstrate that with increasing age they have become more liberal (Glenn, 1974). These changes should not be attributed to age or maturation but to societal shifts toward liberalism (Glenn, 1974). It is also attributable to the individual's level of education, which Glamser (1974) found to be twice as important as age in explaining political views. However, when compared with younger persons, older persons are more conservative in their opinions on issues such as the desirability of racial integration of schools and neighborhoods, sexual mores, drug use, religious values, and law enforcement (Fengler and Wood, 1972; Glamser, 1974; Hunt, 1960; Marascuilo and Penfield, 1966).

POLITICAL PARTICIPATION. Political participation is reflected in a number of different forms such as voting, party affiliation, and holding political office. Each of these forms will be discussed.

Voting. Voting participation studies have shown that voting is lowest for the youngest age groups (21 to 24), increases until people reach late middle age, reaches a plateau when individuals are in their 50s, and declines when people reach their 60s and 70s (Riley and Foner, 1968), with voters in their 80s still voting more than voters in their early 20s (Atchley, 1980). Voter decline by age is attributable to health and transportation problems (Glenn and Grimes, 1968), the objective and subjective involvement in the total life of the community (Turk, Smith, and Myers, 1966), and widowhood and divorce (Gubrium, 1972). Variables with a significant impact on the age pattern of voting are sex (men at almost all ages vote more frequently than women) and education (those with higher levels of education vote more frequently than those with low levels of education) (Brotman, 1977; Cutler and Schmidhauser, 1975). Future trends point to greater levels of participation in old age as successive generations of older persons are better educated and overcome hindrances such as lack of transportation (Glenn and Grimes, 1968; Olsen, 1972).

Party affiliation. Party affiliation increases with age, but, unlike voting, it does not decline in the later years (Atchley, 1980). Older voters are more likely than younger voters to give their party preference as Republican (Riley and Foner, 1968), but people do not appear to shift from the Democratic to the Republican party as they age (Glenn and Hefner, 1972).

Political office. Political office is very accessible to older people. In fact, "older people appear to be better represented than young people among the elite who play strategic roles in the body politic" (Riley and Foner, 1968, p. 475). Presidents, cabinet members, supreme court justices, senators, and representatives in the United States are older than their counterparts from the 1700s and 1800s (Fischer, 1977; Lehman, 1953). In the 95th Congress about one third of the senators and one fifth of the representatives were over 60 years old (U.S. Bureau of the Census, 1978). Although many of those in political power are older, this does not necessarily mean that older persons and their interests are being overrepresented; there is no evidence that politicians vote on the basis of age.

AGE-BASED ORGANIZATIONS. Age-based organizations, emerging in the 1930s, may be viewed as the beginning of the "senior movement" in the United States. The Townsend Movement, named for Dr. Francis Townsend, emerged in California and attracted over a million members who were supportive of Dr. Townsend's plan to provide a $200 a month pension for retirees age 60 and over. George McLain's Citizens Committee for Old Age Pensions claimed a national membership of 250,000 people supportive of improving the economic conditions of the elderly (Crandall, 1980; Ward, 1979). The Townsend Movement was brought to an end as a result of the passage of Social Security legislation in 1935, and McLain's committee lost momentum as a result of the improved economic conditions of the 1940s (Crandall, 1980). However, a number of age-based organizations have appeared since the attempts of the 1930s and 1940s. These organizations are of two types: mass membership organizations of older persons and organizations with age-based interests.

Mass membership organizations of older persons. Four mass membership organizations of older persons to be considered are the combined National Retired Teachers Association and the American Association of Retired Persons (NRTA-AARP), the National Council of Senior Citizens (NCSC), the National Association of Retired Federal Employees (NARFE), and the Gray Panthers.

National Retired Teachers Association and the American Association of Retired Persons. The National Retired Teachers Association and the American Association of Retired Persons (NRTA-AARP) are two separate organizations (NRTA founded in 1947 and AARP founded in 1958) that function as a single unit. It has over 10 million dues-paying members age 55 and older; provides its members with life insurance, an information network, travel and prescription discounts, and the monthly magazine *Modern Maturity;* and maintains a Washington, D.C. office to track legislation of interest in its members.

NRTA-AARP serves as an advocate of federal programs for older persons and supports education and research in gerontology. It advocates national health insurance and federally supported senior volunteer programs. It has supported the establishment of the Davis School of Gerontology and the Andrus Gerontology Center at the University of Southern California.

National Council of Senior Citizens. The National Council of Senior Citizens (NCSC) was formed in 1961 with funds and the encouragement of the American Federation of Labor and Congress of Industrial Organizations (AFL-CIO) for the purpose of passing Medicare legislation; it has since broadened its base of concern to advocacy, providing prescription drugs, planning travel, and publishing the monthly newsletter *Senior Citizens News*. Membership is more than 3 million nationally in 3,000 senior citizen councils and clubs and is open to both union and nonunion retirees. However, the membership is recruited quite heavily from the ranks of organized labor.

National Association of Retired Federal Employees. The National Association of Retired Federal Employees (NARFE), founded in 1921, has over 200,000 members who are former federal employees and directs its efforts to obtaining larger federal pension benefits through the monitoring of Congressional activities related to the pension system. It publishes the magazine *Retirement Life* for its members.

Gray Panthers. The Gray Panthers, founded in 1970, is an organization that has achieved wide media attention because of its name and popular, charismatic founder and leader, Maggie Kuhn. They have sought to increase the visibility of public issues concerning the elderly in the areas of social justice, health care, nursing home reform, consumer fraud, and public transportation.

Organizations with age-based interests. Organizations with age-based interests may be grouped under the headings of trade associations, organizations of health and welfare agencies, and professional associations.

Trade associations. Trade associations active nationally are the American Association of Homes for the Aged, the American Health Care Association, and the National Association of Health Care Services. These associations lobby for beneficial legislation and regulations that would not hinder members' rights to retain their financial backing or realize profits.

Organizations of health and welfare agencies. Organizations of health and welfare agencies include the National Council of Health Care Services, the National Association of State Units on Aging, and the National Council on the Aging. They are concerned with expanding services, funding programs, and consulting with organizations dealing with older persons. The National Council on the Aging deserves special mention because of the extent of its services, which include centers for public policy and the arts, institutes of industrial gerontology and senior centers, and a variety of other services.

Professional associations. Professional associations are exemplified by the Association for Gerontology in Higher Education, the Gerontological Society, and the National Caucus on the Black Aged. The Association for Gerontology in Higher Education is largely composed of educators involved in training practitioners to provide services for the elderly. The Gerontological Society, founded in 1945, has over 5,000 members concerned with the scientific study of aging and application of research findings. The National Caucus on the Black Aged engages in research, curriculum development, and the training of black professionals in gerontology.

Religion

Older persons are often presumed to be more religious than when they were younger because of their closeness to death. However, the relationship of religion and aging is complex and not easily reduced to simple relationships. Religion and aging will be examined from the perspectives of church attendance, life satisfaction, and the relationship of the church and the older adult.

CHURCH ATTENDANCE. People's church attendance begins to increase when they are in their later 20s, peaks in their late 50s and early 60s, and declines slightly after they reach age 80 (National Council on the Aging, 1975; Riley and Foner, 1968). The decline is primarily due to poor health, lack of transportation, the inability to afford nice clothing, or because a younger religious leader has ignored them (Moberg, 1972, 1974).

Attendance is associated with many variables. For example, women attend more frequently than men (Riley and Foner, 1968), blacks attend more frequently than whites (Hirsch, Kent, and Silverman, 1972; Kent, 1971), and white-collar workers attend more frequently than blue-collar workers (Blazer and Palmore, 1976; Wingrove and Alston, 1971). Although church attendance declines with age, the elderly compensate for the absence by participating in in-home activities such as reading the Bible, praying at home, and listening to or watching religious broadcasts on the radio or television (Hammond, 1969; Mindel and Vaughan, 1978; Moberg, 1970, 1972). The Duke Longitudinal Studies of older persons who have been followed for 17 years found that, although religious *activity* declines, there remains a stability of religious *attitudes* (Blazer and Palmore, 1976). It thus appears that older persons still maintain an interest in religion, even though church attendance may decline.

LIFE SATISFACTION. Religion and life satisfaction have been shown to be significantly related, with indicators such as frequent church attendance, Bible reading at home, listening to religious radio broadcasts, and watching religious television programs correlated with high life satisfaction, high morale, and high personal adjustment (Blazer and Palmore, 1976; Cutler, 1976; Edwards and Klemmack, 1973; Moberg, 1965, 1970, 1974; Riley and Foner, 1968; Spreitzer and Snyder, 1974). The consequences of religious involvement are not clear; it may be that those who are more adjusted are simply the ones more likely to be religiously active.

THE CHURCH AND THE OLDER ADULT. The church performs many functions with older adults. Counseling and pastoral calling are two of the most prevalent, with estimates of from one third to one half of counseling and pastoral calling time of ministers being devoted to the elderly (Hammond, 1969; Moberg, 1975). Many ministers have mixed feelings about working with the elderly. Longino and Kitson (1976), in a study of Baptist minister's attitudes toward their older parishioners, found that ministering to the needs of the aged was not their "most enjoyable" activity nor was it the "least enjoyable." Other important functions of the church are comforting the sick, bereaved, and dying (Ailor, 1973; Moberg, 1970); offering chapel services and visiting programs in institutions (Moberg, 1974); supplying social services such as housing and nursing homes (Jacobs, 1974); and providing programs that stimulate individuals to return to the community and the church (Ailor, 1973).

Family

The family is a major source of primary social and emotional relationships. Most individuals are members of two families: the *family of orientation* is the family individuals are born or adopted into and consists of themselves, brothers, sisters, and parents; the *family of procreation* is the family created when one marries and reproduces, making an individual a husband or wife, widow or widower, father or mother, and grandparent. This section will examine several aspects of the family—the family life cycle, family relationships, and sexuality in older persons.

FAMILY LIFE CYCLE

Married aged. Marriage is an important source of satisfaction for older persons. Lowenthal, Thrunher, and Chiriboga (1975) found that after the departure of children most married couples experience greater closeness and companionship, increased mutual dependence, and the possibility for more undivided attention from each other. Most retired couples seem relatively satisfied with their marriages (Dressler, 1973; Riley and Foner, 1968; Rollins and Feldman, 1970), with the happy marriages described as relationships in which greater emphasis is on the *expressive* functions of sharing and cooperation rather than the *instrumental* functions of being a "good housekeeper" or "good provider" (Clark and Anderson, 1967).

Marriage is beneficial to the psychological well-being and longevity of older persons. Married aged have less frequent feelings of loneliness (Tibbitts, 1977) and lower rates of mental illness (Gove, 1973) than those who are not married. Married individual live longer than nonmarried individuals (Civca, 1967; Rose, 1964), with the loss of a lifelong spouse being detrimental to the survivor (Rose, 1964).

Widowed. Widowhood is a difficult experience for the elderly. However, there is disagreement as to whether widowhood is more difficult for the older woman or for the older man. Bell (1971) has concluded that widowhood is more difficult for women because of sex-role socialization and importance of the marital role, less encouragement and opportunity to remarry, bleaker financial futures, and fewer financial management skills. However, Berardo (1968) suggests that older men have more difficulty in adjusting to widowhood because of their lack of preparation in household management (e.g., cooking and cleaning) and their difficulty finding a substitute source of emotional intimacy, since men's friendships are less close and expressive than those of women. These findings suggest that the development of multidimensional social relationships through activities with family, friends, or voluntary associations can make widowhood less traumatic.

Never married. Although never-married elderly do not experience the isolating results of the death of a spouse, Gubruim (1975) found the never married to be more socially isolated. However, they are *not* lonelier than married persons and prefer greater independence and more solitary pursuits. Clark and Anderson (1967) found that the never married have learned to live with aloneness and have developed the autonomy so often required of older persons.

Divorced. Few data exist on divorced older persons (e.g., in areas such as causes of divorce and the impact of divorce on the older person's life). It is known that in 1977 3.8 percent of men and 3.1 percent of women between the ages of 65 and 74 were divorced, and that the age group 75 and older had 1.8 percent men and 2.2 percent women divorced (U.S. Bureau of the Census, 1978).

FAMILY RELATIONSHIPS

Adult children. Older persons are generally not isolated from their nuclear family. About 82 percent of the aged have living children (Brody, 1978). Of those with adult children, Tibbitts (1977) found that 52 percent reported seeing at least one of their children daily, 26 percent reported seeing at least one of their children once a week, and only 13 percent reported occasionally or never seeing their children.

Intergenerational exchanges exist between the aged and their adult children. Johnson and Bursk (1977) found that 93 percent of the aged who had adult children help those children in a number of ways (e.g., giving gifts and financial aid, helping when someone is ill, taking care of grandchildren, shopping or running errands, and fixing things around the house) (National Council on the Aging, 1975). About 70 percent of the aged receive assistance from their adult children in forms such as housework, transportation, meal preparation, and financial assistance (Crandall, 1980, p. 425). Older parents realize that they can count on adult children when the need arises and that they do not have to feel that they are a burden (Sussman, 1976). Adult children are often responsible for keeping their parents out of a nursing home (Shanas, 1979a).

Grandchildren. Currently the role of grandparent occurs at a much earlier age than in the past because individuals were marrying at a younger age and completing their families earlier. It is becoming increasingly common to have middle-aged grandparents, many in their early 40s and 50s.

The role of grandparent is not a source of universal pleasure (Clavan, 1978; Manney, 1973). The most extensive study of grandparents was conducted by Neugarten and Weinstein (1964), who found that although most grandparents were comfortable with their role, 36 percent of grandmothers and 29 percent of grandfathers felt some type of discomfort from the strain of seeing oneself in an alien role, disagreed with the way grandchildren were being raised, or felt indifference toward their grandchildren.

Most grandchildren appear to have a strong affection for their grandparents. Robertson (1976), in a study of 86 adult grandchildren ages 18 to 24, found that more than 50 percent claimed that they visited their grandparents out of love and for the pleasure of being with them and tended to view them as friends rather than elders. In the Robertson study there were indications that the grandparent role had few behavioral expectations beyond gift giving and being the repository of family history.

Siblings. Older persons are more likely to have living siblings than any other living relative in the family of orientation (Cicirelli, 1977; Clark and Anderson, 1967). About 80 percent of older persons have living sisters and/or brothers (Riley and Foner, 1968), who become particularly important after the death of a spouse when contact and interaction between siblings is often resumed (Shanas, 1979b).

Sibling ties are very important in the lives of older persons, especially for the widowed, divorced, and never married (Shanas, 1979b). Siblings are a source of support and may provide older persons with a permanent home (Atchley, 1980, p. 356).

Friends. Interaction with friends may supplement if not replace in importance the interaction with family. Petrowsky (1976) found high morale to be more associated with interaction with friends and neighbors than with adult children. This is because of the similarity of experiences and interests with friends and neighbors and the inability to attain an equal exchange of goods and services between older persons and their adult children.

A number of factors may influence the selection of friends. Friends tend to be individuals of similar characteristics such as age, sex, marital status, and socioeconomic status (Riley and Foner, 1968, pp. 571-573). The social context in which an older person lives is important for friendships and often depends on factors such as long-term residence in one area (Riley and Foner, 1968) and a higher density of older persons in a neighborhood (Atchley, 1980, p. 364; Ward, 1979, p. 319).

Friendships are important in the lives of older persons. Lowenthal and Haven (1968) found that the presence of one intimate friend can serve as a buffer against social losses such as retirement and widowhood, enabling the older person to experience declining social participation with considerably less depression. Friends can provide assistance in shopping for those who live alone, rides to doctors' offices, and aid in emergencies and illness (Riley and Foner, 1968).

SEXUALITY. Stereotypes often portray sex as neither necessary nor possible in old age (Lobsenz, 1974; Rubin, 1968). There is no physiological basis for most older persons not having a satisfying sex life; studies clearly show continuing sexual activity for most and even increasing activity for some (Masters and Johnson, 1966; Pfeiffer, Verwoerdt, and Davis, 1972). Continued sexual activity depends on previous sexual experience and behavior, with such activity being greater among individuals of higher socioeconomic status or good health (Masters and Johnson, 1966; Pfeiffer and Davis, 1972).

Several factors serve to limit sexual performance. For older males the most important reason for declining sexual performance is the "fear of failure" (Masters and Johnson, 1966, p. 269), and for older women the most frequent reasons are the spouse's death, illness, or inability (Pfeiffer, Verwoerdt, and Davis, 1972). The "fear of failure" in males can lead a wife to feel rejected if she does not understand her husband's fear and can create severe problems for older people. Sexual expression of older couples may also be ridiculed or censured by younger persons, as this example illustrates:

> I was told of a recently remarried 78-year-old man whose daughter greets him every morning with a derisive "How did it go last night?" A Florida psychiatrist reported two instances where children tried to commit their parents to a mental institution because they had moved in with friends of

Southern Illinoisan Staff Photo by Jerry Lower

What will be the impact on the delivery of leisure services if the older population is better educated, more economically secure and health conscious, and increasingly involved in the political, religious, and family spheres of society?

the opposite sex. It's not just coincidence that we never refer to even the most profligate youth as a "dirty young man," but are quick to label any older person who shows some interest in sex as a "dirty old man." (Lobsenz, 1974)

SUMMARY

A demographic analysis of the characteristics of older persons in the United States reveals that the aged represent more than 10 percent of the population, more than doubling since 1900. Life expectancy has expanded, with most men looking forward to almost 70 years of life and women to 75 years or more. Because women tend to live longer than men, there is a lower ratio of males to females. Most older males are married, whereas most older females are widowed, and this is reflected in living arrangements, with older women more likely to live alone. The place of residence of older persons is differentially distributed among the states, with the aged more likely to live in urban settings and concentrated in the central city. More than 90 percent of the elderly are white; the remainder are classified as black or "other" (e.g., Asian American and American Indian).

Physiological changes may occur as individuals age. These changes are:

1. Loss of nerve cells, resulting in slower response rate
2. Interruption of blood flow to heart and brain, increasing risk of high blood pressure and stroke
3. Reduction of lung capacity to expand, decreasing the ability of lung tissue to absorb oxygen
4. Inefficient functioning of digestive system
5. Decline in kidney efficiency and peristalsis in alimentary canal, increasing the possibility of kidney problems and constipation
6. Decrease in bone mass, calcification around joints, thinning of cartilage, and decrease in joint lubrication, often causing painful movement and bone deterioration or breaking
7. Decline in muscle function and mass
8. Reduction in coordination of endocrine system, altering normal metabolic process
9. Loss of skin's ability to regulate body temperature

Exercise, proper diet, and other good health practices can help overcome these changes.

Research on the psychological characteristics of older persons has shown that aging often produces changes in sensory processes, psychomotor performance, and mental functioning and may result in psychological disorders. The sensory processes of vision, hearing, and the ability to feel sensations in the skin tend to decline as a result of age, whereas taste and smell may decline as a result of some pathological or environmental condition. Psychomotor performance may be limited by factors such as an increase in reaction time and a decline in speed and accuracy, with the impact being greater on complex motor performance. The evidence from research on mental functioning suggests that intelligence does not decline; that learning continues provided that pacing, environmental conditions, and types of tasks are considered; and that both short-term and long-term memory tend to decline. Psychological disorders in the elderly affect perception, memory, and emotional response and may be functional (having no apparent physical or organic cause) or organic (caused by physical impairment or physical damage, being either reversible or irreversible).

A number of social characteristics are examined in the last section of this chapter. They are education, economic status, health status, political status, religion, and family. Currently, the older a person is, the less formal education a person is likely to have, although this gap between the elderly and other age groups is likely to narrow in the future. Older persons continue to be one of the most economically deprived groups, with poverty being particularly prevalent among blacks, the Spanish speaking, and older women not living with families. Acute health conditions tend to decline with age, although their impact might be more severe on older persons, whereas chronic conditions increase significantly with age, the most frequent being arthritis, hearing and visual impairments, high blood pressure, and heart conditions. An examination of the political status of older persons reveals that the elderly are generally more conservative than younger persons, although as the current population ages the elderly are becoming more liberal; that they vote more frequently than voters in their early 20s; that they are more likely to give their party preference as Republican; that they are often a part of the political leadership; and that they are members of or are represented by age-based organizations. Older persons still maintain an interest in religion, even though church attendance may decline. It has been shown that religion and life satisfaction are significantly related to a variety of church and in-home religious practices, with ministers and church members providing many beneficial services for older persons. The family is a major source of primary social and emotional relationships for older persons. Marriage is a major source of satisfaction and well-being, and widowhood often results in poverty and social and emotional isolation. The never-married elderly prefer more independence and autonomy. Older persons are not generally isolated from their adult children, often engage in intergenerational exchanges of various kinds, and generally are comfortable with their roles as grandparents. They are more likely to have living siblings than other living relatives in the family of orientation. They are able to use friends to supplement family interaction and serve as support for social losses. Sexuality can continue and even increase for some older persons; there is no physiological basis for most older persons not having a satisfying sex life.

REFERENCES

Ailor, J.W.: The church provides for the elderly. In Boyd, R.R., and Oakes, C.G., editors: Foundations of practical gerontology, ed. 2, Columbia, S.C., 1973, University of South Carolina Press.

Atchley, R.C.: The social forces in later life: an introduction to social gerontology, ed. 3, Belmont, Calif., 1980, Wadsworth Publishing Co.

Bahrick, H.P., Bahrick, P.O., and Wittlinger, R.P.: Fifty years of memory for names and faces: a cross-sectional approach, J. Exp. Psychol. |Gen.| 104:54-75, 1975.

Baltes, P.B., and Schaie, K.W.: The myth of the twilight years, Psychol. Today 10:35-40, 1974.

Bell, R.: Marriage and family interaction, Homewood, Ill., 1971, The Dorsey Press.

Berardo, F.: Widowhood status in the U.S.: perspectives on a neglected aspect of the family life cycle, Fam. Coordinator 17:191-203, 1968.

Birren, J.E., and Schaie, K.W., editors: Handbook of the psychology of aging, New York, 1977, Van Nostrand Reinhold Co.

Bischof, L.J.: Adult psychology, New York, 1976, Harper & Row, Publishers, Inc.

Blazer, D., and Palmore, E.: Religion and aging in a longitudinal panel, Gerontologist 16:82-85, 1976.

Botwinick, J.: Aging and behavior, ed. 1, New York, 1973, Springer Publishing Co., Inc.

Botwinick, J.: Aging and behavior, ed. 2, New York, 1978, Springer Publishing Co., Inc.

Botwinick, J., and Thompson, L.W.: Age differences in reaction time: an artifact, Gerontologist 8:25-28, 1968.

Brody, E.M.: The aging family, Annals 438:13-27, 1978.

Bromley, D.B.: The psychology of human ageing, ed. 3, Baltimore, 1974, Penguin Books.

Brotman, H.B.: Income and poverty in the older population in 1975, Gerontologist 17:23-26, 1977.

Burnside, I.M.: The special senses and sensory deprivation. In Burnside, I.M., editor: Nursing and the aged, New York, 1976, McGraw-Hill, Inc.

Butler, R.N., and Lewis, M.I.: Aging and mental health: positive psychosocial and biomedical approaches, ed. 3, St. Louis, 1982, The C.V. Mosby Co.

Canestrari, R.E.: Paced and self-paced learning in young and elderly adults, J. Gerontol. **18**:165-168, 1963.

Canestrari, R.E.: The effects of commonality on paired-associates learning in two age groups, J. Genet. Psychol. **108**:3-7, 1966.

Carp, F.: Housing and living environments of older people. In Binstock, R., and Shanas, E., editors: Handbook of aging and the social sciences, New York, 1976, Van Nostrand Reinhold Co.

Cicirelli, V.G.: Relationship of siblings to the elderly person's feelings and concerns, J. Gerontol. **32**:317-322, 1977.

Civca, A.: Longevity and environmental factors, Gerontologist **7**:196-205, 1967.

Clark, M., and Anderson, B.: Culture and aging, Springfield, Ill., 1967, Charles C Thomas, Publisher.

Clavan, S.: The impact of social class and social trends on the role of grandparent, Fam. Coordinator **27**:351-357, 1978.

Corso, J.F.: Auditory perception and communication. In Birren, J.E., and Schaie, K.W., editors: Handbook of the psychology of aging, New York, 1977, Van Nostrand Reinhold Co.

Craik, F.I.: Age differences in human memory. In Birren, J.E., and Schaie, K.W., editors: Handbook of the psychology of aging, New York, 1977, Van Nostrand Reinhold Co.

Crandall, R.C.: Gerontology: a behavioral approach, Reading, Mass., 1980, Addison-Wesley Publishing Co., Inc.

Cutler, N.E., and Schmidhauser, J.R.: Age and political behavior. In Woodruff, D.S., and Birren, J.E., editors: Aging: scientific perspectives and social issues, New York, 1975, D. Van Nostrand Co.

Cutler, S.J.: Membership in different types of voluntary associations and psychological well-being, Gerontologist **16**:335-339, 1976.

Dressler, D.: Life adjustment of retired couples, Aging Hum. Dev. **4**:335-349, 1973.

Edwards, J.N., and Klemmack, D.L.: Correlates of life satisfaction: a reexamination, J. Gerontol. **28**:497-502, 1973.

Engen, T.: Taste and smell. In Birren, J.E., and Schaie, K.W., editors: Handbook of the psychology of aging, New York, 1977, Van Nostrand Reinhold Co.

Ernst, M., and Shore, H.: Sensitizing people to the processes of aging: the in-service educator's guide, Dallas, 1975, Dallas Geriatric Research Institute.

Fengler, A., and Wood, V.: The generation gap: an analysis of attitudes on contemporary issues, Gerontologist **12**:124-128, 1972.

Finch, C.B.: Biological theories of aging. In Burnside, I.M., editor: Nursing and the aged, New York, 1976, McGraw-Hill, Inc.

Fischer, D.: Growing old in America, New York, 1977, Oxford University Press, Inc.

Glamser, F.D.: The importance of age to conservative opinions: a multivariate analysis, J. Gerontol. **29**:549-554, 1974.

Glenn, N.D.: Age and conservatism. In Eisele, F.R., editor: Political consequences of aging, Philadelphia, 1974, American Academy of Political and Social Science.

Glenn, N.D., and Grimes, M.: Aging, voting, and political interest, Am. Sociol. Rev. **33**:563-575, 1968.

Glenn, N.D., and Hefner, T.: Further evidence on aging and party identification, Public Opinion Q. **36**:31-47, 1972.

Gove, W.R.: Sex, marital status, and mortality, Am. J. Sociol. **79**:45-67, 1973.

Gubrium, J.F.: Continuity in social support, political interest, and voting in old age, Gerontologist **12**:421-423, 1972.

Gubrium, J.F.: Being single in old age, Aging Hum. Dev. **6**:29-41, 1975.

Hammond, P.E.: Aging and the ministry. In Riley, M.W., Riley, J.W., and Johnson, M.E., editors: Aging and society, vol. 3, Aging and the professions, New York, 1969, Russell Sage Foundation.

Harris, C.: Fact book on aging: profile of America's older population, Washington, D.C., 1978, National Council on the Aging, Inc.

Harris, R., and Frankel, L.J., editors: Guide to fitness after fifty, New York, 1977, Plenum Press Corp.

Heron, A., and Chown, S.: Age and function, Boston, 1967, Little, Brown & Co.

Herr, J.J.: Psychology of aging: an overview. In Burnside, I.M., editor: Nursing and the aged, New York, 1976, McGraw-Hill, Inc.

Hirsch, C., Kent, D.P., and Silverman, S.L.: Homogeneity and heterogeneity among low-income negro and white aged. In Kent, D.P., Kastenbaum, R., and Sherwood, S., editors: Research planning and action for the elderly: the power and potential of social science, New York, 1972, Behavioral Publications, Inc.

Hulicka, I.M., Sterns, H., and Grossman, J.: Age-group comparisons of paired-associates learning as a function of paced and self-paced association and response time, J. Gerontol. **22**:274-280, 1967.

Hunt, C.: Private integrated housing in a medium size nothern city, Soc. Problems **7**:196-209, 1960.

Jacobs, J.: Fun city: an ethnographic study of a retirement community, New York, 1974, Holt, Rinehart & Winston.

Johnson, E.S., and Bursk, B.J.: Relationships between the elderly and their adult children, Gerontologist **17**:90-96, 1977.

Kausler, D.H., and Lair, C.V.: Associative strength and paired-associate learning in elderly subjects, J. Gerontol. **21**:278-280, 1966.

Kenshalo, D.R.: Age changes in touch, vibration, temperature, kinesthesis, and pain. In Birren, J.E., and Schaie, K.W., editors: Handbook of the psychology of aging, New York, 1977, Van Nostrand Reinhold Co.

Kent, D.: The negro aged, Gerontologist **11**(1, part 2):48-51, 1971.

Kinsbourne, M., and Berryhill, J.L.: The nature of the interaction between pacing and the age decrement in learning, J. Gerontol. **27**:471-477, 1972.

Lehman, H.C.: Age and achievement, Princeton, N.J., 1953, Princeton University Press.

Lobsenz, N.: Sex and the senior citizen, *N.Y. Times* Magazine, January 20, 1974.

Longino, C.F., and Kitson, G.C.: Parish clergy and the aged: examining stereotypes, J. Gerontol. **31**:340-345, 1976.

Lowenthal, M., and Haven, C.: Interaction and adaptation: intimacy as a critical variable, Am. Sociol. Rev. **33**:20-31, 1968.

Lowenthal, M.F., Thrunher, M., and Chiriboga, D.: Four stages of life, San Francisco, 1975, Jossey-Bass, Inc., Publishers.

Maddox, G., and Douglass, E.B.: Self-assessment of health. In Palmore, E., editor: Normal aging II, Durham, N.C., 1974, Duke University Press.

Manney, J.D.: Aging in American society, Institute of Gerontology, University of Michigan-Wayne State University, 1973.

Marascuilo, L., and Penfield, K.: A northern urban community's attitudes toward racial imbalances in schools and classrooms, School Rev. **74**:359-378, 1966.

Masters, W., and Johnson, V.: Human sexual response, Boston, 1966, Little, Brown & Co.

Mindel, C.H., and Vaughan, C.E.: A multidimensional approach to religiosity and disengagement, J. Gerontol. **33**:103-108, 1978.

Moberg, D.O.: Religiosity in old age, Gerontologist **5**:78-87, 111-112, 1965.

Moberg, D.O.: Religion in the later years. In Hoffman, A.M., editor: The daily needs and interests of older people, Springfield, Ill., 1970, Charles C Thomas, Publisher.

Moberg, D.O.: Religion and the aging family, Fam. Coordinator, **21**:47-60, 1972.

Moberg, D.O.: Spiritual well-being in late life. In Gubrium, J.F., editor: Late life: communities and environmental policy, Springfield, Ill., 1974, Charles C Thomas, Publisher.

Moberg, D.O.: Needs felt by the clergy for ministries to the aging, Gerontologist **15**:170-175, 1975.

National Council on the Aging: The myth and reality of aging in America, Washington, D.C., 1975, National Council on the Aging.

Nesselroade, J.R., Schaie, K.W., and Baltes, P.B.: Ontogenetic and generational components of structural and quantitative change in adult behavior, J. Gerontol. **27**:222-228, 1972.

Neugarten, B.L., and Weinstein, K.K.: The changing American grandparent, J. Marriage Fam. **26**:199-204, 1964.

Olsen, M.E.: Social participation and voting turnout: a multivariate analysis, Am. Sociol. Rev. **37**:317-333, 1972.

Osborn, M.O.: Nutrition of the aged. In Hoffman, A.M., editor: The daily needs and interests of older people, Springfield, Ill., 1970, Charles C Thomas, Publisher.

Palmore, E.: Facts on aging: a short quiz, Gerontologist **17**:315-320, 1977.

Palmore, E., and Luikart, C.: Health and social factors related to life satisfaction, J. Health Soc. Behav. **13**:68-80, 1972.

Petrowsky, M.: Marital status, sex, and the social networks of the elderly, J. Marriage Fam. **38**:749-756, 1976.

Pfeiffer, E.: Psychopathology and social pathology. In Birren, J.E., and Schaie, K.W., editors: Handbook of the psychology of aging, New York, 1977, Van Nostrand Reinhold Co.

Pfeiffer, E., and Davis, G.: Determinants of sexual behavior in middle and old age, J. Am. Geriatr. Soc. **20**:151-158, 1972.

Pfeiffer, E., Verwoerdt, A., and Davis, G.: Sexual behavior in middle life, Am. J. Psychiatry **128**:1262-1267, 1972.

Riley, M., and Foner, A.: Aging and society, vol. 1, An inventory of research findings, New York, 1968, Russell Sage Foundation.

Robertson, J.F.: Significance of grandparents: perception of young adult grandchildren, Gerontologist **16**:137-140, 1976.

Rollins, B., and Feldman, H.: Marital satisfaction over the family life cycle, J. Marriage Fam. **32**:20-28, 1970.

Rose, C.L.: Social factors in longevity, Gerontologist **4**:27-37, 1964.

Ross, E.: Effects of challenging and supportive instructions on verbal learning in older persons, J. Educ. Psychol. **59**:261-266, 1968.

Rossman, I.: Human aging changes. In Burnside, I.M., editor: Nursing and the aged, New York, 1976, McGraw-Hill, Inc.

Ruben, R.: Aging and hearing. In Rossman, I., editor: Clinical geriatrics, Philadelphia, 1971, J.B. Lippicott Co.

Rubin, I.: The "sexless older years": a socially harmful stereotype, Annals **376**:86-95, 1968.

Schaie, K.W.: Translations in gerontology: from lab to life, Am. Psychol. **29**:802-807, 1974.

Schaie, K.W.: Age changes in adult intelligence. In Woodruff, D.S., and Birren, J.E.: editors: Aging: scientific perspectives and social issues, New York, 1975, D. Van Nostrand Co.

Shanas, E.: The family as a social support system in old age, Gerontologist **19**:169-174, 1979a.

Shanas, E.: Social myth as hypothesis: the case of the family relations of old people, Gerontologist **19**:3-9, 1979b.

Shanas, E., and Maddox, G.L.: Aging, health, and the organization of health resources. In Binstock, R., and Shanas, E., editors: Handbook of aging and the social sciences, New York, 1976, Van Nostrand Reinhold Co.

Shanck, A.H.: Musculoskeletal problems in aging. In Burnside, I.M., editor: Nursing and the aged, New York, 1976, McGraw-Hill, Inc.

Shock, N.W.: Physiological aspects of aging in man. In Hall, V.E., et al., editors: Annu. Rev. Physiol. **23**:97-122, 1961.

Shock, N.W.: The physiology of aging, Sci. Am. **206**:100-110, 1962.

Shock, N.W.: Physiology of aging. In Bier, W.C., editor: Aging: its challenge to the individual and to the society, New York, 1974, Fordham University Press.

Sidney, K.H., and Shephard, R.J.: Activity patterns of elderly men and women, J. Gerontol. **32**:25-32, 1977.

Siegel, J.: Demographic aspects of aging and the older population in the United States, Current Population Reports: Special Studies, Series P-23, U.S. Bureau of the Census Pub. No. 59, Washington, D.C., 1976, U.S. Government Printing Office.

Solomon, N., Shock, N.W., and Aughenbaugh, P.S.: The biology of aging. In Hoffman, A.M., editor: The daily needs and interests of older people, Springfield, Ill., 1970, Charles C Thomas, Publisher.

Spirduso, W.W.: Reaction and movement time as a function of age and physical activity level, J. Gerontol. **30**:435-440, 1975.

Spreitzer, E., and Snyder, E.E.: Correlates of life satisfaction among the aged, J. Gerontol. **29**:454-458, 1974.

Sussman, M.B.: The family life of old people. In Binstock, R., and Shanas, E., editors: Handbook of aging and the social sciences, New York, 1976, Van Nostrand Reinhold Co.

Taub, H.A., and Long, M.K.: The effects of practice on short-term memory of young and old subjects, J. Gerontol. **27**:494-499, 1972.

Tibbitts, C.: Older Americans in the family context, Aging **270-271**:6-11, 1977.

Turk, H., Smith, J., and Myers, H.: Understanding local political behavior: the role of the older citizen. In Simpson, I., and McKinney, J., editors: Social aspects of aging, Durham, N.C. 1966, Duke University Press.

U.S. Bureau of the Census: Projections of the population of the United States, by age and sex (interim revisions): 1970 to 2020, Current Population Reports, Series P-25, Pub. No. 448, Washington, D.C., 1970, U.S. Government Printing Office.

U.S. Bureau of the Census: Census of population, 1970, detailed characteristics, Final Report PC(1)-D1, Washington, D.C., 1973a, U.S. Government Printing Office.

U.S. Bureau of the Census: Some demographic aspects of aging in the United States, Current Population Reports, Series P-23, Pub. No. 43, Washington, D.C., 1973b, U.S. Government Printing Office.

U.S. Bureau of the Census: Demographic aspects of aging and the older population in the United States, Current Population Reports, Series P-23, Pub. No. 59, Washington, D.C., 1976a, U.S. Government Printing Office.

U.S. Bureau of the Census: Statistical abstracts of the United States (97th Annual Edition), Washington, D.C., 1976b, U.S. Government Printing Office.

U.S. Bureau of the Census: Statistical abstracts of the United States, Washington, D.C., 1977, U.S. Government Printing Office.

U.S. Bureau of the Census: Statistical abstracts of the United States, Washington, D.C., 1978, U.S. Government Printing Office.

U.S. Bureau of the Census: Statistical abstracts of the United States, Washington, D.C., 1981, U.S. Government Printing Office.

U.S. Bureau of the Census: America in transition: an aging society, Current Population Reports, Series P-23, Pub. No. 128, Washington, D.C., 1983, U.S. Government Printing Office.

Ward, R.A.: The aging experience: an introduction to social gerontology, New York, 1979, J.B. Lippincott Co.

Warrington, E.K., and Silberstein, M.: A questionnaire technique for investigating very long term memory, Q. J. Exp. Psychol. **22:**508-512, 1970.

Watkins, M.J.: Concept and measurement of primary memory, Psychol. Bull. **81:**695-711, 1974.

Weg, R.: Changing physiology of aging, normal, and pathological. In Woodruff, D.S., and Birren, J.E., editors: Aging: scientific perspectives and social issues, New York, 1975, D. Van Nostrand Co.

Weg, R.: Normal aging changes in the reproductive system. In Burnside, I.M., editor: Nursing and the aged, New York, 1976, McGraw-Hill, Inc.

Welford, A.T.: Psychomotor performance. In Birren, J.E.: editor: Handbook of aging and the individual, Chicago, 1959, University of Chicago Press.

Wershow, H.: Reality orientation for gerontologists: some thoughts about senility, Gerontologist **17:**297-302, 1977.

Wilder, C.S.: Acute conditions: incidence and associated disability: United States, July 1971 to June 1972, Vital and Health Statistics, Series 10, No. 80, National Center for Health Statistics, Washington, D.C., 1974, U.S. Government Printing Office.

Wingrove, C.R., and Alston, J.: Age, aging, and church attendance, Gerontologist **11:**356-358, 1971.

Woodruff, D.S.: A physiological perspective on the psychology of aging. In Woodruff, D.S., and Birren, J.E., editors: Aging: scientific perspectives and social issues, New York, 1975, D. Van Nostrand Co.

World Health Organization: World health organization charter, Geneva, 1946, World Health Organization.

Zaretsky, H.H., and Halberstam, J.L.: Age differences in paired-associate learning, J. Gerontol. **23:**165-168, 1968.

SUGGESTED READINGS

Atchley, R.C.: The social forces in later life: an introduction to social gerontology, ed. 3, Belmont, Calif., 1980, Wadsworth Publishing Co.

Birren, J.E., and Schaie, K.W., editors: Handbook of the psychology of aging, New York, 1977, Van Nostrand Reinhold Co.

Butler, R.N., and Lewis, M.I.: Aging and mental health: positive psychosocial and biomedical approaches, ed. 3, St. Louis, 1982, The C.V. Mosby Co.

Crandall, R.C.: Gerontology: a behavioral approach, Reading, Mass. 1980, Addison-Wesley Publishing Co.

Ward, R.A.: The aging experience: an introduction to social gerontology, New York, 1979, J.B. Lippincott Co.

Social theories of aging

The scientific interest in the study of aging and the aged has greatly increased in recent years with the growth of the aged population. The study of aging is in a state of ferment as new ideas replace old ones. Several theoretical frameworks have been developed in an attempt to explain the social process of aging. This chapter will examine some of the common terminology used by scientists who study aging and the aged, the emergence of the scientific study of aging or gerontology, and some of the theories that gerontologists have developed to explain the behavior of the aged.

DEFINITION OF TERMS
Gerontology

The term *gerontology* has its roots in two Greek words: *geros,* meaning "old age," and *logos,* meaning "the study of." Gerontology is thus the study of old age or aging. It is a very broad field of study, encompassing traditional academic fields of study such as biology, psychology, sociology, and economics, as well as areas of human service such as medicine, nursing, social work, and recreation. Almost every area of study or human service has included in it some relationship to human aging.

Social gerontology

Social gerontology is a subfield of gerontology concerned with the social aspects of aging. Clark Tibbitts (1964, p. 139) described social gerontology as "concerned with the development and group behavior of adults following maturation and with the social phenomena which give rise to and arise out of the presence of older people in the population." Thus social gerontology is concerned with the relationship of the older individual to society.

Geriatrics

Geriatrics is a subfield of gerontology that focuses on the causes and treatment of physical pathological conditions in old age. Geriatrics is thus the study of the medical aspects of aging.

Senescence

Senescence is the organism's increasing vulnerability as it moves through its life span. It is a term used in biology to refer to the physiological aspects of growing old and comes from the Latin verb *senescere,* "to grow old."

Aging

The term *aging* is the process of growing older. There are various biological, psychological, and social changes that occur when mature individuals advance in age. Individuals are socially defined as aging when these changes produce noticeable effects, occurring for most people during their 40s.

Aged, older persons, elderly

The terms *aged, older persons,* and *elderly* are often used synonymously to describe adults 65 years of age or older. The age 65 is a somewhat arbitrary indicator adopted out of necessity for legislative purposes and everyday use; it is not based on the appearance of noticeable effects or symptoms.

EMERGENCE OF GERONTOLOGY

The study of human aging has a long history. Francis Bacon, the eminent scholar who proposed the scientific method, wrote *The History of Life and Death* in which he proposed that significant increases in life expectancy would result from improved hygienic practices (Freeman, 1965). Quetelet, a nineteenth century Belgian astronomer-mathematician, is considered to be the first gerontologist because of his statistical description of how abilities, skills, and strengths varied by age (Ward, 1979, p. 3). Sir Francis Galton conducted the first large survey, assessing 17 physical characteristics from a sampling of 9,000 visitors to the International Health Exhibition in London in 1884. He found that reaction time, visual and auditory acuity, and grip strength differ by age (Hendricks and Hendricks, 1977, p. 18). In the late nineteenth century the Russian scientist S.P. Botkin conducted a survey of nearly 3,000 of the poor of St. Petersburg to determine the differences between normal and pathological aging. He found that women tended to live longer, that married persons outlived single persons, and that older men had a higher incidence of atherosclerosis than older women (Birren and Clayton, 1975; Chebotarev and Duplenko, 1972).

The scientific study of aging began in earnest during the twentieth century. In 1922 G. Stanley Hall, a psychologist with a background in child and adolescent psychology, published the classic *Senescence, the Second Half of Life* (1922). In 1939 E.V. Cowdry's edited volume *Problems of Ageing* (1939) brought together some of the best minds of the period. Also in 1939 a group of British scientists established the Club for Research in Ageing, and in the same year this group was responsible for the establishment of the American Research Club on Ageing in the United States (Philibert, 1964) from which the Gerontological Society was formed in 1945.

Gerontological research began to accelerate following World War II, coinciding with the growing number of older persons and increased life expectancy. The late 1950s and early 1960s was a period of increasing interest in the social processes associated with aging. The literature published between 1950 and 1960 equaled the literature of the previous 115 years (Birren and Clayton, 1975). A bibliography of biomedical and social science research for 1954 to 1974 yielded 50,000 titles (Woodruff, 1975).

SOCIAL THEORIES OF AGING

One of the difficulties associated with the increase in social gerontological research is the necessity for conceptual frameworks. Data collected in the many studies of aging need to be cumulative, not just an expansion of descriptive studies, so that the knowledge base can be expanded beyond facts to the development of linkages. Integration of knowledge has been slow in coming, but efforts within the past 25 years to develop theoretical conceptual frameworks are the beginning of a holistic grasp of the issues. The remainder of this chapter will examine seven of these theories.

Disengagement theory

The disengagement theory maintains that high levels of life satisfaction in old age are associated with older persons reducing the number and importance of societal roles (Cumming and Henry, 1961). Happiness in old age consists of the recognition by older persons that they are no longer young and that more competent individuals are available to fill their roles. By phasing older persons out of important roles, their deaths do not disrupt the functioning of society. Disengagement is therefore a gradual, inevitable, universal, and mutually satisfying withdrawal of the individual from society that normally occurs to provide an optimum level of personal gratification and an uninterrupted continuation of the social system.

The disengagement theorists were heavily influenced by the sociological theory *structural functionalism*. The leading exponent of structural functionalism in American sociology is Talcott Parsons. According to Parsons, the United States has a social structure built on instrumental activism, meaning structures and ways of operating that produce visible, material things that are immediately useful. Instrumental activities usually favor the young and operate to the disadvantage of older persons who are not as strong or agile (Parsons, 1960, 1962).

Disengagement theory was based on the Kansas City studies of the 1950s, a cross-sectional survey analysis of 275 people ranging in age from 50 to 90. In these studies Cumming and Henry (1961) noted that with increasing age there was a significant decline in the number of current roles, current role activity, ego involvement in current roles, and in social interaction. It was felt that these declines were logical, natural, normal, and satisfying, leading to the process called disengagement.

Disengagement theory represented the first major theoretical system attempted by social gerontologists, and from its inception it has generated criticism. The major criticism of the theory is that it is too simplistic—there are many older persons who do not disengage and who do not suffer from their engagement. Other analyses of the Kansas City studies suggest that the typical pattern is actually high engagement and high satisfaction rather than low engagement and high satisfaction (Havighurst, Neugarten, and Tobin, 1968). Disengagement may not represent the desire to disengage on the part of older persons but the failure of society to provide opportunities, as illustrated in a study by Roman and Taietz (1967), who found that if given the opportunity for role continuity emeritus professors preferred not to disengage from research, teaching, consulting, and administration. Thus disengagement theory may be criticized for its presumed inevitability, universality, and mutually satisfying withdrawal of the individual from society.

Activity theory

Activity theory was formulated in response to the disengagement theory, although activity had been a persistent theme in the literature (Crandall, 1980, p. 111). Activity theory claims that personal satisfaction and positive self-images of older persons are maintained through continued active participation in socially valued middle-aged roles, and that it is important to *replace* these roles through *substitution* to avoid feelings of uselessness and decline (Havighurst, Neugarten, and Tobin, 1968). The activity theory essentially states that the greater the activity, the greater the life satisfaction, and that the more roles that are lost but not replaced, the greater the drop in life satisfaction.

The activity theory of aging is an application begun by Ernest W. Burgess (1960) of symbolic interaction theory to social gerontology. Burgess observed that older persons were becoming a distinct social group in American society, but that the society was not accustomed to accepting them as fully participating members in the normal daily activities of society and that this resulted in a "roleless role" for older persons (Burgess, 1960). Burgess felt that old age did not have to be devoid of socially meaningful activity but could be a new role leading to a meaningful existence built on responsibilities and obligations.

Activity theory has also been the subject of a number of criticisms. One of the major criticisms is that high activity may not be the major determinant of high morale but that high morale may enable individuals to remain more active than those with low morale (Crandall, 1980, p. 112). Another criticism is that the necessity of remaining active to successfully age would be a tremendous burden on those who are not or cannot remain active, which would thus result in a sense of failure, anxiety, and worthlessness (Atchley, 1980, p. 27; Crandall, 1980, p. 113; Ward, 1979, pp. 104-105). Studies have questioned the basic assumptions on which activity theory is built, noting that high morale was not

Do older persons disengage from society by choice or because they are not given opportunities to remain active and socially involved?

determined by the number of roles an individual had but by an intimate and stable relationship with at least one person (Lemon, Bengston, and Peterson, 1972; Lowenthal and Haven, 1968). On the other hand, both cross-cultural studies (Havighurst, Munnichs, Neugarten, and Thomae, 1969) and longitudinal studies (Palmore, 1970) of old age have found a positive relationship between activity and morale. However, there have been very few empirical studies to test activity theory.

Subculture theory

The subculture theory of aging, proposed by Arnold Rose (1965), asserts that the aged have developed a distinctive aged subculture as a result of more interaction among themselves than with individuals of other categories. This interaction develops an aging group consciousness that fosters "an awareness of belonging to a particular group and not simply a chronological category" (Hendricks and Hendricks, 1977, p. 113). Higher status within the aging subculture is conferred on those having good physical and mental health and greater social activity levels; money, occupation, and educational achievement are less influential than during earlier years.

Rose (1965), the initial advocate of the subculture theory, observed that there were a variety of conditions within the society contributing to an aged subculture. The number of persons 65 and older who are healthy and able to interact because of proximity in inner city neighborhoods, rural areas, and retirement communities has promoted greater age identification. Social services for older persons, elderly participation in voluntary associations, and greater publicity given elderly concerns have tended to develop group self-consciousness.

The subculture theory and the activity theory have an interactionist framework that is concerned with the relationships of roles and social identities to life satisfaction. Whereas the activity theory assumes a continuity between middle age and old age of socially valued middle-aged roles, the subculture theory stresses the development of a distinctive aged subculture. However, neither is able to explain the discontinuities between middle age and old age or the diversity of the aged.

Personality theory

The personality theory of aging views the aging person within the context of lifelong development in which there has been an interaction among biological, personal, and social changes that have resulted in the individual's own coping style. *Personality* is the term used to describe distinctive psychological and behavioral patterns that individuals use to meet the tasks of living. These patterns are rooted in the past and have been built over time into relatively stable characteristics of the self, yet they are dynamic, adapting, and continually evolving (Birren, 1964; Havighurst, 1968). Thus personality lends continuity to old age, while allowing change according to the new demands of aging.

Gerontologists have been able to identify a number of personality types based on empirical descriptions, even though personality is highly individual. Havighurst, Neugarten, and Tobin (1968) developed a description of personality types using the Kansas City data employed by Cumming and Henry (1961). The "reorganizers" substitute new activities for those that have been lost, corresponding closely to the activity theory's approach to successful aging. The "focused" are selective in their activities, withdrawing from some and maintaining or even increasing others. The "disengaged" are content in their voluntary withdrawal from involvements and responsibilities. The "holding on" defend themselves from the threats of aging by clinging to middle-age patterns, while the "constricted" close in their world by erecting defenses against anxiety. The "succorance-seekers" satisfactorily maintain themselves as long as they can lean on others to meet their dependence needs. The "apathetic" maintain long-standing patterns of passivity and low activity, and the "disorganized" show low activity accompanied by poor psychological functioning.

The personality theory points out the individual variability of reactions to aging—variability not captured by the disengagement, activity, or subculture theories—while addressing the problems of discontinuity between middle age and old age. However, the theory does not address the reciprocal relationship between the personal resources that older persons possess and the social environments to which older persons belong.

Exchange theory

The exchange theory of aging is based on the assumption that each person in an interaction is seeking to maximize the benefits of that interaction while minimizing the costs in terms of loss of prestige, self-esteem, or other rewards. Thus individuals continue personal exchanges only as long as the benefits of the interaction outweigh the costs. Older persons may voluntarily withdraw from exchange relations in their social environments when they find themselves without valued skills and the opportunities to initiate rather than be the recipient and are thus left with only the capacity to comply (Dowd, 1975) or simply to cultivate the appearance of "mellowness" (Blau, 1973).

The exchange theory has a potential to analyze almost any interaction as an exchange by asking what are the benefits and what are the costs in relationship to control of the environment and the physiological and social factors in the adjustment process of the elderly (Dowd, 1975). However, individuals vary as to what they count as costs or benefits, and this results in problems of application to the full range of social behavior (Hess and Markson, 1980, p. 21).

Age stratification theory

The age stratification theory developed by Riley, Johnson, and Foner (1972) views age not only as an individual characteristic but also as a component of society. Central to this theory is the observation that society in the process of age grading develops a hierarchy of *age strata*, with every individual being a member of a *birth cohort* (a group of individuals born at about the same time). Each birth cohort has a *life course dimension*, sharing a general biological history and common experiences in role performance (e.g., student, worker, parent, and so on) and a *historical dimension,* sharing a particular historical period with its unique characteristics (e.g., depression, war, natural catastrophies, and so on). Every birth cohort experiences a *cohort flow,* or demographic history, starting with a definite size, slightly more males than females, and certain ethnic and racial composition. But during its life cycle each cohort will change its sexual, racial, and ethnic composition because of differences in life expectancies. The members of every cohort will experience changes in the roles they perform at different ages, according to the processes of *allocation* (assigning or reassigning people of various ages to suitable roles) and *socialization* (learning how to perform new roles, adjusting to changing roles, and relinquishing old roles). As individuals move from one age stratum to another, there are age-related role expectations and sanctions to enforce these expectations to prevent individuals from behaving inappropriately. Thus each age stratum develops its own subculture as it moves through time, and because history presents each cohort with unique conditions, each stratum manifests distinctive patterns of aging (Riley, Johnson, and Foner, 1972).

The age stratification theory is the most comprehensive theoretical perspective yet developed in social gerontology (Hendricks and Hendricks, 1977, p. 124). It has the advantage of allowing each age stratum to be looked at in terms of its own history and characteristics and at the same time viewing each age stratum in relationship to other strata (Decker, 1980, p. 145). The theory, however, has been criticized because it does not take into account the perceptions and expectations of different social classes and ethnic and racial groups (Crandall, 1980, p. 122) or the practical problems of operationally defining age strata for purposes of empirical research (Atchley, 1980, p. 22).

Phenomenological theory

The phenomenological theory of aging is concerned with the meanings attributed to aging by those who are aging, seeing "everyone as ultimately assigning his or her own meaning to aging" (Decker, 1980, p. 146). Not everyone may have a unique view of aging, since meanings are influenced by interaction with others and various settings. Gubrium (1975) documented the meaning of life in a nursing home by living in the setting to determine how residents, staff, administrators, and visitors perceived and interpreted this environment. Marshall (1975), in a study of a retirement community, described the social meaning of death and how it was defined as a routine occurrence that should not be disruptive, with residents learning "not to make a great fuss about their dying" (Marshall, 1975, p. 1140). Thus the basic idea behind the phenomenological theory of aging is to understand the perceptual framework through which older persons "selectively perceive and interpret the world" (Crandall, 1980, pp. 122-123).

Phenomenology is a philosophical movement begun in Germany by Edmund Husserl and practiced by philosophers such as Max Scheler, Nicolai Hartmann, and Martin Heidegger (Caponigri, 1971). This approach began to have an

Southern Illinoisan Staff Photo by Jerry Lower

These older persons represent a birth cohort that experienced the Great Depression and World War II at approximately the same age during each of their life spans.

impact on American behavioral science through the works of Snygg (1941) and Combs and Snygg (1959) and has resulted in the sociological school known as Phenomenological Sociology or Ethnomethology. Social gerontologists such as Gubrium (1975), Jacobs (1975), and Marshall (1975) have used the phenomenological approach in their ethnographic case studies of retirement communities and a nursing home.

The phenomenological theory of aging attempts to individualize the understanding of the aging process. Rather than seeking to determine the general process of aging applicable to everyone, as do most of the social theories of aging reviewed in this chapter, it is concerned with interpreting aging according to individual circumstances. Unlike the age stratification theory, it is not an event such as the depression of 1930s that is important but the individual's perception and interpretation of the event that is important. The theory has been praised because of its comprehensive and complete nature but has been criticized because of its abstractness and the difficulty of conducting scientific research using this approach (Crandall, 1980, p. 123).

The future of social theories

The social theories of aging are each an effort to understand the social world of older persons. They strive to integrate theory with application and serve to stimulate inquiry and further growth in explanation. It is apparent that attempts to develop a general theory of aging to explain the multiple dimensions of aging have not been successful, but each new effort has served to sharpen and focus the critical issues and thus lay the foundations for future efforts. The development of social theories of aging must continue if programmatic interventions are to be of social consequence and if life is to be more satisfying for older persons.

SUMMARY

The scientific study of aging and the aged has led to the emergence of common terminology. Terms now used on a regular basis are *gerontology* (the study of old age or aging), *social gerontology* (a subfield of gerontology concerned with the social aspects of aging), *geriatrics* (the study of the medical aspects of growing old), *aging* (the process of growing older), and the synonymous terms *aged, older persons,* and *elderly* (adults who are 65 years of age or older).

The scientific study of human aging has a long history. Examples of scholars involved in gerontological study are Francis Bacon, Quetelet, Sir Francis Galton, S.P. Botkin, G. Stanley Hall, and E.V. Cowdry. Gerontological research began to accelerate after World War II and has seen a rapid expansion of interest and research during the last 2 decades.

A number of social theories of aging have emerged in social gerontology in an effort to develop theoretical conceptual frameworks. The first major theoretical system was the disengagement theory, which states that high levels of life satisfaction in old age are associated with older persons reducing the number and importance of societal roles, with this disengagement being gradual, inevitable, universal, and mutually satisfying to the individual and society. Activity theory was formulated in response to the disengagement theory and essentially states that personal satisfaction and positive self-images of older persons are maintained through continued active participation in socially valued middle-age roles. This theory states that the more roles lost and not replaced through substitution, the greater the drop in life satisfaction. Whereas activity theory assumes a continuity between middle age and old age of socially valued middle-age roles, subculture theory stresses the development of a distinctive aged subculture as a result of more interaction among older persons, thus fostering group consciousness and age identification. The individual variability of reactions to aging not addressed by the previous three theories is captured by the personality theory of aging, which views the aging person as having developed distinctive and relatively stable psychological and behavioral patterns, lending continuity but allowing change to meet the demands of aging. The reciprocal relationship between personal resources and social environments to which older persons belong is addressed by the exchange theory of aging, which is based on the assumption that individuals continue personal exchanges as long as the benefits of the interaction outweigh the costs in terms of loss of prestige, self-esteem, and other rewards. The age stratification theory of aging is a comprehensive theoretical perspective that views aging not only as an individual characteristic but as a component of society. It views society as made up of age strata composed of birth cohorts, having a life course dimension and a historical dimension, resulting in each age stratum manifesting distinctive patterns of aging and developing its own subculture as it moves through time. Unlike the age stratification theory, which stresses the events within the life course and historical dimensions, the phenomenological theory of aging puts its emphasis on the individual older person's perception and interpretation of events, while attempting to understand the perceptual framework of older persons that has been influenced and developed by social interaction and various settings. Each of these seven theories is an attempt to develop a general theory of aging and to explain the multiple dimensions of aging.

REFERENCES

Atchley, R.C.: The social forces in later life: an introduction to social gerontology, ed. 3, Belmont, Calif. 1980, Wadsworth Publishing Co.

Birren, J.E.: The psychology of the aging, Englewood Cliffs, N.J., 1964, Prentice-Hall, Inc.

Birren, J.E., and Clayton, V.: History of gerontology. In Woodruff, D.S., and Birren, J.E., editors: Aging: scientific perspectives and social issues, New York, 1975, Van Nostrand Reinhold Co.

Blau, Z.: Old age in a changing society, New York, 1973, New Viewpoints.

Burgess, E.W.: Aging in western societies, Chicago, 1960, University of Chicago Press.

Caponigri, A.: Philosophy from the age of positivism to the age of analysis, Notre Dame, Ind., 1971, University of Notre Dame Press.

Chebotarev, D.F., and Duplenko, Y.K.: On the history of the home gerontology movement. In Chebotarev, D.F., editor: The main problems of Soviet gerontology, Kiev, 1972, U.S.S.R. Academy of Social Sciences.

Combs, A., and Snygg, D.: Individual behavior: a perceptual approach to behavior, New York, 1959, Harper & Row, Publishers, Inc.

Crandall, R.C.: Gerontology: a behavioral approach, Reading, Mass., 1980, Addison-Wesley Publishing Co., Inc.

Cumming, E., and Henry, W.E.: Growing old: the process of disengagement, New York, 1961, Basic Books, Inc., Publishers.

Decker, D.: Social gerontology: an introduction to the dynamics of aging, Boston, 1980, Little, Brown & Co.

Dowd, J.: Aging as exchange: a preface to theory, J. Gerontol. 30:584-594, 1975.

Freeman, J.T.: Medical perspectives in aging (12-19 century), Gerontologist 5(1, part 2):1-24, 1965.

Gubrium, J.: Living and dying at Murray Manor, New York, 1975, St. Martin's Press, Inc.

Havighurst, R.: A social-psychological perspective on aging, Gerontologist 8:67-71, 1968.

Havighurst, R., Neugarten, B., and Tobin, S.: Disengagement and patterns of aging. In Neugarten, B., editor: Middle age and aging, Chicago, 1968, University of Chicago Press.

Havighurst, R., Munnichs, M., Neugarten, B., and Thomae, H.: Adjustment to retirement: a cross-national study, New York, 1969, Humanities Press, Inc.

Hendricks, J., and Hendricks, C.D.: Aging in mass society: myths and realities, Cambridge, Mass., 1977, Winthrop Publishers, Inc.

Hess, B., and Markson, E.: Aging and old age: an introduction to social gerontology, New York, 1980, Macmillan Publishing Co., Inc.

Jacobs, J.: Older persons and retirement communities: case studies in social gerontology, Springfield, Ill., 1975, Charles C Thomas, Publisher.

Lemon, B., Bengston, V., and Peterson, J.: An exploration of the activity types and life satisfaction among inmovers to a retirement community, J. Gerontol. 27:511-523, 1972.

Lowenthal, M.F., and Haven, C.: Interaction and adaptation: intimacy as a critical variable. In Neugarten, B., editor: Middle age and aging, Chicago, 1968, University of Chicago Press.

Marshall, V.: Socialization for impending death in a retirement village, Am. J. Sociol. 80:1124-1144, 1975.

Palmore, E.: Normal aging, Durham, N.C., 1970, Duke University Press.

Parsons, T.: Toward a healthy maturity, J. Health Hum. Behav. 2:163-173, 1960.

Parsons, T.: Aging in American society, Law Contemp. Prob. 27:22-35, 1962.

Philibert, M.A.: An essay on the development of social gerontology, Ann Arbor, Mich., 1964, University of Michigan, Division of Gerontology.

Roman, P., and Taietz, P.: Organizational structure and disengagement: the emeritus professor, Gerontologist 7:147-152, 1967.

Rose, A.M.: The subculture of the aging: a framework for research in social gerontology. In Rose, A.M., and Peterson, W., editors: Older people and their social worlds, Philadelphia, 1965, F.A. Davis Co.

Riley, M., Johnson, M., and Foner, A.: Elements in a model of age stratification. In Riley, M., Johnson, M., and Foner, A., editors: Aging and society, vol. 3, A sociology of age stratification, New York, 1972, Russell Sage Foundation.

Snygg, D.: The need for a phenomenological system of psychology, Psychol. Rev. **48:**404-434, 1941.

Tibbitts, C.: The future of research in social gerontology. In Hansen, P., editor: Age with a future, Copenhagen, 1964, Munksgaard.

Ward, R.A.: The aging experience: an introduction to social gerontology, New York, 1979, J.B. Lippincott Co.

Woodruff, D.S.: Introduction: multidisciplinary perspectives of aging. In Woodruff, D.S., and Birren, J.E., editors: Aging, scientific perspectives and social issues, New York, 1975, Van Nostrand Reinhold Co.

SUGGESTED READINGS

Crandall, R.C.: Gerontology: a behavioral approach, Reading, Mass., 1980, Addison-Wesley Publishing Co., Inc.

Decker, D.: Social gerontology: an introduction to the dynamics of aging, Boston, 1980, Little, Brown and Co.

Hendricks, J., and Hendricks, C.D.: Aging in mass society: myths and realities, Cambridge, Mass., 1977, Winthrop Publishers, Inc.

Hess, B., and Markson, E.: Aging and old age: an introduction to social gerontology, New York, 1980, Macmillan Publishing Co., Inc.

Ward, R.A.: The aging experience: an introduction to social gerontology, New York, 1979, J.B. Lippincott Co.

Leisure and aging

Leisure and aging has been the subject of many myths and stereotypes because of the lack of understanding of what leisure is, how it is manifested during the life cycle, and what its impact is on individuals in the latter phase of life. A review of the literature on leisure and aging is a necessary prerequisite for an understanding of leisure services with the elderly. This chapter examines conceptualizations of leisure in the leisure and gerontological literature, leisure and the life cycle, leisure and the elderly, and implications for leisure services with the elderly.

CONCEPTUALIZATION OF LEISURE

The term *leisure* has had many meanings in leisure and gerontological literature, resulting in a number of different conceptualizations. This section will examine a variety of these conceptualizations.

Leisure literature

LEISURE AS A STATE OF MIND. Leisure as a state of mind is the classical view of leisure that emerged in ancient Greece and was developed by Aristotle (348-322 BC). Aristotle viewed leisure (*schole* in Greek) as a state of mind free from the necessity of being occupied by work or any other form of obligation, a state in which activity is performed for its own sake or as an end in itself (DeGrazia, 1962). Leisure is not contrasted with activity, because it is considered the highest form of activity of the part of the soul possessing rational principle, especially of the speculative division. It is contrasted, however, with "occupation" *(ascholia)* or the type of activity that is not pursued for its own sake but for the sake of something else. Leisure is also distinguished from "recreation" *(anapausis)* and "amusement" (*paidia,* the things of children), since recreation and amusement mean rest after occupation or preparation for occupation. The activity of leisure for Aristotle is *diagoge,* or the cultivation of the mind, with *schole* being spent in *diagoge* and *diagoge* being pursued in *schole.* Particular activities of leisure desirable for their own sake would be listening to noble music and poetry, conversation and interaction with friends, and exercise of the speculative faculty. The Aristotelian view of leisure, according to DeGrazia (1962) and Pieper (1963), is thus a mental and spiritual attitude; representing a state of freedom; characterized by calm, openness, and contemplation; and providing an opportunity for spiritual and intellectual enlightenment.

LEISURE AS DISCRETIONARY TIME. One commonly used conceptualization in the sociological literature is leisure as discretionary time, which views leisure as the time remaining after the basic requirements of subsistence (working) and existence (meeting the biological requirements of eating, sleeping, and so on) have been satisfied (Murphy, 1981, p. 26). This equating of leisure with "spare time" or "free time" implies that leisure is determined by work and is set apart from work (Murphy, 1981, p. 28) and has "led to the separation of work and leisure and places an emphasis on economically productive functions as the most significant aspects of life" (Murphy, 1981, p. 27).

LEISURE AS FUNCTIONAL ACTIVITY. Leisure may also be viewed as "nonwork activity in which people engage during their free time" (Kraus, 1978, p. 40). Leisure as activity may serve various functions.

The psychological function of leisure is to contribute to the life satisfaction of the individual through participation in activities that satisfy certain psychological needs. In a study by Tinsley, Barrett, and Kass (1977) it was found that needs for sex, catharsis, independence, understanding, getting along with others, and affiliation were satisfied much more through participation in some leisure activities than in others. The psychological function of leisure according to Neulinger (1974, p. xi) "means to be engaged in an activity performed for its own sake, to do something which gives one pleasure and satisfaction, which involves one to the very core of one's being. To leisure means to be oneself, to express one's talents, one's capacities, one's potentials."

The function of leisure in society is to allow for individual self-fulfillment *after* the societal obligations of occupation, family, and so on have been met. Dumazedier (1967, pp. 16-17) sees leisure as "activity—apart from the obligations of work, family, and society—to which the individual turns at will, for either relaxation, diversion, or broadening his individual and his spontaneous social participation, the free exercise of his creative capacity."

LEISURE AS PERCEIVED FREEDOM. The concept of freedom is a dimension of leisure that is an integral part of each of the previously described conceptualizations of leisure—a state of mind free from work or other obligations, discretionary or "free time," and activity apart from obligations to which a person turns to satisfy certain needs. An understanding of an individual's definition or perception of leisure, however, needs to include the term *subjective* or *perceived freedom.*

Perceptions of leisure vary considerably as functions of several factors. Neulinger (1974) suggests that the one essential criterion for leisure is the condition of perceived freedom, followed by motivation for the activity (extrinsic to intrinsic), and the goal orientation of the activity (instrumental to final). Extrinsic motivation is satisfaction derived from the consequences of the activity (e.g., money), whereas intrinsic motivation is engaging in an activity for its own sake. An instrumental activity (e.g., stringing the reel) is engaged in to enable an individual to accomplish the final goal (fishing). Kelly (1972) considered perceived freedom and work relation (the degree to which leisure activities resemble work) to be critical factors. Iso-Ahola (1977, 1979) conducted two quasi-experimental studies to determine whether definitions and perceptions of leisure vary as a function of perceived freedom, extrinsic or intrinsic motivation, goal orientation, or work relation; he found that the effect of perceived freedom had a greater impact than the other variables, although intrinsic motivation, final goals, and low work relation were statistically significant. Leisure is thus brought about by activities engaged in under conditions of perceived freedom.

Gerontological literature

The most comprehensive conceptualization of leisure in gerontological literature was developed by Gordon, Gaitz, and Scott (1976), who built on the distinction between *instrumental* and *expressive* activities emphasized by the "action theory" of Talcott Parsons (1959). Instrumental activity (work and necessary preparatory activity) is oriented toward the attainment of gratification at a later time, whereas expressive activity (symbolic and material interchanges with the environment) involves intrinsic, immediate gratification. Leisure is defined therefore as "discretionary, personal, expressive activity, in which expressive meanings are more important than instrumental themes in the sense that gratification of present needs, wants, desires, or objectives is given precedence over practical preparation for later gratification" (Gordon, Gaitz, and Scott, 1976, p. 333). This definition of leisure draws on the work of individuals who have analyzed the social and psychological functions of leisure activities. Riesman (1952) specified a number of objectives that individuals seek through leisure activities: development, recreation, reverie, and creativity. Havighurst (1957, 1960, 1961, 1972, 1973) delineated the following meanings of leisure: autonomy, creativity, sociability, talent development, services, relaxation, and ego integration. Dumazedier (1967) saw leisure activities fulfilling functions such as relaxation, diversion, knowledge, social participation, and creativity.

A continuum of expressive involvement intensity (Table 3-1) was then developed. This continuum builds on the earlier general distinction between instrumental and expressive activities and the functions of leisure specified by Riesman, Havighurst, and particularly Dumazedier, with *sensual transcendence* being added. The five major functions of leisure activities are asserted to be relaxation, diversion, development, creativity, and sensual transcendence, with the positioning of the leisure activities along an expressive intensity continuum beginning with relaxation, assuming increasing intensities of physical, cognitive, and emotional involvement but not implying a grading as to reward, costs, and risks. Using this continuum Gordon, Gaitz, and Scott (1976, p. 316) further define leisure as "personally expressive discretionary activity, varying in intensity of involvement from relaxation and diversion at the low end of the continuum, through personal development and creativity at higher levels, up to sensual transcendence at the highest levels of cognitive, emotional, and physical involvement."

TABLE 3-1   **A continuum of expressive involvement intensity**

			Forms of leisure activity
Intensity of expressive involvement (Cognitive, emotional and physical)	Very high	Sensual transcendence	Sexual activity Psychoactive chemical use Ecstatic religious experience Aggression, "action" (physical fighting, defense or attack, verbal fighting) Highly competitive games and sports Intense and rhythmic dancing
	Medium high	Creativity	Creative activities (artistic, literary, musical, etc.) Nurturance, altruism Serious discussion, analysis Embellishment of instrumental (art or play in work)
	Medium	Developmental	Physical exercise and individual sports Cognitive acquisition (serious reading, disciplined learning) Beauty appreciation, attendance at cultural events (galleries, museums, etc.) Organizational participation (clubs, interest groups) Sight-seeing, travel Special learning games and toys
	Medium low	Diversion	Socializing, entertaining Spectator sports Games, toys of most kinds, play Light conversation Hobbies Reading Passive entertainment (as in mass media usage)
	Very low	Relaxation	Solitude Quiet resting Sleeping

From Gordon, C., Gaitz, C., and Scott, J.: Leisure and lives: personal expressivity across the life span. In Binstock, R., and Shanas, E., editors: Handbook of aging and the social sciences. New York, 1976, Van Nostrand Reinhold Co., p. 314.

Leisure patterns are related to developmental issues and tasks that individuals face at different stages in the life cycle, and in many cases these patterns will be shaped by the preoccupations and needs of individuals at each stage. This section considers leisure through the life cycle by examining different age groups or life-cycle categories.

LEISURE AND THE LIFE CYCLE

Play is the main leisure form of infancy and childhood. Theories of play stress the importance of providing challenge and security during play. Berlyne (1969) showed that play follows the sequence of tension, uncertainty, and excitement, ending with the pleasurable reduction of arousal and relief from conflict and tension. Ellis (1973) stressed the necessity of optimum arousal as the key to play motivation. Hunt (1969), rather than speaking of arousal, referred to this motivational behavior as incongruity seeking. A proper interaction of the organism with the environment should not offer too much incongruity or, as Seligman (1975) has found, the child may develop feelings of helplessness and withdrawal rather than mastery, thus affecting the child's emerging self-concept. There needs to be an appropriate match between child and environment, providing optimally arousing and incongruous play environments and security.

Infancy and childhood

Play contributes to the child's cognitive development through enhancement of problem-solving ability and creativity. Hunt (1969) reported that experiences with progressively more complex environments enhance the growth of the child's central brain structures and helps develop problem-solving ability. Bruner (1975) found that children playing on their own with materials needed in problem solving performed as well as children given the complete solution for the task and that they learned to transfer this knowledge to nonplay situations involving the same materials. Feitelson and Ross (1973) determined that free play provides a means for acquiring and rehearsing skills conducive to the development of creative behavior. Bishop and Chase (1971) were able to show that mothers having an abstract, flexible, unorthodox, and nonauthoritarian cognitive style tended to provide a more playful, engendering environment for their children, resulting in the development of a wide repertoire of responses for creatively manipulating novel materials. Thus play serves as a forerunner for adult competence in both problem solving and creativity (Caplan and Caplan, 1973).

Socialization through play influences the child's ability to cope in interpersonal relationships and is the beginning of adult leisure behavior (Yoesting and Burkhead, 1973). With increasing age there is an increase in social and interactive play and play involved with direct personal leadership in both giving and carrying out orders (MacDonald, McGuire, and Havighurst, 1949). Children's play with peers involving the themes of leadership, control, and role playing are important for the development of self (Turner, 1956, 1962) and provide opportunities for relatively safe role experimentation and consequent sex role definition (Sutton-Smith, Rosenberg, and Morgan, 1963).

The play experiences of infancy and childhood are "serious business" (Bruner, 1975; Sutton-Smith, 1971). These experiences "lay the foundations for future leisure . . . and . . . provide the setting and direction for individual changes in leisure patterns during the later stages of life" (Iso-Ahola, 1980, p. 101).

Adolescence (ages 12 to 21)

The developmental thrust of early adolescence (approximately ages 12 to 15) is directed toward achievement versus acceptance, and late adolescence (approximately ages 16 to 20) is directed toward autonomy versus intimacy (Gordon, 1971a, 1971b). Leisure in early adolescence is concerned with developing skills and competencies to be rewarded with social acceptance by the adolescent's peers (Bishop, 1970; Witt, 1971). Leisure is used by late adolescents "to promote and maintain autonomy from their parents by first increasing intimacy with close peers" (Gordon, Gaitz, and Scott, 1976, p. 320).

Leisure activities help to socialize male and female adolescents to adult attitudes and roles. Jersild (1963), in a study of 5,000 high school students of varying social backgrounds, found that the adolescents most accepted by peers were those who were most willing to enter extracurricular activities such as sports, music, publications, and social activities and who were able to suggest and initiate group projects and social events with liveliness, cheerfulness, and spontaneity. The mass media (radio, television, and records) contribute to escape from parental authority (Kline and Clarke, 1971). Csikszentmihalyi, Larson, and Prescott (1977) found "talking with peers" to be the most important activity for adolescents, absorbing most of their time and making them the most happy. Interpersonal intimacy is fostered by sexual competence (Hunt, 1974) that leads to the development of connections with loved ones in the next life-cycle category.

Young adulthood (ages 21 to 29)

Occupational and marital commitments characterize this life-cycle category. Kelly (1974, 1975) found that leisure choices were shaped by crucial variables such as occupational situation, monetary resources, available time, family roles, and marital and career stage, with the arrival of the first child making the most significant impact on leisure patterns of the young married. Leisure is important for marital satisfaction because it provides an environment for personal communication, sharing of experiences, and family cohesiveness through joint planning of leisure activities (Orthner, 1975, 1976). Joint activities encourage interaction and shared commitments, both significant to family formation (Carise, 1975).

Early maturity (ages 30 to 44)

Work and family continue to be the dominant themes in early maturity. Husband and wife are concerned with attaining the rewards of occupational and/or household accomplishments while increasing the growth and stability of marriage and family. Leisure activities of this life-cycle category are often home and

Southern Illinoisan Staff Photo by Jerry Lower

Leisure during retirement may be more home centered, autonomous, and media based.

family centered and provide a means of achieving marital and family growth (Gordon, Gaitz, and Scott, 1976).

The drive for acquisition of goods and the rewards of accomplishment tend to decrease in full maturity, with greater emphasis being placed on evaluating past accomplishments and maintaining dignity, respect, and control over activities and life patterns as individuals begin to experience physical changes (e.g., menopause and weight gain) (Gordon, Gaitz, and Scott, 1976). Leisure activities

Full maturity (ages 45 to retirement)

TABLE 3-2 "A lot of time" personally spent doing various activities by public 65 and over compared with public 18 to 64

	Percentage 18-64	Percentage 65 and over	Net difference
Socializing with friends	55	47	− 8
Caring for younger or older members of the family	53	27	−26
Working part-time or full-time	51	10	−41
Reading	38	36	− 2
Sitting and thinking	37	31	− 6
Gardening or raising plants	34	39	+ 5
Participating in recreational activities and hobbies	34	26	− 8
Watching television	23	36	+13
Going for walks	22	25	+ 3
Participating in sports like golf, tennis, or swimming	22	3	−19
Sleeping	15	16	+ 1
Participating in fraternal or community organizations or clubs	13	17	+ 4
Just doing nothing	9	15	+ 6
Doing volunteer work	8	8	—
Participating in political activities	5	6	+ 1

From The myth and reality of aging in America, 1975, published by The National Council on the Aging, Inc. p. 57.

TABLE 3-3 Leisure participation as a function of increased age

Activity	Males	Females
Dancing and drinking	−0.77*	−0.75*
Movies	−0.67*	−0.69*
Sports and exercise	−0.56*	−0.54*
Outdoor activities	−0.43*	−0.53*
Travel	−0.38*	−0.37*
Reading	−0.36*	−0.36*
Cultural production	−0.34*	−0.25*
TV viewing	−0.17*	−0.19*
Discussion	−0.16*	−0.17*
Spectator sports	−0.14*	−0.19*
Cultural consumption	−0.17*	−0.08
Entertaining	−0.17*	−0.06
Number of clubs	−0.02	−0.07
Home embellishment	+0.03	−0.01
Cooking	+0.59*	−0.25*
Solitary activities	+0.26*	+0.40*

From Gordon, C., Gaitz, C., and Scott, J.: Leisure and lives: personal expressivity across the life span. In Binstock, R., and Shanas, E., editors: Handbook of aging and the social sciences, New York, 1976, Van Nostrand Reinhold Co.
*Statistically significant at the 0.05 level or better.

may become less home and family centered as fewer family responsibilities and increased economic resources provide opportunities for more evenings out, travel, and other less home-oriented leisure. Marital satisfaction may be enhanced as couples interact and share interests (Orthner, 1975, 1976), thus helping to overcome the sadness caused by the "empty nest" as children leave home. Individuals sometimes need to rediscover or develop new leisure interests as the work career diminishes and retirement approaches (Ward, 1979).

Retirement

The transition from full maturity to retirement is characterized by efforts to maintain personal autonomy and social integration (Gordon, Gaitz, and Scott, 1976). Retirement can result in the relinquishment of social roles, reduction in economic resources, and decreased social involvement. Leisure can provide a context for autonomous decision making and social integration with meaningful other persons, thus supporting and encouraging the very important life-cycle transition to old age.

LEISURE AND THE ELDERLY

Leisure can provide a means of social integration and new sources of personal meaning for the elderly. This section will discuss leisure and personal adjustment.

Leisure activity patterns

Leisure activity patterns of the elderly are related to and conditioned by a number of demograhpic, social, and environmental factors. The factors to be examined are age, sex, socioeconomic status, and mobility.

AGE. Older persons engage in many of the same activities as younger persons, but there are a few age differences. Data from the National Council on the Aging (1975, p. 57) (Table 3-2) show that activities such as reading, sitting and thinking, gardening and raising plants, walking, sleeping, participating in fraternal or community organizations, doing nothing, doing volunteer work, and participating in political activities do not considerably decrease when persons age. However, the older respondents were less likely than younger ones to socialize with friends, participate in recreational activities and hobbies, and participate in sports (e.g., golf, tennis, and swimming) and were more likely to watch television.

Leisure participation tends to decline as age increases. Gordon, Gaitz, and Scott (1976), in a Houston sample of 1,441 adults ranging in age from 20 to 94 years, found that with age there was a greater decline in leisure participation in the following activities (Table 3-3): dancing and drinking, movies, sports and exercise, outdoor activities, travel, reading, cultural production such as television viewing, discussion, spectator sports, cultural consumption, and entertaining. It appears therefore that leisure participation tends to decline most with age in activities "that can be characterized as highly active, external to the home, and physically demanding," whereas "home-centered forms of sociability and media-based symbolic interaction" continued well into old age (Gordon, Gaitz, and Scott, 1976, p. 333).

SEX. There is little variation in the decline of leisure participation with age for females and males, as an examination of the Gordon, Gaitz, and Scott (1976) data shows (see Table 3-3). However, solitary activities significantly increased for females (+0.4), whereas cooking increased for males (+0.59) but declined for females (−0.25). Overall the findings that males increased their participation in home embellishment, cooking, and solitary activities support the earlier findings of Zborowski (1962) that men appear to become more home centered in their activities as they age.

SOCIOECONOMIC STATUS. Leisure patterns of older persons are related to socioeconomic status. Middle-class elderly tend to be more community oriented in their leisure, preferring clubs and organizations, cultural events, parties, and travel, whereas the working and lower classes tend to be more home centered, preferring family socializing, television watching, and hobbies (Havighurst, 1973; Havighurst and Feigenbaum, 1959). Reduction in income for those older persons who formerly had middle-class incomes creates a barrier to community involvement (Atchley, 1976) in activities such as entertaining, attending movies and concerts, and travel (Atchley, 1980; Carp, 1972; Friedsam and Martin, 1973).

MOBILITY. Mobility deficiencies may severely limit leisure participation. Clubs, church activities and socials, libraries, theaters, restaurants, parks, recreation centers, sporting events, and visiting may not be "convenient" because of physical limitations to mobility or because of lack of transportation (National Council on the Aging, 1975; Atchley, 1980).

Meanings of leisure activities

The focus of the previous subsection on activities engaged in by the elderly only considered the overt content of leisure behavior and did not examine the deeper personal meanings attached to various activities by individuals. Two studies have sought to determine how specific activities are viewed by the elderly.

Donald and Havighurst (1959), in an early study, asked respondents in Kansas City to indicate reasons why they engaged in various activities. They found the most commonly expressed reasons to be: just for the pleasure of it (68 percent), a welcome change from work (48 percent), a new experience (42 percent), contact with friends (28 percent), a chance to achieve something (23 percent), and makes time pass (23 percent). Different activities had different meanings; for example, handicrafts resulted in feelings of achievement but not new experiences or contacts with friends, whereas fishing was viewed as pleasurable and a welcome change from work but not as a source of new experience or creativity.

Havighurst (1961) listed a number of meanings according to which activities can vary: autonomy as opposed to other directedness, creativity, enjoyment as opposed to killing time, opportunities to develop talents, instrumental as opposed to expressive outlets, physical energy, complementary or competitive relationships to work, gregariousness, service as opposed to personal pleasure, status or prestige, relaxation from anxiety, and ego integration. Havighurst found that more middle-class than lower-class older persons were likely to engage in activities involving creativity, enjoyment, opportunities to develop talent, and status or prestige. High personal adjustment was related to activities characterized by the following meanings: autonomy, creativity, enjoyment, opportunities to develop talent, instrumental, physical energy, gregariousness, service to others, status or prestige, and ego integration. Thus it would appear that not all activities have the same meanings or are related to personal adjustment.

Leisure and personal adjustment

The impact of leisure on personal adjustment in old age is a key issue in retirement literature. Stephen Miller (1965), in an often-quoted article, argues that retirement is a degrading and traumatic experience because it means the loss of the work role, a major source of identity providing essential social and psychological benefits. According to Miller, leisure roles cannot replace this lost identity because society does not generally consider leisure to be a legitimate source of identity; it does not replace the work identity nor does it compensate for the loss. The retired person may have difficulty developing a positive self-image and feelings of adequacy unless leisure is granted social approval as a legitimate role replacement for work and a source of identity and self-respect.

Atchley (1971), a frequently cited critic of Miller, found after an examination of a number of studies that leisure can be a legitimate source of identity after retirement. Although the work role was important, identity loss is minimized by continuity in other roles such as those provided by family, friends, church, and community. These roles create retirement cohorts for individuals and provide identity continuity to legitimize leisure. Prime predictors of retirement adjustment were an adequate retirement income and retired friends with whom to share the leisure role, suggesting that loss of income rather than work accounts for negative retirement effects. Activities that build on skills and interests of preretirement should provide a foundation for personal adjustment and life satisfaction after retirement.

The importance of leisure continuity between preretirement and postretirement and the relationship of leisure continuity to life satisfaction have further support in the literature. DeCarlo (1974) reported a positive correlation (0.48) between recreative pursuits (classified according to sensory-motor, cognitive, and affective behavioral elements) and successful aging (mental and physical health and intellectual performance) during middle age and old age, with those participating regularly from middle age to old age having a higher correlation than those who sporadically participated. Palmore and Kivett (1977), using longitudinal data from individuals 46 to 70 years old, determined that social participation (sexual relations and organizational activity) was positively correlated with life satisfaction for both sexes, with the single best predictor of later life satisfaction being satisfaction at an earlier time. Lemon, Bengston, and

Peterson (1972) found a positively significant correlation between informal activity with friends and life satisfaction; as social activity with friends increases so does life satisfaction. Graney (1975) reported a significant relationship between social participation (especially face-to-face interaction with friends and relatives) and happiness among women ages 62 to 89, with decreases in the levels of activity having a negative impact on happiness.

IMPLICATIONS FOR LEISURE SERVICES WITH THE ELDERLY

The importance of leisure to life satisfaction should *not* lead to the conclusion that satisfaction is achieved in *all* cases through active leisure participation. The leisure service provider needs to consider the individual differences among older persons and to allow for both continuity and change. The importance of *continuity* is stressed by Atchley (1977, p. 27) when he states, "as the individuals grow older, they are predisposed toward maintaining continuity in habits, associations, preferences, and so on." However, these predispositions are subject to *change* because of "interactions among personal preferences, biological and psychological capabilities, situational opportunities, and experience" (Atchley, 1977, p. 27). Lawton and Nahemow (1973, p. 666) address the issue of continuity and change in a discussion of their theory of man-environment transactions, stating that environmental planners for the elderly need "to provide maximum motivation for exercise of skills without overstepping the individual's limits of tolerance and stress." Davis and Teaff (1980) describe how continuity and change can be implemented in a leisure service setting through the creation of roles (e.g., hostess, organizer, entertainer, reporter, musician, artist, signmaker, receptionist, and so on) that draw on a variety of current leisure service needs within the environment yet build on past individual experiences, habits, and preferences. Creating roles also involves an evaluation of the individual's current physical, psychological, social, and leisure functioning through personal interviews and observations. The leisure service provider thus needs to promote continuity through leisure services that support past associations, preferences, and habits and to promote change through leisure services that challenge without overburdening with stress.

Perceived personal control is vital to the physical and psychological well-being of older persons and must be the cornerstone of leisure services that challenge older persons through choice and responsibility. Schulz (1976) and Schulz and Hanusa (1978) found that increased social interaction through a planned visitation program in a private retirement home improved physical and psychological well-being, provided that the frequency and duration of these visits by college students were predictable and controllable by the older persons. Langer and Rodin (1976) and Rodin and Langer (1977) showed that nursing home residents given the opportunity to make meaningful choices and to exercise personal responsibility were more active, more sociable, more mentally alert, and had lower mortality than residents who did not have "responsibility-induced" opportunities (e.g., deciding what recreation they wanted and when, types of plants they wanted to have, and what room arrangement they preferred). The importance of a controllable environment and the relationship of environment and level of competence is well stated in the Lawton and Simon "environmental docility hypothesis" (1968). This hypothesis proposes that the less competent the older person is in health, intelligence, ego strength, and social role performance, the more the older person will be affected by the immediate environment, which results in a preference for simplicity and passivity in that environment. Leisure services should challenge older persons to exercise coping and adapting skills, allowing them to enjoy the consequent sense of mastery and to overcome the preference for simplicity and passivity. At the same time these services should provide a supportive and not overly demanding environment so as not to exceed the limits of stress, pressure for activity, sociability, group conformity, and privacy. The critical issue for the leisure specialist is how much *challenge* and how much *support* to build into environmental and individual leisure services.

SUMMARY

Leisure has been conceptualized in a variety of ways in both leisure and gerontological literature. In leisure literature it has been conceptualized as: a state of mind free from the necessity of being occupied; discretionary time remaining after subsistence and existence requirements have been met; functional activity satisfying a variety of psychological and social needs; and perceived freedom. The most comprehensive conceptualization of leisure in gerontological literature was proposed by Gordon, Gaitz, and Scott (1976), who developed a continuum of expressive involvement intensity that assumes increasing intensities of physical, cognitive, and emotional involvement varying from relaxation and diversion at the low end of a continuum through personal development and creativity to sensual transcendence.

Leisure through the life cycle is shaped by individual needs at different stages of life. During infancy and childhood play that provides both challenge and security contributes to a child's cognitive development and socialization and lays the foundations for leisure patterns later in life. Leisure in adolescence (ages 12 to 20) helps in the socialization process by providing opportunities to develop skills rewarded by peer acceptance, autonomy from parents, and intimacy with close peers, leading to sexual competence and connections with loved ones in young adulthood. Young adulthood (ages 21 to 29) is characterized by occupational and marital commitments, with leisure enhancing marital satisfaction and family cohesiveness. Work and family are the dominant themes of early maturity (ages 30 to 44), and leisure is home and family centered. Leisure during full maturity (age 45 to retirement) may become less home and family centered as children leave, thus allowing individuals to rediscover or develop new leisure interests as retirement approaches. Retirement and the transition to old age may be eased through a leisure that supports autonomous decision making and social integration.

Leisure and the elderly may be viewed from perspectives such as activity patterns, meanings, and personal adjustment. Leisure activity is related to and conditioned by factors such as age (participation tending to decline in activities that are highly active, external to the home, and physically demanding but increasing in home-centered and media-based activities), sex (solitary activities significantly increasing for females and home-centered activities such as home embellishment and cooking increasing for males), socioeconomic status (community-oriented activities being preferred by the middle class and home-centered activities being preferred by the working and lower classes), and mobility (physical limitations and lack of transportation impeding involvement in community leisure settings). Meanings of leisure activities differ, and personal adjustment is related to activities having various meanings. Leisure has an impact on personal adjustment and is a legitimate source of identity after retirement, provided there is continuity of roles, skills, and interests between middle age and old age.

There are a number of implications for leisure services with the elderly that may be drawn from leisure and gerontological literature. The leisure service provider needs to promote *continuity* of past associations, preferences, and habits, as well as *change* through services that challenge without overburdening with stress. Perceived personal control can challenge older persons through choice and responsibility and help overcome the preference for simplicity and passivity, while providing a supportive and not overly demanding environment that does not exceed the limits of stress, pressure for activity, sociability, group conformity, and privacy.

REFERENCES

Atchley, R.: Retirement and leisure participation: continuity or crisis, Gerontologist 11:13-17, 1971.

Atchley, R.: The sociology of retirement, Cambridge, Mass., 1976, Schenkman Publishing Co., Inc.

Atchley, R.: The social forces in later life, ed. 2, Belmont, Calif., 1977, Wadsworth Publishing Co.

Atchley, R.C.: The social forces in later life: an introduction to social gerontology, ed. 3, Belmont, Calif., 1980, Wadsworth Publishing Co.

Berlyne, D.: Laughter, humor, and play. In Lindzey, G., and Aronson, E., editors: Handbook of social psychology, ed. 2, Reading, Mass., 1969, Addison-Wesley Publishing Co., Inc.

Bishop, D.: Stability of the factor structure of leisure behavior: analyses of four communities, J. Leisure Res. 2:160-170, 1970.

Bishop, D., and Chase, D.: Parental conceptual systems, home play environment, and potential creativity in children, J. Exp. Child Psychol. 12:318-338, 1971.

Bruner, J.: Play is serious business, Psychol. Today 8:81-83, 1975.

Caplan, F., and Caplan, T.: The power of play, Garden City, N.Y., 1973, Doubleday & Co., Inc.

Carise, C.: Family and leisure: a set of contradictions, Fam. Coordinator 24:191-197, 1975.

Carp, F.: Retired people as automobile passengers, Gerontologist 12:66-72, 1972.

Csikszentmihalyi, M., Larson, R., and Prescott, S.: The ecology of adolescent activity and experience, J. Youth Adolesc. 6:281-294, 1977.

Davis, N., and Teaff, J.: Facilitating role continuity of the elderly through leisure programming, Ther. Recreation J. 14:32-36, 1980.

DeCarlo, T.: Recreation participation patterns and successful aging, J. Gerontol. 29:416-422, 1974.

DeGrazia, S.: Of time, work and leisure, New York, 1962, Doubleday & Co., Inc., Twentieth Century Fund.

Donald, M., and Havighurst, R.: The meanings of leisure, Soc. Forces 37:355-360, 1959.

Dumazedier, J.: Toward a society of leisure, New York, 1967, The Free Press.

Ellis, M.: Why people play, Englewood Cliffs, N.J., 1973, Prentice-Hall, Inc.

Feitelson, D., and Ross, G.: The neglected factor: play, Hum. Dev. 16:202-223, 1973.

Friedsam, H., and Martin, C.: Travel of older people as a use of leisure, Gerontologist 13:204-207, 1973.

Gordon, C.: Role and value development across the life cycle. In Jackson, J., editor: Role: sociological studies IV, London, 1971a, Cambridge University Press.

Gordon, C.: Social characteristics of early adolescence, Daedalus 100:931-960, 1971b.

Gordon, C., Gaitz, C., and Scott, J.: Leisure and lives: personal expressivity across the life span. In Binstock, R., and Shanas, E., editors: Handbook of aging and the social sciences, New York, 1976, Van Nostrand Reinhold Co.

Graney, M.: Happiness and social participation in aging, J. Gerontol. 30:701-706, 1975.

Havighurst, R.: The leisure activities of the middle-aged, Am. J. Sociol. 63:152-162, 1957.

Havighurst, R.: Life beyond family, and work. In Burgess, E., editor: Aging in western societies, Chicago, 1960, University of Chicago Press.

Havighurst, R.: The nature and values of meaningful free-time activity. In Kleemeier, R., editor: Aging and leisure: a research perspective into the meaningful use of time, New York, 1961, Oxford University Press.

Havighurst, R.: Life style and leisure patterns: their evolution through the life cycle, Proc. Int. Course Soc. Gerontol. 3:35-48, 1972.

Havighurst, R.: Social roles, work, leisure, and education. In Eisdorfer, C., and Lawton, M.P., editors: The psychology of adult development and aging, Washington, D.C., 1973, American Psychological Association.

Havighurst, R., and Feigenbaum, K.: Leisure and life style, Am. J. Sociol. 64:396-404, 1959.

Hunt, J.: The challenge of incompetence and poverty, Urbana, Ill., 1969, University of Illinois Press.

Hunt, M.: Sex in the seventies, Chicago, 1974, Playboy Press.

Iso-Ahola, S.: Social psychological determinants of perceptions of leisure, Paper presented at the NRPA Research Symposium, National Recreation and Park Association, Las Vegas, October, 1977.

Iso-Ahola, S.: Basic dimensions of definitions of leisure, J. Leisure Res. 11:28-39, 1979.

Iso-Ahola, S.: The social psychology of leisure and recreation, Dubuque, Iowa, 1980, Wm. C. Brown Co., Publishers.

Jersild, A.: The psychology of the adolescent, New York, 1963, Macmillan, Inc.

Kelly, J.: Work and leisure: a simplified paradigm, J. Leisure Res. 4:50-62, 1972.

Kelly, J.: Socialization toward leisure: a developmental approach, J. Leisure Res. 6:181-193, 1974.

Kelly, J.: Life styles and leisure choices, Fam. Coordinator 24: 185-190, 1975.

Kline, G., and Clarke, P., editors: Mass communications and youth: some current perspectives, Beverly Hills, Calif., 1971, Sage Publications, Inc.

Kraus, R.: Recreation and leisure in modern society, ed. 2, Santa Monica, Calif., 1978, Goodyear Publishing Co., Inc.

Langer, E., and Rodin, J.: The effects of choice and enhanced personal responsibility for the aged: a field experiment in an institutional setting, J. Personality Soc. Psychol. 34:191-198, 1976.

Lawton, M.P., and Nahemow, L.: Ecology and the aging process. In Eisdorfer, C., and Lawton, M.P., editors: The psychology of adult development and aging, Washington, D.C., 1973, American Psychological Association.

Lawton, M.P., and Simon, B.: The ecology of social relationships in housing for the elderly, Gerontologist 8:108-115, 1968.

Lemon, B., Bengston, V., and Peterson, J.: An exploration of the activity types and life satisfaction among in-movers to a retirement community, J. Gerontol. 27:511-523, 1972.

MacDonald, M., McGuire, C., and Havighurst, R.: Leisure activities and the socio-economic status of children, Am. J. Sociol. 54:505-519, 1949.

Miller, S.: The social dilemma of the aging leisure participant. In Rose, A.M., and Peterson, W., editors: Older people and their social worlds, Philadelphia, 1965, F.A. Davis Co.

Murphy, J.: Concepts of leisure, ed. 2, Englewood Cliffs, N.J., 1981, Prentice-Hall, Inc.

National Council on the Aging: The myth and reality of aging in America, Washington, D.C., 1975, National Council on the Aging.

Neulinger, J.: The psychology of leisure, Springfield, Ill., 1974, Charles C Thomas, Publisher.

Orthner, D.: Leisure activity patterns and marital satisfaction over the marital career, J. Marriage Fam. 37:91-102, 1975.

Orthner, D.: Patterns of leisure and marital interaction, J. Leisure Res. 8:98-111, 1976.

Palmore, E., and Kivett, V.: Change in life satisfaction: a longitudinal study of persons aged 46-70, J. Gerontol. 32:311-316, 1977.

Parsons, T.: An approach to psychological theory in terms of the theory of action. In Koch, S., editor: Psychology: the study of a science, vol. 3, New York, 1959, McGraw-Hill, Inc.

Pieper, J.: Leisure: the basis of culture, New York, 1963, The New American Library, Inc.

Riesman, D.: Some observations on changes in leisure activities, Antioch Rev. 12:417-436, 1952.

Rodin, J., and Langer, E.: Long-term effects of control-relevant intervention with the institutionalized aged, J. Personality Soc. Psychol. 35:897-902, 1977.

Schulz, R.: Effects of control and predictability on the physical and psychological well-being of the institutionalized aged, J. Personality Soc. Psychol. 33:563-573, 1976.

Schulz, R., and Hanusa, B.: Long-term effects of control and predictability-enhancing interventions: findings and ethical issues, J. Personality Soc. Psychol. 36:1194-1201, 1978.

Seligman, M.: Helplessness: on depression, development and death, San Francisco, 1975, W.H. Freeman & Co., Publishers.

Sutton-Smith, B.: Child's play: very serious business, Psychol. Today 5:67-69, 87, 1971.

Sutton-Smith, B., Rosenberg, B., and Morgan, E.: Development of sex differences in play choices during preadolescence, Child Dev. 34:119-126, 1963.

Tinsley, H., Barrett, T., and Kass, R.: Leisure activities and need satisfaction, J. Leisure Res. 9:110-120, 1977.

Turner, R.: Role-taking, role-standpoint, and reference group behavior, Am. J. Sociol. 61:316-328, 1956.

Turner, R.: Role-taking: process versus conformity. In Rose, A., editor: Human behavior and social process: an interactionist approach, Boston, 1962, Appleton-Century-Crofts.

Ward, R.: The aging experience: an introduction to social gerontology, New York, 1979, J.B. Lippincott Co.

Witt, P.: Factor structure of leisure behavior for high school age youth in three communities, J. Leisure Res. **3:**213-219, 1971.

Yoesting, D., and Burkhead, D.: Significance of childhood recreation experience on adult leisure behavior: an exploratory analysis, J. Leisure Res. **5:**25-36, 1973.

Zborowski, M.: Aging and recreation, J. Gerontol. **17:**302-309, 1962.

SUGGESTED READINGS

Atchley, R.: The sociology of retirement, Cambridge, Mass., 1976, Schenkman Publishing Co., Inc.

Gordon, C., Gaitz, C., and Scott, J.: Leisure and lives: personal expressivity across the life span. In Binstock, R., and Shanas, E., editors: Handbook of aging and the social sciences, New York, 1976, Van Nostrand Reinhold Co.

Havighurst, R.: Social roles, work, leisure, and education. In Eisdorfer, C., and Lawton, M.P., editors: The psychology of adult development and aging, Washington, D.C., 1973, American Psychological Association.

Iso-Ahola, S.: The social psychology of leisure and recreation, Dubuque, Iowa, 1980, Wm. C. Brown Co., Publishers.

Ward, R.: The aging experience: an introduction to social gerontology, New York, 1979, J.B. Lippincott Co.

PART TWO
Leisure service settings

The network of services available to older persons is increasingly being viewed along a continuum that attempts to match need with appropriate services. Part Two is organized along a continuum of leisure service settings, spanning voluntary associations and volunteerism (Chapter 4), multipurpose senior centers (Chapter 5), planned community housing (Chapter 6), and institutions for the elderly (Chapter 7). The underlying dimension of this continuum is the level of independence of the older persons and the requirement for assistance with leisure services according to service setting. Thus at one end of the continuum the older person may not require extensive assistance (voluntary associations and volunteerism), whereas further along the continuum greater levels of dependence may require more assistance (multipurpose senior centers and planned community housing), ultimately ending in full dependence and full-time assistance (institutions for the elderly). The major question therefore is not whether one service setting is better than another but whether there is a matching of need with appropriate leisure services within the setting.

4

Voluntary associations and volunteerism

The French traveler Alexis de Tocqueville commented well over a century ago on the vitality of voluntary associations in the United States. The number and variety of such associations continue to the present day both at national and local levels. There are very few aspects of life not directly touched by political, religious, labor, trade, charitable, fraternal, veterans', social, athletic, and recreation associations. The proliferation of voluntary associations from civic to recreation provides many opportunities for older persons to participate. This chapter will examine age-integrated and age-homogeneous voluntary associations, the importance of these associations to older persons, the volunteer service role and its contributions to older persons and society, the development of the volunteer service role, and the use of older volunteers in leisure services.

TYPES OF VOLUNTARY ASSOCIATIONS

There are age-related patterns to voluntary association participation. This section examines age-integrated and age-homogeneous voluntary associations.

Age-integrated associations

Age patterns of participation in voluntary associations may vary according to gender, race, health, income, and education. Older men are more likely than older women to belong to fraternal groups (e.g., Rotary), farm organizations, and political clubs, whereas older women are more likely to belong to church-affiliated groups and professional or academic associations (Cutler, 1976a; Payne and Whittington, 1976). Blacks have higher rates of participation than whites, with blacks being more likely to belong to church-affiliated groups and whites more likely to belong to fraternal groups, nationality groups, and senior citizen clubs (Clemente, Rexroad, and Hirsch, 1975). Association participation is greater for individuals with better health, higher income, and more education (Riley and Foner, 1968).

Age patterns of participation may also vary according to type of association. Data in Table 4-1 show these patterns for a representative sample of persons in the United States 18 years of age and older (Cutler, 1976a, p. 464). Persons 65 or older are most likely to belong to fraternal groups, church-affiliated groups, labor unions, and veterans' groups. It can be seen that the percentage belonging to fraternal and church-affiliated groups increases with age, which Cutler (1976a) suggests is due to generational differences in association appeal. Membership in sports groups, labor unions, veterans' groups, and service clubs reaches a peak in middle age and declines thereafter. This decline in membership and participation has been traditionally attributed to increasing age and has been taken as evidence to support the disengagement theory. However, Cutler (1977) reported two longitudinal studies that indicated a basic pattern of engagement, with those who either increased or maintained a stable level of participation far outnumbering those whose participation declined. These declines may be due to poor health and relinquishing of work and family roles (Cutler, 1976a; Ward, 1979a), lower socioeconomic status (Cutler, 1977), or simply changes from job-related, political, or civic associations to fraternal, recreational, service, or age-homogeneous associations (Trela, 1976).

TABLE 4-1   **Percentage belonging to 16 types of voluntary associations by age**

Type of association	Age						
	18-24	25-34	35-44	45-54	55-64	65-74	75+
Fraternal groups	3	9	14	15	15	17	23
Church-affiliated groups	27	34	46	45	48	48	52
Sports groups	26	23	23	19	12	8	5
Labor unions	13	16	17	21	22	11	7
Professional or academic societies	12	15	17	13	10	9	5
School service groups	8	22	31	18	8	5	1
Youth groups	13	11	19	10	5	4	1
Veterans' groups	2	4	9	14	13	8	11
Service clubs	4	8	11	13	9	8	8
Literary, art, discussion, or study groups	7	13	8	9	9	8	7
Farm organizations	3	3	4	6	6	4	4
Political clubs	2	5	6	4	4	4	7
Hobby or garden clubs	8	12	10	7	10	9	9
School fraternities or sororities	5	6	4	5	3	4	3
Nationality groups	3	3	3	4	2	3	3
Other groups	7	11	10	9	7	12	11

From Cutler, S.: J. Gerontol. **31**:464, 1976. Reprinted by permission of the Journal of Gerontology.

The level of participation in voluntary associations organized for or by older persons is relatively low. The National Council on the Aging (1975) found that only 8 percent of individuals 55 to 64 years old and 18 percent of those over 65 years old had attended a golden age club or senior citizen center during the previous year, with those most likely to attend being women, blacks, and the lowest income group. The National Council on the Aging also found that 19 percent of those over 55 years old (39 percent of blacks) stated that they would like to attend but lacked convenient facilities, adequate transportation, good health, or the time. Participation may also be limited by social class, with an organization such as the National Retired Teachers Association-American Association of Retired Persons (NRTA-AARP) more likely to have upper-middle-class members who are more skilled at interpersonal relationships, who make friends more readily, and who are better able to exercise leadership (Tissue, 1971; Ward, 1979a). The inability to easily accommodate individuals from different social classes limits the ability of these voluntary associations to serve the poor and disadvantaged (Taietz, 1976; Tissue, 1971).

Age-homogeneous associations

Gerontologists generally agree that voluntary associations are an important mechanism for maintaining the social integration of older persons (Hendricks and Hendricks, 1981). Such associations help to overcome the loss of instrumental roles and often provide a substitute for family roles through the development of friendships and informal support networks (Rosow, 1974; Trela and Jackson, 1979). Through age-homogeneous associations older persons are brought into contact with other older persons, enabling friendships to blossom and mutual information exchanges to take place.

IMPORTANCE OF VOLUNTARY ASSOCIATIONS

Gerontologists have not generally agreed on the relationship of voluntary association participation and life satisfaction; activity theorists support such a relationship, and disengagement theorists support the opposite view. Earlier research tended to support the assumption of the positive relationship between participation in voluntary associations and life satisfaction (Riley and Foner, 1968). However, research by Cutler (1973, 1976b), Edwards and Klemmack (1973), and Bull and Aucoin (1975) has shown that when the effects of socioeconomic status and subjective or self-rated health are taken into consideration the impact of voluntary association participation on life satisfaction is not significant. That is, socioeconomic status and health rather than voluntary participation are the significant contributors to life satisfaction.

The lack of a significant relationship between voluntary association participation and life satisfaction may reflect a lack of personally meaningful involvement. Ward (1979b) found that individuals with higher life satisfaction said they participated in voluntary associations because associations offered new experiences, opportunity for achievement, and development of creativity and because participating made them feel of help to society and other people.

These findings suggest that the volunteer service role will be experienced as meaningful because it provides opportunities for help to society and others.

THE VOLUNTEER SERVICE ROLE

The volunteer service role has greater participation and interest among older persons than is generally reported. Studies by ACTION (1974) found that 14 percent of older persons surveyed in April of 1974 had volunteered during the past year; the National Council on the Aging (1975) reported that 22 percent of individuals over 65 years of age do volunteer on a regular basis and another 10 percent said they would like to volunteer. This section examines the contributions of the volunteer service role to older persons and society.

Contributions to older persons

The volunteer service role can be a source of meaningful personal activity for older persons. Volunteering offers the older person an opportunity to increase feelings of usefulness, to neutralize the effects of loneliness, to satisfy the need for communication, to fill unused time, and to create a functional role (Dye, Goodman, Roth, Bley, and Jensen, 1973; Hunter and Linn, 1980-81; Katz, 1970; Lambert, Guberman, and Morris, 1964; Rosenblatt, 1966; Sainer and Zander, 1971). Fred Clarke, a school volunteer with Dedicated Older Volunteers in Educational Services (DOVES) in Los Angeles, expressed how volunteering affected him (Williamson and Ware, 1977, p. 1):

> At my time of life, age 75, to find people . . . who encourage me to do my little bit . . . has been so rewarding. It has given me more than I could ever give the children I help . . . .

Contributions to society

Older volunteers can be providers of services that benefit society. Under authority of the Older Americans Act of 1965, the federal government established ACTION in 1971, and through its Older Americans Volunteer Programs implemented four major programs.

RETIRED SENIOR VOLUNTEER PROGRAM. The Retired Senior Volunteer Program (RSVP) enables individuals 60 years of age or older to do volunteer service in a variety of "volunteer stations" such as day care centers for children, hospitals, nursing homes, senior centers, libraries, museums, courts, parks, zoos, and schools. Tracing its roots to the very successful project Serve and Enrich Retirement by Volunteer Experience (SERVE), developed by the Community Service Society of New York in 1965, RSVP provides reimbursement for transportation to and from the site of volunteer service and out-of-pocket expenses, as well as accident and liability insurance.

FOSTER GRANDPARENTS PROGRAM. The Foster Grandparents Program pays a modest stipend to low-income persons 60 years of age and over, reimbursement for meals and transportation, and accident insurance to enable older persons to work on an individual basis with children who have special needs. Foster grandparents have direct contact and do simple activities with children in settings such as homes for the mentally retarded or emotionally disturbed, correctional facilities, pediatric wards, day care centers, and schools.

SENIOR COMPANION PROGRAM. The Senior Companion Program (SCP) is modeled after the Foster Grandparents Program, except that the service recipients are older persons. Older low-income persons receive a modest stipend, reimbursement for transportation and meals, and accident insurance to enable them to provide services to frail or disabled elderly in their homes, hospitals, and nursing homes. Duties may include personal hygiene, simple housekeeping, cooking, letter writing, or reading.

SERVICE CORPS OF RETIRED EXECUTIVES. The Service Corps of Retired Executives (SCORE), a program jointly sponsored by ACTION and the Small Business Administration, places retired businessmen and businesswomen in small businesses such as restaurants, bakeries, groceries, and pharmacies. The experience and knowledge gained by the retired executives in the working world is made available to individuals setting up new businesses. SCORE volunteers are reimbursed for any out-of-pocket expenses they may incur while volunteering.

This and the other programs described have been shown to be beneficial to the service recipients and to the older volunteers. An example of a small scale evaluation is a study by Saltz (1971), who evaluated one Foster Grandparents program, finding a "family" feeling between older volunteers and institutionalized children; in spite of the temporary nature of the relationship the experience was conducive to life satisfaction, health, and general vigor of the older volunteer. In addition, it was found that the "grandparents" had good attendance, good job stability records, and favorable ratings from supervisors.

Payne (1977, p. 357) proposed for the volunteer service role a Social Restructuring Model (Fig. 4-1) that builds on the Kuypers and Bengston (1973) social reconstruction model and introduces the volunteer role as an intervention strategy that may provide social support, role continuity, enhanced self-concept, and life satisfaction. This model is based on the assumptions that:

DEVELOPMENT OF VOLUNTEER SERVICE ROLE

1. Older persons have learned and developed a pool of skills through a lifetime of roles.
2. These skills are adequately and appropriately used.
3. Old age is felt to be a different but valuable time that needs to be restructured.
4. Different sorts of roles than those at other periods of the life cycle need to be filled.
5. An individual's sense of identity depends on the kind of social valuing he or she experiences.
6. Appropriate feedback is given from a significant group that makes the older person feel useful.

An examination of Fig. 4-1 shows a cyclical system that is a dynamic interaction or exchange between the individual older person and his or her social setting or context (inner circle of the figure) and inputs (*A* through *E*) that can assist the older person in restructuring roles and providing social participation continuity. This model will be used to illustrate and integrate some of the key elements of the volunteer service role.

Recruitment and selection

The recruitment and selection of older volunteers can be facilitated through an understanding of the characteristics that have been shown to distinguish older volunteers from nonvolunteers. Research by Dye, Goodman, Roth, Bley, and Jensen (1973) found the central variable distinguishing the older volunteer from the nonvolunteer was past patterns of organizational participation. Monk and Cryns (1974) found the volunteer service role to be most attractive to older persons who were younger, owned their own homes, were better educated, had a belief in their capacity to make a service contribution, were interested in organized activities, and had a broad range of social interests. Volunteers were found to have a significantly higher degree of life satisfaction, fewer symptoms of depression, and possessed a stronger will to live than nonvolunteers (Hunter and Linn, 1980-1981).

A variety of techniques may be used in the recruitment and selection of older volunteers. Examples of techniques may be drawn from DOVES, a group of more than 2,300 older persons volunteering in more than 350 Los Angeles area schools. When the program began in 1974 an intensive publicity campaign was launched through local media, service organization bulletins, and industrial house organs. As the program developed, organizations such as RSVP, senior centers and clubs, school teachers and principals, and PTAs were used to recruit. A DOVES volunteer recruitment committee was formed to set up a citywide program and even included speakers bureau workshops to help enthusiastic volunteers improve their public speaking skills. In the selection process each DOVES applicant must complete a detailed questionnaire and be carefully screened before he or she is accepted for orientation. Volunteers are sought who have "a good attitude toward children, a desire to serve, good health and character, talent or experience that can help a child, command of English, an outgoing personality, and an ability to communicate" (Williamson and Ware, 1977, p. 3).

Placement and training

Placement and training of older volunteers must be an integrated process. The newly recruited older volunteer needs to be given a variety of placement opportunities consistent with his or her background, experience, and interests and *not* simply with the agency's current needs. Given an opportunity to observe a variety of assignments, older volunteers will be able to choose where they are able to use the skills they have developed over a lifetime and will feel

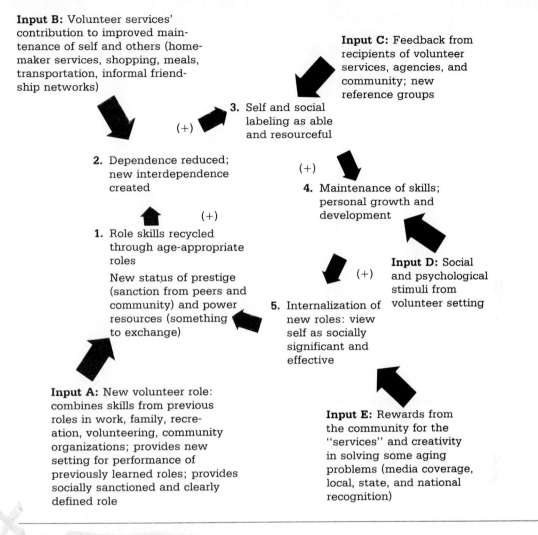

Input B: Volunteer services' contribution to improved maintenance of self and others (homemaker services, shopping, meals, transportation, informal friendship networks)

Input C: Feedback from recipients of volunteer services, agencies, and community; new reference groups

3. Self and social labeling as able and resourceful

(+)

2. Dependence reduced; new interdependence created

(+)

4. Maintenance of skills; personal growth and development

(+)

1. Role skills recycled through age-appropriate roles

New status of prestige (sanction from peers and community) and power resources (something to exchange)

Input D: Social and psychological stimuli from volunteer setting

(+)

5. Internalization of new roles: view self as socially significant and effective

Input A: New volunteer role: combines skills from previous roles in work, family, recreation, volunteering, community organizations; provides new setting for performance of previously learned roles; provides socially sanctioned and clearly defined role

Input E: Rewards from the community for the "services" and creativity in solving some aging problems (media coverage, local, state, and national recognition)

Fig. 4-1. Social restructuring model.

From Payne, B.P.: Gerontologist **17**:357, 1977. Reprinted by permission of The Gerontologist.

competent and comfortable (see Fig. 4-1, *Inputs A* and *B*). Older volunteers are happier when they can move quickly into an assignment (Babic, 1972) and are *at the same time* provided with ongoing orientation and on-the-job training, which lessens the fear that they might not be able to successfully perform the tasks at hand (a particular fear of older volunteers with lower socioeconomic status). Formal training sessions tend to intimidate older persons (Babic, 1972) and imply that they are being tested (Sainer and Zander, 1971). The most effective placement and training is informal, ongoing, and adjusted to the volunteer's level of development and pace, rather than the predetermined pace of someone else (Babic, 1972).

Supervision

The *group approach* to supervision has been shown to be most valuable (Babic, 1972; Sainer, 1976; Sainer and Zander, 1971). This approach focuses on group placement and the training of a group of older volunteers who accept individual assignments but who come as a group on a selected day of the week. Such an approach provides the older person without volunteer experience peer support from veteran volunteers, as well as the social contact and friendship so needed by many older persons. The group approach has benefits for the agency because group meetings can facilitate communication of general information and discussion of shared problems and can encourage the development of new volunteer programs and responsibilities.

Older volunteers also need an *individual supervisor*. This supervisor performs a variety of functions such as listening to complaints from volunteers, following up on volunteers who are absent or drop out, promoting understanding and relations with agency staff (particularly the "line" supervisor), exploring new placement opportunities, and recruiting and welcoming new volunteers (Babic, 1972; Sainer, 1976; Sainer and Zander, 1971).

Retention

Retention of the older volunteer is facilitated by the practices employed in the process of recruitment and selection, placement and training, and supervision previously discussed. Recognition and transportation, however, need further discussion because they are directed specifically toward retention of older volunteers.

RECOGNITION. The older volunteer needs recognition from the agency and the larger community (see Fig. 4-1, *Inputs C, D,* and *E*). Sainer and Zander (1971, pp. 203-204) list a number of ways that the older volunteer has been recognized in project SERVE, with "words of praise from SERVE and agency staff, newspaper and magazine articles, comments from friends and acquaintances, and plaudits from city, state, and federal officials, whom he sees as powerful and approving, and as giving community sanction." Recognition from a variety of sources makes the volunteer role a position of prestige and enables the older person to feel needed and valued.

TRANSPORTATION. Transportation is essential to the retention of the older volunteer because of the diminished strength of the older person, the lack of convenient transportation, and the difficulty of reaching many agencies because of their inaccessibility (Sainer, 1976). Transportation does not simply mean reimbursement of car fare but may necessitate providing vans or cars so that volunteers can go as a group to the placement agency.

Southern Illinoisan Staff Photo by Jerry Lower

Special transportation is often necessary to enable the older volunteer to fulfill the service role and provides opportunities for conversation with fellow volunteers.

Older volunteers have not been effectively used as a resource by leisure service agencies. The National Council on the Aging (1975) found leisure services to be one of the volunteer areas preferred by older persons who were not currently committed to volunteering.

USE OF OLDER VOLUNTEERS IN LEISURE SERVICES

The leisure service delivery system offers many features attractive to the older volunteer. Responsible, meaningful positions may be assigned on an ongoing basis, provided the leisure service agency is flexible in matching tasks to the older volunteer's interests and experiences. Leisure service agencies have a long tradition of volunteer use and experience in training volunteers with nonthreatening teaching approaches. The group approach is the predominant form of leisure service delivery and can be easily adapted to supervision of older volunteers. The public visibility of leisure services and the use of a variety of media for public relations enable the older volunteer to be recognized and rewarded by the agency and the larger community. Transportation of groups of participants can be adapted to the transportation of older volunteers either singularly (by each agency) or cooperatively (with other agencies).

Leisure service agencies that do not currently employ a coordinator or supervisor of volunteers should consider the benefits of such a position. The justification for a coordinator or supervisor's position, presented in terms of the number of hours of volunteer time that may be generated multiplied by the minimum hourly wage, results in dollars saved, or "earned." The job description should include the recruitment, selection, placement, training, supervision, and retention of volunteers. The job applicant should have leadership, programming, and management skills and knowledge of human growth and development, particularly in social gerontology. Such a position in a leisure service setting would be attractive because it would allow both individual contact with service recipients and management opportunities.

Declining monetary resources, an increasing pool of available older persons, and renewed interest in voluntarism in the public sector make it incumbent on leisure service agencies to use older persons as volunteers for both direct service and as advisory board members. It would be a service to older persons, the agency, and society.

SUMMARY

Voluntary associations, touching all aspects of life in the United States, can be of two types: age integrated and age homogeneous. Age patterns of participation in age-integrated associations may vary according to individual characteristics such as gender, race, health, income, education, and type of association. The level of participation in age-homogeneous associations organized for or by older persons is relatively low for associations such as senior centers or golden age clubs because of the lack of convenient facilities, adequate transportation, good health, or time. The most likely attendees are women, blacks, and the lowest income group.

Voluntary associations are important for older persons. They help to socially integrate older persons by enabling friendships and informal support networks to develop. However, voluntary association participation was found to be not significantly related to life satisfaction when the effects of socioeconomic status and self-rated health were taken into consideration. This possibly reflects a lack of personally meaningful involvement of older persons in voluntary associations that do not provide help to society and others.

The volunteer service role makes important contributions to older persons and society. The volunteer service role can be a source of meaningful personal activity for older persons because it offers an opportunity to increase feelings of usefulness, neutralizes the effects of loneliness, satisfies the need for communication, fills unused time, and creates a functional role. Older persons can be providers of services that benefit society through a number of federally sponsored programs such as the Retired Senior Volunteer Program (RSVP), Foster Grandparents Program, Senior Companion Program (SCP), and Service Corps of Retired Executives (SCORE).

The development of the volunteer service role as an intervention strategy providing benefits for the older person and society depends on a number of key elements. The recruitment and selection of older volunteers is facilitated through a consideration of the characteristics that distinguish older volunteers from nonvolunteers and a variety of techniques illustrated by the Dedicated Older Volunteers in Educational Service (DOVES) program. Placement and training must be integrated and quick and must draw on the background, experience, interests, and choices of older volunteers. Ongoing orientation and training must also be provided, while avoiding formal training sessions whose format might intimidate the elderly or imply that they are being tested. Supervision may be conducted through the group approach, which provides peer support, social contact, and friendship opportunities, or it may be conducted by an individual supervisor. Retention of the older volunteer is enhanced through recognition of his or her contribution to the agency and the larger community and through consideration of the transportation needs of older persons.

Older volunteers have generally been underutilized by leisure service agencies, yet leisure services offer many features consistent with the key elements for the development of the volunteer service role. The employment of a coordinator or supervisor of volunteers by a leisure service agency can be justified on the basis of fiscal soundness and attractiveness to prospective employees because of the duties, competencies, and rewards to be gained through leadership and management opportunities. It also provides service to older persons, agencies, and society.

REFERENCES

ACTION: Americans volunteer, Washington, D.C., 1974, ACTION.

Babic, A.: The older volunteer: expectations and satisfactions, Gerontologist 12:87-90, 1972.

Bull, C., and Aucoin, J.: Voluntary association participation and life satisfaction: a replication note, J. Gerontol. 30:73-76, 1975.

Clemente, F., Rexroad, P., and Hirsch, C.: The participation of the black aged in voluntary associations, J. Gerontol. 30:469-472, 1975.

Cutler, S.: Voluntary association membership and life satisfaction: a cautionary research note, J. Gerontol. 28:96-100, 1973.

Cutler, S.: Age profiles of membership in sixteen types of voluntary associations, J. Gerontol. 31:462-470, 1976a.

Cutler, S.: Membership in different types of voluntary associations and psychological well-being, Gerontologist 16:335-339, 1976b.

Cutler, S.: Aging and voluntary association participation, J. Gerontol. 32:470-479, 1977.

Dye, D., Goodman, M., Roth, M., Bley, N., and Jensen, K.: The older adult volunteer compared to the nonvolunteer, Gerontologist **13**:215-218, 1973.

Edwards, J., and Klemmack, D.: Correlates of life satisfaction: a reexamination, J. Gerontol. **28**:497-502, 1973.

Hendricks, J., and Hendricks, C.: Aging in mass society, ed. 2, Cambridge, Mass., 1981, Winthrop Publishers.

Hunter, K., and Linn, M.: Psychosocial differences between elderly volunteers and nonvolunteers, Int. J. Aging Hum. Dev. **12**:205-213, 1980-1981.

Katz, A.: Self-help organizations and volunteer participation in social welfare, Soc. Work **15**:51-60, 1970.

Kuypers, J., and Bengston, V.: Social breakdown and competence: a model of normal aging, Hum. Dev. **16**:181-201, 1973.

Lambert, C., Guberman, M., and Morris, R.: Reopening doors to community participation for older people: how realistic? Soc. Serv. Rev. **38**:42-50, 1964.

Monk, A., and Cryns, A.: Predictors of voluntaristic intent among the aged: an area study, Gerontologist **14**:425-429, 1974.

National Council on the Aging: The myth and reality of aging in America, Washington, D.C., 1975, National Council on the Aging.

Payne, B.: The older volunteer: social continuity and development, Gerontologist **17**:355-361, 1977.

Payne, B., and Whittington, F.: Older women: an examination of popular stereotypes and research evidence, Soc. Problems **23**:488-504, 1976.

Riley, M., and Foner, A.: Aging and society, vol. 1, An inventory of research findings, New York, 1968, Russell Sage Foundation.

Rosenblatt, A.: Interest of older persons in volunteer activities, Soc. Work **11**:87-94, 1966.

Rosow, I.: Socialization to old age, Berkeley, Calif., 1974, University of California Press.

Sainer, J.: The community cares: older volunteers, Soc. Policy **7**:73-75, 1976.

Sainer, J., and Zander, M.: Guidelines for older person volunteers, Gerontologist **11**:201-204, 1971.

Saltz, R.: Aging persons as child-care workers in a foster-grandparent program: psychosocial effects and work performance, Aging Hum. Dev. **2**:314-340, 1971.

Taietz, P.: Two conceptual models of the senior center, J. Gerontol. **31**:219-222, 1976.

Tissue, T.: Social class and the senior citizen center, Gerontologist **11**:196-200, 1971.

Trela, J.: Social class and association membership: an analysis of age-graded and non-age-graded voluntary participation, J. Gerontol. **31**:198-203, 1976.

Trela, J., and Jackson, D.: Family life and community participation in old age, Res. Aging **1**:233-251, 1979.

Ward, R.A.: The aging experience: an introduction to social gerontology, New York, 1979a, J.B. Lippincott Co.

Ward, R.A.: The meaning of voluntary association participation to older people, J. Gerontol. **34**:438-445, 1979b.

Williamson, J., and Ware, M.: The older volunteer, Washington, D.C., 1977, National Center for Voluntary Action.

SUGGESTED READINGS

Babic, A.: The older volunteer: expectations and satisfactions, Gerontologist **12**:87-90, 1972.

Sainer, J.: The community cares: older volunteers, Soc. Policy **7**:73-75, 1976.

Sainer, J., and Zander, M.: Guidelines for older person volunteers, Gerontologist **11**:201-204, 1971.

Senior centers

Senior centers across the United States are emerging as focal points for older persons living in the community. This chapter provides introductory background information and information on the organization and management of senior centers.

The concept of the senior center as a community focal point for older persons is emphasized in the National Institute of Senior Centers (NISC) definition of a senior center:

DEFINITION AND DESCRIPTION

> A senior center is a community focal point of aging where older persons as individuals or in groups come together for services and activities which enhance their dignity, support their independence and encourage their involvement in and with the community. (National Institute of Senior Centers, 1978, p. 15)

A description of senior centers is provided by the 1974 national survey of senior group programs conducted by the National Institute of Senior Centers (Leanse and Wagner, 1975). This national survey identified 4,870 senior group programs of which 51 percent were senior centers, 46 percent were clubs, and 3 percent were neither senior centers nor clubs. Most of the senior centers are in urban or suburban settings; about 25 percent are in rural areas. Sponsorship was almost evenly divided between voluntary nonprofit organizations and public or government agencies, with recreation departments being the municipal agency most often entrusted with the development and management of senior centers under public or government sponsorship. Although data on funding sources were incomplete, 47 percent reported receiving funding entirely from public sources, 34 percent reported a combination of public and private sources, and 18 percent reported support entirely from private sources. Only 26 percent of senior centers own their facilities. The remaining use donated facilities (66 percent make no direct payment for space). Only 20 percent use new facilities, 42 percent use renovated facilities, and the remaining use facilities that have not been altered to suit program needs. The majority of the senior

EXAMPLE 5-1

CELESTE CAMPBELL SENIOR COMMUNITY CENTER
155 High Street, Eugene, Oregon

At the Celeste Campbell Senior Community Center, four paid staff and about 200 volunteers work together for the recreational, educational, and social benefit of persons over the age of 55. Operated by the Parks and Recreation Department since 1963, the Center is located near two senior housing projects and on a major transit line. More than 5,500 people participate in the Center's activities each month.

The Campbell Center is open 5 days a week. Regular programs include opportunities for older persons to be involved in community service projects, to keep current on legal assistance, health education and consumer information, and to be out of doors with senior swimming, golf, fishing, and intrastate travel. Bicycling, canoeing, bird watching, and camping programs are also included. Social opportunities include dances, card parties and clubs, potlucks, birthday parties and meetings of retirement groups, such as the American Association of Retired Persons and the Retired Railroaders. In addition, Spanish, German, French, creative writing, and speed reading classes are also held.

Volunteers, most of whom are older persons, help maintain the programs and services of the Center as hostesses, office helpers, drivers, and field trip assistants. Since all class instructors are volunteers, there are no class registration fees. Volunteers with an aptitude for sewing make quilts and layettes that are distributed by community social welfare department. Other volunteers cook and provide cleanup for the Center's Wednesday Fun Night, a program that includes an evening meal, cards, and bingo. In addition, each Thursday the Center is host to elderly persons living in nursing homes, foster homes and sheltered care facilities, and the homebound; 12 to 16 volunteers plan and supervise activities for the 90 participants, visiting with them, playing cards and ping pong, and assisting with crafts.

Recruiting of volunteers is done through Voluntary Action Centers, the Retired Senior Volunteer Program (RSVP) and by word of mouth. The paid staff members rotate in coordinating volunteers in the various programs. A general orientation and welcome is held for new volunteers as a group, then each individual is assigned someone, usually another volunteer, to advise and train him or her. Monthly meetings are held for feedback, suggestions and problem solving. Recognition for volunteers is given at brunches and in newsletters. Accident insurance is handled by a local insurance broker, and RSVP participants are covered by federal insurance.

centers employ one or more full-time paid staff persons. In multipurpose senior centers (centers offering three or more services) it was found that 84 percent offered the three basic services of recreation, education, and either counseling or information and referral services. The most commonly offered recreation activities are sedentary recreation (e.g., cards, bingo, movies, spectator sports, and parties), offered by 87 percent of centers; creative activities (e.g., arts and crafts, drama, music, and preparing bulletins or newspapers), offered by 86 percent of centers; and active recreation (e.g., hiking, dancing, sports, and exercise classes), offered by 55 percent of centers. Example 5-1 is a description of a senior center and its programs.

HISTORY

Senior centers are a relatively new service for older persons. The first senior center was the William Hodson Community Center established in New York City in 1943 (Leanse, Tiven, and Robb, 1977). This center was established because of the need for a setting to help alleviate the loneliness and to fill the unobligated time so often observed among older persons by social workers in the city's department of welfare. Participation was encouraged by its location in a working class neighborhood and by the provision of services such as recreation, social casework, education, and other personal services needed to maintain older persons in the community.

California was the site of the next two senior centers. The San Francisco Senior Center was founded in 1947. From the very beginning it was a multipurpose senior center, focusing on recreation and educational services supervised by a professional staff in a facility supplied by the Department of Parks and Recreation (Kent, 1978). Little House opened in 1949 in Menlo Park and had a unique feature—middle-class retirees planned and carried out a full recreation and educational program that benefited the entire community through active involvement of older persons in a variety of community projects (Maxwell, 1962).

The growth of senior centers has been accelerated as a result of the passage of the Older Americans Act of 1965. Although senior centers continue to be sponsored and funded by local community organizations, public agencies, privately contributed United Way dollars, and tax dollars from local recreation, adult education, and public health agencies, federal dollars have enabled senior centers to expand their services and develop special services for the unserved or underserved elderly. Federally sponsored nutrition programs have considerably increased the number of service sites for older persons, and many of these programs have moved beyond the daily meal to become senior centers.

PHILOSOPHY AND RATIONALE

The philosophy of senior centers is built on the concept that older persons have value, dignity, and the same basic needs that all people have. This philosophy is articulated by the National Institute of Senior Centers (1978, p. 5):

> The philosophy of the senior center movement is based on the premises that aging is a normal developmental process; that human beings need peers with whom they can interact and who are available as a source of encouragement and support; and that adults have the right to have a voice in determining matters in which they have a vital interest.

The rationale for the senior center is based on a recognition of the unique characteristic of a senior center:

> A planned program; location in a facility; being directed to older persons; meeting the interrelated needs of the total individual; helping older people to help themselves; providing a locus for service providers for the aging; assisting them in bringing their services to the neighborhood; combining public and private resources to benefit older persons; serving as a community resource for information or training about older people, as well as bringing to the community older people's skills, talents, and experiences. (Leanse, Tiven, and Robb, 1977, p. xiii)

MODELS

There are a number of different models according to which senior centers may be categorized. Fowler (1974) developed three different ways to categorize senior centers: *activities generated* (services, activities, individual services and casework, or a combination of all three), *administration* (centralized, decentralized, or central location with satellites), and *origin of services* (center staff, center staff and community agencies, or community agencies with center staff providing coordination). The National Institute of Senior Centers' (Leanse and Wagner, 1975) national survey of senior group programs categorized centers according to size and complexity of operation into multipurpose senior centers, senior centers, clubs for older persons, and programs for all persons with special activities available for the elderly; the differences between clubs and centers is that centers are more likely to offer a wide variety of services and activities, sponsor groups that meet several days per week, have a paid staff and a permanent facility, and be incorporated with a board of directors. Taietz (1976, p. 219) classified senior centers according to the *social agency model,* which views senior centers as "programs designed to meet the needs of the elderly and postulates that the poor and the disengaged are the more likely candidates for participation in senior centers." The alternative *voluntary organization model* hypothesizes that "the elderly who are more active in voluntary organizations and who manifest strong attachments to the community are also the ones who make use of senior centers."

ORGANIZATION AND MANAGEMENT

Senior center organization and management require considerable skill and expertise if the senior center is to fulfill its capacity and commitment to older people. This section addresses a number of the critical areas important for the successful organization and management of senior centers.

The development of a new senior center requires a sound plan of action based on informed leadership. Planning requires the identification and adoption of certain strategies by the initiating or sponsoring group. The following are strategies proposed to give guidance and direction in the planning process.

Planning

FORMATION OF A PLANNING COMMITTEE. The initiators or sponsors of a proposed senior center should establish a small planning committee. Such a planning committee may want to appoint an advisory committee composed of community representatives from the initiating or sponsoring agency; related community agencies; older persons; and business, civic, and religious segments of the community, as well as enlist the expertise of professionals from fields such as gerontology, psychology, leisure services, social work, city planning, real estate, and law. If the planning committee decides that additional guidance may be needed, a consultant may be employed to guide the project through the planning stages by identifying essential tasks, helping to establish realistic priorities, and providing financial and time management strategies to enable the committee to reach achievable goals. The committee needs to develop a budget to cover initial planning expenses and an action plan for setting forth tasks to be accomplished, persons responsible for each of these tasks, and completion time for each task.

NEED DETERMINATION. An action plan should provide specific information required for establishing the need for a senior center. The community's needs may be documented through an examination of census data on the characteristics of the older population as to numbers and community distribution and through interviews with older community residents and elderly advocacy and service providers at the local, county, and state levels (e.g., departments of health, education, and social services; housing authority; human services; and area agency on aging). The examination of census data will help to define the appropriate service area based on elderly population concentration, and interviews will help to identify currently existing services to avoid duplication.

FUNDING SOURCES. Identification of funding sources is a necessary but difficult task, ultimately spelling success or failure for the center. The planning committee may appoint a subcommittee to accomplish this task or assign or engage a consultant who is familiar with funding sources. Federal funding is not the only source of capital funding. There are also public bond issues; special grants from municipal, county, or state funds; capital fund campaigns; corporate gifts; grants from private foundations; grants from private trusts; appropriations by religious or philanthropic groups; board donations; and individual gifts.

PRELIMINARY PLAN DEVELOPMENT. A preliminary plan is developed from the information that has been gathered. It consists of three documents: a *program plan,* a *facility plan,* and an *operating plan* (Jordan, 1978). The program plan attempts to determine in as much detail as possible the types of services that the center should provide based on the needs and resource possibilities previously decided on. The facility plan is a preliminary analysis of the number, types, and sizes of rooms, yielding a space analysis that may be used to determine facility size. The operating plan, or management plan, establishes critical elements such as sponsorship, board of directors, staffing, and other key management elements related to the center's administrative structure. It must be stressed that all three plans are interrelated; the program plan affects facility and operations planning, the facility plan is based on program and operations needs, and the operating plan follows logically from program needs and facility design. The following sections will discuss the implementation of each of these plans.

Program

A senior center's program includes all of the services offered by the center and those made accessible through linkages with other agencies.

SERVICES. Although senior center programming is diverse, there are still a number of identifiable services available through a senior center.

Leisure services. Leisure services are the types of programs most commonly viewed as the central component of a senior center (Gelfand and Olsen, 1980). Common activities are arts and crafts, music, drama, dance, movies, physical fitness, sports, table games, camping, tours, outings, trips, parties, celebrations, and hobby and special interest groups.

Education. Education covers a wide range of activities. Activities may include lectures, forums, and round tables on nutrition, home safety, health, consumerism, law, creative writing, defensive driving, Bible study, and leadership development.

Information, counseling, and referral. Information, counseling, and referral may include general information, intake, registration, use of resource files, and personal counseling in topics such as housing, health, nutrition, transportation, finances, family, religion, retirement, law, and any number of other areas.

Health. Health programs may be developed in conjunction with city or county health departments, outpatient clinics, hospitals, extended care facilities, doctors, and nurses. Services may include screening clinics for high blood pressure, glaucoma, hearing, and other health concerns. Specialty services such as dentistry, podiatry, pharmacy, and health education may also be provided.

Housing. Housing services may be operated in senior centers to advise older persons on the availability of housing with appropriate cost, location, and safety. Trips to apartments, rooms, or houses may be arranged to alert older persons to problems that they might overlook when choosing housing.

Employment. Employment assistance may be provided through job referral. Guttman and Miller (1972) propose that centers develop employment services that could include employment counseling, job aptitude testing, job training, and job placement.

Financial aid and counseling. Related to employment is the provision of financial aid and counseling. This may include financial aid in emergencies, consumer counseling on eligibility for Supplemental Security Income (SSI), budgeting and spending of limited resources, and avoidance of dishonest salespersons.

Legal aid. Legal aid may be provided to advise the elderly in preparation of a will, guardianship or commitment proceedings brought by family or friends, personal abuse, and fraud.

Nutrition. Senior centers may provide food stamp information and serve as sites for congregate or group meals provided by the nutrition program of the Older Americans Act. Home-delivered meals or "meals-on-wheels" may also be directed from or coordinated through the senior center.

Transportation. Lack of mobility is a major problem for many older persons who often live in communities where transportation systems are nonexistent, inadequate, or too expensive. The senior center may arrange for transportation through center-owned or center-operated vans or buses or by using volunteers on a scheduled basis.

Services for the homebound. Senior centers may provide services to the homebound such as telephone reassurance and friendly visiting. These services can assist senior center members who are sick or potential members who need an incentive to come to the center.

Homemaker assistance. Homemaker assistance can help maintain older persons in their homes. Included under homemaker assistance are services such as housecleaning, occasional cooking, yard work, and minor home repairs.

Daycare. Daycare provides an alternative to the nursing home for older persons who want to remain in their own homes but whose families cannot be with them at all times because of work or other responsibilities. Daycare allows older persons to spend the entire day at the senior center, be fed a hot meal, and participate in leisure activities.

SERVICE DELIVERY SYSTEM. The senior center is a delivery system making services available to older persons. Outreach and community linkages are two approaches to more effective service delivery.

Outreach. Outreach has been developed to reach out to the more isolated or hard-to-reach older person. The *single site center* often employs outreach workers, who are specially trained community or participant volunteers, to identify and provide appropriate service either in the home of the older person or through encouraging and often personally escorting the older adult to the center. Another form of outreach is the creation of the *satellite center,* which may be established in a variety of spaces such as that available in storefronts, libraries, churches, or planned housing for the elderly. Satellite centers have several advantages. They have the increased capacity to respond to more defined target areas (e.g., specific neighborhoods), save resources by sharing certain administrative functions (e.g., by maintaining centralized management, information and referral systems, and highly technical personnel and services), and permit the development of site councils fostering consumer participation and community linkages.

Community linkages. The senior center must establish linkages with community planning and service agencies.

Community planning. Senior center involvement in community planning can be facilitated by participation on boards of other agencies planning services for older persons (e.g., area agency on aging) and by broad community input into the center's own program planning process (Leanse, Tiven, and Robb, 1977). This participation on the boards of other agencies may be performed not only by center staff but also by center board members and participants. Involvement of the larger community in the center's program planning is an effective technique that may lead to a commitment of resources to support the center's programs.

Service agencies. Linkages with service agencies help to provide a healthy competition among agencies providing similar services (Leanse, Tiven, and Robb, 1977) and helps to avoid duplication of services. Communication among agencies can be enhanced through regular meetings of local agency service providers, which enables each agency to better understand the goals and the programs of other agencies.

OVERCOMING PARTICIPATION BARRIERS. Effective senior center programming requires the overcoming of participation barriers. Strategies for overcoming these barriers are discussed in this section.

Treating older persons as adults. Senior center services must be geared to treating older persons as adults. Programming practices must be oriented to doing *with* and not simply *for* older adults. Working with older adults fosters decision making and a deep involvement in center programming, thus creating a climate of independence rather than dependence. Encouraging older persons to assume as much responsibility as they can and want should be the goal of every senior center.

Providing a range of choices. Senior center programming must reflect a range of choices, since older adults have varied needs, interests, and abilities. The provision of a variety of services will attract more older participants and demonstrate to the community that older persons are capable of leading well-rounded lives.

Fostering accessibility and acceptability. Conscious efforts must be made to make senior centers accessible and acceptable to a variety of older users. Participation may be unconsciously limited to certain social and ethnic groups, women rather than both women and men, healthy rather than both healthy and frail elderly, and so on. The center must provide a climate that is warm and accepting, realistic in its expectations, and committed to reaching out to the unserved and the underserved.

Individualizing programs. Program planning must attempt to respond to the individual differences among older persons. Senior center staff need to make an effort to assess each participant individually, reviewing life experiences, present conditions and situations, special interests, and abilities. The assessment effort should be made immediately after an older person has shown an interest in participating.

Maslow's "hierarchy of needs" (Maslow, 1968), which classifies human needs that may be met through a variety of services, can be used to facilitate individualized programming (Leanse, Tiven, and Robb, 1977). Human needs and examples of senior center services to meet the appropriate need are:

1. *Physiological needs,* met by group meals, meals-on-wheels for the homebound, sex education, exercises, games, and sports

2. *Security needs,* met by transportation, neighborhood crime watch, direct deposit of social security checks, health screening, 24-hour emergency hot line, telephone reassurance, housing, and legal services

3. *Love needs,* met by opportunities for friendships, family contacts, and friendly visiting

4. *Esteem needs,* met by recognition through employment programs, craft projects, service in center advisory group, political activities, and activism

5. *Self-actualization needs,* met by self-fulfillment through the arts

The choice of a facility is an important component of senior center development, since a facility's design has a bearing on programming and successful functioning of participants, staff, volunteers, and agencies delivering services in or through the center. This section will discuss important considerations involved in choosing the facility, selecting a location, and developing a facility plan.

Facility

CHOOSING THE FACILITY. The choice of the facility for a senior center requires the examination of a number of possibilities such as accepting a donated facility, renovating a facility, or building a facility. A number of the advantages and disadvantages of each of these are discussed, using Jordan (1978) as a resource.

Accepting a donated facility. A senior center may occupy space either free of charge or for a nominal fee in an existing facility that has received little or no design changes to meet special needs of older persons. Examples of such facilities are unused or abandoned schools, post offices, libraries, storefronts, church halls, municipal buildings, and so on. A senior center occupying such a facility would have the *advantages* of requiring little or no capital investment, annual rent, or start-up time and could be either centrally located in the community or used as a satellite center. This type of facility may have certain *disadvantages,* such as steps at entrances or between floors; no fire alarms or fire-fighting systems; little parking or outdoor recreation space; poor lighting, heating, and ventilation; and few smaller rooms for specialized activities such as counseling, adult education, and arts and crafts.

Sharing a facility. A senior center may share space and program opportunities on a full-time or part-time basis in an intergenerational facility such as a church, synagogue, YMCA, YWCA, YMHA, YWHA, school building, recreation center, fraternal organization meeting hall, or other community facility. The *advantages* of a senior center in such a facility are no capital cost (since the building would be provided by others), low operating cost (since annual rental cost would be low), good building quality (since facilities are complete and first rate), and there may be varied spaces such as auditoriums, swimming pools, arts and crafts areas, exercise rooms, and so on. The *disadvantages* of such a facility might include scheduling conflicts with the activities of other users, sharing of maintenance staff who may not be available when needed, and the sacrificing of public visibility and sense of identity through use of another's facilities.

Renovating a facility. A senior center may occupy space renovated to provide for the special needs of older persons after it is purchased by the sponsor or rented through a long-term lease agreement. Many of the facilities presented previously under donated facilities may be renovated. *Advantages* of renovated space are capital cost is usually less than new construction, provided that minimum alterations are needed; funding for acquisition and renovation may be obtained from local, state, and federal sources; location of a senior center in elderly-concentrated sections of town may be more suitable in existing buildings; and renovations often save time in the design and construction stages and allow new uses of existing resources. *Disadvantages* of a renovated facility may include unsightly ramps and costly elevators, the high cost of meeting fire regulations and adding other safety features, and the difficulty of achieving a character to a renovated building appropriate for a senior center.

Building a new facility. A senior center may occupy space in a new facility especially designed for older persons. A new facility has the *advantages* of achieving a high level of accessibility through the avoidance of architectural barriers, safety through fireproof construction and warning systems, functional arrangement, flexibility for growth and change, special design features, and funding from local, state, and federal sources. *Disadvantages* include a higher cost than the cost of renovation, a longer period to design and build a new facility, and the lack of an appropriate location near concentrations of older people.

SELECTING A LOCATION. The selection of the location for a senior center requires the examination of a number of characteristics. Jordan (1978) suggests that these characteristics be organized under the headings of community, neighborhood, and site.

Community characteristics. Selecting the location of a senior center must be based on an examination of community characteristics such as intended service area (neighborhood, city, county, or region), general concentration of the elderly population, and location of other agencies or services (e.g., shopping and medical facilities). The facility must be conveniently located near public or private transportation to serve a dispersed older population or within comfortable walking distance if it is to be a neighborhood center.

Neighborhood characteristics. The neighborhood in which a senior center is located should allow older persons to be reasonably safe from personal harassment, mugging, or robbery; should be zoned to be compatible with senior center purposes; and should be in an area where property values promise to remain reasonably stable. The safety and security of older participants and staff are of particular importance.

Site characteristics. The senior center serving as a focal point for older persons in the community should have a prominent site to enhance its visibility; should provide the necessary space for the building, parking, and outdoor recreation; and should have a price consistent with property values in the area. Barrier-free access for handicapped older persons should be stressed in site selection.

Thomas O. Byerts

Using a lounge to accommodate too many activities may result in conflicts and competition for space.

DEVELOPING A FACILITY PLAN. The development of a facility plan is necessary regardless of whether donated, shared, renovated, or new facilities are used. One way of developing a facility plan is to examine the variety of spaces that may be necessary for program and administrative services occurring within a senior center.

Entrance lobby. The entrance lobby may serve a number of purposes. Its main purpose is to be a reception area where participants and visitors may register and receive direction to proper services, persons, or rooms. The entrance lobby may also serve as a lounge for chatting and observing the arrival and departure of other participants and visitors.

The design of the entrance lobby should convey warmth and a welcoming graciousness. The participant or visitor should be able to easily find the reception area, clothing storage area or coatroom, main bulletin board, rest rooms, connecting hallways, stairs, and elevators. A display area or gift shop in the vicinity of the lobby can display salable items for fundraising and participant recognition.

Lounge. The lounge is the focal point of the center, serving as the family room or living room of the center. A variety of activities can take place in the lounge—card games, conversation, television watching, reading, listening to music, or simply watching others in activity.

The design of the lounge should forcefully state one of the senior center's purposes: socialization and fellowship. To make this statement the lounge needs to be located near the entrance lobby and the activity center of the facility, yet it should not be a circulation area or path for participants going to and from other areas. Accommodating the variety of activities that may occur requires a sensitivity to multiple use and avoidance of the domination of one activity or group of users (e.g., card players, television watchers, readers, or music fans). Whenever possible, alcoves or room divisions should be created to provide special differentiation.

Multipurpose room. The multipurpose room is a space for a variety of activities that typically bring a large number of participants together. It may be used for dancing, dining, table games, exercise, parties, special events (e.g., exhibits, craft fairs, and voting), and special programs (e.g., lectures and movies).

The multipurpose room should be centrally located in the senior center. Its proximity to the entrance lobby and the lounge will enhance traffic flow and its multipurpose use.

Trying to accommodate too many purposes may result in a no-purpose room, which may be avoided or reduced by movable partitions so that several groups can use the room at the same time.

Dining room and kitchen. Dining is important not only for the balanced nutrition it provides but also for the social interaction it fosters. Facilities may require a rather heavy financial investment because of the kitchen, but it is worth the investment considering the number of daily participants that dining attracts and the potential impact on health and general welfare of nutritious food.

The decision to set aside a special room for dining rather than simply using the multipurpose room is warranted by the attractiveness and comfort of a separate room, the opportunity for a longer meal period, and the availability of a large room in which events can be scheduled simultaneously with events in the multipurpose room. If the decision is made to have a separate dining room, consideration must be given to local health regulations concerning the relationship of dining room, kitchen, and delivery area for food and other supplies; the problem of a premeal line that may spill into hallways and other spaces; and the importance of acoustical materials to keep down the noise level.

Meeting rooms and classrooms. Senior centers may have an impressive variety of meeting rooms and classrooms, depending on center goals and purposes, interests of participants, attitude of the center director, and availability of volunteer instructors. Critical considerations in the design of meeting rooms and classrooms are the need for an array of room sizes to accommodate a variety of group sizes, separate entrances into each room so that one does not have to pass through other rooms, and sound amplification systems (particularly in larger meeting rooms).

Special-purpose rooms. Multipurpose rooms and other adaptable spaces cannot always be used for certain activities or functions that may require spe-

Thea Lorin Breite

A craft room should be able to accommodate several activities at the same time and provide a storage wall of open shelving for work in progress.

cial purpose or single use spaces. Examples of special-purpose rooms are:

1. *Craft room,* which is designed as a single-purpose room because crafts may require special equipment (such as a kiln for ceramics), often generate dirt and noise, may require storage space for expendable craft materials and work in progress, and may require that space be rearranged to meet the needs of a particular craft class

2. *Game room,* which is designed as a single-purpose room because billiard and ping pong tables are heavy and not easily moved to accommodate other activities

3. *Physical fitness room,* which may be warranted when there is a regular physical fitness program of exercise, calisthenics, yoga, or modern dance that meets 5 days a week or that requires stationary equipment too heavy to easily move

4. *Music room,* which is warranted in a large center with instrumental and choral groups that practice on a regular basis or that have instruments, music stands, chairs, risers, and other pieces of equipment requiring storage

5. *Medical examination/treatment room,* which may be necessary because an active health promotion program of physical examinations, glaucoma tests, and so on requires the allocation of a special space for examination, treatment, consultation, and counseling

Outdoor recreation space. Outdoor recreation space may be developed to supplement available indoor facilities. The decision to develop outdoor recreation space must be based on a consideration of factors such as age, health, and interests of participants; available space; climate; budget; and functions to be served. Outdoor space at a senior center can provide a number of programming options (e.g., lawn bowling, croquet, shuffleboard, horseshoes, gardening, outdoor cooking, and picnics). The design should provide opportunities for privacy, temperature variation options (i.e., full sun, partial shade, and full shade), and accessibility.

Administrative services. Administrative office space is needed for center staff such as the director, coordinator of services, nutrition director, volunteer director, and secretary/receptionist. An important consideration in office design is the issue of privacy versus accessibility, with these decisions based on the need to handle confidential information or the necessity of being near participants, volunteers, or the center of activity.

Management

Management of a senior center requires the consideration of a number of issues critical to the effective organization and operation of the program and the facility. This section examines the development of purpose and goal statements, organization, personnel, fiscal management records and reports, and evaluation.

PURPOSE AND GOAL STATEMENTS. Purpose and goal statements are the foundation of the senior center's organization and operation (National Institute of Senior Centers, 1978, p. 19). These statements serve to orient the community, staff, and participants; to assist the program planning process; and to support requests for funds. Purpose and goals need to be consistent with the philosophy of the senior center.

Purpose. The purpose statement is a written expression of the senior center's character, scope, mission, and aspirations. An example of a purpose statement is:

> The purpose of the Senior Center is to increase the comprehensiveness and continuity of quality services to older persons in order to optimize their successful integration into and prevent their exclusion from the community. (Leanse, Tiven, and Robb, 1977, p. 31)

The purpose statement should be developed and regularly reviewed by the governing board, staff, and participants and should be available for distribution

Thomas O. Byerts

Trees and umbrellas provide needed shade in this outdoor space. Note bird cage to the left of the picture.

in a suitable form to interested persons. The purpose statement serves as the basis for the center's goals.

Goals. Goal statements are guidelines for the center's program development; they identify in written, measurable form what accomplishments the center seeks to achieve in a year or in a longer period (National Institute of Senior Centers, 1978, p. 20). A goal statement might read: ''A goal of this center is to provide leisure services that respond to older citizens' interests, stimulate growth, and facilitate community participation.'' Broad, long-range goals are often not specific enough for the center's daily operation or for funding sources; more specific, short-term goals are required. As with the purpose statement, goal statements should be developed and reviewed on a regular basis by the governing board, participants, and staff to reflect program change and should be made available in a suitable form to interested persons.

ORGANIZATION. The accomplishment of the senior center purpose and goals requires the creation of an organization that specifies the relationships among the governing or advisory body, participants, and staff. The essential components of the center's organization are examined in this section.

Governing documents. Governing documents such as a written constitution, charter, and bylaws convey to the governing and advisory bodies, participants, staff, and concerned persons in the community the responsibilities and roles of each of the above components of the center's organization. Governing documents are generally required for incorporation—a process establishing the organization's legal existence and securing legal rights and safeguards (e.g., property ownership and protection of individual assets from legal action against the center).

Organizational structure. An organizational chart is necessary to explain the organizational structure and formal communication network among all center components (governing and advisory bodies, participants, and staff) and if necessary the parent body and other centers. An organizational chart should be written and circulated to all center components and used in center management.

Governing and advisory bodies. Governing and advisory bodies are the means through which the community demonstrates its support of an agency and exercises its authority either in a governing or advisory capacity.

Governing body. The term *governing body* refers to the board of an independent senior center. The governing body of an independent, incorporated senior center establishes policy and has the legal responsibility for decisions in areas such as planning, policy, budget and finance, program development and implementation, securing physical facilities, hiring and firing of the executive, public relations, and evaluation of staff and programs. The governing body should have representation from center participants, influential community leaders, and individuals with technical skills and expertise. Written bylaws establish and define procedures such as job qualifications, job duties, election and tenure, officers, committee structure, and procedures for conduct of meetings.

Advisory body. The term *advisory body* refers to a board established by the governing body of the parent organization when the senior center is a subunit of that larger public or private parent organization. The advisory body is frequently appointed by the governing body of the parent organization and serves to assist the governing body in policy and practice formulation, problem solving, and effective program functioning. Although the advisory body does not have legal responsibility, its influence is considerable when its members have special expertise, are deeply committed, and are well informed. Its composition and operation according to written bylaws is similar to what was previously stated for the governing body.

Governing and advisory bodies are often assisted by a participant organization. Such an organization enhances communication among participants, staff, and governing or advisory body and represents the interests of center participants. Another very important function is providing the opportunity for participant leadership and decision making—both vital to elderly well-being.

PERSONNEL. The senior center's effectiveness is very much related to the quality of its personnel. The employment, supervision, and training of senior center personnel are discussed in this section.

Chief administrator. The chief administrator is the key to center development. The employing of the chief administrator is the responsibility of the sponsoring agency or the governing body to whom the chief administrator is accountable for the center's effective operation and programming. The responsibilities of the chief administrator may include fiscal management and budgeting, fund raising, personnel management, staff training and development, program development, community relations, and overall evaluation of the center operation. The chief administrator should have graduate-level professional training in fields such as recreation or therapeutic recreation, adult education, or social work with specialized training in gerontology and experience in administration of public or voluntary organizations. The chief administrator must be able to deal with the complexity of interactions among agency board, staff, and participants. Some centers may have only a chief administrator who is responsible for the daily operation, whereas other centers may have a variety of staff.

Staff. There are a number of possible staff positions within a senior center (in addition to secretarial, maintenance, and housekeeping staff), depending on the center's budget, size, and program diversity.

Center director. The center director is responsible for the daily operation of a center in coordination with the chief administrator or executive director. This individual should have a background similar to the qualifications described for the chief administrator.

Coordinator of services. The coordinator of services is responsible for the variety of center services (e.g., leisure, education, and counseling). Educational backgrounds preferred are in recreation or therapeutic recreation, adult education, or social work.

Nutrition director. The nutrition director is responsible for nutrition programs (e.g., congregate meals and meals-on-wheels). This individual should be a dietitian or food service specialist.

Volunteer director. The volunteer director is responsible for recruiting, training, placing, and supervising volunteers from the center and/or the community. Qualifications required may be specialized training, or a volunteer may be willing to assume this responsibility.

Volunteers. Volunteers are an important source of additional personnel for a senior center. As Leanse, Tiven, and Robb (1977, p. 105) state:

> Volunteers expand and supplement the Center's resources; increase the Center's capacity in volume, type and level of offered services; bring fresh and innovative ideas, and provide services otherwise unavailable. Also, since both Center participants and community members function as volunteers, they serve as an important link with the larger community, communicating what is going on at the Center to people who otherwise would not know.

The use of volunteers requires a coordinated plan that should include a number of steps.

Job descriptions. Job descriptions must be developed before recruitment and be based on the roles and tasks available at the center. The description should be specific but should also have some flexibility to allow for some special interests and skills. Elements to be included are job title, responsibilities, hours, necessary skills, and nature of the job (permanent or temporary).

Recruitment and selection. Recruitment and selection must be controlled to assume an adequate number of volunteers selected to fill positions that are open and for which they have the qualifications. Names and additional information (e.g., skills and availability) should be listed for future reference if positions are not currently available.

Orientation. Orientation must be provided before the volunteer begins work and should include the center's purposes, policies, procedures, staff, and facilities. A tour of the facility should alert the new volunteer to lounges, bathrooms, the dining area, telephone facilities, and the location of the supervisor.

Supervision. Supervision must include a formal supervisor to turn to for assistance and support in solving problems related to work performance and in handling feelings and reactions to the job and the people with whom they are working.

Evaluation and recognition. Evaluation and recognition must be ongoing to allow volunteers the opportunity to assess strengths and weaknesses and to enhance their sense of belonging and worth. Training to enable volunteers to improve performance and increase competence should be provided. Recognition to make volunteers feel wanted and needed are provided informally by treating them with respect and formally through certificates, recognition luncheons, and so on.

Termination. Termination must be conducted in the same way as with paid staff—with a tactful and sensitive approach. Whenever possible, alternative placement either within the center or in some other program should be investigated and critically evaluated.

Personnel policies and practices. Sound personnel policies and practices established in writing and continually updated are essential for employment and retention of personnel; they provide personnel with a clear and concise understanding of the goals of the organization and expectations of their jobs. The formal determination and statement of personnel policies and practices promote continuity and consistency of center services and contribute to the impartiality and uniformity of staff relationships.

A policies and practices manual or handbook should include the following topics:

1. *Organizational chart,* clearly delineating areas of responsibility, authority, and lines of communication among board, staff, and participants
2. *Employment terms and conditions,* including recruitment, selection, orientation, schedule and hours, performance appraisal, promotion, and termination
3. *Staffing patterns,* clearly defining each staff position, with a job description stating job title, duties and responsibilities, scope of authority, qualifications, salary range and benefits, and lines of communication for reporting and supervision
4. *Compensation and benefits,* including issues such as salaries (e.g., pay periods and deductions), leave (e.g., sick, maternity, military, jury, annual, and holiday), vacations, compensatory and/or overtime, retire-

ment, and insurance (e.g., accident, health, life, unemployment, and workmen's compensation)

5. *Employer and employee relations,* including channels of internal communication, labor and management relations, and grievance procedures

Training. A formal system of staff training helps improve performance, develops abilities, and solidifies staff relationships to the center. Such a formal system should provide:

1. *Training for new staff,* providing orientation to the center's goals, objectives, practices, programs, and characteristics of older persons in the center

2. *Continuing education,* enabling staff to maintain and improve their skills and competence in their professional field, as well as in knowledge of human aging

Staff training and development can be facilitated through a program of in-service education; resource materials such as films, books, and magazines; encouragement; time off; and financial assistance to cover expenses to attend conferences, seminars, and other types of training sessions offered by colleges and universities, public schools, and state and national organizations.

FISCAL MANAGEMENT. The effective management of a senior center requires the practice of fiscal planning and sound management. Some of the principles and practices of fiscal management will be discussed in this section.

Funding. The ability of the senior center to generate its own sources of financial support requires the development of a funding plan. Planning requires the consideration of a variety of funding sources:

1. *United Way* is a community-based organization that raises contributions from the community and funds programs that have demonstrated their value to the community.

2. *Donations* can be solicited from individuals or businesses through an organized fund-raising program.

3. *Fund-raising events* not only provide income from events such as bazaars, dances, carnivals, craft fairs, and so on but can also be a center program having impact on board, staff, and participants.

4. *Deferred giving* does not usually provide substantial immediate income but can provide long-term income through means such as wills, trusts, annuities, and bequests.

5. *Foundations and trusts* usually provide funding from 1 to 3 years to establish a particular program or service that the center is particularly capable of rendering, that concords with the general purpose of the foundation or trust, and that is within its funding locale.

6. *Membership fees* should be equitable, with provisions for those unable to pay.

7. *Governmental sources,* including sources at all levels of government (local, county, region, state, and federal), should be considered. It is

important to work closely with the local Area Agency on Aging (AAA) for information on these sources.

A center should pursue funding sources that are feasible financially and whose regulations are compatible with the center's purposes.

Budgeting. Budgeting is the process by which the administration of the senior center allocates its resources to achieve its goals and objectives. The budget serves to translate planning decisions into monetary terms, is a fiscal control device determining the center's efficiency of operation, and is useful for soliciting support and resources for the center because it is a series of goals and objectives with attached price tags.

The budget should be prepared by the administrative staff in consultation with program development staff, accounting, housekeeping, and maintenance. The budget should be presented to and approved by the governing body.

Accounting. Accounting is a set of procedures "designed to collect, clarify and communicate information about an organization's financial affairs" (Leanse, Tiven, and Robb, 1977, p. 74). The accounting procedures should not only comply with legal requirements but should also communicate with maximum disclosure to bodies such as funding agencies, contributors, the general public, and the participants.

Accounting procedures need to be established for cash control and purchasing. Written procedures need to be developed for depositing cash funds, recording cash expenditures and receipts, and authorizing individuals to handle cash and sign checks. Purchasing procedures should include a purchase approval system, a process for competitive bidding, and a list of persons authorized to purchase or contract for the center.

Fiscal monitoring is necessary for record consistency and freedom from bias. There should be a separation of cash handling from record keeping and purchasing from receiving. The management of the risk of misuse or loss of funds is minimized through bonding of employees handling money or financial records, requiring more than one signature for authorizing withdrawals or payment of funds, and stipulating an annual audit by an independent auditor.

Each senior center should seek the assistance of an accountant or develop accounting procedures suitable to its needs. Such procedures should communicate information relative to particular programs, allow for the production of quarterly and annual reports, and show the dollar value of in-kind contributions (e.g., donated equipment and services).

A good accounting system makes it possible to track funds, readily collect or retrieve data, and construct future financial plans. A system successfully planned and implemented reflects well on the center director and the board and enhances the possibility of the center's survival and the public willingness to contribute.

RECORDS AND REPORTS. Records and reports are vital to the effective management of a senior center. Information should be collected through a record keeping system and disseminated in the form of reports, which are a source of specific information basic to planning, operation, evaluation, and overall accountability. Accurate and current records and reports allow easy access to and retrieval of current information, help to determine gaps in services, reduce waste and errors, provide continuity during personnel change of staff and board, inform and educate the public, and help document the center's history.

The development of an efficient data collection and dissemination system requires the determination of the critical information needs for which records must be kept and reported on. Advanced planning and consultation with a specialist will avoid unnecessary data collection and dissemination. The following are some common types of records and reports.

Participant. The participant's background and involvement in the center's program must be recorded, reported, and reviewed for accuracy and usefulness. Background information should include name, address, telephone number, sex, birth date, marital status, living arrangement (alone or with another), emergency information (physician's name, health problems, emergency phone numbers for family, hospital preference, and next of kin), and interests and skills. Participant involvement may include attendance information and volunteer activities.

Program. Program records and reports provide information on services, thus documenting operations for funding sources and for the community. Records should include a description of services, names and numbers of persons served by types of services, and participant evaluations of services. Periodical and annual reports should be submitted to the board, funding agencies, staff, participants, and the community providing information such as persons served during that period, average daily attendance and for how long, a profile indicating participation patterns for each service (percentage of participants using each service, patterns of regular attendance, and so on), and summaries of participant evaluations.

Administrative. Administrative records and reports should be kept in certain areas:

1. *Financial,* including invoices and receipts for expenditures, in-kind contributions, and inventory of furnishings, equipment, and supplies
2. *Personnel,* including resume, letters of reference, letter of employment, employment date, job title, job description, salaries and wages paid, withholding for taxes and social security, retirement benefits, evaluations of performance, disciplinary actions, and when appropriate the reasons and date of termination
3. *Board meetings,* including attendance records of board meetings, minutes of each meeting, and decisions
4. *Staff meetings,* including attendance, minutes, and decisions
5. *Policies and procedures,* relating to personnel and operation, updated and filed on a regular basis
6. *Public relations,* documenting past and current activities and future plans
7. *Historical records,* including photographs, newspaper articles, newsletters, and interviews

8. *Correspondence and telephone calls,* including letters, telephone calls logged daily, and when necessary a memo summarizing a conversation

9. *Resources,* including items such as volunteer sources, films, speakers, groups for special events, and so on

10. *Health and safety,* including public health inspections, accident reports and procedures, fire inspections, and so on

Confidentiality of all records and reports containing sensitive or personal information should be controlled and monitored. Procedures for ensuring confidentiality may include special provisions for storage and access to confidential information, protection for the identity of individuals to be cited in reports, and permission from the individual before releasing confidential information.

EVALUATION. Evaluation of senior center program and operations is one of the major responsibilities of the board and the center administrator. Effective evaluation requires that this process be planned in advance; implemented on a formal, regular basis; conducted by a committee consisting of board, staff, and participants; and funded adequately. The definition, purposes, types, and process of evaluation will be examined in this section.

Definition. The National Institute of Senior Centers (1978, p. 59) defines senior center evaluation as:

> An objective review of a senior center's program or operation for a particular period of time or program cycle. The evaluation may range from an overall inventory of the center's operation to an assessment of one aspect of its program.

Purposes. A senior center may undertake an evaluation of its program or operation for a variety of reasons. A number of purposes of evaluation are:

1. To determine whether the center is achieving its stated goals
2. To determine whether needs that led to the establishment of a program are being met
3. To determine whether each program is accomplishing its objectives
4. To compare the use of financial or human resources in relation to results or output

Types. Evaluation of senior center program or operations may include two types of evaluation: *qualitative,* such as the number of units of service (e.g., meals served) or the number of persons acquiring a new skill after participating in a crafts class, and *qualitative,* such as the determination that a particular leisure service reduces social isolation and contributes to reintegration of withdrawn persons or the determination that health is improved as a result of health services.

Process. The evaluation process is most often concerned with the determination of whether a senior center is meeting its goals and objectives. In Fig. 5-1 the evaluation process is illustrated. This process involves formulating objectives with measurable criteria, selecting activities to meet the objectives,

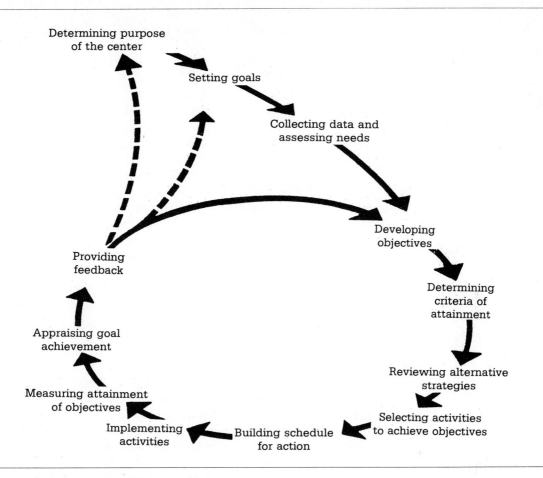

Fig. 5-1. A planning and evaluation model.

From Leanse, J., Tiven, M., and Robb, T.: Senior center operation: a guide to organization and management, published by The National Council on the Aging, Inc., p. 71.

measuring the outcomes according to criteria, determining the degree to which the objectives are being attained, and recommending continuation, change, termination, or expansion of a program or operation.

The process of evaluation requires that certain elements be considered:
1. The objectives of the program or operation must be stated with clarity.
2. The criteria must be related to the objectives.
3. The selection of only activities that have easily measurable outcomes should be avoided.
4. The objectives when attained must contribute to goal attainment.
5. Results must be disseminated to the board, staff, and participants.

6. The results of the evaluation must be integrated into the planning process.

USE OF LEISURE SERVICE PERSONNEL IN SENIOR CENTERS

The continued use of leisure service personnel in senior centers is difficult to predict, but available data suggest that employment of leisure service personnel in senior centers will continue. Earlier in the chapter it was noted that leisure service agencies have sponsored senior centers from the beginning of the senior center movement and that leisure services are provided in a variety of forms in almost all centers. An educational background in leisure services is one of the preferred areas for the chief administrator, center director, and coordinator of services in a senior center.

An individual desiring employment in a senior center has a number of sources of assistance (National Recreation and Park Association, 1982). The local telephone book may list senior centers and recreation centers that might provide leisure services for the elderly. Public libraries often have in a reference area directories of services for the elderly. The state agency on aging should have ready access to addresses and telephone numbers of all senior centers (see Appendix A for a list of state agencies).

Qualifications for employment in senior centers vary with the type of position (National Recreation and Park Association, 1982). Entry level positions are open to recent leisure service graduates wishing to be program specialists for a variety of leisure activities such as music, drama, art, fitness, sports, aquatics, and so on. More experienced individuals or individuals with both advanced degrees in leisure service and experience are qualified for supervisory and managerial positions such as coordinator of services, center director, and chief administrator.

SUMMARY

Senior centers as focal points for older persons living in the community are a relatively new service designed to provide services and activities supportive of independence and community involvement of the elderly. Beginning in 1943 with the William Hodson Community center in New York City, followed by the San Francisco Senior Center in 1947 and Little House in Menlo Park, California in 1949, senior centers have become a nationwide effort, accelerating in growth as a result of the Older Americans Act of 1965. The philosophy and rationale of senior centers build on the principles that older persons are adults in need of social support, interaction, and voice in self-determination—all of which senior centers are uniquely capable of providing through a variety of services and activities delivered under a variety of models.

The organization of a senior center requires considerable effort in the planning of program and facility. Preliminary efforts at senior center development necessitate the formation of a planning committee responsible for the documentation of community need, identification of funding sources, and the development of a preliminary plan concerned with program, facility, and operations. A senior center's program may include a variety of services (e.g., leisure services, education, information, counseling and referral, health, housing, employment, financial aid and counseling, legal aid, nutrition, transportation, services to the homebound, homemaker assistance, and daycare) delivered directly by the senior center or through a system of outreach and community linkages. A center's program is designed to overcome participation barriers through a variety of strategies (e.g., treating older persons as adults, providing a range of choices, fostering accessibility and acceptability, and individualizing programs). Planning for the facility requires the consideration of the advantages and disadvantages of accepting a donated facility with little or no design changes, sharing a facility with another agency, renovating a facility to provide for the needs of the elderly, or building a new facility. Selecting a location requires the examination of a variety of community characteristics (e.g., elderly concentration, medical services, transportation, and location of shopping), neighborhood characteristics (e.g., stable property values and safety and security of staff and participants), and site chracteristics (e.g., necessary building space, parking, outdoor recreation, and barrier-free access). Developing a facility plan requires the provision of the necessary spaces for program and administration (e.g., entrance lobby, lounge, multipurpose room, dining room and kitchen, meeting rooms and classrooms, special program rooms, outdoor recreation space, and administrative office space).

Effective management of program and facility are enhanced through the development of purpose and goal statements, an organizational structure, qualified personnel, sound fiscal planning and management, a system of record and reports, and an evaluation process. Purpose and goal statements serve as the foundation of the senior center's organization and operation, with the purpose statement being the foundation from which short- and long-term goals flow. The center's organization is specified in detail through governing documents such as a written constitution, a charter, and bylaws; through an organizational structure specifying the formal communication network within the organization; and through a governing body that has the legal responsibility for all aspects of center management or through an advisory body that assists the governing body in various aspects of policy and practice. Personnel may include the chief administrator, a variety of staff (e.g., center director, coordinator of services, nutrition director, and director of volunteers), and volunteers—all of whom are provided with a clear and concise understanding of the organization through a policies and practices manual and a system of training and continuing education. Sound fiscal planning and management require the consideration of funding sources from both the private and public sectors, budgeting of these funds through an appropriate type of budget format, and accounting procedures to monitor cash handling and purchasing. A system of record keeping and reporting of information requires the gathering of information on participants, program, and administration, while controlling and monitoring the dissemination of information of a personal and sensitive nature. Planned, regular, funded evaluation involving board, staff, and participants is the key to the determination of center success in meeting its goal and objectives.

Use of leisure service personnel in senior centers will continue because leisure service agencies sponsor many senior centers, leisure services are provided in almost all senior centers, and leisure services as an educational background is one of the preferred areas for senior center management. Information on employment possibilities in senior centers may be obtained from a variety of sources (e.g., telephone directories, directories of services for the elderly, and state agencies on aging), with employment qualifications being based on education, experience, and the type of position sought.

REFERENCES

Fowler, T.: Alternatives to the single site center, Washington, D.C., 1974, National Council on the Aging.

Gelfand, D., and Olsen, J.: The aging network: programs and services, New York, 1980, Springer Publishing Co., Inc.

Guttman, D., and Miller, P.: Perspective on the provision of social services in senior citizen centers, Gerontologist **12**:403-406, 1972.

Jordan, J.: Senior center design: an architect's discussion of facility planning, Washington, D.C., 1978, National Council on the Aging.

Kent, D.: The how and why of senior centers, Aging **283**:2-6, 1978.

Leanse, J., Tiven, M., and Robb, T.: Senior center operation: a guide to organization and management, Washington, D.C., 1977, National Council on the Aging.

Leanse, J., and Wagner, S.: Senior centers: report of senior group programs in America, Washington, D.C., 1975, National Council on the Aging.

Maslow, A.: The need-hierarchy. In Wadia, M.S., editor: Management and the behavioral sciences, Boston, 1968, Allyn & Bacon, Inc.

Maxwell, J.: Centers for older people, Washington, D.C., 1962, National Council on the Aging.

National Institute of Senior Centers: Senior center standards: guidelines for practice, Washington, D.C., 1978, National Council on the Aging.

National Recreation and Park Association: Leisure services for older Americans, Employ **8**:1-7, 1982.

Taietz, P.: Two conceptual models of the senior center, J. Gerontol. **31**:219-222, 1976.

SUGGESTED READINGS

Jordan, J.: Senior center design: an architect's discussion of facility planning, Washington, D.C., 1978, National Council on the Aging.

Leanse, J., Tiven, M., and Robb, T.: Senior center operation: a guide to organization and management, Washington, D.C., 1977, National Council on the Aging.

National Institute of Senior Centers: Senior center standards: guidelines for practice, Washington, D.C., 1978, National Council on the Aging.

6

Planned community housing

The variety and number of planned community housing units for the elderly have been the result of a commitment to provide adequate housing for older persons. Characteristics of that housing, however, interact with other characteristics of the environmental context to form a "life setting in its physical and social entirety, the context for living" (Carp, 1976, p. 245). This "living environment" includes elements such as physical characteristics, the surrounding neighborhood, interpersonal and social environment, and the availability and convenience of services (Lawton and Nahemow, 1973). The importance of the interpersonal and social environment coupled with the availability and convenience of services provide an environmental context supportive of leisure services. This chapter will examine the environmental context of planned housing, research issues about planned housing, facilitating leisure life-styles through leisure services, and employment opportunities for leisure service specialists in planned community housing.

A theoretical framework or model useful for understanding the interactions between older persons and the environment is the "ecological model of adaptation and aging" proposed by Lawton and Nahemow (1973). Fig. 6-1 presents a graphic representation of this model. Individual *competence* (from low to high) is shown on the ordinate and is defined as the individual's capacity to function in the biological, cognitive, and sensory-motor domains (Lawton, 1972). *Environmental press* (from weak to strong) is shown on the abscissa and is defined as the demand quality of the physical environment setting, having the potential to evoke the desired behavior. The maximum performance, according to this

**ENVIRONMENTAL
CONTEXT OF
PLANNED
HOUSING**

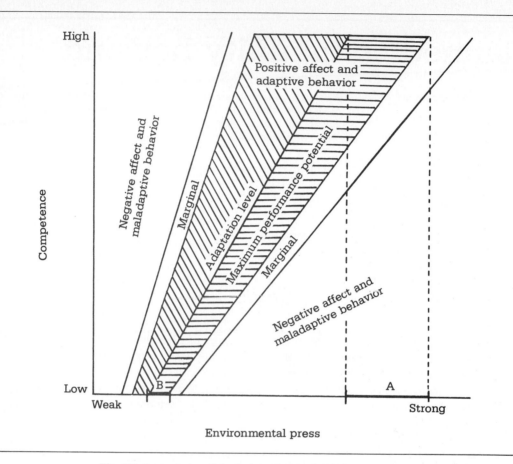

Fig. 6-1. Ecological model of adaptation and aging.

From Lawton, M.P., and Nahemow, L. In Eisdorfer, C., and Lawton, M.P., editors: The psychology of adult development and aging, Washington, D.C., 1973, American Psychological Association, p. 661. Copyright 1973 by the American Psychological Association. Reprinted by permission of the author.

model, will occur when the *environmental press* is within the range of the individual's *competence,* particularly when the demand quality approaches the maximum capacity of the individual. A further examination of Fig. 6-1 indicates that a person of high competence has a higher maximum performance potential over a larger range of environmental situations (Fig. 6-1, *A*) than a less competent individual (Fig. 6-1, *B*). On the other hand, the constricting width of the adaptive range of the less competent (Fig. 6-1, *B*) suggests that those of lower competence may be more easily removed from their area of environmental mastery than those of higher competence.

The Lawton and Nahemow (1973) concepts of competence and environ-

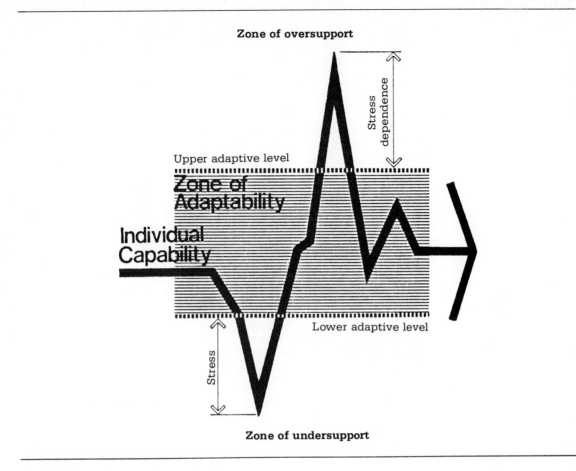

Fig. 6-2. Man-environment interaction.

From Gelwicks, L., and Newcomer, R.: Planning housing environments for the elderly, 1974, published by The National Council on the Aging, Inc., p. 41.

mental press are further illustrated by Gelwicks and Newcomer (1974), who speak of the "man-environment interaction" of the elderly in terms of individual capability, zone of adaptability, and zone of support (Fig. 6-2). The ability of the individual to perform is a combination of capability and support. Gelwicks and Newcomer (1974, p. 40) state:

> The concept implies that when high ability is matched by low supports, the individual is able to maximize his independence. If ability declines, environmental supports must increase in order for the individual to be functioning at his highest level of independence. If environmental supports, on the other hand, are not increased when needed, the individual would be overstressed and unable to cope.

In reverse, the theory maintains that if environmental support is too high for the individual's ability, he would experience boredom, sensory deprivation or excessive dependency.

Kahana (1980) conceptualized environmental transactions of the elderly in terms of "person/environment congruence." Underlying this concept is the concern to make an environment as person specific as possible through the matching of environment to the type and strength of personal needs. The matching of needs and abilities and the level of support and challenge can assist in prolonging independence and can avoid creating dependence. It is therefore necessary to have a proper balance between support and challenge.

The maintenance and encouragement of adaptive behavior and the matching of person with the environment are important in planning for housing for the elderly. With varying competencies among older persons, it is necessary to have a proper person/environment congruence, which may be achieved through the provision of a wide range of living environments for older persons. The following sections will examine this range of planned community housing environments.

Public housing

The largest number of planned community housing units for the elderly is supported by the federal public housing program, which began with the United States Housing Act of 1937 and extended to the elderly in the Housing Act of 1956 (Gelfand and Olsen, 1980; Lawton, 1980). The purpose of public housing is to provide low-cost shelter to low-income older persons, with some space provided for services such as leisure services but with no funds provided for such services through the U.S. Department of Housing and Urban Development (HUD). Public housing is managed by a local housing authority with a variety of service personnel involved in the daily operations of the projects. Although the majority of housing units are for families, most new units in recent years have been constructed for the elderly and handicapped. To be eligible for such housing, older persons must have an income below a defined local level, be 62 years of age or older, or be the spouse of a person 62 or older.

Private nonprofit rental housing (Section 202 housing)

The Housing Act of 1959, Section 202, provided low-cost federal loans to nonprofit sponsors (e.g., church groups, labor unions, nonprofit organizations, and fraternal groups) for the construction or rehabilitation of existing structures as housing for the elderly. Such housing often includes support services and space for dining and leisure services and is staffed by an administrator and varying numbers of personnel from service backgrounds. Research by Lawton (1975) has shown a tendency in such housing to have formally organized services and activity programs geared to the personal needs of the tenants.

Thomas O. Byerts

The presence of younger families in public housing provides opportunities for intergenerational interaction. Play spaces are a forum for such interaction.

Congregate housing

Congregate housing was authorized in the provisions of the Housing and Urban Development Act of 1970, but it was only in 1978 that federal funds were made available to pay for congregate services. The term *congregate* is applied to housing "that offers a minimum service package that includes some on-site meals served in a common dining room, plus one or more of such services as on-site medical/nursing services, personal care, or housekeeping" (Lawton, 1976, p. 239). The provision of meals in a social setting fosters a social milieu often absent in traditional housing, and the addition of other services often allows a marginally independent older person to remain in a community-based residential situation.

Nonsubsidized housing (Section 231 housing)

The Housing Act of 1959, Section 231, authorized federally insured loans but no direct subsidy, thus enabling a sponsor to obtain favorable interest rates in the commercial loan market. This type of housing has typically served the more affluent older person, since there are few cost restrictions in the legislation and the environments created tend to provide more services on the site such as leisure services and facilities, larger living units, lavish furnishings, medical services, and in some cases intermediate and skilled nursing care (Lawton, 1980).

Life care and founders' fee communities

Life care and founders' fee communities derive their names from the types of nonsubsidized financial arrangements that the relatively affluent enter into as a prerequisite for joining these communities. Both the life care and founders' fee communities require a large lump sum on entry (partially refundable in some cases if the person dies or leaves within a specified limited period) and a monthly maintenance fee (increasing as costs rise or higher levels of care or support are required by the older person). Federal assistance is not permitted to life care communities.

Retirement communities

Retirement communities are relatively recent phenomena resulting from the large number of individuals retiring with good retirement incomes. Heintz (1976, p. 8) defines retirement communities as "planned, low-density, age restricted, developments constructed by private funds and offering extensive recreational services and relatively low cost housing for purchase." Such communities generally have entrance requirements and complete community planning Retirement communities are usually located in warm climates outside of urban centers but are often near urban or metropolitan areas. The age limit for purchase is usually 50 to 55, and although the original intent was to have a community of healthy and independent older persons, the aging of their populations has resulted in the development of nursing care facilities.

Effects of supportive services

Retirement communities, as well as other forms of planned community housing in the process of evolution, have provided supportive services, often without the encouragement of federal legislation or the support of planners and managers. The effects of supportive services on older persons living in planned housing were tested by Lawton (1976) in two housing sites, one congregate and the other traditional planned housing. In comparison with tenants in traditional planned housing, congregate housing tenants had an increase in their sense of well-being but had a reduction in general activity, particularly in activity external to the housing environment. Thus it appears that the increased sense of well-being resulted at the expense of external housing activity involvement, alerting leisure service staff to the importance of intervening to encourage tenant involvement in the community beyond the housing site.

Planned community housing offering supportive services can be useful to older persons who range in competence from full independence to dependence requiring institutionalization. Having supportive services to choose from or to use as the need arises can help maintain the independence of the occupants of planned housing. Carefully determined supports provided in a planned housing site could enable the site to function as an alternative to institutionalization, thus accommodating the "frail," marginally competent older person.

Thomas O. Byerts

Retirement communities foster leisure life-styles through the provision of a variety of leisure spaces. Note not only the swimming pool but also the individual balconies.

A number of important issues related to planned housing for the elderly have been of concern to researchers. The following sections will examine issues such as the impact of planned housing and age integration and age segregation.

RESEARCH IS-SUES CONCERN-ING PLANNED HOUSING

Housing specifically designed for the elderly has a potentially decisive impact on the well-being of residents within those environments. A number of major studies evaluating the impact of planned housing will be discussed in this section.

Impact of planned housing

An excellent example of the impact of planned housing on the well-being of elderly residents is provided by a series of studies on Victoria Plaza, a public housing development for the elderly in San Antonio, Texas (Carp, 1966, 1975a, 1975b). This housing development consists of an eight-story apartment building with a senior center on the ground floor. Because of the excess of applicants, the research staff was able to compare those who eventually moved into the development with the those who were not accepted. In a series of follow-up interviews conducted 12 to 15 months after the move, it was found that although nonmovers showed little change, the movers showed an increase in morale, self-rated health, housing satisfaction, number of friends, and participation in activities. In a follow-up study of the movers and nonmovers after 8 years (Carp, 1978), it was found that movers increased their activity levels in areas such as "regular responsibility" activities (e.g., lobby receptionist, church work, and responsibilities at the senior center) and pastimes (e.g., visiting, club meetings, and table games). Additional follow-up data (Carp, 1975a, 1975b) after 8 years reported that movers had lower mortalities and better health than the nonmovers.

Lawton and Cohen (1974), using data from five different housing environments (public housing sites in Reading, Pennsylvania and Jersey City, New Jersey and Section 202 housing in Philadelphia and Atlantic City, New Jersey), assessed the psychological and social characteristics of tenants before a move and 12 months after, comparing the movers to a group of residents in the community who had not applied for planned housing and who remained in the same residence. Statistically controlling for (removing the effects of) health, certain background characteristics, and a variety of measures of well-being, change scores indicated that planned housing had a favorable impact on perceived change for the better, satisfaction with the status quo, housing satisfaction, and involvement in activities external to the housing sites.

Sherwood, Greer, and Morris (1979) assessed the impact of Highland Heights of Fall River, Massachusetts, a public housing project physically linked to a hospital whose services were provided in a well-planned approach to elderly and handicapped tenants. Rehoused (experimental groups) and nonrehoused (control groups) were randomly assigned by a multivariate matching technique that employs a large number of health, background, psychological, and social characteristics by which subjects were matched. Changes were assessed, and gains were noted in the rehoused in self-rated health, housing satisfaction, participation in formal activities, and satisfaction with the level of social activity. During a 5-year follow-up it was found that rehoused subjects were less likely to be institutionalized and had significantly lower death rates than the nonrehoused subjects.

Planned housing can have a favorable impact on older persons as these research projects have shown. Particularly important is the impact on activity level, as evidenced by increased interaction with friends, on-site formal activity participation, involvement with activities external to the housing site, and general satisfaction with the level of social activity.

Age integration and age segregation

The advantages and disadvantages of older persons living in an age-integrated setting, surrounded by younger families, or in an age-segregated setting such as apartments for the aged or retirement communities are part of a long-standing discussion. This discussion began in earnest when activity theorists claimed that age-integrated settings facilitated the maintenance of a middle-aged lifestyle. The disengagement theorists, on the other hand, favored segregated settings because such settings would facilitate the process of disengagement. This section will examine the research on these issues in two types of settings—apartments for the aged and retirement communities.

APARTMENTS FOR THE AGED. One of the most impressive and influential works in the area of social integration of the aged was done by Rosow (1967). He sought to determine the relationship between the degree of concentration or density of aged peers in apartment buildings (private and public housing) and social interaction of older persons living in those buildings. He sampled 1,200 elderly working-class and middle-class tenants from buildings classified according to degree of old-age concentration or density: *normal housing* (households with 1 to 15 percent aged members), *concentrated housing* (households with 33 to 49 percent aged members), and *dense housing* (households with more than 50 percent aged members). For both the working-class and middle-class tenants, the presence of more peers of the same age was associated with greater interaction with neighbors (working-class tenants were more dependent on neighbors as a source of friends, whereas middle-class tenants had a larger number of nonneighbor friends). A number of individual elderly tenant characteristics were associated with greater sensitivity to local concentration of the elderly, age (75 and over), sex (female), and marital status (single), especially when they occur in combination. Thus buildings containing a larger proportion of units occupied by elderly tenants represent significant advantages for friendship formation and socialization, particularly for the working class, the very old, women, and the single. These findings appear to support the Lawton and Nahemow (1973) "ecological model of adaptation and aging," since those of less competence (the working class and the very old) were not as free as the more competent (particularly the middle class, who are possibly less constrained by income, distance, and transportation) to choose friends beyond the housing site.

Messer (1967) sought to determine the interaction between age density, social interaction, and morale in two public housing projects (one age integrated and one age segregated). In the age-integrated project higher rates of social interaction were associated with higher morale, whereas in the age-segregated project there was no association between social interaction and morale. Messer suggests, as an explanation for these findings, that older persons who are not active in an age-integrated environment (where activity is important for younger persons) may feel guilty. On the other hand, the tenants of the age-segregated setting can become less active and not feel guilty. Thus a concentration of age peers encourages the development of expectations and groups of older persons who are supportive of a less active life-style, resulting in the development of social values and norms appropriate to the older tenants rather than what the larger community demands as appropriate.

Teaff, Lawton, Nahemow, and Carlson (1978) sought to determine the relationship between age mixing and indicators of well-being other than social interaction as in previous studies. Using a national probability sample of both subjects (2,000 elderly tenants) and settings (103 public housing sites), the relationship between age mixing and measures of elderly well-being (activity participation, housing satisfaction, mobility, morale, peer interaction, and family interaction) were examined. After statistically removing the effects of personal background characteristics and the social and physical characteristics of the housing environment, it was found that elderly tenants living in the more age-segregated environments had higher participation in organized activities within the housing environment, morale, housing satisfaction, and neighborhood mobility. Two possible explanations of why age-segregated public housing has positive effects on elderly public housing tenants may be attributed to feelings of security (because there are no children and teenagers from problem families) and to the emergence of age-specific norms and activity patterns (because of the freedom from negative opinions and stereotypes expressed about older persons).

One additional study will be presented that is less quantitative than those previously presented. This study is based on participant observation, employing the case study research method referred to as ethnography. Data from ethnographic research are no less scientific and do provide a more personal report on the everyday lives of people.

Hochschild (1973) engaged in an ethnographic research project at Merrill Court in San Francisco, an apartment complex housing 43 residents, of whom 37 were women. The women were socially homogeneous, being mostly widowed, rural born, Protestant, and working class. These background characteristics set the scene for the emergence of a community that was further fostered by the architectural design and events in the housing site. The architectural design facilitated social interaction through certain characteristics. The building was a five-story building with only 10 apartments per floor. A recreation room, mail room, and only one apartment were on the ground floor. There was a long porch outside all of the apartments on the second floor, enabling residents to observe the coming and going of neighbors. Events occurring in the housing site facilitated activity. The installation of a coffee machine in the recreation room resulted in tenants gathering around the machine to talk, and the recreation director began to participate in the conversation from which events, clubs, and organizations emerged. Interaction fostered by formal activities soon spread to the floors where regular visiting occurred among residents and their families, and patterns of assistance were evident, taking the form of help during illness, sharing recipes, and assisting in home repair. The sense of community is illustrated by examples such as the collection committee gathering a large amount of money and pushing it under the door of a tenant who was robbed, or the observation that tenants received an average of one phone call per hour. The community formed in Merrill Court was thus engaged and active and from all appearances was a group of satisfied individuals.

RETIREMENT COMMUNITIES. Retirement communities originated in Florida after World War II (Mangum, 1973) and were initially an effort to provide low-cost housing for retired members of unions, churches, and fraternal groups. Private builders only later entered the market. Retirement communities satisfy

Porches and balconies are an extension of an apartment's living space. They provide opportunities to observe the behavior of others and to informally interact.

older retirees' need for easily maintained housing that is smaller and cheaper. They also assist retirees in developing a leisure life-style.

Bultena and Wood (1969) compared older men who had moved from the Midwest after retirement to regular, age-integrated communities with those who had moved to planned, age-segregated retirement communities. Morale was found to be significantly higher for men in the planned retirement communities than for those in the age-integrated communities, even after the effects of age, occupational status, income, educational attainment, and perceived health status were removed through statistical procedures. Bultena and Wood suggest two reasons for the high levels of morale found among the men in the planned retirement communities. First, migrant retirees to the planned retirement communities had significantly higher preretirement occupational status, education, current income, and perceived health status. Second, planned retirement communities have certain structural features such as a physical concentration of age peers of similar social backgrounds that serves to expedite the formation of new friendship ties and leisure life-styles. In addition, Bultena and Wood (1970) examined leisure orientation and recreation activities within planned retirement communities. They found that individuals who had moved into these communities were leisure oriented, with such orientation being supported by a wide range of activities, facilities, and a peer group supportive of leisure. In fact, only 10 percent of the residents of these retirement communities were not regularly involved in leisure activities.

Retirement communities are not always the best of all possible worlds, although most studies indicate the satisfaction to be considerable. Jacobs (1974), in an ethnographic study of a retirement community that he called "Fun City," found a considerable amount of dissatisfaction. Fun City was described as a planned retirement community of approximately 6,000 residents, with an average age of 71 years, and being primarily white and middle-to-upper class. This self-sustaining community is located about 90 miles from a large metropolitan area in an isolated, rural community and has a nearby shopping center of approximately 40 businesses catering to Fun City residents. On site there is an activity center housing 92 clubs and organizations consisting of hobby, sports, service, fraternal, political, and church groups. Jacobs found, however, that even with many recreation opportunities only about 500 of the 6,000 residents participated on a daily basis. There were a number of reasons given for this nonparticipation and inactivity. First, there was a lack of public transportation so necessary because many residents were too disabled to get to the various meetings and events. Second, the exceptionally hot weather kept many from walking and participating in sports such as golf (except in the early morning, when they could escape the afternoon sun). Third, poor health such as a "bad" heart and severe arthritis fostered inactivity. Fourth, some individuals found that the air conditioning was aggravating their arthritis, so they stopped going to the activity center. Jacobs described Fun City as an unnatural setting that fostered social isolation. One resident summed up Fun City as a "false paradise."

The review of literature on age-integrated and age-segregated planned housing suggests that there are varying benefits. Age-segregated housing is often not a panacea, as Jacobs (1974) found in Fun City. However, age-segregated housing does appear to offer some real benefits to older persons:

1. Friendship formation and socialization (Rosow, 1967)
2. Development of a new normative reference group not dependent on high activity for high morale (Messer, 1967)
3. Higher on-site organized activity participation, morale, housing satisfaction, and neighborhood mobility (Teaff, Lawton, Nahemow, and Carlson, 1978)
4. Sense of community and mutual assistance (Hochschild, 1973)
5. Facilitation of leisure life-styles (Bultena and Wood, 1969, 1970)

FACILITATING LEISURE LIFE-STYLES THROUGH LEISURE SERVICES

Sherman's research (1971, 1972, 1974, 1975) showed that age-segregated planned housing does not always facilitate leisure. Comparing residents in six age-segregated settings (a retirement hotel, a rental village, an apartment tower, a purchase village, a cooperative village, and a life care facility), Sherman found only a moderate relationship between activity and morale. She suggested that this moderate relationship was a consequence of variations in continuity of life-style, styles of aging, available activities, and site facilities. This section will propose a role continuity model of leisure services and suggest design criteria for leisure service site facilities.

Role continuity model of leisure services

Davis and Teaff (1980) presented a role continuity model of leisure services that has been implemented at the Byer Activity Center at the Dallas Home for Jewish Aged, Dallas, Texas. Participants at the Byer Activity Center are residents of the on-site apartment units and persons from the nearby community.

RATIONALE FOR THE MODEL. Atchley (1977, p. 27) proposed that "as individuals grow older, they are predisposed toward maintaining continuity of habits, associations, preferences, and so on." These predispositions are also evolving "from interactions among personal preferences, biological and psychological capabilities, situational opportunities, and experience" (Atchley, 1977, p. 27). Leisure services provide many situational opportunities for role continuity because of the variety of meanings that leisure may have for individuals. Havighurst (1972) found leisure to have meanings such as an opportunity for service to others, a source of prestige or status, an environment for social participation, a time to make new friends, a source of new experiences, and a way to make time pass.

ASSESSMENT PROCEDURES. Assessment procedures are an important first step in the construction of situational opportunities for role continuity. Important areas of assessment are social history, physical and mental functioning, and leisure preferences.

Social history. An individual's social history is an essential part of the assessment. Davis (1982, p. 307), in a follow-up of the Davis and Teaff article (1980), suggests that certain information be gathered:

1. Name of client
2. Date and place of birth
3. Ethnic or cultural background
4. Religious preference
5. Family relationships
6. Marital status
7. Children (number, sexes, and ages)
8. Educational background
9. Work and occupational history
10. Places of residence
11. Retirement (reasons for and satisfaction with)
12. Economic status
13. Interests and pleasures
14. Hobbies
15. Community involvement and affairs
16. Friendships and social patterns
17. Associations
18. Interesting anecdotes about the individual

Physical and mental functioning. The assessment of physical and mental functioning may be gathered from information provided by the resident or by the staff. Certain critical questions should be answered (Davis, 1982, p. 308):

1. Are there any physical limitations?
2. What is the degree of ambulation?
3. What is the level of the ability for personal care?
4. Are there any chronic disorders?
5. Have there been any falls or injuries lately?
6. Is there any hearing impairment?
7. Is there any visual impairment?
8. What are the current physical problems and medications?
9. What are any other special problems?

Leisure preferences. Personal habits, associations, and preferences may be determined by asking a series of open-ended questions. Examples of such questions are (Davis, 1982, p. 310):

1. Describe how you spend a typical day.
2. Describe a perfect holiday.
3. What is the most boring time of your day?
4. What honors have you received?
5. What unique experiences have you had in life?
6. Tell me some of your most pleasant memories.
7. What types of things did you do on your job?
8. Did you have many friends at work?
9. What is your motto?

Leisure preferences may also be determined through a series of closed-ended activity questions, requiring a "yes" or "no" response. Closed-ended activity questions are useful in an initial effort to get an overview of activity interests. Open-ended questions, on the other hand, are useful as a follow-up and may take a number of forms. First, leading questions may be employed—for example, "I understand you are interested in clubs. What types of clubs do you belong to?" Second, based on activity participation interests, an individual can be asked a forced-choice question such as, "If you had a choice, would you visit friends, attend a lecture, or watch T.V.?" If the answer is "attend a lecture," the next question might be, "What subjects do you prefer?"

Leisure assessment may be conducted for the withdrawn through a walking tour of the facility. Activity participation questions may be asked of the older person as programs are observed—for example, "Do you enjoy singing?" Many nonverbal cues may be observed—for example, the examination of ceramic items for sale may indicate a past or present interest.

CREATION OF A ROLE. The information gained from the various assessment procedures is then used to integrate each older participant into a variety of activities and to create a role based on past habits, associations, and preferences. Examples of roles and the activities related to each of the roles follow.

Hostess. "'The Hostess' greets and welcomes guests for a party, serves on the welcoming committee, plans refreshments for the tea, helps make decorations in the craft group for a luau. All these activities allow the continuance of the preference for hostessing" (Davis and Teaff, 1980, p. 34).

Salesman. "'The Salesman' helps with the raffle for the women's group, helps run the gift shop, organizes flea markets, white elephant sales, the annual bazaar, serves on the committee for fund-raising projects" (Davis and Teaff, 1980, p. 34).

Organizer. "'The Organizer' serves as president of the council, helps on the program committee, brings helpful hints and ideas from all newspaper sources, helps call for activities, and sets up games such as bridge" (David and Teaff, 1980, p. 34).

Entertainer. "'The Entertainer' who has always enjoyed the limelight is the bingo caller, tells jokes at social gatherings, helps provide entertainment for parties, is a member of the drama club, and is the master of ceremonies for talent shows and grandchildren's day" (Davis and Teaff, 1980, p. 34).

Humanitarian. "'The Humanitarian' helps with service projects, cancer society bandages, crocheting for shut-ins, knitting for babies, friendly visiting with the sick, phone calling, helping with the sunshine committee, sending get well cards and reporting on human interest stories at the current events groups" (Davis and Teaff, 1980, p. 34).

Motherer. "'The Motherer' has always had a preference for caring for others. She enjoys those activities in which she can lend a hand and taking a mothering role. She bakes for others as well as for many activities and lunches. She helps with the cooking group, suggests recipes for the recipe book and adds helpful hints to the center newsletter. She also participates in the tutoring program and children's storytelling" (Davis and Teaff, 1980, p. 34).

Reporter. "'The Reporter' knows lots of information on a variety of subjects. The activities of the reporter involve announcing community events, acting as secretary to the Resident Council, and interviewing members for the 'Mystery Resident'" (Davis and Teaff, 1980, pp. 34-35).

Musician. "'The Musician' helps with all music endeavors, acts as a link to community resources for performers, helps with the choral group, plays the piano, assembles sing-along books and participates actively in music listening and music appreciation groups" (Davis and Teaff, 1980, p. 35).

Businessman. An example to illustrate how a role can be created and how an individual can be integrated into a variety of activities is provided through a case study of Mr. X:

> Mr. X is a retired businessman. He retired from his own business seven years ago, is widowed, lives alone and says he "has nothing to do." Mr. X has few leisure skills, since he is a product of the work ethic and had little time for community and civic affairs. His associations have been through business. Mr. X has limited physical capabilities, having suffered a stroke several years ago. His speech is slurred. Mr. X is extremely bright and alert. Since he commuted quite a distance to work, he has always gotten up early, been very efficient, and prides himself on being exact in every detail. His preference is for work related activity, providing an opportunity to be productive.
>
> Because Mr. X has become increasingly more lonely and depressed, his daughter inquired about the possibility of his becoming involved at the Byer Activity Center. Feeling useless, Mr. X was withdrawn at first. During an interview with Mr. X, his preferences, past experiences and habits were learned. Mr. X likes responsibility, figures and money, has dabbled in the stock market, had knowledge of jewelry and says he doesn't like to waste time. He is always dressed in suit, tie and hat.
>
> The role of "Businessman" is designed for him. Both individual and group activities are suggested to him where he can perform the role of businessman. The activities which are suggested include: counting money from the soft drink machine, collecting fees for luncheons and trips, serving as the treasurer of the organization's council, helping on the membership committee, reporting on business and stock market changes at the men's discussion group, and operating the center's "post office" where stamps and envelopes are sold. By providing the opportunities for Mr. X to continue his past preferences and experience, he is able to gain status and recognition while participating in a leisure program that is meaningful to him (Davis and Teaff, 1980, p. 35).

Less active roles. It is important to note that not all individuals will have an active role but may simply have the role of visitor or observer. Some individuals may have a variety of roles within the leisure program.

EVALUATION OF ROLE PERFORMANCE. An ongoing evaluation of each individual's role performance is vital. Each older person participating for the first time in leisure services in the new environment must be assisted by the leisure services staff in identifying activities that might provide meaningful opportunities for role continuity. The matching of activities with individual should result in recognition, status, and sense of identity, helping to socially integrate the older person into the planned community housing environment and foster a leisure life-style.

The leisure service specialist must be sensitive to changes in an individual's personal preferences and in biological and psychological capabilities. Consistent with the Lawton and Nahemow (1973) "ecological model of adaptation and aging" and illustrated by Gelwicks and Newcomer (1974), environmental supports may need to be increased by the leisure service staff as competence declines.

The design criteria to be described are selected from a large number of criteria developed by Gelwicks and Newcomer (1974) and are addressed to a variety of design concerns in planned housing for the elderly. These design criteria are to serve as guiding principles for leisure service site facilities.

Design criteria for leisure service site facilities

ENTRANCE AREA

Management policies and the design of physical spaces should encourage social interaction between residents, residents and staff, and residents and the community. (Gelwicks and Newcomer, 1974, p. 95)

Lawton (1970), in observations of resident behaviors in 12 housing projects, found the area around the front door and the elevator entrance to be high activity areas. Older persons used these areas of maximum traffic and pedestrian movement for sitting and watching the behavior of staff members and visitors. The entrance area should therefore be designed as a space for traffic, sitting, watching, and social interaction. Managers and leisure service personnel should encourage this multiple use by designing a large enough entrance area and furnishing them to serve as true social spaces.

FURNITURE

The furniture design and layout in interior and exterior common spaces should encourage small informal group formations, as well as permit an individually selected pattern of privacy and one-to-one conversation. (Gelwicks and Newcomer, 1974, p. 119)

Social interaction can be fostered and privacy respected through the clustering of chairs in a number of small groupings. Light-weight, comfortable chairs that are easily movable by older persons allow the social interaction and use of space to be controlled according to the desired level of social interaction or degree of privacy.

ACTIVITY SPACES

Activity spaces of all types—i.e., recreation lounge, lobby and service should have individual identities but conceived and interrelated as a series of interacting spaces. (Gelwicks and Newcomer, 1974, p. 116)

Activity spaces with individual identities and opportunity for interactions and interrelationships provide a variety of activity options. Large, multipurpose activity spaces should be avoided whenever possible because they are undefined and lack an individual identity that often decreases use, particularly when older persons are interested in a particular activity and do not want to compete with the noise of other activities. Interacting places such as a lounge adjacent to the dining room or a recreation room adjoining the lobby provide a variety of activity and contact options for older persons entering an area. Interrelationships of spaces such as those with more obligatory uses (e.g., dining room and laundry) near those with less obligatory uses (e.g., craft room and greenhouse) increase use of the less obligatory spaces.

SENIOR CENTER

A community multi-purpose senior citizen center where both residents and people from the community can meet for social activities and services should be included on the site of the housing project. This is best located immediately adjacent to the project's central facilities, but not as an integral part of either the central facilities or the living units. (Gelwicks and Newcomer, 1974, p. 102)

A senior center can be a focus of activity for the neighborhood and the entire community, as well as a resource center for older persons. If the location of the housing site is in a neighborhood having the requisite density of older persons and available transportation, then a senior center located on site would be ideal because the resources of the senior center can be shared with residents of the housing site. However, it is important to note that Carp (1966) found that the senior center located within the main high-rise building constituting Victoria Plaza created some resentment on the part of the tenants who felt their territory was being invaded by neighborhood elderly. The problem of territoriality can be solved by locating the senior center on site without integrating it into living units or central facilities.

OUTDOOR SPACES

The design of outdoor spaces should be given as much consideration as indoor spaces. (Gelwicks and Newcomer, 1974, p. 117)

Outdoor spaces provide opportunities for social interaction and exercise. Outdoor activity spaces should be located near areas of pedestrian movement and should include outdoor furniture and seating arrangements that foster observation of activity and conversation. Pathways and walkways encourage exercise through the provision of opportunities for walking, jogging, and biking. Maximum use of walkways and pathways can be realized provided that they are safe from crime and dangerous conditions such as ice and snow and have resting points such as benches.

This chapter has documented how leisure services and other life supporting and enriching services in planned community housing are increasingly being viewed as vital to the maintenance of older persons in the community. Research on the impact of planned housing and the effects of age-segregated planned community housing support the benefits of such housing on friendship, organized activity participation, and facilitation of leisure life-styles.

EMPLOYMENT OPPORTUNITIES FOR LEISURE SERVICE SPECIALISTS IN PLANNED COMMUNITY HOUSING

Leisure services are increasing in planned community housing. Federally subsidized and privately constructed housing are providing leisure services in a variety of forms, depending on federal regulations and the demands of the consumers. The necessity of having professionally planned and administered leisure services is evident from the unsuccessful experience of residents of Fun City.

Leisure service specialists interested in employment in planned community housing should consult a number of resources currently available for locating housing for the elderly. The American Association of Retired Persons (see Appendix C) has published a comprehensive guide to housing for the elderly titled *National Directory of Retirement Facilities.* Individuals interested in employment in a life care facility should check their state department of health or state office on aging and the directory of homes for the aging available from the American Association of Homes for the Aging (see Appendix C), which lists about 400 life care facilities. Information on retirement communities in a variety of geographical locations in the United States may be obtained from two books by Peter A. Dickinson (1980, 1981), both of which are available from E.P. Dutton. Community park and recreation departments should be contacted, since these agencies often provide services for planned community housing, particularly public housing.

Planned community housing for older persons is an environment for living. The interactions between an older person and the planned housing environment may be viewed from a number of perspectives. The Lawton and Nahemow (1973) "ecological model of adaptation and aging" views this interaction in terms of *competence* and *environmental press,* with the maximum performance occurring when environmental press is within the older person's individual competence. Gelwicks and Newcomer (1974) speak of the man-environment interaction as a combination of *capability* and *support,* with high ability matched by low environmental support and declining ability matched by increasing environmental support. Kahana's (1980) concept of "person/environment congruence" is concerned with the matching of the environment and the type and strength of needs, balancing *support* and *challenge* to prolong independence. The maintenance and encouragement of adaptive behavior and the matching of person with environment may be achieved through the provision of a wide range of living environments. Various types of planned community hous-

SUMMARY

ing have been developed: public housing; private, nonprofit rental housing; congregate housing; nonsubsidized housing; life care and founders' fee communities; and retirement communities. Leisure services and other types of life supporting and life enriching services have been provided at varying levels in each of the preceding types of planned community housing, often accommodating the marginally competent older person.

The impact of planned community housing and age integration and age segregation in planned community housing have been two important areas of concern to researchers. The impact of planned community housing on older persons is significant for a variety of measures of well-being, particularly important for activity level (e.g., increased interaction with friends, on-site formal activity participation, involvement in activities external to the housing site, and general satisfaction with the level of social activity). The research on age integration and age segregation of planned community housing such as apartments for the aged and retirement communities has found age-segregated housing to offer a number of benefits in the area of activity involvement (e.g., friendship formation and socialization, higher on-site organized activity participation, neighborhood mobility, and facilitation of leisure life-styles).

Leisure life-styles may be facilitated through leisure services that are focused on role continuity and concerned with the provision of site facilities. The role continuity model of leisure services is concerned with the assessment of the individual's physical, social, psychological, and leisure functioning; the creation of a role that integrates a variety of activities related to that role, thus increasing status and sense of identity; and evaluation of role performance, paying particular attention to changes in personal preferences and biological and psychological capabilities. Leisure service site facilities should be guided by certain design criteria:

1. Physical spaces such as entrance areas should encourage social interaction through design and furnishings.
2. Furniture design and clustering of chairs in small groupings should allow both social interaction and privacy.
3. Activity spaces of all types should have individual identities, interact with other spaces to provide a variety of activity and contact options, and interrelate obligatory and less obligatory uses.
4. A senior center located on site but not within the central facilities or the living units can serve the needs of residents of the housing site, the neighborhood, and the entire community.
5. Outdoor spaces, pathways, and walkways foster social interaction, providing they have seating and are safe.

Employment opportunities for leisure service specialists in planned community housing are increasing in federally subsidized and privately financed housing. Leisure services professionally planned and administered help to maintain older persons in the community and avoid unsuccessful experiences like those of "Fun City." A number of resources currently exist to aid in locating a variety of planned community housing sites that might be of interest to the leisure service specialist looking for employment.

REFERENCES

Atchley, R.: The social forces in later life, ed. 2, Belmont, Calif., 1977, Wadsworth Publishing Co.

Bultena, G., and Wood, V.: The American retirement community: bane or blessing? J. Gerontol. **24:**209-217, 1969.

Bultena, G., and Wood, V.: Leisure orientation and recreational activities of retirement community residents, J. Leisure Res. **2:**3-15, 1970.

Carp, F.: A future for the aged, Austin, Tex., 1966, University of Texas Press.

Carp, F.: Impact of improved housing on morale and life satisfaction, Gerontologist **15:**511-515, 1975a.

Carp, F.: Long-range satisfaction with housing, Gerontologist **15:**68-72, 1975b.

Carp, F.: Housing and living environments of older people. In Binstock, R., and Shanas, E., editors: Handbook of aging and the social sciences, New York, 1976, Van Nostrand Reinhold Co.

Carp, F.: Effects of the living environment on activity and use of time, Aging Hum. Dev. **9:**75-91, 1978.

Davis, N.: The role continuity approach to aging: implications for leisure programming. In Teague, M., MacNeil, R., and Hitzhusen, G., editors: Perspectives on leisure and aging in a changing society, Columbia, Mo., 1982, University of Missouri Press.

Davis, N., and Teaff, J.: Facilitating role continuity of the elderly through leisure programming, Ther. Recreation J. **14:**32-36, 1980.

Dickinson, P.: Sunbelt retirement: a complete state-by-state guide to retiring in the South and West of the United States, New York, 1980, E.P. Dutton, Inc.

Dickinson, P.: Retirement Edens: outside the sunbelt, New York, 1981, E.P. Dutton, Inc.

Gelfand, D., and Olsen, J.: The aging network: programs and services, New York, 1980, Springer Publishing Co., Inc.

Gelwicks, L., and Newcomer, R.: Planning housing environments for the elderly, Washington, D.C., 1974, National Council on the Aging.

Havighurst, R.: Life style and leisure patterns: their evolution through the life cycle. In Leisure in the IIIrd age, Conference, Dubrovnik, Yugoslavia, Paris, 1972, International Center for Social Gerontology.

Heintz, K.: Retirement communities: for adults only, New Brunswick, N.J., 1976, Center for Urban Policy Research.

Hochschild, A.: The unexpected community, Englewood Cliffs, N.J., 1973, Prentice-Hall, Inc.

Jacobs, J.: Fun city: an ethnographic study of a retirement community, New York, 1974, Holt, Rinehart & Winston General Book.

Kahana, E.: A congruence model of person-environment interaction. In Lawton, M.P., Windley, P., and Byerts, T.O., editors: Aging and the environment: direction and perspectives, New York, 1980, Garland Press, Inc.

Lawton, M.P.: Public behavior of older people in congregate housing. In Archea, J., and Eastman, C., editors: Proceedings of Environmental Design Research Association II, Pittsburgh, 1970, Carnegie-Mellon University.

Lawton, M.P.: Assessing the competence of older people. In Kent, D., Kastenbaum, R., and Sherwood, S., editors: Research, planning, and action for the elderly, New York, 1972, Behavioral Publications.

Lawton, M.P.: Planning and managing housing for the elderly, New York, 1975, John Wiley & Sons, Inc.

Lawton, M.P.: The relative impact of congregate and traditional housing on elderly tenants, Gerontologist **16:**237-242, 1976.

Lawton, M.P.: Environment and aging, Monterey, Calif., 1980, Brooks/Cole Publishing Co.

Lawton, M.P., and Cohen, J.: The generality of housing impact on the well-being of older people, J. Gerontol. **29:**194-204, 1974.

Lawton, M.P., and Nahemow, L.: Ecology and the aging process. In Eisdorfer, C., and Lawton, M.P., editors: The psychology of adult development and aging, Washington, D.C., 1973, American Psychological Association.

Mangum, W.: Retirement villages. In Boyd, R., and Oakes, C., editors: Foundations of practical gerontology, Columbia, S.C., 1973, University of South Carolina Press.

Messer, M.: The possibility of age-concentrated environment becoming a normative system, Gerontologist **7:**247-251, 1967.

Rosow, I.: Social integration of the aged, New York, 1967, Free Press.

Sherman, S.: The choice of retirement housing among the well elderly, Aging Hum. Dev. **2:**118-138, 1971.

Sherman, S.: Satisfaction with retirement housing: attitudes, recommendations and moves, Aging Hum. Dev. **3:**339-366, 1972.

Sherman, S.: Leisure activities in retirement housing, J. Gerontol. **29:**325-335, 1974.

Sherman, S.: Provision of on-site services in retirement housing, Aging Hum. Dev. **6:**229-247, 1975.

Sherwood, S., Greer, D., and Morris, J.: A study of the Highland Heights apartments for the physically impaired and elderly in Fall River. In Lawton, M.P., Windley, P., and Byerts, T.O., editors: Aging and the environment: directions and perspectives, New York, 1979, Garland Press, Inc.

Teaff, J., Lawton, M.P., Nahemow, L., and Carlson, D.: Impact of age integration on the well-being of elderly tenants in public housing, J. Gerontol. **33:**126-133, 1978.

SUGGESTED READINGS

Carp, F.: Housing and living environments of older people. In Binstock, R., and Shanas, E., editors: Handbook of aging and the social sciences, New York, 1976, Van Nostrand Reinhold Co.

Gelwicks, L., and Newcomer, R.: Planning housing environments for the elderly, Washington, D.C., 1974, National Council on the Aging.

Lawton, M.P.: Planning and managing housing for the elderly, New York, 1975, John Wiley & Sons, Inc.

Lawton, M.P.: Environment and aging, Monterey, Calif., 1980, Brooks/Cole Publishing Co.

Institutions for the elderly

Only about 5 percent of individuals 65 and older reside in institutions—a surprising fact considering the general public image of older persons as being sick and disabled. However, such statistics are somewhat misleading; the figure rises to 10 percent of those over 75, with the probability that one of every five older persons 65 and over will spend *some* time in an institution (Palmore, 1976). The institution may have an impact on a substantial number of older persons and their younger families, as well as the public in general, who are asked to support care facilities through tax dollars. The quality of the care available in institutions is of great concern to older persons and should be of concern to the general public. Leisure services in institutions are an important component of quality care. This chapter will present a short history of institutional care, the types of institutions for the elderly, characteristics of institutions and their residents, the impact of institutionalization on older persons, rehabilitation programs, development of leisure services, and employment opportunities for leisure service specialists in institutions for the elderly.

Institutional care of older persons has a long history. The Elizabethan Poor Law of 1601 was the foundation for welfare legislation in England and the United States (Hess and Markson, 1980). This legislation provided for the care of the aged and poor in an almshouse, or poorhouse, where custodial care became the responsibility of municipal government. Because the elderly were cared for along with the sick, the mentally ill, the destitute, and criminals in an undifferentiated institution, the institutionalization of the aged was viewed as a penalty for "improvident or dissolute life" (Townsend, 1964, p. 15). This attitude continues today and contributes to the stigma attached to residence in an institution.

**HISTORY OF
INSTITUTIONAL
CARE**

Isolation of the aged and infirm continued to be the predominant social policy of the nineteenth century. Following the Revolutionary War and the Poor Law of England passed in 1834, almshouses and public poorhouses became increasingly popular (Gelfand and Olsen, 1980). Financing of these facilities was the responsibility of cities and counties, not of the state or federal government. Residents were often forced to work for very meager wages as a means of providing some support for themselves and the institution.

New concepts of income support began the expansion of the types of institutional care available for older persons in the twentieth century. The Old Age Assistance Act of 1929 began to offer alternatives to institutionalization in a number of states. The early versions of the Social Security Act of the 1930s prohibited federal financial support of institutions because public institutions were viewed as a state responsibility, with the legislative intent being to encourage older persons to live at home (Cohen, 1974). The effect of this legislation, however, was to encourage the movement of older persons from public to private facilities such as boarding homes. Boarding homes later added nurses to staffs, resulting in the emergence of the term *nursing home* (Moss and Halmandaris, 1977). Some could not afford to move to the boarding homes and so remained in institutions at public expense (Drake, 1958).

Federal involvement in funding institutional care of the elderly was greatly expanded during the 1950s and 1960s. In 1953 the federal government began to assist older persons with the costs of private institutionalization, but the law prohibiting public institutional payments continued. The 1950s saw the passage of the Hill Burton Act and the National Housing Act, which authorized grant and loan funds for constructing and equipping institutions. The passage of Medicare (Title XVIII) in 1965 and Medicaid (Title XIX) in 1967 established major funding sources for institutions. It also established common definitions and basic national standards for service delivery (Winston and Wilson, 1977).

TYPES OF INSTITUTIONS

There are a variety of types of institutions serving the needs of older persons. The term *institution* is used to refer to "care provided in an institutional setting over an extended period of time" (Cohen, 1974, p. 18). The care provided can range from activities of daily living (ADL) (e.g., feeding, bathing, and dressing) to the provision of medical life support systems. As institutions, they require older persons to adjust to being removed from individual or family living and submit to constraints on choice in a variety of daily living situations. Institutions are operated under public, private nonprofit, or proprietary auspices and may include chronic care hospitals, Veterans' Administration facilities, psychiatric hospitals, homes for the aged, and public and profit nursing homes. There are various types of institutions that provide different levels of care and that are certified under Medicare and Medicaid (extended, skilled, and intermediate care), as well as board and care, personal care, and domiciliary facilities.

Extended care facilities (ECFs), certified for Medicare, provide extensive professional nursing and support staff. According to Cohen (1974, p. 20):

> The extended care facility is a short-term convalescent care facility
> specifically arranged to take care of carefully selected patients coming
> from hospitals. . . . It involves aspects of rehabilitation, social work, high-
> quality medical and nursing care, and supportive services—that is, those
> services usually associated with long-term care of high quality.

There are very few ECF beds actually in use because Medicare defines eligibility for extended care so narrowly (in terms of length of stay, origin of patient, and rehabilitation potential of patient, rather than in terms of types of services actually provided). In actuality the beds that are available are usually in skilled nursing facilities.

Extended care facilities

Skilled nursing facilities (SNFs) may be characterized as institutions that provide care for severely ill patients. SNFs are required to provide "the emergency and ongoing services of a physician, nursing care, rehabilitation services, pharmaceutical services, dietetic services, laboratory and radiological services, dental services, social services, and activity services" (Glasscote et al., 1976, p. 34). Attending physicians must visit every 30 days of the patient's first 90 days of stay; after that visits may be reduced to every 60 days. Nursing services must be supervised by a full-time registered nurse, with a registered nurse being in charge on the day shift and either a registered nurse or a licensed practical nurse being on the afternoon and night shifts. A patient care plan should be prepared and regularly reviewed so that the patient's changing conditions are appropriately translated into services needed. Rehabilitative, laboratory, radiological, dental, and social services may be provided by formal contractural agreements with outside sources. Regular activity services and programs are required to be provided by on-site personnel.

Skilled nursing facilities

Intermediate care facilities (ICFs) were defined in the Medicaid legislation of the 1960s and were developed because of the need of elderly poor for health supervision and access to various health services but not the need for full-time professional staff (Glasscote et al., 1976). Many of the regulations are the same as those for SNFs, but there are some differences (Glasscote et al., 1976, p. 39):

> Regulations for construction, sanitation, safety, and the handling of drugs
> are very similar. Theoretically and philosophically the difference is that the
> SNF is a "medical" institution and the ICF is a health institution. In the
> ICF, social and recreational policy is to be given near equal emphasis with
> medical policy.

One major difference is in supervisory nursing requirements; for example, nursing services on the day shift must be supervised by either a licensed practical

Intermediate care facilities

TABLE 7-1   **Percentage distributions of institutions by sponsorship, size, and certification status, 1973-1974**

	Nonprofit (3900 institutions)	Proprietary (11,900 institutions)
Number of beds		
Fewer than 50	36	42
50-99	36	35
100-199	20	21
200 or more	8	2
	100	100
Certification status		
Both Medicare and Medicaid	24	27
Skilled nursing or both skilled and intermediate	26	21
Intermediate care only	24	29
Note certified	25	22
	99	99

From National Center for Health Statistics: Selected operating and financial characteristics of nursing homes, Vital and Health Statistics Series 13, Pub. No. 22, Rockville, Md., 1975, U.S. Department of Health, Education, and Welfare.

TABLE 7-2   **Characteristics of nursing home residents and community resident elderly (percentages)**

Characteristic	Nursing home	Community
Sex		
Male	28	41
Female	72	59
Race		
White	95	91
Nonwhite	5	9
Marital status		
Married	12	54
Widowed	69	37
Divorced or separated	3	3
Never married	15	6
Age		
65-74	17	63
74+	83	37

From National Center for Health Statistics: Characteristics, social contacts, and activities of nursing home residents, Vital and Health Statistics Series 13, Pub. No. 27, Rockville, Md., 1977, U.S. Department of Health, Education, and Welfare.

nurse or a registered nurse. It is important to note that, as in the case of skilled nursing care, the definition of intermediate care is based on the level of care provided and *not* the facility providing the care (e.g., SNFs, and hospitals).

The level of care of board and care, personal care, and domiciliary care homes is difficult to describe because no federal licensing classification exists for these facilities. Each state adopts its own regulations. In general it may be said that this level of care provides a protective environment, some personal care, and meals but does not provide medical or leisure services.

Board and care, personal care, and domiciliary care homes

Homes for the aged may also be included under this category. Homes for the aged are usually nonprofit and very often church-sponsored homes that provide personal care, social services, and comprehensive leisure services. Although homes for the aged provide some personal care, persons entering such homes are usually required to be healthy and able to maintain themselves in their own room. They freely select leisure activities and come and go as they desire. Many of these homes have intermediate or skilled nursing care facilities, should a resident's health decline.

The number of institutions and the number of beds for elderly institutional residents have increased since the 1930s. The United States in 1939 had 1,200 institutions containing 25,000 beds. Between 1960 and 1976 the number of beds increased from 331,000 to 1,327,358 (a 302 percent increase) and the number of patients increased from 290,000 to over 1 million (a 245 percent increase); the 65 and older population increased from 17 to 21 million—only a 23 percent increase (Moss and Halmandaris, 1977). These figures reflect a number of changes within society: an increase in the older population, changes in federal financing as a result of Medicare and Medicaid, and a willingness by institutions to accept a greater variety of patients (Cohen, 1974; Manard, Kart, and van Gils, 1975).

CHARACTERISTICS OF INSTITUTIONS AND THEIR RESIDENTS

Institutions may be further examined through characteristics such as sponsorship, size, and certification status. Table 7-1 shows that the majority of the institutions are proprietary, 75 percent have fewer than 100 beds, and 50 percent are giving either intermediate care only or both intermediate and skilled nursing care (National Center for Health Statistics, 1975).

The nursing home has the greatest number of residents of all the types of institutions. Nursing home residents differ from elderly living in the community, as Table 7-2 shows. Almost 75 percent of nursing home residents are female and 95 percent are white. They are more likely to be widowed or never married than their community counterparts and to be 74 years of age or older (National Center for Health Statistics, 1977a).

Nursing home residents have a variety of physical, functional, and mental conditions impeding independent living outside the institution. Table 7-3 shows a number of common conditions reported by staff members; notable impairment

TABLE 7-3　　　　　**Selected physical, functional, and mental capacities
of nursing home residents**

Condition	Percentage of residents
Arthritis	34
Heart trouble	34
Diabetes	13
Paralysis due to stroke	11
Impaired vision	47
Impaired hearing	32
Impaired speech	26
Impaired ability to bathe	86*
Impaired ability to dress self	68*
Impaired mobility	65*
Impaired continence	45*
Impaired ability to eat	32*
Senility	58
Agitation or nervousness	42
Depression	39
Sleep disturbance	19
Abusiveness or aggressiveness	17
Other behavioral problem	5

From National Center for Health Statistics: Profile of chronic illness in nursing homes, Vital and
Health Statistics Series 13, Pub. No. 29, Hyattsville, Md., 1977, U.S. Department of Health,
Education, and Welfare; and National Center for Health Statistics: A comparison of nursing home
residents and discharges from the 1977 National Nursing Home Survey, Advance Data, Pub. No. 29,
Hyattsville, Md., 1978, U.S. Department of Health, Education, and Welfare.
*1977 data; all other data from 1973-1974.

occurs in self-maintenance skills (e.g., bathing, dressing, and mobility), as well
as in physical and mental functioning (National Center for Health Statistics,
1977b, 1978).

Nursing homes are increasingly being used as care centers for the very
old, many of whom have no close family to rely on, and who may have some
functional, mental, or physical impairment. Nursing homes are becoming chronic disease hospitals for physically and mentally impaired older persons rather
than care centers and homes for the ambulatory who are not self-sufficient
(Tobin and Lieberman, 1976). This change in the population of nursing homes
has resulted in care becoming more medical than social and psychological in
nature. However, as Tobin and Lieberman (1976, p. 236) caution, "the loss of
physical or psychological self-sufficiency does not automatically mean the loss
of social needs; the consequences will indeed be dire if we retreat to ware-
housing these most needly elderly and do not make every effort to provide
life-sustaining social as well as physical supports."

In Chapter 6 the Lawton and Nahemow (1973) "ecological model of adaptation and aging" stressed the relationship between environmental press and competence. Residents of institutions for older persons are likely to have reduced competence with the result that the older individual will be increasingly shaped by the environment rather than shaping the environment to meet individual needs. The impact of institutionalization will be examined from the perspectives of institutional transfer and the institutional environment.

IMPACT OF INSTITUTIONAL- IZATION ON OLDER PERSONS

Relocation from home to institution or from one institution to another can have a variety of physical, psychological, and social consequences. Aldritch and Mendkoff (1963), in a study of an elderly sample relocated after the closing of their institution, compared expected mortalities (data from the previous 10 years at the institution) with mortalities following the move, finding that mortalities increased for all ages, primarily in the first 3 months. Aldritch and Mendkoff (1963, p. 190) use the following case as an illustration:

Institutional transfer

> Miss E.W., aged 85, had been in the Home for twenty-four years following a back injury. She walked with a cane and had been an active and alert participant, requiring no nursing supervision. She was anxious about the Home's closing, expressed fear of any change in her situation, and became depressed and withdrawn. After arranging her belongings and taking care of her personal affairs, she withdrew further and lost all interest in the daily activities of the Home. She frequently spoke of death and stated that she had no reason to live. While efforts were being made for transfer, she died, apparently of arteriosclerosis.

The stress of relocation can be alleviated in a number of ways (Lieberman, 1974; Schulz and Brenner, 1977). Traumatic adjustments can be lessened by involving patients in the decisions related to the move, conducting trial visits, and attempting to make the new environment as similar to the old one as possible. The new environment should encourage integration into the outside community, social interaction, and personal autonomy. Liebowitz (1974) suggested that the most severe negative impact will occur when older persons are moved into cold and dehumanizing environments that foster dependence.

Erving Goffman (1961) used the term *total institution* when referring to places such as mental hospitals and prisons that cut individuals off from the world and impose regimented schedules for eating, sleeping, working, and playing. The degree of institutional "totality" of a nursing home may be determined by a variety of criteria (Bennett and Nahemow, 1965; Kiyak, Kahana, and Lev, 1975). Some criteria related to life in the nursing home are: involuntary recruitment, formalized rules and sanctions, little resident involvement in governance, few provisions for personal property, and institution scheduling of all activities. Criteria related to access to the outside world include: allowances for leaving during the day or for the weekend, availability of private phones, ease of travel

Institutional environment

to the community, and scheduled activities outside the institution. Individual older persons in a "total" nursing home that provides a custodial, protected environment for its residents are increasingly perceived as having little capacity for personal growth and autonomy and become oriented to the world of the institution and isolated from the outside world, thereby losing the capacity to function independently of the institution.

The labeling and treating of older persons as incompetent, particularly for the elderly who are dependent and confused, may result in what Zusman (1966) calls the *social breakdown syndrome*. Examples may be gleaned from the literature to illustrate various aspects of the social breakdown syndrome such as loss of privacy (Townsend, 1964), loss of personal possessions (Gubrium, 1975), and loss of friends and the capacity to care (Townsend, 1964):

> The staff took the attitude that the old people had surrendered any claims to privacy. The residents were washed and dressed and conveniently arranged in chairs and beds—almost as if they were made ready for a daily inspection. An attendant was always present in the bathroom, irrespective of old people's capacity to bathe themselves. The lavatories could not be locked and there were large spaces at the top and bottom of the doors. The matron swung open one door and unfortunately revealed a blind old woman installed on the w.c. She made no apology. In a dormitory she turned back the sheets covering one woman to show a deformed leg—again without apology or explanation. (Townsend, 1964, p. 5)

> "It isn't home here. I woulda' liked to have stayed with the children. We had a cat and I miss that cat quite a bit. I miss my little radio and the window I had where you could see the dog in the yard next door. Sometimes I really miss that nice little carpet I had next to my bed. I was used to that." (Gubrium, 1975, p. 87)

> The residents of Weldon Manor are actively discouraged from helping one another, as I saw for myself during the two days I was there. One of the women said, "We are not supposed to help. It does seem shortsighted to a good few of us here. I think it's made me rather unkind." Another added to this, "I'm not supposed to lift a finger for anybody and I'm not even allowed to wash up. I'd like to . . .. We're not always good-tempered with each other. It's a lonely life, you know, with nothing to do and plenty of time to do it in." (Townsend, 1964, p. 82)

Nursing homes are particularly likely to isolate residents from the larger community and from interactions with staff and other residents, which results in an incapacity for self-initiated activity (Curry and Ratliff, 1973; Lowenthal and Robinson, 1976). Gottesman and Bourestom (1974) conducted an observational study in which the behavior of 1,144 nursing home residents was observed in 44 nursing homes during a 2-day period. In an analysis of activity and social interaction they found that 56 percent of residents' waking time was spent "doing nothing" (passive, null, noncategorizable behavior). Although 23 percent of the observations noted personal care behavior (e.g., bathing and dressing), only 4.5 percent of personal care was spent with staff members. Only 17 percent of the observations noted contacts with other persons (including doctors and nurses), and of these contacts only 7.5 percent were with nonstaff.

Joseph D. Teaff

Moving into an institution requires the giving up of home, a lifelong expression of individuality and personal choice.

Miller and Beer (1977), in a study to determine what amount of companionship nursing home residents have in nursing homes, asked residents if they had formed friendships with any of the staff. They reported that 76 percent of the residents felt close to someone on the staff, 13 percent were not close to anyone, and 11 percent liked all of the staff (a response interpreted to mean that they were not close to anyone on the staff). Disabled residents were much more likely to feel close to the nursing staff, whereas those who were more mobile were the more likely to feel close to the activity staff. Studies would seem to indicate that staff maintain a considerable social distance from residents, and when staff members develop close friendships it is based on a perceived professional relationship and expected level of physical performance.

These studies imply that nursing homes, because of their characteristics as total institutions, create residents who are passive and withdrawn. It has been assumed that negative behaviors are caused by the institutional environment, yet researchers only studied the residents *after* they were admitted to a nursing home. Therefore the question needs to be asked: were the characteristics present before the individual's institutionalization? In an effort to answer this question Tobin and Lieberman (1976) attempted to separate the effects of the institution from explanations such as *selection bias* (physical illnesses accounting for residents' psychological status), *preadmission effects* (feelings of separation and rejection and negative attitudes toward institutionalization), and *impact of relocation* (entrance into a new environment). They interviewed 100 people living in the community and awaiting admittance to three nursing homes, then reinterviewed those who entered (85 persons) at 2 months and at 1 year after admission. They also interviewed two comparison groups—a sample of community residents and a sample of relatively healthy persons who had lived 1 to 3 years in the three nursing homes that the 85 persons had entered. They found that "most of the psychological qualities attributed to the adverse effects of entering and living in an institution were already present in people on the waiting list" (Tobin and Lieberman, 1976, p. 77). They also found that persons on the waiting list were more similar to the institutional sample than the community sample, and in some ways worse than those already institutionalized, leading Tobin and Lieberman to suggest that the most difficult transition may be from community to waiting list because of the deteriorating social networks, losses, and dependence. The first few months were the most critical for institutional adjustment because older persons left prized possessions, felt resentment toward their families, and had low status in the resident social system. Nevertheless preadmission characteristics generally persisted. In the 1-year follow-up Tobin and Lieberman found that among those who had not shown extreme deterioration or died, there was no evidence of psychological deterioration. This study cautiously concluded that some of the negative or even destructive influences of the nursing home as an environment may have been overstated.

The creation of passive, dependent, and withdrawn institutional populations is not inevitable. Institutions can have a beneficial impact on the social and psychological functioning of residents, yet staff often perceive the physical and mental disorders of the institutionalized aged as irreversible (Tobin and Lieberman, 1976). Staff should view themselves as workers who can rehabilitate older persons or who can at least prevent further decline of psychological and social skills.

REHABILITATION PROGRAMS

Gerontologists have recently been involved in implementing and evaluating a number of different rehabilitation programs for older persons in institutions. Several of these programs will be described.

Thomas O. Byerts

Large boards are used in reality orientation programs.

Reality orientation

Reality orientation was first organized in 1958 by James C. Folson at the Winter Veterans' Administration Hospital in Topeka, Kansas (Butler and Lewis, 1982). It was designed to be used on a 24-hour basis by all who came in contact with confused or disoriented elderly placed on psychiatric wards (Allen, 1970; Stephens, 1975). Reality orientation alleviates the manifested confusion and disorientation by having all contact persons reiterate basic personal and current information. It is assumed that when someone has forgotten his or her name, current place of residence, the date, and other information, the best chance of relearning is by hearing and repeating what has been heard. All who come in contact with the older person are instructed to remind the individual about simple aspects of the immediate environment, and the older person is always requested to repeat the statements. Clear responses are encouraged and digressions checked using approaches such as approval for success, active friendliness, and firmness.

In addition to the 24-hour milieu therapy approach, structured reality orientation classes are held with a small number of more confused patients, since the presence of others in the group is an effective factor in providing a motivational force for improvement (Taulbee and Folsom, 1966). These formal daily classroom sessions are usually about 30 minutes and can be taught at basic and advanced levels. At the basic level a variety of visual aids are used such as a large clock, a calendar with large numbers, and a notice board that lists daily information (e.g., date, weather, and menu) and permanent information (e.g., institution, place, and upcoming holiday) in large print. During the basic-level sessions personal and current information are presented again and again to each group member, beginning with the person's name, where he or she is, and the date and followed by the daily and permanent information. During the more advanced sessions, group members are expected to identify themselves and other members of the group, use maps to identify different places, and generally exhibit a longer attention span as manifested through greater interaction and personal exchanges of more complex and abstract terms.

The early practitioners of reality orientation reported the technique to be generally successful (Folsom, 1968; Stephens, 1970), but formal reported research is quite limited.

Barnes (1974) studied six patients (mean age of 81) involved in 6 weeks of classroom reality orientation. He found that the patients were less confused and more manageable, according to observations reported by the staff, but there was no change in scores on a test devised by Barnes.

Brook, Gegun, and Mather (1975) applied reality orientation techniques to a 16-week experimental group actively engaged in various tasks using materials found in the room. A control group was exposed to the materials in the room, but therapists remained passive. They found that intellectual and social functioning improved for both groups during the first 2 to 4 weeks, but only the experimental group continued to show improvement.

Harris and Ivory (1976) conducted an evaluation of reality orientation with matched experimental and control groups, using pre and post outcome variables of ward behavior, verbal interaction, and patient orientation. The findings indicated that the experimental group interacted more, demonstrated better recognition skills, and were more likely to know their names, the date, and the names of others. These findings should be viewed with caution because of methodological issues such as pretest differences between the groups and the fact that patients were rated by psychiatric aides who were involved in the reality orientation sessions.

Citrin and Dixon (1977) compared a control group (mean age of 84) and an experimental group receiving 24-hour reality orientation and the classroom

Thomas O. Byerts

The monthly activity calendar can be used in a reality orientation program to alert residents to current and future leisure programs.

method. The staff attending the control group were specifically forbidden to use reality orientation approaches with their patients. The experimental group had a significant increase in scores on the Reality Orientation Information Sheet (ROIS), whereas the untreated control group showed a slight decline in scores on the ROIS.

Zepelin, Wolfe, and Kleinplatz (1977) compared an experimental group of residents in a home for the aged who received 24-hour reality orientation for a year with a control group. The control group showed deterioration, whereas the experimental group after 6 months showed statistically significant improvement on the Mental Status Questionnaire (MSQ). However, there were no favorable effects on ratings of ADL or interpersonal behaviors.

Gotestam (1979) conducted a reality orientation program for five patients between the ages of 70 and 89 years (mean age of 81.4). After baseline data were gathered, the patients were exposed to a number of training procedures: training in a special room designed to enhance time orientation with a large wall clock and calendars; training in person orientation through saying their names and other names while rolling a ball to that person; and training in room orientation through the use of town, county, and country maps placed on the walls. The results clearly showed improved orientation as to time and room while the patient was in the training situation, but there was no lasting effect outside of this situation.

Leisure service personnel can easily implement many of the reality orientation approaches in their programs. The program leader can introduce himself or herself and have members of the group introduce themselves. The program leader can orient the group as to time and date and describe any other programs to be presented in the near future. During a program, if a participant becomes confused, the program leader can provide additional information to orient that participant. Large monthly activity calendars are also a prop to assist in the reality orientation of institutional residents.

Remotivation

Remotivation has been defined as restoring that which causes action but has been dormant or willingly repressed for some reason (Stracke, 1970). A therapist working in a remotivation group attempts to bring each person in the group to a higher level of social and emotional functioning in the group as measured through greater independence, self-confidence, and interaction (Nevruz and Hrushka, 1969).

Remotivation programs are usually 12 weeks long and meet twice a week for about 45 minutes in groups numbering between 10 and 15 persons. During each session five basic steps are followed (Butler and Lewis, 1982, p. 315):

1. *The climate of acceptance,* the first step, is concerned with establishing a warm, friendly relationship in the group. The leader may use techniques such as greeting each member of the group by name and giving some background information on each member of the group. This step usually takes about 5 minutes.
2. *A bridge to reality,* the second step, is the reading of an article from a news magazine or the reading of poetry. The leader should introduce the topic for discussion, being sure to pick a subject that members are aware of. This step usually lasts 15 minutes.
3. *Sharing the world,* the third step, is designed to further develop the topic introduced in step 2 through the asking of questions and using various ''props'' such as pictures. This step also lasts about 15 minutes.
4. *Appreciation of the work of the world,* the fourth step, involves a discussion of what jobs would be related to the subject under discussion. This step usually lasts about 15 minutes.
5. *Climate of appreciation,* the fifth step, provides the group leader with

an opportunity to express enjoyment at getting together and appreciation for the participation of all the members. Participants may also decide on the topic for the next session. This step lasts about 5 minutes.

Several studies have attempted to document improvement in functioning as a result of participation in remotivation. Abstracts of these studies follow.

Bowers, Anderson, Blomeier, and Pelz (1967) measured individual behaviors and social functioning before and 6 months after group remotivation. Significant improvement was reported for individual behavior and for social functioning.

Birkett and Boltuch (1973) compared conventional group therapy with remotivation. Treatment consisted of 39 geriatric patients participating in 12 weekly 1-hour sessions of remotivation. Results indicated improvement in both groups, but there were not statistical differences between the groups.

Thralow and Watson (1974) compared a control group of 36 patients with 36 patients in an experimental group, who were paired with 36 elementary school students. The experimental patients and students met twice a week for 45 minutes during a 14-week period. Hospital and school staff supervised the students. The experimental and control groups were rated using three instruments: the Nurses Observation Scale for Inpatient Evaluation (NOSIE-30), the Remotivation Self-Evaluation, and Morale Self-Evaluation. The experimental subjects demonstrated significantly more improvement than the controls in the areas of neatness, interest, self-awareness, self-esteem, and reduced irritability. Gains appeared to be lost if there is no continued involvement with therapists.

The basic steps of the remotivation program can be incorporated into a variety of leisure programs. For example, during a music appreciation program, all members of the group can be introduced, a brief article about a composer can be discussed, a composition by that composer can be played, the role of the musician in the world of work can be discussed, and the program closed with appreciation for the participants' attention and planning of the next music program.

Reminiscence

It has often been noted that older persons have a tendency to be concerned with the past. This used to be considered an indication of the loss of recent memory, but Butler (1974) considers the process of reminiscing to be a part of normal life review and a healthy adaptation to the last phase of the life cycle. Butler (1974) proposed that the process of life review served as an adaptation mechanism enabling past experiences to be returned to consciousness and deeply buried conflicts to be resolved. It is a way of coming to terms with failures and imperfections so that a balanced perspective on life can be developed.

Different types of reminiscing have been delineated. Lo Gerfo (1980) suggests from a review of literature that there are three distinct though overlapping categories of reminiscence.

INFORMATIVE REMINISCENCE. Informative reminiscing serves "to provide pleasure and to enhance self-esteem through reliving and retelling past events. Gratification comes not only from the remembrance itself, but also from the tribute to longevity and mental soundness that memory of the distant past celebrates" (Lo Gerfo, 1980, p. 40). This is the most common form of recollection among older persons and may take forms such as storytelling glorifying the "good old days" and reminiscence groups in a social or educational setting involved in an oral history class.

EVALUATIVE REMINISCENCE. Evaluative reminiscence is based on Butler's concept of life review (Butler and Lewis, 1982), which is "an attempt to come to terms with old guilt, conflicts and defeats, and to find meaning in one's accomplishments" (Lo Gerfo, 1980, p. 42). Scrapbooks, pilgrimages to significant places, and genealogies may be used in the process of developing a biography of the entire life cycle, in which guilt and hurt are reduced to small incidents in the larger life perspective.

OBSESSIVE REMINISCENCE. Obsessive reminiscence can be the result of informative and evaluative reminiscence if older persons are unable to accept their pasts and become overwhelmed with guilt or even despair. Techniques such as life review (Butler and Lewis, 1982, pp. 326-327) and psychodrama allow older persons to feel and say what they never truly allowed themselves to express.

Reminiscence has been explored in the research literature from a variety of perspectives.

McMahon and Rhudick (1964), in a study of the patterns of reminiscence among older men, identified a relationship between personality dynamics and patterns of reminiscence. They found that the more depressed group of older men reminisced less than the nondepressed group, with the best adjusted individuals using memories primarily for purposes of storytelling.

Coleman (1974) investigated reminiscing among a sample of older men and women living in planned housing for the elderly in Great Britain. Coleman found that those who were satisfied with their past lives reviewed life to a lesser extent than those who were dissatisfied with their past lives. He concluded that the process of life review helps older persons deal with an unsatisfactory past because it assists with the working through of past conflicts.

Boylin, Gordan, and Nehrke (1976) studied the relationship between the amount of reminiscence and ego integrity among 41 institutionalized elderly veterans. They found a positive correlation between the amount of reminiscence and ego integrity (i.e., the more the reminiscence, the higher the ego integrity, as measured by an ego adjustment scale). It was also found that reminiscing about negative or painful past experiences also correlated with the measure of ego integrity.

A leisure service specialist can easily incorporate reminiscence into leisure programs. For example, during an arts and crafts program each older participant could be encouraged to make a collage of family pictures illustrating

Thomas O. Byerts

A reminiscence program may serve to enable older persons to engage in the life review process. Here a resident's room door is decorated with greeting cards that recall significant persons and events of the past and present.

different life events. Each participant could present the completed collage to the group, acting as a leader of a discussion group on the different events presented in the collage.

Leisure services are essential to the establishment of an environment for the re-habilitation and maintenance of residents in institutions for the elderly. The pri-mary purpose of leisure services is "to create opportunities and reasons for a person affected by a condition requiring long-term care to exercise abilities and

DEVELOPMENT OF LEISURE SERVICES

continue life tasks which he previously took for granted'' (Bachner and Cornelius, 1978, p. 3). A general environment is created to provide all elderly residents with the opportunity to exercise physical, intellectual, and social abilities alone and with others. The opportunity to exercise abilities and continue life tasks must be provided to the elderly resident on his or her own terms, maximizing and reinforcing independence, dignity, and respect. Resources, programming, and evaluation in the development of leisure services in institutions for the elderly will be discussed in this section.

Resources

The development of leisure services for the elderly in institutions requires resources. Such resources are staff, areas and facilities, equipment and supplies, and funds.

STAFF. Staff may be considered in two categories: paid employees and volunteers.

Paid employees. Paid employees may include the director of leisure services, activity leaders, consultants, and resource persons.

Director of leisure services. The director of leisure services may perform a variety of administrative duties, many being similiar to the duties of other administrators. Examples of such duties are:

1. Interpreting the goals and objectives of leisure services to staff members of other departments, volunteers, relatives of the elderly, and the general public
2. Employing, supervising, and providing in-service training for staff
3. Recruiting, training, supervising, and recognizing volunteers
4. Obtaining and maintaining equipment and supplies through purchase, donation, or construction
5. Preparing budget requests and obtaining authorization to expend funds
6. Evaluating administrative resources and programs
7. Preparing reports on the progress of the department
8. Developing a policies and procedures manual for staff and volunteers
9. Attending local, regional, state, and national workshops; conferences; and continuing education programs

The director should be qualified by education and experience to administer leisure services in an institution for the elderly. The director should have a college education in one of the human services (e.g., recreation, gerontology, or social work) and should have experience in working with older persons and have administrative and good communication skills.

Activity leaders. Activity leaders perform a variety of duties related to program planning, implementation, and evaluation. Many of these duties may also be performed by the director of leisure services if activity leaders are not available or if the facility is small. Activity leaders may perform a variety of duties:

1. Performing and documenting the initial assessment of each new resident

2. Supervising and training volunteers
3. Providing bedside leisure services when needed
4. Assisting with the movement of residents to and from leisure activities
5. Leading a variety of activities
6. Developing the activities calendar
7. Supervising the activities of special interest groups (e.g., men's club, resident newspaper, and resident advisory council)
8. Writing quarterly and discharge planning reports for all residents that he or she is directly responsible for
9. Working with relatives of discharged residents and referring them to leisure resources and services available in the community

Activity leaders may come from a variety of backgrounds—recreation, art, music, dance, social service, and so on. The activity leader should possess activity, leadership, and communication skills. Particular attention should be paid to personality and temperament to assess whether the individual can deal effectively with the residents.

Consultants. Consultants may be used in a number of different capacities. For the director, they can be a source of information for concerns such as changes in legislation and standards, funding, community resources, and in-service training. For the activity leader, they can provide information on new programs and equipment, documentation, and use of volunteers.

A number of considerations need to be addressed before the employment of a consultant. State standards need to be examined to determine whether a consultant is required in settings in which activity personnel do not possess certain educational requirements. The setting should be assessed to determine what services are required of a consultant. In the light of service needs, the qualifications and reputation of prospective consultants should be examined before a decision is made. It is important that a contract be developed between the agency and the consultant of choice, specifying what services will be provided, when they will be provided, and at what cost.

Resource persons. Resource persons are available to provide assistance for leisure service personnel. The following sections identify them by title and indicate some types of assistance they may provide.

THE ADMINISTRATOR. The administrator is responsible for all aspects of the management of the institution. Leisure service personnel need the administrator's particular attention in the areas of staffing, funding, allocation of areas and facilities, and the purchase of equipment and supplies. Assistance may also be provided in the development of the organizational structure of the department, of the policies and procedures manual, and of program activities that require residents to leave the facility for outings, tours, picnics, art shows, and so on, since these activities may present certain constraints from legal responsibilities and insurance coverage. Every effort should be made to establish a good working relationship with the administrator through procedures such as regular reports on program participation and significant departmental achievements.

PHYSICIANS. Physicians are responsible for providing important assessment information on each person admitted to the institution and for monitoring resident progress. Physicians are a valuable source of information concerning resident habits and interests, activity needs and limitations, and the overall care of the residents. Leisure service personnel should report to the physician any changes in a resident participating in leisure services, according to institutional policies (e.g., directly or through an intermediary such as the charge nurse).

NURSING PERSONNEL. Nursing personnel are usually the most knowledgable about each resident's condition because of their regular contact with residents. The charge nurse will be able to provide particular information on specific needs and interests of residents. Nurse's aides may provide insights into personalities of residents and adjustments needed in activities based on resident comments. Leisure service personnel should report any significant changes in a resident's condition to the charge nurse, since this could have an effect on the resident's care plan. It is essential that leisure service personnel develop a good relationship with nursing personnel at all levels because they will probably be involved with the program. Nurses should know the nature and purpose of leisure services and the goals and objectives of the care plan of each resident.

FOOD SERVICE. The director of food service and other food service personnel are valuable resources for leisure programming. They can suggest food for parties, cookouts, and snacks that are of proper nutritional value, that conform to the nutritional and special diet requirements of residents, and yet are manageable for nonfood service staff to serve. They can be particularly valuable in assisting with cooking classes enjoyed by both women and men.

HOUSEKEEPING. Housekeeping is responsible for space scheduling and maintenance of institutional spaces. Housekeeping personnel can assist with setting up rooms for particular activities, cleaning up, and rearranging spaces. Leisure service personnel should communicate on a regular basis about use of space requiring scheduling and multipurpose space that may require rapid rearranging.

RELIGIOUS LEADERS. Priests, ministers, rabbis, and lay persons from the community provide an important source of community contact. In addition to religious services, religious leaders may assist with the recruiting of volunteers, trips to community events, use of church buildings, donations of equipment and supplies, and a variety of other functions.

EDUCATORS. Educators with specializations in areas such as art, music, dance, vocational education, and adult education, can assist with the instruction of activities and the recruitment of volunteers. College and university personnel involved with the education of recreation and leisure service personnel should be approached to determine whether the institution could serve as a fieldwork, practicum, or internship site.

LEISURE SERVICE PERSONNEL. Leisure service personnel working in institutional and community settings are often an untapped resource. Leisure service personnel in institutions for the elderly have organized at the state and local levels to establish educational programs, exchange ideas, engage in problem

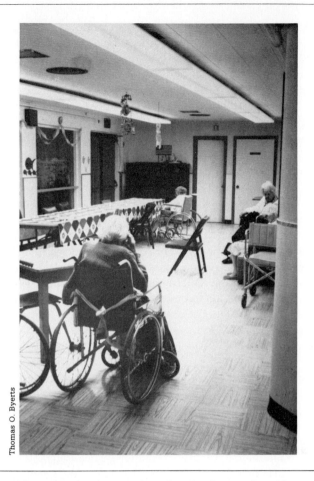

Thomas O. Byerts

Leisure service, nursing, and housekeeping personnel need to develop good working relationships. Why are there remnants of decorations, unattended residents, and a general level of disorganization in this multipurpose space?

solving, and share facilities and equipment. Community leisure service personnel can provide assistance with facilities for community special events and may supply personnel and equipment for a variety of programs in the institution.

INSTITUTIONAL RESIDENTS. Every effort should be made to provide an opportunity for each resident to make a contribution to the leisure services in the institution. The Role Continuity Model of Leisure Services presented in Chapter 6 has equal application within an institutional setting.

OTHERS. There are many others who can serve as resource persons. Additional community resources are librarians, hobby shop personnel, YMCA and YWCA personnel, families of residents, organized volunteer programs such as RSVP and SCP (see Chapter 4), and many others. Institutional personnel may include art therapists, music therapists, occupational therapists, physical therapists, social workers, speech pathologists, and audiologists.

VOLUNTEERS. Volunteers are a vital and necessary link between the institution and the community. Volunteers communicate to elderly residents that the community cares and that the community has not forgotten. This section will examine the process of volunteer use, covering topics such as recruitment, selection, orientation and training, placement, supervision, and recognition.

Recruitment. The recruitment of volunteers may initially require the overcoming of community misconceptions regarding institutions for the elderly. Informing and educating the community may be accomplished by speaking before the public about the role and function of leisure services with older persons, providing guided tours for interested individuals and groups, and maintaining regular contacts with a variety of individuals and groups.

Volunteers may be recruited from a variety of sources.

Children. Children who are members of organizations such as the Brownies, Cub Scouts, Girl Scouts, Boy Scouts, and 4-H clubs, may be recruited as friendly visitors or as holiday entertainers. Friendly visitors may come as a group but visit individually with older persons. Holiday entertainers may provide 2 to 3 hours of entertainment during major holidays. Every effort should be made to spread large group visitations and entertainment throughout the year and not simply at Christmas.

Teenagers. Teenage volunteers may be recruited through high school service organizations such as the Key Club and the Keyette Club, health career classes, and church groups. These volunteers can work on a one-to-one basis reading, playing cards, writing letters, sharing conversation, and so on. They may also help lead large group activities (e.g., calling bingo and helping older persons find the numbers). They should attempt to make a commitment for a set number of hours per week throughout the school year because older persons will begin to look forward to their regular involvement.

College students. College students are another source of reliable and in many cases trained volunteers (e.g., students in recreation, social work, and gerontology). Working in leisure services with the elderly can be a service project of a fraternity or sorority. Students in human services (e.g., recreation, social work, and gerontology) may use this volunteer opportunity to satisfy fieldwork, practicum, or even internship requirements, provided that there is a supervisor available who is qualified by education and experience.

Adults. Adult volunteers can be a source of manpower, donations, and equipment. These individuals can be sought through religious organizations, fraternal organizations (e.g., Lions, Elks, Moose, Masons, Shriners and Eastern Star), business and professional groups (e.g., Jaycees, Rotary, and Kiwanis), clubs (e.g., hobby, garden, drama, music and dance), family and friends of elderly residents, and the elderly themselves.

Selection. It is important that each prospective volunteer be carefully interviewed and screened, with particular attention given to the volunteer who will have regular involvement with the program. In the initial interview one must determine the reasons for volunteering; background (i.e., education, other volunteer experience, physical fitness, and so on); special skills, capabilities, or interests; type of volunteer work sought; hours able to work; and transportation available or needed. References should be contacted for an evaluation of previous volunteer experiences.

Orientation and training. Volunteers need an initial orientation. That orientation should include a tour of the facility and an introduction to the various personnel in the institution. A special effort should be made to introduce the new volunteers to several residents. The initial orientation tour of the facility should avoid the more ill elderly because the new volunteer may be overly frightened.

Each volunteer should participate in a training program. General information about the institution's philosophy, purpose, policies, and procedures that directly affect the volunteer should be stated. The volunteer should be given a very basic background on diseases often encountered, realistic abilities and limitations of persons with those diseases, and some tips to aid the volunteers in working with those individuals. Philosophy, goals, and purposes of leisure services should be explained. Standards of conduct toward residents and staff should be presented, with particular emphasis on the need to be responsible and faithful to promised time commitments. It should be stressed to the volunteers that they have assumed a responsibility and that many persons are depending on them, particularly the residents who see them as friends, sources of enjoyment, people to look forward to seeing, and providers of emotional reassurance unduplicated by paid staff.

Placement. The assignment of responsibilities to each volunteer should be made based on the volunteer's skills, interests, and needs. The matching of volunteers with responsibilities may be assisted by the use of the five volunteer categories proposed by Bachner and Cornelius (1978, pp. 45-46):

1. Those with multiple skills, interests, and capabilities may be assigned to a variety of responsibilities based on their interests and the residents' needs. It is important to periodically change the assignment to promote the volunteer's enthusiasm and make use of capabilities.
2. Those with specialized skills should be assigned based on their special interests. Individuals with skills and experience in woodworking, sewing, ceramics, music, dance, and so on could be assigned to teaching their skills to residents after their leadership skills and ability to work with people have been assessed.
3. Those with few specialized skills can be assigned to perform a variety of tasks, but every attempt should be made to have these persons learn on the job through assisting the more experienced volunteers and paid employees. These volunteers are more likely to become involved with specific residents (e.g., in friendly visiting), so they need support and supervision.
4. Those with special attributes might include children and teenagers.

They have no specialized skills, but their youth makes them special. These attributes should be evaluated in the process of assignment.

5. Guest entertainers are called on periodically for special events such as holiday entertainment, presentations of lectures on a topic of special interest, guest recitals of music and dance, and so on. Such volunteers may be called on a regular basis if they live in the area.

In no case should a volunteer be given an assignment for which he or she is not fully prepared. Every effort should be made to explain the background, interests, habits, and so on of the residents with whom the volunteer will be working. Volunteers working with specific leisure activities should be given instruction and practical experience with each activity. It may be helpful to provide volunteers with reading materials from both published and unpublished sources. However, there are practical limits to the responsibilities and duties that volunteers may be assigned. A sensitivity to these limits is vital to successful placement.

Supervision. Effective supervision of volunteers requires that channels of communication be developed and maintained. The supervisor needs to observe the volunteer's work with residents and to discuss these observations with the volunteer. The supervisor should continually observe volunteer attendance, and if attendance declines it may indicate that a change in assignment is in order or that the volunteer has lost interest.

Facilitywide meetings and in-service education sessions are important forums to increase communication and to foster staff relationships. Meetings should be held on a regular basis to discuss problems, request ideas and suggestions, improve performance, and set up long-range goals and short-term projects. It is important that a friendly atmosphere be maintained so that comments and ideas may be shared by the paid staff and the volunteers.

A number of suggested principles and practices can enhance the volunteer's functioning with residents and aid the supervision process:

1. Each volunteer should check in on arrival at a designated location and pick up his or her assignment and any particular instructions concerning programs or residents.
2. Each volunteer should be told the procedures for informing the supervisor should he or she not be able to keep the assigned commitment.
3. Each volunteer should keep confidential all information regarding residents (e.g., diagnoses, conditions of other residents, and so on). Residents' charts and records are privileged information and should not be accessible to volunteers.
4. The volunteer should encourage residents to do as much as possible on their own. "Suggest and direct but do not force" is an important principle.
5. The volunteer should avoid being condescending, even though resident behavior may be childish at times.
6. Each volunteer should display enthusiasm and avoid discouragement when an activity does not meet with the expected resident acceptance.

Thomas O. Byerts

The central space of the Weiss Institute at the Philadelphia Geriatric Center serves as an informal and formal focal point of leisure services for residents with senile dementia and related pathological brain conditions. Note that all resident rooms face this space—an area of maximum staff interaction, as well as leisure resources.

Recognition. Volunteers must be recognized by both staff and residents. Although the work itself is a source of satisfaction, volunteers receive a special satisfaction when they are publicly recognized. Volunteers may be honored with tangible expressions of appreciation such as banquets, parties, teas, pins, certificates, and the designation "volunteer of the month." Awards made and presented to the volunteers are often the most appreciated. It is important to remember that the residents who volunteer are entitled to similar forms of recognition.

AREAS AND FACILITIES. In most institutions areas and facilities for leisure services are limited, but larger institutions may have more varied spaces to accommodate a larger number of residents. This section will discuss a variety of possible spaces. It is important to remember, however, that the leisure service specialist will often have to use to full advantage whatever space is available.

Large group area. A large group area can serve as a multipurpose room to house a variety of activities. Such an area can be used for large social, religious, or intellectual activities (e.g., parties, dances, Christmas programs, bowling, shuffleboard, church or synagogue services, movies, stage productions, concerts, lectures, group sings, and classes). It should be large enough to seat 75 percent of all those in the facility. The area should be well ventilated, be near bathrooms and running water, have sufficient electrical outlets and cabinet space, and have good general lighting and windows that may also be darkened for movies and slides. Furnishings such as folding tables and chairs should be mobile to allow the room to be easily cleared.

If the facility does not have a large group or multipurpose area, it may be necessary to use other areas. A dining room, lounge, or chapel may have to be adapted. It may even be necessary to use lobbies, corridors, and large wards.

Small group area. The small group area provides a space for activities such as rhythm bands, indoor horseshoes, shuffleboard, pool, and a variety of other musical and game activities. The room should be relatively uncluttered and away from the bedroom area to permit noisy activities.

Game room. The game room may be used for card groups and quiet groups, as well as for a library, conference and meeting room, and club room. Some storage space may be necessary, depending on the type of use.

Lounge. The lounge may serve as a sitting room or day room near the bedroom area. This space should contain a TV; comfortable chairs; good lighting; and small tables for writing, working puzzles, and playing checkers. Families and guests may also use this area for visiting.

Craft room. The craft room is used for craft projects that create dust, noise, odor, and clutter (e.g., ceramics, woodworking, and copper enameling). This single-purpose room allows a project to remain unfinished in a work area, whereas a multipurpose room would have restricted hours, a limited scope of projects, and frequent required cleaning.

Storage area. Space is essential for storage of valuable and easily movable objects, dangerous equipment, and flammable or toxic materials. Valuable and easily movable objects such as tape recorders and players and projectors should be locked up to prevent theft. Dangerous equipment such as drills and saws should be placed in a lockable closet. Flammable or toxic materials such as paints and solvents should be stored in metal cabinets. Large metal storage cabinets may be used in various rooms where additional storage space is needed.

Office area. Office space is needed for staff and volunteer conferences, correspondence, records, and confidential information. There should be a desk with a lockable drawer, telephone, typewriter, and a lockable file cabinet. It is helpful to have the office near the storage area and craft room, particularly when there are ceramic, woodworking, and other crafts that require supervision.

Outdoor recreation area. An outdoor recreation area may be used for lounging, gardening, picnics, and games. A patio area should have a level, paved, smooth surface for easy mobility of wheelchairs and for safety from tripping. Shade and shelter such as a canopy should be provided for all residents— especially for those on medication who may be more sensitive to heat and light. Both gardening space and a greenhouse are welcome because they permit use for more months of the year. Sturdy picnic tables and chairs and nontippable

Joseph D. Teaff

Leisure services should be provided for both men and women. Because of the generally larger number of older women, it is often difficult to have activities for men.

umbrellas provide safe lawn furniture for a variety of activities. Games such as lawn bowling, croquet, and horseshoes are ideal lawn games. Any transition between a grassy and paved area should be smooth and clearly marked.

EQUIPMENT AND SUPPLIES. Equipment and supplies are basic resources necessary for the development of leisure services. Equipment is nonexpendable items that use does not greatly diminish; supplies are expendable items used up in the process of delivering leisure services. This section will discuss a variety of basic equipment and supplies and how they may be obtained.

Equipment. Certain pieces of equipment may already be available; others will have to be obtained. The list on p. 148 is equipment that is commonly used. Whereas some equipment may already be on hand, other equipment may be purchased new or used, made, rented, donated, repaired, or adapted.

EQUIPMENT

Desk	Piano or small organ
File cabinet	Sewing machines
Shelving	Rhythm instruments
Chairs	Table looms
Sink	Easels
Bulletin boards	Ceramics kiln
Portable blackboard	Woodworking tools
Folding tables	Needlecraft equipment
Folding or stacking chairs	Supply transport cart
Tape recorder	Barbecue pit or grill
Slide projector	Popcorn poppers
16 mm sound movie projector	Ice cream freezer
Portable screen	Lawn furniture
Portable record player	

Supplies. Supplies may be purchased directly from a distributor or from a local merchant or supplier or may be donated or "scrounged" from a variety of sources (see lists below). A card file listing suppliers and the items that they sell or donate should be kept.

SUPPLIES

Jigsaw puzzles	Knitting needles	Canvas brushes
Dominoes	Crochet hooks	Liquid embroidery
Checkers	Embroidery hoops	Clay
Chess	Scissors	Copper enameling
Cards	Thimbles	Ceramics
Scrabble	Thread	Candlecraft
Monopoly	Hooked rug materials	Stonecraft
Cribbage	Beads	Woodcraft
Backgammon	Leather lacing	Craftsticks
Bowling set	Large and small frames	Crepe paper
Bingo set	Tile and trivets	Masking tape
Ring toss	Mosaic trays	Glue
Horseshoes	Mosaic tables	Rulers
Croquet	Water paints	Construction paper
Horse racing game	Pastel paints	Yarn
Song sheets	Oil paints	Punched rug materials
Sewing needles		

DONATED OR "SCROUNGED" SUPPLIES

Cardboard	Burlap	Catalogs
Carpet	Linoleum	Greeting cards
Cans	String	Sandpaper
Glass bottles	Stockings	Wire
Plastic bottles	Cotton socks	Wood
Leather	Cotton batting	Spools
Fur	Wallpaper	Broom handles
Felt	Newspaper	Plastic bags
Velvet	Magazines	

FUNDS. Funds for leisure services are usually allocated on the basis of a prepared budget. The budget is prepared in cooperation with the administrator but is based on a suggested budget developed by the director of leisure services and presented to the administrator. There are three basic categories in a budget.

Personnel. The budgetary category for personnel is usually the largest single item within the budget. This category should include salary and fringe benefits (i.e., social security, pension, workmen's compensation, life and health insurance, and so on) for each full and part-time employee. If an individual divides his or her time between two departments, it is important that the salary and fringe benefits reflect this.

Equipment. Equipment includes nonexpendable items that may be further categorized into furnishings (e.g., tables, chairs, and desk) and basic equipment (e.g., tape recorder, and phonograph). Each of these categories represents a capital expense that may be depreciated differently depending on the institution's accounting and bookkeeping system.

Supplies. Supplies are expendable items. Allowances for expenditures in this category should directly reflect the various types of programs being currently offered, as well as anticipated programs. If a painting program is being anticipated, for example, the budget should reflect paints, brushes, canvases, and so on. The cost of these items may be borne entirely by the institution or shared by both institution and participants.

Revenue may be generated by the institution through donations or the sale of craft projects. Donations may be allocated by the resident council for the purchase of more equipment and supplies. Part of the revenue generated by the sale of craft projects might be returned to the resident who made the craft item.

Programming

The programming of leisure services requires the matching of resources to the needs and interests of elderly residents. This section examines various aspects of programming such as assessment, care plan development, program content, and motivation.

ASSESSMENT. The assessment of the elderly resident requires gathering information from a number of sources on a variety of resident characteristics.

Social worker. The social worker is responsible for developing a social history for each resident. Important information is gathered concerning the resident's background (e.g., family and friends, involvement in community groups and organizations, work history, religious preference, and education), intellectual and emotional status (e.g., memory; attention span; orientation to time, place, and person; and mood), and perception of the reasons for placement in an institution and reactions to it. Information useful to the leisure assessment may also have been gathered (e.g., hobbies, reading interests, trips made, and number of friends) (Example 7-1 is a social assessment form).

Health personnel. Physicians, nurses, and therapists of various types are responsible for gathering information about medical and physical conditions. Information about medical problems (e.g., restrictions on diet and allergies) and physical conditions (e.g., range of motion, coordination, exercise tolerance, and level of self-care) is important to know because limitations on activity may be

EXAMPLE 7-1

SOCIAL ASSESSMENT FORM

Interviewer & title _____ Date _____

Source of information: Resident _____ Relative _____ Other _____

Name of resident _____ Age _____ M ____ F ____

Diagnosis _____

Former occupation _____ Religion _____

Number of children _____ Marital status _____

Education: Elementary _____ High school _____ College _____ Degrees _____

Special training/skills _____

Membership in clubs/organizations _____

Hobbies _____

Significant past events _____

Factors leading to placement:

_____ Gradual deterioration resulting in inability to care for self

_____ Sudden onset of acute and/or chronic illnesses becoming a problem

_____ Change in family situation resulting in inability to care for self

_____ Other

What are resident's feelings toward nursing home setting? _____

_____

What are family's feelings? _____

_____

Orientation: Time _____ Place _____ Person _____ Other _____

Ability to recall past events: Good _____ Fair _____ None _____

Is resident: Sociable _____ Withdrawn _____ Senile _____ Unable to respond _____

Special psychosocial needs: (Check) _____ Close one-to-one relationship

_____ Security _____ Social interaction _____ Spiritual _____ Reality orientation

_____ Family interaction _____ Intellectual stimulation _____ Privacy

Activity interest: _____ Current events _____ Resident council _____ Exercise group

_____ Music programs _____ Discussion group _____ Field trips _____ Bingo _____ Arts and crafts

_____ Religious services _____ Sewing _____ Movies _____ Spelling bees _____ Books

_____ Entertainment groups _____ In-room individual activities _____ Competitive sports

_____ Other _____

Physical limitations: _____

Comments:

Courtesy of Silver Leaves Nursing Home, Garland, Texas.

necessitated. A patient care transfer form (Example 7-2) sent with the resident from a hospital or other agency should be consulted, as well as a recent medical workup by a family or house physician.

Leisure service personnel. Leisure service personnel have the major responsibility for the leisure assessment. A preliminary assessment should be

EXAMPLE 7-2

PATIENT CARE TRANSFER FORM

I.

Name _____

Birth date _____ (Last) Sex ____ S.M.W.D. _____ (First)

Home address _____ (Religion)

Directions _____

Floor _____ Apt. _____ Tel. _____

Responsible relative or guardian _____

Address _____ Tel. (Relation) _____

Physician in charge after transfer _____

Hospital no. _____

Transferred from _____ Station or clinic _____

Address _____

Date of admission _____ Date of transfer _____

Transferred to _____

Address _____ Claim no. (Hosp., nursing home, agency) _____

Clinic appt. _____ Date _____

_____ M.D., City _____

II. Advised of transfer and consent given by _____ Date _____
(Name)   (Relation)

III. (Check, explain)

Disabilities		Impairments	
Amputation	___	Mentality	___
Paresis	___	Speech	___
Contracture	___	Hearing	___
Decub. ulcer	___	Vision	___
		Sensation	___

Incontinence

Bowel ___ Bladder ___

Activity tolerance limitations

None___ Moderate___ Severe___

Orders for active care

Bed

Position in good body alignment and change position every_____ hrs.

Avoid _____ position.

Prone position _____ times/day as tolerated.

Sit in chair ___hrs. ___times/day.

Increase as tolerated_____ .

Self-care

Maintain___ Improve___ level.

Interpret progress to family _____ .

Weight bearing

Full___ Partial___ None___

on _____ leg.

Locomotion

Walk _____times/day.

Increase as tolerated _____ .

Exercises

Range of motion _____times/day

to _____

by patient___ nurse___ family___ .

Other as outlined or attached _____ .

Stand ___Min. ___times/day.

Social activities

Encourage group___ individual___

within___ outside___ home.

Transport: Ambulance___ Car___
Car for handicapped___ Bus___

Patient knows diagnosis?_____ Last chest x-ray date _____

Attachments: Diet list___ Lab. report___ Exercise program___ X-ray report___

(Give dates) Important medical history and prognosis (State allergies if any)

Major diagnoses

Physician's order (diet, drugs, etc.)

Physician's sig. _____ Date _____

From Bachner, J., and Cornelius, E.: Activities coordinator's guide, Washington, D.C., 1978, U.S. Government Printing Office.

Continued.

EXAMPLE 7-2, cont'd

PATIENT INFORMATION

Self-care status

Check level of performance. Use S in column for supervision only. Draw line when item is currently inapplicable.

In blank space explain assistance needed in care. Use number from table to identify area discussed. Therapists and social workers include title with signature.

	Independent	Needs assistance	Unable to do	
Bed activity				1. Turns
				2. Sits
Personal hygiene				3. Face, hair, arms
				4. Trunk and perineum
				5. Lower extremities
				6. Bladder program
				7. Bowel program
Dressing				8. Upper trunk, arms
				9. Lower trunk, legs
				10. Appliance, splint
				11. Feeding
Transfer				12. Sitting
				13. Standing
				14. Tub
				15. Toilet
Loco-motion				16. Wheelchair
				17. Walking
				18. Stairs

19. Personal interests
    Music____
    Group singing____   Group games____
    Crafts____   Radio and TV____   Art____
    Plays instrument____
    Other____
20. Mental status
    Lonely____
    Alert____   Forgetful____   Confused____
    Other_____
21. Communications ability   (yes, no)
    Speaks and understands   ____
    Writes intelligibly   ____
    Understands writing   ____
    (If no or any limitations, describe)
    Responds to gestures (describe) ____
22. Other nursing information
    About diagnosis, medications, treatments, medical history, habits, preferences, condition on discharge, etc.
23. Equipment
    Side rails____ Bedboard____ Footboard____
    Long: R____ L____   Short: R____ L____
24. Bed: Low____ Mattress: Firm____ Reg.____
    Other____

Nurse's sig. _____ Tel._____

IV. Social Information (Adjustment to disability, emotional support from family, motivation for self care, socializing ability, financial plan, family health problem, etc.)

Agencies active_____ Sig._____

attempted in the first week of the resident's arrival. It is recommended that a member of the leisure services staff meet the new resident, explain the program, and attempt to determine likes, dislikes, and past interests. A list of activities in a checklist format is *not* recommended; rather persons, places, and things of general interest should be determined. Based on this information, the resident may be invited to participate in activities currently available.

Additional information pertaining to leisure may be gathered from a variety of sources as the new resident becomes familiar with the environment. Staff members—especially nurses, nurse's aides, food service and housekeeping personnel—should be advised to observe what the new resident says, listens to, looks at, or touches. Such observations may indicate interests and unmet needs.

Leisure service personnel should be cautioned not to expect all contacts with residents to provide information or go smoothly. It may be difficult to carry on a meaningful conversation because of a resident's anger or confusion. A resident may, in fact, show hostility or be totally unresponsive. As a consequence, no solid information on interests and needs may be obtained before the team meeting called to develop the initial care plan.

CARE PLAN DEVELOPMENT. The care plan is developed by an interdisciplinary team composed of staff members who have frequent, direct contact with the resident. Appropriate members of the team would be medical personnel (physician, charge nurse, and nurse's aide), social workers, dietitians, and leisure service personnel. The resident and his or her family should also be involved whenever possible.

The interdisciplinary team has a variety of responsibilities. Before the team meeting each discipline having frequent, direct contact with a new resident will prepare information to be presented. During the meeting each discipline will present an initial assessment and approaches to working with the new resident. Intervention decisions will then be made by group consensus, with responsibility for treatment assigned to appropriate team members.

The leisure services care plan is developed to contribute to the team effort. Based on the assessment the leisure services approach will include at least one long-term goal, one short-term goal, and specific actions. The goals are to be resident oriented (i.e., what the resident will accomplish); the specific actions are to be staff oriented (i.e., what the staff will do to help the resident attain the goal). An example of a resident care plan is presented in Example 7-3.

PROGRAM CONTENT. The program content should reflect individual and group decision making in an attempt to help overcome one of the problems of institutional living—the loss of decision making. The individual resident should be able to determine his or her own leisure activities as much as possible, with restrictions based on issues such as physician's orders, religious and moral views, sleeping patterns, and special diet. Group decision making may be encouraged by the formation of a resident advisory council as a planning body to consider interest and needs of residents, past participation and acceptance, and available resources (staff, volunteers, areas and facilities, equipment and supplies, and funds). The advisory council can assist staff in the planning of the monthly activity calendar.

EXAMPLE 7-3

RESIDENT CARE PLAN

Name: Jane Jones   Date of birth: 3/12/02   Admission date: 5/28/82

Marital status: Widowed   Education: Completed sixth grade

Member of organization: Women's   Religious background: Practicing
                        Club   Catholic

Mental status: Semi-confused

Hearing: Good

Vision: Impaired

Social background: Mrs. Jones was married for 50 years. Her husband passed away 2 years ago. She was a housewife and mother of three children. One daughter visits her weekly; the other daughter and son live in California. Her past recreation experiences included attending church every Sunday, secretary of the Women's Club, and needlework. She presently appears overwhelmed and withdrawn socially.

Long-term goal: Improved psychosocial functioning

Short-term goal: Adjustment to nursing home life

Specific actions: Introduce her to the other ladies on the floor who share an interest in crafts. Inform her of the recreation activities that are available to her. Encourage her to attend crafts class once a week. Have her begin work on a large-stitch, bright-colored needlecraft project. Encourage her to attend church weekly.

The planning of the monthly activity calendar is one of the most important responsibilities of leisure service personnel. Steps in the process of developing the calendar are recommended by Bachner and Cornelius (1978, pp. 59-66).

Step one: establishing a "scheduling schedule." The first step is concerned with the determination of the time necessary to assemble the resources to meet the requests of the resident advisory council. The scheduling cycle of other departments must be considered (e.g., nursing may need 3 months advance notice if extra help is needed for a special event). The scheduling process must also allow time for the initial draft to be circulated for staff and resident evaluation. Scheduling must not be put off until the last minute.

Step two: blocking out the schedule. The second step involves the development of a rough draft of the schedule, which may be refined through revision. Consideration should be given to a number of factors in blocking out the schedule.

Routine. The routine of the institution will have an impact on the program scheduled. Regularly scheduled events such as meals, visiting hours, physicians' rounds, and so on affect all residents, whereas medications, reality orientation, and so on may affect only certain residents. Other routines to be considered include scheduling of areas and facilities by other departments and time needed by dietary and housekeeping staff to set up an area.

Residents' interests and time preferences. Interests and time preferences vary from resident to resident, but groups of individuals may have several interests and preferences in common. In blocking out the schedule it is important to consider these interests and time preferences whenever possible, keeping in mind that there is no perfect schedule for everyone.

Group activities. The regular, ongoing scheduling of group activities makes the scheduling process easier but may result in a lack of sensitivity to individual needs and interests. Group activities should be selected and scheduled on a monthly basis to add variety and overcome the boredom that may result from a set schedule.

Individual or independent activities. Individual or independent activities for residents requiring special attention should be based on resident interests, activity anticipated, staff and volunteers required, space available, and group scheduled. Individual resident interests and desires should have a high priority.

Step three: review. A review of the proposed schedule should be conducted by departments and resources involved (e.g., housekeeping, nursing, and dietary staff) and by leisure service personnel. A number of critical questions are posed by Bachner and Cornelius (1978, pp. 61-62):

1. *What needs of the resident are being met?* (Will the activities meet an identified need of persons expected to participate?)
2. *Has the activities plan been reviewed?* (Has the activities plan been reviewed to determine whether scheduled activities relate to care plan goals?)
3. *Has reinforcement been assured?* (Do activities reinforce the care plans and treatment goals of a variety of treatment personnel such as nursing and social work?)
4. *Has past experience been examined?* (Do involvement records show attendance to be low or sporadic?)
5. *Will participation be rewarding?* (Are a small number of activities relied on too heavily, possibly making them boring?)
6. *Is the pattern of activities scheduled acceptable?* (Are scheduled activities for each day properly spaced to allow for resident energy and staff scheduling?)
7. *Has backup planning been done?* (Are alternatives available should there be changes in weather or reduced staff and volunteers?)
8. *Should routine be changed?* (Is it necessary to change another regularly scheduled activity?)
9. *Have precautions been checked?* (What precautions are there to prevent accidents?)

Step four: reviewing equipment and supplies. The fourth step requires a critical review of equipment and supplies. Equipment needs should be examined to determine if equipment is available and to make sure there are not two scheduled activities requiring the same equipment. Supplies should be reviewed on the basis of the anticipated number of participants and the rate of supply use per person to anticipate availability or the necessity of ordering additional supplies.

Step five: assigning staff. Assigning staff to activities that have been blocked out on the proposed schedule requires the matching of activities with available staff. The process of assigning staff should begin with a listing of activities and proposed time slots that also allow for setup and cleanup time. Each activity in the proposed schedule should be analyzed to determine the job tasks required and the number of expected participants in an attempt to decide on the number of personnel and qualifications needed. The last step is to determine available staff and volunteers who meet the qualifications and are available for that day and time and to make the assignment of the appropriate number of qualified staff.

Step six: integrating into total facility program. The integration of the monthly activity schedule into the total facility program requires communicating with all persons and departments involved with supplying personnel, equipment, and space for the program. Communication will be facilitated by a monthly events schedule (Example 7-4) that may be circulated to various departments and personnel, as well as to the administrator, for their suggestions and comments. Since the schedule was circulated for review in step three, there should be few changes in this schedule.

Step seven: ordering equipment and supplies. Equipment and supplies should be inventoried and if necessary additional supplies ordered. Supplies may be ordered from the regular supplier or from a local supplier if needs are immediate.

Step eight: preparing individual assignment sheets. Individual assignment sheets should be prepared for each staff member and volunteer. This assignment sheet should list the activity, when and where it is scheduled, and any special directives. Backup planning may be necessary if there is a possibility that a staff member will not be present for the assigned activity.

Step nine: operationalizing. Operationalizing necessitates the general distribution of the monthly activity calendar to all appropriate personnel and residents. An example of such a calendar in Example 7-5.

Step ten: flexibility. Flexibility is required to deal with unexpected changes in the calendar. Such changes should be expected and anticipated whenever possible.

MOTIVATION. A question constantly asked by leisure service personnel working in institutions is, "How can I get older people more involved in my programs?" The answer is not an easy one; it involves the problem of motivation, which really must come from within the older person. This section will examine some ways that leisure service personnel might stimulate an older person to seek involvement in leisure services.

Explanation of the benefits. Leisure service personnel should clearly

EXAMPLE 7-4

MONTHLY EVENTS SCHEDULE

Events schedule for the month of _____

	Date	Time	Type of activity	Location	Staff	Volunteers
Example:	6/1/77	10 AM	Current events	Library	Ms. Fisher	Mrs. Miles Mrs. Weaver
		11 AM	Open house entertainment committee	Library	Ms. Walker	Mrs. Schultz

Under the "Date" column would go the date of the month indicated above, starting with 1. Under "Time" would be placed the times during which an activity is scheduled, for example, 9 AM-10:30 AM. Under type of activity would go a description which you feel identifies what will be conducted. Under "Location" you will place the site in the facility, or outside the facility. Under "Staff" place the last names and initials of staff members assigned to the activity, and do the same for volunteers under "Volunteers." This form also should include identity of certain individual activities, and so on, although such information would be excluded from the version used for posting. It would not be excluded from the operational version distributed to department heads, staff, and others.

From Bachner, J., and Cornelius, E.: Activities coordinator's guide, Washington, D.C., 1978, U.S. Government Printing Office.

EXAMPLE 7-5

MONTHLY ACTIVITY CALENDAR

Activities room = A
Day room = D
Dining room = E
Library = L
Main lounge = ML
Patio = P

Exercise class—Mon.-Fri. at 9 AM—D
Coffee—Mon.-Saturday at 10 AM—E
Needlework/crafts—Mon.-Fri. 10-4—A

Sunday	Monday	Tuesday	Wednesday	Thursday	Friday	Saturday
			1 10—Current events—L 11—Open house enter. committee—L 12—Picnic lunch—P 2—Menu Comm. (gen.)—L 7—Scripture study—L	**2** 10—Garden class—D 2—Horseshoe tr.—P 3—Music apprec.—L 7—Rhythm band pr.—A	**3** 11—Unit meeting—D 2—Bowling—Hi Lanes 7—Hymn sing—E	**4** 11—Chorus pr.—A 2—Swimming YMCA 7—Board, Resident Council—L
5 9—Worship service—ML 3—Birthday party—Mrs. Boyd—E	**6** 9-12—Library cart 11—Tattler editors' meeting—L 2—Painting class—A 7—Domino tr.—E	**7** 10—Flower arr.—A 11—Unit meet.ng—D 2—Photography cl.—D 3—Music apprec.—L	**8** 11—Unit outing—Lake 2—FDOH menu comm.—L 3—ICS enter. comm.—E 7—Scripture study—L	**9** 10—Garden class—D 2—Debra circle—E 3—Horseshoe tr.—P 7—Rhythm band pr.—A 7—FDOH decor. comm.—L	**10** 11—Unit meeting—D 2—Bowling—Hi Lanes 7—Hymn sing—E	**11** 11—Chorus pr.—A 2—Swimming YMCA 3—Play reading group—L 7—Movie—E "The Near East"
12 9—Worship service—ML	**13** 9-12—Library cart 11—Tattler staff—L 2—Painting class—A 3—Bird watchers—L 7—Domino tr.—E	**14** 10—Flower arr.—A 11—Unit meeting—D 2—FDOH decor. comm.—A 3—Music apprec.—L	**15** 10—Current events—L 10—Tattler staff—A 2—ICS menu comm.—L 3—FDOH decor. comm.—A 7—Scripture study—L	**16** 10—Garden class—D 2—Stamp exch.—L 3—Horseshoe tr.—P 7—Rhythm band pr.—A	**17** 11—Unit meeting—D 2—Bowling—Hi Lanes 3—Violet club—P 7—Hymn sing—E	**18** 11—Chorus pr.—A 2—Swimming YMCA 3—FDOH enter. committee—E
19 9—Worship service—ML 10—FDOH decor. comm.—E 3—Father's Day open house	**20** 9-12—Library cart 10—ICS decor. comm.—L 2—Painting class—A 7—Domino tr.—E finals	**21** 10—ICS enter. comm.—P 11—Photography club—D 2—Music apprec.—L	**22** 10—Current events—L 10—ICS decor. comm.—A 2—Menu comm. (gen.)—L 7—Scripture study—L	**23** 10—Garden class—D 10—ICS decor. comm.—A 2—ICS enter. comm.—E 2—Tattler staff—A 7—Rhythm band pr.—A	**24** 11—Unit meeting—D 2—Bowling—Hi Lanes 2—Tattler distribution 7—Hymn sing—E	**25** 9—ICS enter. pr.—A 10—ICS decor comm.—E, P 11—Chorus pr.—A 2—Midsummer ice cream social
26 9—Worship service—ML	**27** 9-12—Library cart 2—Painting class—A 7—Bingo—E and D	**28** 10—Flower arr.—A 11—Unit meeting—D 2—Book review—ML "The Navigator" 7—"Loyal Helpers' meeting—L	**29** 10—Residents' Council—E (open meeting) 2—Gourmet Club—A 7—Scripture study—L	**30** 10—Garden class—D 2—Stamp Club—L 3—Bulletin board committee—A		

Appreciation = Apprec.
Arrangement = Arr.
Class = Cl.
Committee = Comm.
Decoration = Decor.
Entertainment = Enter.
Father's Day open house = FDOH
Ice cream social = ICS
Practice = Pr.
Tournament = Tr.

From Bachner, J., and Cornelius, E.: Activities coordinator's guide, Washington, D.C., 1978, U.S. Government Printing Office.

state to residents what the benefits of their involvement are expected to be and why they can expect such benefits. The activity leader must be sincerely convinced that what residents are doing is beneficial to them. Written testimonial materials may be gathered from past participants and used to help motivate potential participants.

Avoidance of pretense. Sincerity and respect for the individual participant is manifested in the avoidance of pretense. Rapport is developed and enthusiasm engendered when the resident is praised for achievements or particular accomplishments, but artificial praise and false jolliness should be avoided. Whenever possible the resident's improvements may be presented in detail.

Planning by residents. Every resident should be given an opportunity to help plan the programs. Motivation may be enhanced through the recognition that if one helped plan the program one should also be actively involved in helping to carry it out.

Involvement of family and friends. Family and friends are an encouragement and major support through their participation in programs. Such individuals should be contacted to encourage their participation with the resident. When the resident has the esteem and support of those who mean the most, they are more likely to participate.

Departure from routine. Departure from routine is an ingredient for injecting new life into an activity. Changes in elements such as personnel, leadership style, time scheduling, seating, decorations, resident involvement, and so on help to create excitement and enthusiasm.

Controlled competiton. If properly controlled, competition can present a challenge to residents. Competition not only against someone else but also against one's own performance should be fostered.

Provision of an attractive physical environment. The physical environment associated with leisure services should be attractive. An environment that is cluttered, has poor lighting, is too hot or too cold, and has echoes or extraneous sounds is very unpleasant. An environment communicates messages, often unconsciously.

Evaluation

Each resident's care plan should be evaluated as needed—at least quarterly for all residents and more frequently for new residents. Evaluation should be conducted by the interdisciplinary team working with the resident. The team should consider what problems are diminished, what new problems have arisen, and which approaches are working and which are not. Revisions in the care plan should be based on an evaluation of each resident's progress notes and records of involvement. This section will focus on progress notes and records of involvement as means of evaluation of the care plan.

PROGRESS NOTES. To be an effective means for the evaluation of each resident's care plan, progress notes should follow a format. Each note should be preceded by the date, and the time should be recorded if the event is very

EXAMPLE 7-6

PROGRESS NOTES

Quarterly report

8/27/82   Mrs. Jones has adjusted well to the nursing home environment. She appears less overwhelmed and bewildered. She is no longer as withdrawn. She has befriended four ladies from the arts and crafts class. She has been attending class once a week. Mrs. Jones has just completed a needlepoint pillow; she did experience some difficulty because of her visual impairment. The resident has been attending church once weekly; she appears to follow the service but cannot read the Bible.

Signed: _____

notable. Each note should be a summary of participation related to the care plan, including activities, time involvement, patterns of participation, and any noticeable changes in the resident.

There are a number of techniques that may be employed to ensure clarity and objectivity of progress notes. Comments of all leisure personnel, including volunteers, should be written and kept in a special notebook to be referred to when drafting a progress note. A system of monthly recording of progress notes on all residents should be developed to avoid having to write all monthly notes for all residents on the same day. Another staff member should review and edit a progress note draft before it is entered into a resident's record. All notes entered must be signed. (See Example 7-6 for a progress note written on the resident referred to in Example 7-3).

Progress notes are a vital part of record keeping. They are useful not only for leisure service personnel but also for physicians, nurses, and dietary and other personnel. Future planning is facilitated when there is a record of past performance.

RECORDS OF INVOLVEMENT. Records of involvement are important indicators of institutional life. This section will present and discuss attendance records and records of involvement according to resident characteristics.

Attendance records. A record of attendance may be kept using the form in Example 7-7. This form is used to tally the approximate amount of time residents are in attendance at activities and is not intended to tally specific activities. The blanks across the top of the form under the days of the week may be used to tally attendance by time of day (e.g., morning, afternoon, or evening), by activity classification (e.g., cognitive, affective, psychomotor, or social), or as preferred. Such a form should be used to tally on a daily basis both supervised and unsupervised activity attendance.

EXAMPLE 7-7

ATTENDANCE RECORD FORM

Date_____ Through_____ Activities coordinator_____ Unit_____

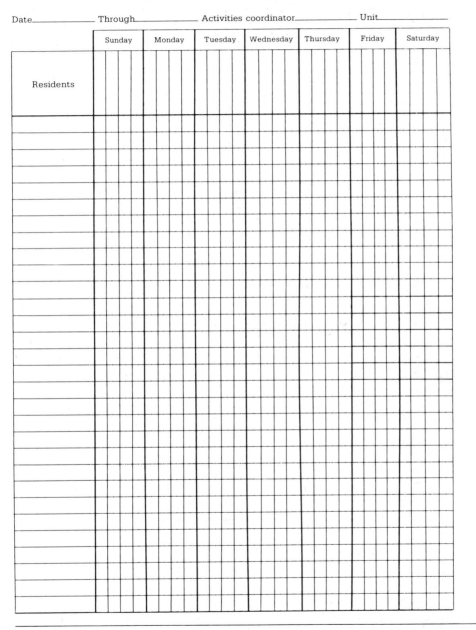

From Bachner, J., and Cornelius, E.: Activities coordinator's guide, Washington, D.C. 1978, U.S. Government Printing Office.

EXAMPLE 7-8

INVOLVEMENT ACCORDING TO RESIDENT CHARACTERISTICS

Characteristic—dependent in 4 or 5 areas of ADL
No. _____ residents with characteristic
_____ % whose care plan identifies activities interests
_____ % whose care plan identifies needs

Percent of residents	Level of involvement			
	Much	Some	Little	None
75-100%				
50-74%				
25-49%				
0-24%				

Impaired hearing
No. _____ residents with characteristic
_____ % whose care plan identifies activities interests
_____ % whose care plan identifies needs

Percent of residents	Level of involvement			
	Much	Some	Little	None
75-100%				
50-74%				
25-49%				
0-24%				

Men
No. _____ residents with characteristic
_____ % whose care plan identifies activities interests
_____ % whose care plan identifies needs

Percent of residents	Level of involvement			
	Much	Some	Little	None
75-100%				
50-74%				
25-49%				
0-24%				

Bedfast
No. _____ residents with characteristic
_____ % whose care plan identifies activities interests
_____ % whose care plan identifies needs

Percent of residents	Level of involvement			
	Much	Some	Little	None
75-100%				
50-74%				
25-49%				
0-24%				

Stroke or arthritis
No. _____ residents with characteristic
_____ % whose care plan identifies activities interests
_____ % whose care plan identifies needs

Percent of residents	Level of involvement			
	Much	Some	Little	None
75-100%				
50-74%				
25-49%				
0-24%				

Disoriented
No. _____ residents with characteristic
_____ % whose care plan identifies activities interests
_____ % whose care plan identifies needs

Percent of residents	Level of involvement			
	Much	Some	Little	None
75-100%				
50-74%				
25-49%				
0-24%				

Definitions:

Much—At least 5 hours of individual and/or group activities on each of five days during the week including one day of the weekend (minimum 25 hours a week).

Some—2-5 hours of individual and/or group activities on each of five days of the week (minimum 10 hours in a week)

Little—15 or less hours of individual and/or group activities some time during the week. (CAUTION—if five hours are all on one day, it may be dangerous to the health of some patients.)

None—Averages less than two hours of activities a week.

From Bachner, J., and Cornelius, E.: Activities coordinator's guide, Washington, D.C., 1978, U.S. Government Printing Office.

Attendance records may be used in a variety of ways in evaluating residents and programs. Patterns of resident participation may be analyzed to graphically show the extent and pattern of involvement, changes and fluctuations in involvement, or a general lack of involvement that may be compared on a weekly, monthly, or quarterly basis for each resident and for all residents. These same data may also be used to assess total program effectiveness by identifying whether attendance at certain types of activities is changing because of changes in resident interests and needs, scheduling gaps or conflicts, quality of leadership, or other reasons.

Involvement according to resident characteristics. It is important to evaluate involvement of residents who have characteristics that may be limiting. Limiting characteristics include difficulties with ADL (e.g., feeding, dressing, toileting, and transferring), impairment of the senses (e.g., hearing and vision), gender (men tend to be less involved than women), lack of ambulation (e.g., chairfast or bedfast), certain diagnoses (e.g., arthritis, stroke, glaucoma, and Parkinson's disease), and mental status (e.g., confused or disoriented). Evaluation using the forms in Example 7-8 may be carried out according to steps recommended by Bachner and Cornelius (1978, pp. 37-39):

1. *Determine resident characteristics to be evaluated for resident involvement.* Example 7-8 identifies six characteristics to be evaluated for resident involvement. A variety of other characteristics may be used, depending on the composition of the resident population.
2. *List residents with each characteristic to be evaluated.* Example 7-9 is a worksheet that will assist in adding columns and determining percentages. The total number of residents having the characteristic being examined are totaled at the bottom of the page under column 1.
3. *Determine whether interests and needs have been identified.* Check columns 2 and 3 of worksheet in Example 7-9 to determine if interests and needs have been identified. Add check marks and enter the total at the bottom of the page under columns 2 and 3.
4. *Determine level of activity involvement.* This may be determined from progress notes and attendance forms. Example 7-8 gives the definitions of levels of involvement on the worksheet in Example 7-9. Check the level of involvement of each resident in column 4 of the worksheet.
5. *Determine percentage of residents having a particular level of involvement.* This may be calculated using data in column 1 (number) and data from column 4 (involvement in activities) in Example 7-9. Data are then transferred to one of the forms in Example 7-8, according to the particular characteristic being evaluated.

Once involvement data have been gathered according to resident characteristics, they may be analyzed. Questions may be asked of the data—for example, "Are most residents well served or are residents having certain characteristics underserved?" A conference of the interdisciplinary team should evaluate the problems and move toward specific solutions.

EXAMPLE 7-9

INVOLVEMENT ACCORDING TO RESIDENT CHARACTERISTICS WORKSHEET

Date _____ Characteristic of residents being evaluated _____

1. Resident's name	2. Interests identified	3. Needs identified	4. Activities involvement			
			Much	Some	Little	None
TOTALS						
	Percent of total					

From Bachner, J., and Cornelius, E.: Activities coordinator's guide, Washington, D.C., 1978, U.S. Government Printing Office.

The number of institutions providing long-term care for older persons, coupled with Medicare and Medicaid requirements for activity programs, provide numerous job possibilities. In 1976 there were more than 1,300,000 beds in 23,000 long-term care institutions for older persons (Gelfand and Olsen, 1980, p. 206). Title XVIII (Medicare), passed in 1965, and Title XIX (Medicaid), passed in 1967, opened up major funding sources for institutions, while requiring activity programs for SNFs and ICFs.

EMPLOYMENT OPPORTUNITIES FOR LEISURE SERVICE SPECIALISTS IN INSTITUTIONS FOR THE ELDERLY

Leisure service personnel seeking employment in institutions for the elderly should evaluate a number of criteria before accepting a job in a particular institution. Bachner and Cornelius (1978, p. 74) suggest criteria that go beyond federal regulation and probably beyond state and local regulations in many cases (Example 7-10). These criteria can be used when interviewing and touring a facility to determine the quality of care currently being provided.

Graduates of therapeutic recreation undergraduate and graduate programs are needed to upgrade the quality of leisure services in institutions for older persons. Activity programs have traditionally been provided by poorly trained staff at minimum levels of compensation, which resulted in high turnover of activity staff. Professionally educated and trained therapeutic recreation specialists have the skills to individualize programs (because of the influence of the Gunn and Peterson (1978) programming approach), to work with the health care team, and to manage persons and resources. Therapeutic recreation specialists could have a dramatic impact on the quality of individual and group leisure services in institutions, and thus upgrade employment qualifications and salaries.

EXAMPLE 7-10

SUGGESTED CRITERIA TO BE USED FOR EVALUATION OF RESOURCES AND ORGANIZATION

(Based on good practice not directly related to any federal or state regulations.)

Resident activities criteria:
Activities meeting the needs and interests of residents are provided daily as an important adjunct to the treatment program, to encourage restoration to self-care, and resumption of normal activities. Residents are guided into appropriate activities but are not required to participate.

A. Principle: *Appropriate activities are available to residents of the facility.*
The activities available meet the needs and interest of all residents including those unable to leave their rooms. Community, educational and recreational resources are used to the extent necessary to provide appropriate activities. The elements to be observed:

1. The activities coordinator is notified of all admissions.
2. Contraindications for activities are noted by the physician in the resident record and on the care plan.
3. The activities coordinator is aware of contraindications and precautions relative to residents whose problems would restrict or limit their activities.

From Bachner, J., and Cornelius, E.: Activities coordinator's guide, Washington, D.C., 1978, U.S. Government Printing Office.
Continued.

EXAMPLE 7-10,
cont'd

SUGGESTED CRITERIA TO BE USED FOR EVALUATION OF RESOURCES AND ORGANIZATION

4. Each resident's individual activities interests and needs are entered on the resident care plan.

5. Each resident is encouraged to develop his interests to meet his needs. (When this is done most residents will have between 6 and 8 hours of independent, organized, individual and/or group activities daily.)

6. There is a listing of all residents on which a daily recording of the approximate hours of each resident's participation in *independent and organized activities is kept.*

7. The participation records, staff knowledge of residents' specific activities, resident care plans (interests and needs) are compared at least monthly to evaluate to what degree interests and needs are being met. Programming and care plans are altered as indicated by evaluation.

8. Notations are made in the residents' records summarizing the monthly evaluation and describing his interests, needs, pattern of participation and changes which have occurred.

9. Residents' requests to see their clergymen are honored and space is provided for privacy during visits.

10. Residents who are able and who wish to do so are assisted to attend religious services.

11. Residents are provided opportunities to participate in the community outside the facility.

B. Principle: *A staff member is designated as responsible for coordinating resident activities.* This person has experience and education in directing activities for the ill and aged and receives consultation from a registered therapeutic recreation specialist or occupational therapist registered. Elements to be documented:

1. The activities coordinator is a certified occupational therapy assistant or registered therapeutic recreation technician with supervised experience in resident activities in a long-term care setting or has equivalent education and experience.

2. Consultation is provided on a regularly scheduled basis by an experienced therapeutic recreation specialist, or occupational therapist registered.

3. The activities coordinator has sufficient time to adequately carry out his responsibilities (minimum 2/3 hour a week per resident).

4. The activities coordinator participates in the resident care planning and facility in-service education program.

5. The activities coordinator is allowed to attend educational programs which are outside the facility and are related to resident activities.

C. Principle: *Daily visiting hours are flexible and posted to encourage visiting by friends, relatives, and community representatives.* The elements to be documented are:

1. Daily visiting hours are posted and flexible.

2. Visitors are restricted only on the written order of a physician.

3. Friends and relatives are encouraged to participate with residents in activities.

4. Volunteers are available to assist residents in the development of their interests a minimum of 2 hours a week per resident.

D. Principle: *Safe supplies, equipment, and space are available to carry out suitable activities.* The elements to be observed are:

1. Space suitable for activities of interest to the residents is provided.

2. The environment (heat, light, noise, and ventilation) is controlled and maintained.

3. Supplies, equipment and other resources are provided in sufficient quantity and variety to conduct the organized and independent activities to satisfy the individual interests of residents.

4. Appropriate storage space is provided for all supplies and equipment including hazardous materials such as darts, shellac, turpentine, and power tools.

5. Mechanical safety devices are provided to protect operators of equipment.

6. Safety procedures related to activities and for resident protection are known and followed by personnel, volunteers, and residents.

7. Safety procedures and warning precautions are appropriately posted.

The Elizabethan Poor Law of 1601 was the foundation for welfare legislation in England and the United States. Isolation of the aged and infirm continued to be the predominant social policy of the nineteenth century in England and the United States. Residents of almshouses, or poorhouses, were required to work for meager wages to support the institutions because the responsibility for these facilities rested on city and county governments. Types of institutional care in the United States began to expand in the twentieth century with federal involvement in legislation such as the Old Age Assistance Act of 1929, which offered alternatives to institutionalization, and the Social Security Act of the 1930s, which prohibited financial support of public institutions to encourage older persons to stay home. Federal involvement in funding institutional care was greatly expanded in the 1950s and 1960s with the passage of the Hill Burton Act, the National Housing Act, and Medicare and Medicaid.

There are a variety of institutions serving the needs of older persons. Institutions are operated under public, private nonprofit, or proprietary auspices. Institutions may be classified (according to the level of care provided and certification under Medicare and Medicaid) as extended care facilities (ECFs), which provide extensive professional nursing and support staff; skilled nursing facilities (SNFs), which care for severely ill patients; and intermediate care facilities (ICFs), which provide access to various health services but not delivery by the level of professional staff required in an SNF. Board and care, personal care, and domiciliary care homes have no federal licensing classification but are controlled by state regulations.

Institutions and their residents have increased since the 1930s as a result of an increase in the older population, changes in federal financing as a result of Medicare and Medicaid, and a willingness by institutions to accept a greater variety of patients. The majority of institutions are proprietary, have fewer than 100 beds, and provide either intermediate care only or both intermediate and skilled nursing care. Nursing homes have the greatest numbers of residents of all the types of institutions, with the majority of residents being female, white, widowed or never married, and 74 years of age or older. Nursing home residents have a variety of physical, functional, and mental conditions, most notably impairment of self-maintenance skills (e.g., bathing, dressing, and mobility). Nursing homes are increasingly becoming chronic disease hospitals for physically and mentally impaired older persons rather than care centers and homes for the ambulatory who are not self-sufficient.

Institutional transfer and the institutional environment have been shown to have an impact on older persons. Institutional transfer or relocation has been demonstrated to have a variety of physical, psychological, and social consequences that may be alleviated by involving patients in decisions related to the move and avoiding placement in cold and dehumanizing environments that foster dependence. The "total institution" provides a custodial, protected environment for its residents that results in older persons losing the capacity to function independently of the institution. Treating older institutional residents

SUMMARY

as incompetents because of their dependence and confusion may result in the social breakdown syndrome, manifested through loss of privacy, personal possessions, friends, and the capacity to care. Nursing homes are particularly likely to isolate residents from the larger community and from interactions with staff and other residents, which results in an incapacity for self-initiated activity. Some of the negative or destructive resident characteristics attributed to nursing homes as an environment, however, may already be present in older persons before entry and so should not always be attributed to the nursing home environment.

Institutions can have a beneficial impact on the social and psychological functioning of residents through a variety of rehabilitation programs. Reality orientation is designed to alleviate the confusion and disorientation of older persons through staff reiterating basic personal and current information to the older persons. Remotivation seeks to bring each person in a remotivation group to a higher level of social and emotional functioning through a five-step process. Reminiscence has been delineated into three distinct but overlapping categories: informative, evaluative, and obsessive. All of the rehabilitative programs discussed have been studied from a variety of research perspectives, and each program may be integrated into leisure services.

The development of leisure services in institutions for the elderly requires resources such as staff, areas and facilities, equipment and supplies, and funds. Staff includes paid employees (e.g., the director of leisure services, activity leaders, consultants, and resource persons) and volunteers—all of whom perform a variety of duties and functions depending on the setting. Areas and facilities for leisure services may include spaces such as a large group area, small group area, game room, lounge, craft room, storage area, office space, and an outdoor recreation area, but leisure service personnel must often take advantage of whatever space is available. Equipment is nonexpendable items that may be already available or need to be purchased, made, rented, donated, repaired, or adapted; supplies are expendable items that may be purchased, donated, or "scrounged" from a variety of sources. Funds for leisure services are usually allocated on the basis of a prepared budget and are categorized into personnel (salaries and fringe benefits), equipment (furnishings and basic equipment), and supplies. Revenue is often generated through donations or the sale of craft projects.

The programming of leisure services should include assessment of residents, care plan development, program content, and motivation. Assessment of each elderly resident requires the gathering of information on a variety of resident characteristics from the social worker, health personnel, and leisure service personnel as soon as the resident enters the facility and again when the resident becomes more familiar with the environment. The care plan is developed by an interdisciplinary team with leisure service personnel contributing to the team effort through a leisure services plan that should include the assessment, the leisure services approach, at least one long-term goal, one short-term goal, and specific actions. Program content should reflect individual resident and group decision making by a resident advisory council, with the resulting monthly program content being expressed in a monthly activity calendar that integrates scheduling of activities with the needed resources. Motivation of residents to seek involvement in leisure services may be facilitated by explaining the benefits of involvement, avoiding pretense, planning by residents, involving family and friends, departing from routine, instituting properly controlled competition, and providing an attractive physical environment.

Evaluation of leisure services should focus on the progress notes and records of involvement as a means of evaluating the care plan. Progress notes should follow a predetermined format and should be clear and objective. Records of involvement include attendance records of both supervised and unsupervised involvement according to a variety of resident characteristics.

Employment opportunities for leisure service specialists in institutions for the elderly are potentially numerous because of the number of institutions and Medicare and Medicaid requirements for activity programs. Leisure service personnel, however, should evaluate institutional resources and the organization of a particular setting before accepting a job.

REFERENCES

Aldritch, C., and Mendkoff, E.: Relocation of the aged and disabled: a mortality study, J. Am. Geriatr. Soc. **11**:185-194, 1963.

Allen, V.: Motivation therapy with the aging geriatric veteran patient, Milit. Med. **135**:1007-1010, 1970.

Bachner, J., and Cornelius, E.: Activities coordinator's guide, Washington, D.C., 1978, U.S. Government Printing Office.

Barnes, J.: Effects of reality orientation classroom on memory loss, confusion and disorientation in geriatric patients, Gerontologist **14**:138-142, 1974.

Bennett, R., and Nahemow, L.: Institutional totality and criteria of social adjustment in residences for the aged, J. Soc. Issues **21**:44-76, 1965.

Birkett, D., and Boltuch, B.: Remotivation therapy, J. Am. Geriat. Soc. **21**:368-371, 1973.

Bowers, M., Anderson, G., Blomeier, E., and Pelz, K.: Brain syndrome and behavior in geriatric remotivation groups, J. Gerontol. **22**:348-352, 1967.

Boylin, W., Gordan, S., and Nehrke, M.: Reminiscing and ego integrity in institutionalized elderly males, Gerontologist **16**:118-124, 1976.

Brook, P., Gegun, G., and Mather, M.: Reality orientation: a therapy for psychogeriatric patients—a controlled study, Br. J. Psychiatr. **127**:42-45, 1975.

Butler, R.: Successful aging and the role of the life review, J. Am. Geriatr. Soc. **22**:529-535, 1974.

Butler, R., and Lewis, M.: Aging and mental health, ed. 3, St. Louis, 1982, The C.V. Mosby Co.

Citrin, R., and Dixon, D.: Reality orientation: a milieu therapy used in an institution for the aged, Gerontologist **17**:39-43, 1977.

Cohen, E.: An overview of long-term care facilities. In Brody, E., editor: A social work guide for long-term care facilities, Rockville, Md., 1974, National Institute for Mental Health.

Coleman, P.: Measuring reminiscence characteristics from conversation as adaptive features of old age, J. Aging Hum. Dev. **5**:281-294, 1974.

Curry, T., and Ratliff, B.: The effects of nursing home size on resident isolation and life satisfaction, Gerontologist **13**:295-298, 1973.

Drake, J.: The aged in American society, New York, 1958, Ronald Publishing Co.

Folsom, J.: Reality orientation for the elderly mental patient, J. Psychiatr. **1**:291-307, 1968.

Gelfand, D., and Olsen, J.: The aging network: programs and services, New York, 1980, Springer Publishing Co., Inc.

Glasscote, R., et al.: Old folks at homes, Washington, D.C., 1976, American Psychiatric Association and Mental Health Association.

Goffman, E.: Asylums, Garden City, N.Y., 1961, Anchor Books.

Gotestam, K.: Training in reality orientation of patients with senile dementia. In Levi, L., editor: Society, stress and disease: aging and old age, London, 1979, Oxford University Press.

Gottesman, L., and Bourestom, N.: Why nursing homes do what they do, Gerontologist **14**:501-506, 1974.

Gubrium, J.: Living and dying at Murray Manor, New York, 1975, St. Martin's Press, Inc.

Gunn, S., and Peterson, C.: Therapeutic recreation program design: principles and procedures, Englewood Cliffs, N.J., 1978, Prentice-Hall, Inc.

Harris, C., and Ivory, P.: An outcome evaluation of reality orientation therapy with geriatric patients in a state mental hospital, Gerontologist **16**:496-503, 1976.

Hess, B., and Markson, E.: Aging and old age: an introduction to social gerontology, New York, 1980, Macmillan Publishing Co., Inc.

Kiyak, A., Kahana, E., and Lev, N.: The role of informal norms in determining institutional totality in residence for the aged. Unpublished paper presented at the Annual Meeting of the Gerontological Society, 1975, Louisville, Ky.

Lawton, M.P., and Nahemow, L.: Ecology and the aging process. In Eisdorfer, C., and Lawton, M.P., editors: The psychology of adult development and aging, Washington, D.C., 1973, American Psychological Association.

Lieberman, M.: Relocation research and social policy, Gerontologist **14:**494-500, 1974.

Liebowitz, B.: Impact of intra-institutional relocation, Gerontologist **14:**293-295, 1974.

Lo Gerfo, M.: Three ways of reminiscence in theory and practice, Int. J. Aging Hum. Dev. **12:**39-48, 1980.

Lowenthal, M., and Robinson, B.: Social networks and isolation. In Binstock, R., and Shanas, E., editors: Handbook of aging and the social sciences, New York, 1976, Van Nostrand Reinhold Co.

Manard, B., Kart, C., and Van Gils, D.: Old age institutions, Lexington, Mass., 1975, Lexington Books.

McMahon, A., and Rhudick, P.: Reminiscing in the aged: an adaptational response. In Levin, S., and Kahana, R., editors: Psychodynamic studies on aging: creativity, reminiscing, and dying, New York, 1964, International Universities Press, Inc.

Miller, D., and Beer, S.: Patterns of friendship among patients in a nursing home setting, Gerontologist **17:**269-275, 1977.

Moss, F., and Halmandaris, V.: Too old, too sick, too bad, Germantown, Md., 1977, Aspen Systems Corp.

National Center for Health Statistics: Selected operating and financial characteristics of nursing homes, Vital and Health Statistics Series 13, Pub. No. 22, Rockville, Md., 1975, U.S. Department of Health, Education, and Welfare.

National Center for Health Statistics: Characteristics, social contacts, and activities of nursing home residents, Vital and Health Statistics Series 13, Pub. No. 27, Rockville, Md., 1977a, U.S. Department of Health, Education and Welfare.

National Center for Health Statistics: Profile of chronic illness in nursing homes, Vital and Health Statistics Series 13, Pub. No. 29, Hyattsville, Md., 1977b, U.S. Department of Health, Education, and Welfare.

National Center for Health Statistics: A comparison of nursing home residents and discharges from the 1977 National Nursing Home Survey, Advance Data, Pub. No. 29, Hyattsville, Md., 1978, U.S. Department of Health, Education, and Welfare.

Nevruz, N., and Hrushka, M.: The influence of unstructured and structured group psychotherapy with geriatric patients on their decision to leave the hospital, Int. J. Group Psychother. **19:**72-79, 1969.

Palmore, E.: Total chance of institutionalization among the aged, Gerontologist **16:**504-507, 1976.

Schulz, R., and Brenner, G.: Relocation of the aged: a review and theoretical analysis, J. Gerontol. **32:**323-333, 1977.

Stephens, L.: Reality orientation, Washington, D.C., 1970, Hospital and Community Psychiatry Service, American Psychiatric Association.

Stephens, L.: Reality orientation, Washington, D.C., 1975, Hospital and Community Psychiatry Service, American Psychiatric Association.

Stracke, D.: Climates in remotivation in therapeutic recreation, Ther. Recreation J. **4:**9-12, 44, 1970.

Taulbee, L., and Folsom, J.: Reality orientation for geriatric patients, Hosp. Community Psychiatry **17:**133-135, 1966.

Thralow, J., and Watson, C.: Remotivation for geriatric patients using elementary school students, Am. J. Occupational Ther. **28:**469-473, 1974.

Tobin, S., and Lieberman, M.: Last home for the aged, San Francisco, 1976, Jossey-Bass, Inc., Publishers.

Townsend, P.: The last refuge, London, 1964, Rutledge & Kegan Paul of America, Ltd.

Winston, W., and Wilson, A.: Ethical considerations in long-term care, St. Petersberg, Fla., 1977, Eckerd College Gerontology Center.

Zepelin, H., Wolfe, C., and Kleinplatz, F.: Evaluation of a year-long reality orientation program, J. Gerontol. **36:**70-77, 1977.

Zusman, J.: Some explanations of the changing appearance of psychotic patients: antecedents of the social breakdown syndrome concept, Milbank Mem. Fund Q. **64:**363-394, 1966.

SUGGESTED READINGS

Bachner, J., and Cornelius, E.: Activities coordinator's guide, Washington, D.C., 1978, U.S. Government Printing Office.

Butler, R., and Lewis, M.: Aging and mental health, ed. 3, St. Louis, 1982, The C.V. Mosby Co.

PART THREE
Special leisure services

Attention has been focused in recent years on a variety of special leisure services provided within the network of services available to older
persons. Part Three seeks to highlight four areas of special leisure services: Exercise (Chapter 8), Creative Arts (Chapter 9), Education (Chapter 10), and Outdoor Recreation (Chapter 11). Each chapter presents
pertinent theory and research, as well as procedures for the development of the special leisure service under discussion.

8

Exercise

Exercise is vital to the total well-being of older persons (Crandall, 1980; Harris and Frankel, 1977). Regular exercise will strengthen heart and lungs and help decrease the likelihood of heart attack; in the event of an attack, it may lessen the severity. Increased exercise combined with proper dietary controls can produce weight loss through a reduction of excessive body fat. Ailments such as daily fatigue, sore joints, stiffness, and poor circulation may gradually disappear as a result of increased exercise. Improved digestion and elimination and more restful sleep may be promoted. Exercise may improve an older person's personal appearance by shaping and toning muscles, improving complexion, increasing strength and flexibility, and improving posture. Regular exercise may improve feelings of well-being, accomplishment, and pride and may therefore motivate an individual to give up smoking, unnecessary drugs, and other unhealthy habits. It may provide a release of tension, relaxation, the opportunity to develop interpersonal relationships, and enjoyment.

Today there is a growing concern to provide exercise programs that older persons may engage in, whatever the leisure service setting. Until recently, physical exercise or other activities that increase heart rate or put strain on the body have generally been avoided by the elderly and by individuals working with the elderly. This chapter will examine the benefits of exercise for older persons as documented by research and the process of developing an exercise program for older persons.

BENEFITS OF EXERCISE

Data from exercise specialists are demonstrating the benefits of exercise for the elderly. It has been shown in research that continued exercise has physiological and psychological benefits for older persons. This section will consider the benefits of exercise as illustrated by selected pieces of physiological and psychological research.

Physiological benefits

Flexibility is an important factor in helping older persons to remain ambulatory (deVries, 1976). Chapman, deVries, and Swezy (1972), in a joint flexibility study of 20 young and 20 elderly subjects, found that after 6 weeks of a weight training program both young and old could remedy joint stiffness, even though older subjects began the program with greater joint incapacitation. Frekany and Leslie (1975), in a study of ankle and hamstring/lower-back flexibility of 15 women ages 71 to 90, found that after 7 months of stretching and mild calisthenics for 30 minutes twice a week subjects showed significant improvements in both ankle and lower-back flexibility on pre and post indices. Lesser (1978), in a study of 60 older persons ages 61 to 89, sought to determine the impact of a 30-minute, twice weekly, 10-week rhythmical exercise to music program; she found statistically significant improvements in shoulder, elbow, knee, and plantar flexion and dorsiflexion. It is evident from these three studies that gains in flexibility are consistent, even though different exercise formats were used.

Research suggests that older persons are able to improve their cardiovascular fitness. deVries (1970), in a study of the impact of exercise on various functions of 112 males ages 52 to 80 (mean age of 69.5), showed that after 6 weeks of training (1 hour per day, three times weekly) involving calisthenics, jogging, and either stretching exercises or aquatics significant improvements occurred in the cardiovascular parameters of fitness, even though subjects were limited to exercise intensities of 145 heartbeats per minute or less. In a later report (deVries, 1971) he suggested that cardiovascular improvement could be made, except for highly conditioned men, through a program of vigorous walking that raised the heart rate to between 100 and 120 beats per minute for 30 to 60 minutes daily. Adams and deVries (1973) also conducted a study to determine the effects of a systematic exercise program on older women (ages 52 to 79). The women participated in a three-phase program (calisthenics, aerobic exercise, and stretching exercise) that met three times per week for 1 hour; significant improvement occurred in the cardiovascular system after a 3-month exercise program at 60 percent of maximum heart rate. Thus elderly males and females need not exercise at heart rates as high as younger persons to show improved cardiovascular fitness.

Improvements in cardiovascular fitness have been noted in institutionalized geriatric patients. Stamford (1972), in a carefully controlled 3-month exercise program that met 5 days per week, found significant gains in cardiovascular functioning (decreased heart rate and blood pressure) in 25 institutionalized male geriatric patients participating in a 70 percent of maximum heart rate training program. Stamford (1973) found that the chronically ill patients manifested improvements sooner than the recently admitted patients, although both the chronically ill and recently institutionalized patients responded favorably to the 18-week program of treadmill exercise. It is interesting to note that improvements were observed even when patients exercised from only 9 to 20 minutes per session.

Bone mass may be increased as a result of physical exercise. Aloia (1981),

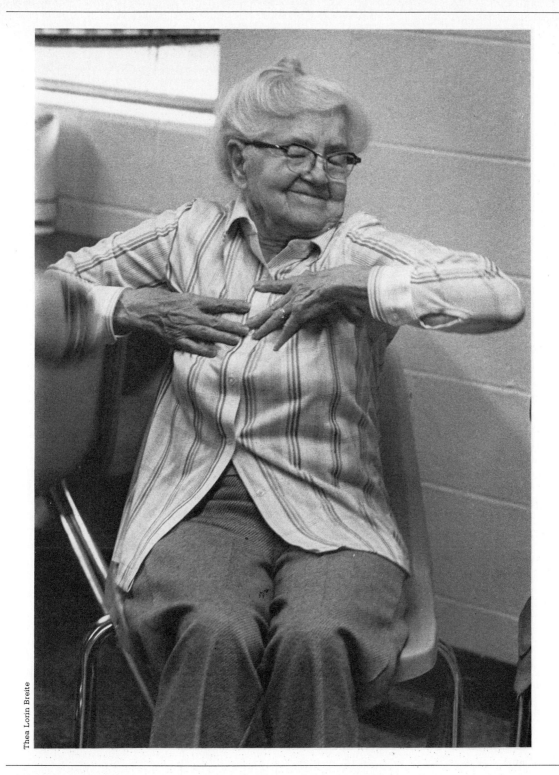

Exercise has been shown to provide a variety of physiological and psychological benefits for older persons.

in a review of experimental evidence supporting the hypothesis that involutional bone loss (the reduction of skeletal mass) can be prevented by physical exercise, concluded that studies have demonstrated an increase in bone mass after a program of physical exercise. He recommended that a program to maintain skeletal health may require the revision of the current training programs, which are primarily directed to the improvement of maximum oxygen intake. Further research is needed, however, to determine the effectiveness of specific types and duration of exercise.

Psychological benefits

Stamford, Hambacher, and Fallica (1974) studied the psychological effects of a 12-week exercise program on institutionalized geriatric patients. Nine men were in the experimental group (mean age 71.5), and eight men were in the control group (mean age of 65.2). Psychological tests of self-concept (Draw-A-Person Test), memory (two sections of the Wechsler Adult Intelligence Scale), and environmental awareness (questionnaire on ward activities) were administered in a pretest, posttest design. The treatment consisted of graduated exercise sessions (from 6 minutes to 20 minutes by the end of the study) Monday through Friday in the form of walking on a treadmill. Results indicated significant psychological changes in the experimental group on the Wechsler Adult Intelligence Scale General Information and Questionnaire; no similar changes occurred in the control group.

Powell (1974) investigated the effects of a 12-week mild exercise program on selected psychological and behavioral characteristics of institutionalized geriatric patients. Thirteen men and eleven women (mean age of 69) were randomly placed into two treatment groups and one control group. One treatment group received exercise, the second participated in social activities, and the control group received no special treatment. The 12-week program was conducted 5 days a week for 1 hour for each treatment group. Exercise included rhythmical movements such as arm swings, trunk rotation and flexion, leg flexion, toe raising, walking, and postural exercises. The social activities consisted of arts and crafts, music, and games. Subjects in both treatment groups were evaluated before and after treatment on the basis of three psychological tests (Wechsler Memory Scale, Progressive Matrices Test, and Memory for Designs Test) and two behavioral scales (Nurses Observation Scale and the Geriatric Assessment Scale). An analysis of variance showed that the cognitive scores on the Progressive Matrices Test and Wechsler Memory Scale improved significantly for the exercise group compared with the social activities and control groups. No significant changes in behavior were found either in the exercise group or in the social activities group. Powell (1974, p. 161) concluded that "social interaction was not the most important factor in contributing to cognitive improvement found in the exercise treatment group."

Diesfeldt and Diesfeldt-Groenendijk (1977) sought to determine the impact of 4 weeks of group gymnastics on the memory performance of geriatric mental patients with symptoms of disorientation, decreased ability to dress, incontinence, and inertia. Forty subjects were divided into an exercise group (mean age 80.9) and a control group (mean age 82.6) and matched on dependence scores. The results showed that exercise significantly improved total recall (measured on the posting-box error scores), but no changes were observed in cooperation and mood. Exercise thus had a significant effect on memory performance.

Blumenthal and Williams (1982), in a study of an experimental group of 16 men and women (age 65 to 75 years) who participated in a 10-week exercise program of walking and jogging and a matched control group of adults who maintained their sedentary life-styles, found regular exercise to be associated with changes in the psychological condition of older participants. The exercise program participants had lower scores on the measures of anxiety, depression, tension, confusion, and fatigue than did members of the control group; the exercise group also scored higher on the vigor subscale than did the control group. The results of this study provide evidence that psychological benefits can be obtained from a 10-week walking and jogging program.

DEVELOPMENT OF AN EXERCISE PROGRAM

This section is a basic guide for the development of an exercise program. Steps in the process of program development are staffing, organizing, scheduling, providing appropriate setting and equipment, taking precautions, motivating, choosing types of exercises, structuring the exercise sessions, providing complementary activities, and evaluating.

Staffing

Supervision of an exercise program should be the responsibility of a person who has professional training in leisure services, recreation, gerontology, exercise physiology, and related fields, as well as training and experience in working with older persons. Professional training is especially important if more vigorous exercise routines are to be followed (deVries, 1975). The supervisor should be certified in first aid and cardiopulmonary resuscitation (CPR).

Trained older persons may also be highly effective. They may be elected, appointed, or the group may take turns leading the exercises. Members of the group should be encouraged to demonstrate and lead both new exercises and the old favorites. Involvement of older persons helps to ensure program continuation and continuity should regular leadership be absent.

Organizing

Publicity is the first step in getting an exercise program organized. Publication by word of mouth, newsletters, and other sources is an effective means of letting older persons know that a program is being considered.

An organizational meeting should be called to give all interested older persons the opportunity to express interest and make suggestions and requests that they feel are important. At this meeting the need for and benefits of exercise should be presented along with types of exercises being considered, location and time, and other pertinent information.

Scheduling

A regularly scheduled group exercise meeting can provide the structure that is needed. Exercise must be regular and consistent if it is to be effective. Many individual exercise programs fail because most people have a difficult time exercising on a regular basis when they are on their own.

Exercising daily is the most beneficial way to exercise. However, it may be difficult for a group to meet this often. Leslie and McLure (1975) suggest that 15- to 30-minute daily sessions are best for older persons. Group meetings two or three times per week may be combined with individual sessions on the other days (Leslie and McLure, 1975).

Older persons have individual preferences as to the best time of day to exercise. Leslie and McLure (1975) found that the most popular times for older persons to exercise are before the noon or evening meals. However, the group will have to agree on a time that is most suitable for all of its members. Immediately after meals is not a good time for vigorous exercise, although a leisurely walk might help digestion and some gentle exercises just before going to bed might help one to relax (Leslie and McLure, 1975).

Setting and equipment

A number of factors should be considered when selecting a setting for a regular exercise program. The exercise group should meet in a room where the traffic flow is light, yet it should be convenient and accessible for older persons. The room should have enough space for everyone to move about freely and a minimum amount of furnishings so as not to interfere with free movement. Wall space should be available for exercises performed against the wall. Health and fitness centers and community recreation centers are often ideal locations.

A minimum amount of special equipment is needed for a basic exercise program. Each group member should have a sturdy, stable, straight-backed chair with a firm seat and no arms (Leslie and McLure, 1975). Floor exercises may be facilitated by exercise mats, but such mats are not absolutely necessary. Exercise routines may require or be facilitated by items such as balls, balloons, wands, scarfs, towels, surgical tubing for stretching, and so on.

Precautions

Approval should be obtained from each participant's physician to assure protection for both the older person and the exercise staff. The request for physician approval should include a letter stating the types of exercise, pacing, length and frequency of sessions, and who is responsible for the program. The form should provide space for physician recommendations and special limitations and be enclosed with a stamped, self-addressed envelope to encourage a

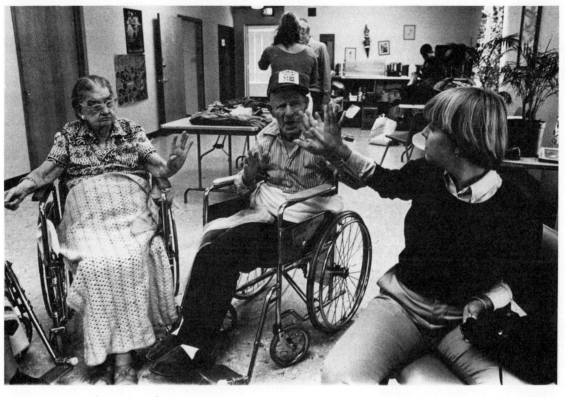

Thea Lorin Breite

Institutionalized semiambulatory older persons should be given the opportunity to participate in a program of regularly scheduled exercise.

quick response (Example 8-1). The physician should be encouraged to ask the older person how he or she feels about his or her health, to recommend modifications of the program to suit individual needs, or to eliminate exercises that might be harmful, especially for older persons who have not had much recent physical activity or who have certain limitations.

Exercise staff should be alert to two common problems. First, an older person might not have a personal physician who is familiar with his or her history and conditions. In this case referral should be made to the public health office, a local hospital, or the local medical society. Second, spontaneous participation in the exercise sessions by older persons who do not have medical approval is common. This can be decreased by watching for new faces and checking for medical approval.

EXAMPLE 8-1

REQUEST FOR PHYSICIAN APPROVAL

Dear Doctor:

AHOY is a program to maintain and improve the physical health of older adults. It consists of very basic exercise movements that will be designed to meet individual needs. The exercises will be done slowly and gently, will begin with few repetitions, and will be increased gradually. Please note any limitations that this individual may have. Your cooperation is appreciated. For specific details, contact _____, _____.
Thank you.   Name   Phone

Name _____ Age _____
    Sex _____ Weight _____ Height _____
Description of physical condition:
    Blood pressure _____ Resting pulse _____
    Heart condition _____
    Respiratory condition _____
    Joint or bone disorders _____
    Hernia _____ Diabetes _____
    Allergies _____
    Other physical conditions _____
    _____
    Medications _____
Additional comments _____
_____
_____

This individual has my approval to participate in the AHOY program of gentle, basic movements and activities. In my opinion, this individual is reasonably able to determine their own limitations regarding exercise, although the program director should note the above information.

                                    _____
                                          (Doctor's signature)

                                    _____
                                    (Phone number)   (Date)

From McEachern, M.: Ahoy: add health to our years, Raleigh, N.C., 1980, M. McEachern.

Motivation

Motivation to begin exercising will not be easy for older persons if they are not used to exercising, if they have become increasingly sedentary, or if they are in poor physical condition. There are ways to assist older persons to motivate themselves:

1. Education can provide an understanding of how the body works, the importance of physical fitness, and the benefits of a regular program of exercise.

2. Experiencing some of the benefits of exercise after a relatively short time often converts older persons to the value of exercise, and many may share the benefits and value with their friends.

3. Some older persons may be attracted to an exercise group through the opportunities to show affection, to touch and be touched, to make new friends, to escape from loneliness, and to share a common experience.

4. Individual attention, recognition, and certificates of achievement may help.

5. Exercise may be "prescribed" by a physician to help the older person regain fitness, prevent illness, or recover from an accident or illness.

6. Periodically measuring progress through various forms of evaluation (e.g., questionnaires and informal discussions) and individual feedback has been shown to be of value (McLure and Leslie, 1972).

Types of exercise

There are two types of exercise programs for older adults. The first is designed to maintain and improve muscle tone, flexibility, kinesthetic awareness, balance and posture; this type of exercise does not raise the heart rate above the normal daily routine. The second is designed to maintain and improve cardiovascular fitness through a program of endurance activities that "exercise" the circulatory system; examples of endurance activities are jogging, swimming, biking, and walking. Cardiovascular exercises warrant a complete and thorough medical checkup and close medical supervision.

FLEXIBILITY, MUSCLE STRENGTH, AND ENDURANCE. Exercise programs to increase flexibility should allow stretching of the muscles serving the major joints of the body; muscle strength and endurance exercises should involve the lifting of a relatively light load, increasing the load over time. An example of an exercise program satisfying these provisions is a program titled "Join the Active People Over 60!" (Example 8-2) (National Association for Human Development, 1976).

CARDIOVASCULAR FITNESS. Exercise programs to increase cardiovascular fitness enhance the ability of the lungs, heart, and vascular system to process and supply the necessary oxygen to the body during work. The measurement of maximum oxygen uptake is called aerobic capacity. The determination of the aerobic capacity for a person over 60 is 220 beats per minute minus the person's age (e.g., $220 - 60 = 160$ beats per minute) (Shivers and Fait, 1980, p. 263). The efficiency of the cardiovascular system can be maintained or increased by participation in an activity that results in the heartbeat increasing to the target heart rate. The target heart rate is the pulse rate obtained by taking the percentage of estimated aerobic capacity measured by pulse rate. A formula for determining how high the pulse rate should be raised, as compared with the estimated aerobic capacity, would be to use a conservative aerobic capacity of 40 percent (deVries, 1980, p. 289) (e.g., [220 − age] − resting pulse rate [0.4] + resting pulse rate = target rate). For example, a target rate for a person 60 years of age with a resting heart rate of 80 would be $(220 - 60) - 80(0.4) + 80 = 112$ (Shivers and Fait, 1980, p. 264). Improvement of aerobic capacity requires the

Text continued on p. 186.

EXAMPLE 8-2

JOIN THE ACTIVE PEOPLE OVER 60!

Warm-up

Before conditioning exercises or circulatory activities are attempted, the body should be warmed up to increase respiration and body temperature and to stretch ligaments and connective tissue. The warm-up is necessary to gear up the body for the more strenuous exercises that follow. Some simple warm-up activities are:

1. Shake arms at the side.
2. Lift one foot off the ground and shake it until it feels loose, then repeat with the other foot.
3. Jog or walk in place.

Arms only

Arm circles

Starting position: Stand with feet about 1 foot apart, arms at side.

Exercise: Move arms, making small circles and gradually expanding to larger circles.

The movement of the arms helps to keep the shoulder joints flexible while strengthening shoulder muscles.

Arm swings

Starting position: Stand with feet together, arms at side.

Exercise: Keep feet together, swing arms.

This exercise stimulates circulation in the arms and relaxes the shoulder muscles.

Overhead and shoulder touch

Starting position: Stand with feet together, hands touching shoulders.

Exercise: Touch shoulders, extend arms overhead, repeat.

This movement limbers and strengthens the muscles of the upper back and shoulders.

Shoulder touch, arms out

Starting position: Stand with feet together, hands touching shoulders.

Exercise: Touch shoulders, extend arms out, repeat.

This motion stimulates circulation in the arms and strengthens the biceps.

Arms up, arms down

Starting position: Stand with arms at side, legs together.

Exercise: Keeping arms straight, lift arms to position even with shoulders, repeat.

Shoulder, back, and chest muscles are strengthened in this exercise.

Modified from National Association for Human Development: Join the active people over 60! Washington, D.C., 1976, National Association for Human Development, pp. 12-16.

EXAMPLE 8-2,
cont'd

Legs only

Knees up

Starting position: Lie flat on back, legs together, arms at side.

Exercise: Bring right knee up, return to floor, bring left knee up, return to floor, repeat.

This exercise strengthens the abdominal muscles and improves the flexibility of the hip and knee joints.

Walking in place

Starting position: Stand with legs together, arms at side.

Exercise: Bring right knee up, return, bring left knee up, return.

This exercise strengthens muscles and improves circulation.

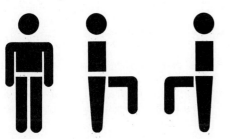

Head only

Head circles

Starting position: Stand with hands on hips, legs together.

Exercise: Do head circles to the right, head circles to the left.

Firming of the chin line and loosening and relaxation of the neck muscles can be accomplished with this exercise.

Yes-no

Starting position: Stand with hands on hips, legs together.

Exercise: Shake head yes, shake head no.

This motion helps to relax and loosen muscles of the neck.

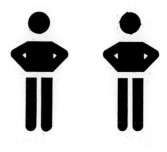

Feet only

Foot circles

Starting position: Stand with one foot lifted off the ground.

Exercise: Circle foot to the right, circle foot to the left.

This exercise helps improve balance, enhances posture, and develops the muscles in the upper leg.

Continued.

**EXAMPLE 8-2,
cont'd**

JOIN THE ACTIVE PEOPLE OVER 60!

Shoulder exercises

Ear-shoulder exercise

Starting position: Stand with legs together, arms at side.

Exercise: Raise shoulder and touch right ear, raise shoulder and touch left ear.

This movement relaxes the neck and shoulder muscles and loosens the shoulder joints.

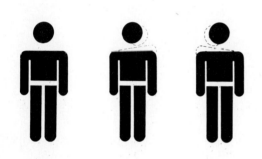

Up-down

Starting position: Stand with legs together, arms at side.

Exercise: Raise both shoulders, lower them, repeat.

This exercise also strengthens shoulder and back muscles and aids expansion of the lungs.

Elbow touch

Starting position: Stand with hands on shoulders.

Exercise: Touch elbows, return to original position, repeat.

A conditioning and strengthening of the shoulders, arms, and wrists, as well as expansion of lungs, is accomplished in this movement.

Arm and leg exercises

Angel in the snow

Starting position: Lie on back, arms and legs together.

Exercise: Bring legs apart and move arms overhead, keeping both legs and arms straight.

This exercise helps improve posture and strengthens the abdominal muscles.

EXAMPLE 8-2,
cont'd

Elbow exercises
Forearm raise

Starting position: Stand with hands touching shoulders.
Exercise: Circle left elbow, circle right elbow.

This motion loosens and relaxes shoulder joints and muscles and increases muscle tone in the upper arm.

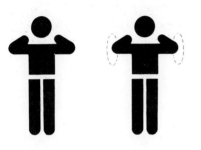

Knee push up

Starting position: Kneel with body and arms straight.
Exercise: Bend arms and lie on floor, keeping knees straight.

This exercise strengthens arms and shoulders and helps tighten the stomach muscles.

Body exercises
Bending left to right

Starting position: Stand with legs together, arms over head, hands together.
Exercise: Stretch the body to the right, then to the left.

This exercise helps limber and stretch the trunk, legs, and arms of the body and expands the rib cage to augment breathing.

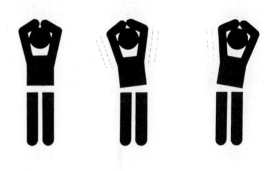

Body circles

Starting position: Stand with legs together, arms over head, hands together.
Exercise: Circle the body to the right, then to the left.

This exercise stretches the abdominal muscles, strengthens shoulder and upper arm muscles, and enhances posture.

participant to reach the target rate and hold it for 15 to 20 minutes through activities such as jogging, swimming, bicycling, and vigorous walking.

Structuring the exercise sessions

It is important to provide time for warming up and cooling off. A period of warming up and loosening up before getting involved in any vigorous activity is especially important for older persons. Vigorous activity should be alternated with less strenuous activity. The amount (number of repetitions, length of activity, and so on) should be increased very gradually but steadily to achieve improved fitness. When the session is over, there should be a cooling off period during which the body is allowed to slowly return to its normal temperature, heart rate, and so on. This does not mean a sudden cessation of activity but a slowing down and gradual stopping of activity.

No two persons in the program will be alike, so it is important that the program be flexible enough to allow individualization. Older persons with medical conditions such as arthritis and cardiac and circulatory problems will require some individual adaptations. Most older persons are capable of determining their own limits and stopping when these limits have been reached, but to avoid discouragement or serious injuries the group leader should specify the number of repetitions and when to stop.

The group leader should structure the sessions to include variety. Suggested leadership guidelines are:

1. Make the sessions a social experience through conversation, jokes, and the sharing of new ideas and successes.
2. Include variations and innovations in the exercise routine by slowly demonstrating and helping the older person move through the new routine, perhaps even using manipulation of the body parts involved.
3. Incorporate creative movement into the exercise routine whenever possible; it provides multisensory stimulation through rhythm, drama, dance, and music.
4. Experiment with the inclusion of innovations such as Tai Chi Chuan to improve balance and grace and yoga to improve breathing and relaxation.

Complementary activities

The following are complementary activities that offer older persons opportunities for physical exercise. Programming hints pertaining to each activity are provided.

SWIMMING. Swimming has a number of special qualities. Exercising in the water can be easier because the water provides some support, while resisting an older person's movements to increase the workout. Swimming is relaxing yet involves all major muscle groups. For too many older persons it is an activity vigorously enjoyed in childhood but reduced during the middle and later years to a "quick dip" on a hot, summer afternoon.

A swimming program for older persons should consider:

1. *Consultation with the physician* to determine if the program being proposed is too vigorous for the older person in his or her care
2. *Facility design* such as clean and well-equipped dressing and shower rooms, handrails and slide-resistant floor stripping for easy access into and out of the pool, and capacity to keep the water temperature between 82 and 90 degrees (However, prolonged or excessive use of a heated pool can affect the ability to regulate the body temperature.)
3. *Publicity* such as films, demonstrations, and workshops to introduce the program
4. *Staff* such as certified lifeguards, leaders aware of the physical limitations of the participants, and use of older persons as leaders if possible
5. *Programming* such as a 15-minute warm-up period, exercises (e.g., leg thrash, knees drawn up to chest and stretched out, and rhythmical clapping) and a half hour of free swim or movement
6. *Scheduling* during times when children and adolescents are not using the facility to avoid noise

CYCLING. Cycling can be both an individual and a group exercise program. A stationary bicycle exerciser allows an older person to exercise at his or her convenience but does require knowledge of exerciser operation and placement of the exerciser in an attractive and conveniently located area. A biking group or club may be organized for those older persons interested in such a group experience. Some programming suggestions for organizing a bicycle group or club are:

1. The agency may want to purchase or seek donations for the purchase of bicycles for those older persons who do not own a bike or who cannot afford to buy one.
2. It is important to conduct an informational seminar or workshop to provide information on the benefits of biking, bike safety, and bike use.
3. Registration should be kept open so that new persons can join at a later time; the success of the program should result in new enrollees.
4. All enrollees should be evaluated on their riding skills and their knowledge of bike safety.
5. Leaders should have a sound knowledge of the maintenance and repair of bikes, as well as a knowledge of older persons' needs.
6. Riding routes should be planned to avoid major streets and include points of interest.
7. Distance tours and drive-ride tours are two program innovations that could be included as the program develops.

A cycling program suitable for institutionalized elderly was developed at the Veterans' Administration Medical Center in Butler, Pennsylvania (Frost, 1978). Fifteen residents (ages 50 to 90) from the nursing home unit (ambulatory care residents) were involved in a cycling program using four 26-inch adult tricycles donated by a volunteer service organization. The residents were instructed in proper riding techniques that could be practiced in the parking lot adjacent to the nursing home. Once the residents had mastered proper riding techniques, a scenic tricycle trail around the hospital grounds was developed. The program was run daily for 90 minutes under the supervision of a corrective therapist who monitored each older person. The program format was a break from the routine of clinic activities, got the residents outside, and was of benefit physiologically (increased muscle strength and endurance) and psychologically (emotional outlet for withdrawn and hyperactive individuals).

WALKING. Walking is another individual or group exercise program with many advantages. It is readily available, inexpensive, and can be done almost anytime. As a group activity, it can be organized in a variety of settings such as senior centers, planned community housing sites, and institutions. Programming suggestions for organizing a walking group or club are:

1. Informational meetings should be held to explain the benefits of a regularly scheduled walking program and the value of walking with a group. It should be stressed to prospective participants that for a walking group or club to be effective, older persons must view walking as a planned part of their daily routine.

2. Participants should not be required to pay registration fees or dues. Registration should be kept open for new members to join at anytime.

3. Walking should be out of doors in parks, along nature trails, or in shopping centers with enclosed walkways. Planned walking tours might be scheduled to places of special interest as an incentive.

4. Motivation for regular participation may be enhanced through a system of recording on a master sheet the dates, times, and places walked. Acknowledgment of achievements may be made through announcements, certificates, awards, and so on.

An innovative walking exercise program for older persons has been developed by Gamefield Concept Company.* The program involves a series of 15 pieces of equipment and instructional signs along a trail. The necessary walking stations may be located within a mile or more or in an area no larger than 30 by 40 feet. The walking exercise program was designed especially for older persons, with each station having three different exercise levels. Games are structured to provide warm-up, gradually increasing the activity level, and then cooling the body off through a gradual reduction in motion. The program is popular because it appeals to the need for improved fitness and health, while providing a novel walking game and social meeting place.

JOGGING. Jogging is increasing in popularity as older persons become more aware of the importance of physical fitness. Emphasis should be placed on physical fitness, but every effort should also be made to maximize social outcomes. Organizing a successful jogging program may be facilitated through the use of certain programming suggestions:

1. Medical approval and supervision are mandatory. A qualified and high-

---

*Gamefield Concept Company, 2088 Union Street, Suite One, San Francisco, 94123; (415) 563-2805.

ly respected physician can greatly assist with the promotion of this activity in an agency.

2. The program may be promoted through newsletter announcements, feature stories in newspapers, radio, television, and so on. An informational and planning meeting should be scheduled to answer the questions of prospective participants and to present the benefits of such a program.

3. It is important that older persons wear the correct clothing while jogging. Well-fitting socks, jogging shoes, and nonrestrictive clothing appropriate to the weather are a must.

4. Walking and jogging should be alternated, gradually increasing the proportion of jogging to walking. Many older persons jog 2 to 5 miles per day, but the distance for the beginner must be gradually increased while reactions are monitored. Calisthenics or other conditioning exercises should be added to the session because, although jogging is excellent for the circulatory system, it does not provide a balanced workout.

5. Consistent monitoring and evaluation will serve as a strong motivational force. Progress charts, achievement awards, public recognition, and so on are useful motivational techniques.

COMPETITIVE ATHLETICS AND GAMES. The Senior Olympics is one of the largest programs of athletics and games designed to promote physical fitness and competition through activities that meet the physical and social needs of older persons. There are several examples of Senior Olympic programs.

Illinois Senior Olympics. The Illinois Senior Olympics is an annual competition held in Springfield and cosponsored by the Springfield Recreation Department, the Illinois Governor's Council on Health and Fitness, and the Illinois Park and Recreation Association. The events draw about 500 participants annually, with at least 10 states sending delegates. Olympic events include swimming, tennis, track and field, handball, racquetball, road and sprint bike races, and a 6-mile run. Special events include miniature golf, horseshoes, shuffleboard, bowling, table tennis, badminton, archery, trap shooting, rope skipping, and basketball throwing.

Golden Olympics. The Golden Olympics is sponsored by the Virginia Recreation and Parks Society, the State Commission of Outdoor Recreation, and Blue Cross/Blue Shield of Virginia. It began in 1979 with 240 participants; events include track and field, tennis, 18-hole golf, a 10-kilometer run, a 1-mile walk-run, duck-pin and 10-pin bowling, and games such as bridge, croquet, checkers, chess, and pool. Age categories are 55 to 59, 60 to 64, 65 to 69, 70 to 74, 75 to 79, and 80 and over. There are separate divisions for men and women in all events except bridge, croquet, checkers, and chess.

Nursing home olympics. The nursing home olympics is a series of adapted sports and games organized to give nursing home residents the opportunity to compete against one another or against other nursing homes. An example of nursing home olympics was held in Houston, Texas with competitors from four nursing homes participating in horseshoes, frisbee throwing, bowling, darts, basketball tossing, watermelon-seed spitting, wheelchair racing, and croquet (Reed, 1979, pp. 7-9).

Evaluation

A variety of data on each exercise participant should be gathered and constantly updated. There should be a medical history that is periodically updated and reevaluated as the individual participates in a program. A record of medications should be taken and summarized in the form of a medication list that is readily available in the event of an emergency. All information should be considered confidential and filed in an individual folder for each participant.

The participants should be encouraged to take their pulse rates at the beginning, during, and immediately on ending the exercise session. The pulse is taken applying pressure with the fingers on the inside of the wrist. Pulse rate may be determined by taking the heart rate for 15 seconds and multiplying by 4 (adding a 0 to the number calculated). Pulse rate should be computed immediately on completion of the exercise session because the rate slows very quickly when exercising stops.

The exercise leader should be aware of the warning signs that may indicate excessive exercise. Reactions or symptoms may include:
1. Pain or tightness in the chest
2. Labored breathing or extreme breathlessness
3. Excessive perspiration
4. Dizziness, nausea, trembling, clumsy movements
5. Blueness in fingers and lips or lighter cast or pallor
6. Irregular heart rate, elevated heart rate, or failure of pulse to slow after exercise
7. A significant drop in blood pressure

If the reactions or symptoms increase in severity or persist, a physician should be contacted to evaluate the situation.

Each participant's progress may be monitored with specialized equipment and data sheets. Olson and White (1979, p. 55), reporting on an innovative sports and exercise program called RASCAL sponsored by the Rockville, Maryland Department of Recreation and Parks, refer to several pieces of equipment that were purchased to monitor participants' progress:
1. Scale (for taking accurate body weight)
2. Skin caliper (for measuring the fat content in the folds of the skin)
3. Fabric tape measures (for measuring the different body areas)
4. Skan-A-Graf (for evaluating posture)
5. Universal Goniometer (for measuring range of motion)
6. Pulse Minder (for taking pulse rates accurately and quickly)
7. Sphygmomanometer and stethoscope (for taking blood pressure)

Olson and White (1979, pp. 53-54) also mention a variety of data sheets for weight, daily food consumption, blood pressure, pulse rate, body measurement, body fat composition, posture, and range of joint motion. It is important to note that the types of specialized equipment and data sheets very much depend on the types of exercise programs being implemented. Photographs (before and after) and caloric expenditure charts according to activity may also be used.

SUMMARY

Research demonstrates that exercise has physiological and psychological benefits for older persons. Physiological benefits include increased flexibility and cardiovascular fitness for both community and institutionalized older persons. Psychological benefits have been particularly significant for institutionalized older persons who have shown improvement as measured by a variety of psychological tests.

The developer of an exercise program should consider a number of components. Supervision should be the responsibility of a person with the proper educational background, training, and experience in fitness and in working with older persons. Publicity through a variety of means is essential for informing older persons that an exercise program is being considered. Exercise should be scheduled on a regular basis, preferably daily for 15 to 30 minutes. The setting should be a room convenient and accessible with special equipment (e.g., chairs, exercise mats, and "props"). Certain precautions should be observed—for example, approval from the older person's personal physician or another physician should be obtained. Helping older persons motivate themselves can be done by instituting a formal education program, allowing them to experience the benefits of exercise, and fostering the social aspects of the experience. The types of exercise may focus on flexibility, muscle strength, and endurance, as well as cardiovascular fitness. The exercise sessions should be structured to provide for warming up and cooling off, for alternating between vigorous and less vigorous, and for individualizing and adapting. Complementary activities are swimming, cycling, walking, jogging, and competitive athletics and games. Each exercise participant should be evaluated thoroughly.

REFERENCES

Adams, G., and deVries, H.: Physiological effects of an exercise training regimen upon women ages 52 to 79, J. Gerontol. **28:** 50-55, 1973.

Aloia, J.: Exercise and skeletal health, J. Am. Geriatr. Soc. **29:** 104-107, 1981.

Blumenthal, J., and Williams, R.: Exercise and aging: the use of physical exercise in health enhancement, Center Reports on Advances in Research, Duke University Center for the Study of Aging and Human Development **6**(3):1-5, 1982.

Chapman, E., deVries, H., and Swezey, R.: Joint stiffness: effects of exercise on young and old men, J. Gerontol. **27:**218-221, 1972.

Crandall, R.: Gerontology: a behavioral approach, Reading, Mass., 1980, Addison-Wesley Publishing Co., Inc.

deVries, H.: Physiology effects of an exercise training regimen upon men ages 52 to 88, J. Gerontol. **25:**325-336, 1970.

deVries, H.: Exercise intensity threshold for improvement of cardiovascular-respiratory function in older men, Geriatrics **26:** 94-101, 1971.

deVries, H.: Fitness after fifty, J. Phys. Educ. **47:**47-49, 1976.

deVries, H.: Physiology of exercise and aging. In Woodruff, D., and Birren, J., editors: Aging: scientific perspectives and social issues, New York, 1975, D. Van Nostrand Co.

deVries, H.: Physiology of exercise for physical education and athletics, ed. 3, Dubuque, Iowa, 1980, Wm. C. Brown Co., Publishers.

Diesfeldt, H., and Diesfeldt-Groenendijk, H.: Improving cognitive performance in psychogeriatric patients: the influence of physical exercise, Age Aging **6:**58-64, 1977.

Frekany, G., and Leslie, D.: Effects of an exercise program on selected flexibility measurements of senior citizens, Gerontologist **15:**182-183, 1975.

Frost, G.: Adult tricycle program in a nursing home, Am. Correct. Ther. J. **32:**191, 1978.

Harris, R., and Frankel, L., editors: Guide to physical fitness after fifty, New York, 1977, Plenum Publishing Corp.

Leslie, D., and McLure, J.: Exercises for the elderly, Iowa City, Iowa, 1975, The University of Iowa.

Lesser, M.: Effects of rhythmic exercise on the range of motion in older adults, Am. Correct. Ther. J. **32:**118-122, 1978.

McEachern, M.: AHOY: add health to our years, Raleigh, N.C., 1980, M. McEachern.

McLure, J., and Leslie, D.: Guidelines for an exercise program leader for senior citizens, J. Health Phys. Educ. Recreat. **43:**72-73, 1972.

National Association for Human Development: Join the active people over 60! Washington, D.C., 1976, National Association for Human Development.

Olson, R., and White, J.: RASCAL: Rockville's seniors pep up with exercise, Parks Recreat. **14:**52-56, 96, 1979.

Powell, R.: Psychological effects of exercise therapy upon institutionalized geriatric mental patients, J. Gerontol. **29:**157-161, 1974.

Reed, P.: Nursing home olympics, Houston Chronicle, Texas Magazine, June 24, pp. 7-9, 1979.

Shivers, J., and Fait, H.: Recreational service for the aging, Philadelphia, 1980, Lea & Febiger.

Stamford, B.: Physiological effects of training upon institutionalized geriatric men, J. Gerontol. **27:**455, 1972.

Stamford, B.: Effects of chronic institutionalization on the physical working capacity and trainability of geriatric men, J. Gerontol. **28:**441-446, 1973.

Stamford, B., Hambacher, W., and Fallica, A.: Effects of daily physical exercise on the psychiatric state of institutionalized geriatric mental patients, Res. Q. **45:**34-41, 1974.

SUGGESTED READINGS

Harris, R., and Frankel, L., editors: Guide to physical fitness after fifty, New York, 1977, Plenum Publishing Corp.

McLure, J., and Leslie, D.: Guidelines for an exercise program leader for senior citizens, J. Health Phys. Educ. Recreat. **43:**72-73, 1972.

Mobily, K.: Physical activity and aging. In Teague, M., MacNeil, R., and Hitzhusen, G., editors: Perspective on leisure and aging in a changing society, Columbia, Mo., 1982, The University of Missouri.

9

Creative arts

Leisure service personnel are increasingly recognizing that older persons have creative ability, and as a consequence arts programs are being provided in environments in which creativity can flourish. Participation by older persons in arts programs of varying quality and scope is not new, but the emphasis on enhancing artistic and creative expression in older persons is new. Arts programs should no longer be considered just "busy work" or entertainment but an opportunity to have older persons share their lifetimes of experiences with others. This chapter examines research on arts and the elderly and the organization and management of arts programs.

Creativity in later life and the impact of arts on the elderly are the categories in which research on the arts and the elderly will be reviewed. Unfortunately, the literature in this area is contradictory and rather sparse.

RESEARCH ON ARTS AND THE ELDERLY

Research on creativity in later life is contradictory because of the difficulty in determining what creativity is and how it is measured. Lehman (1953, 1956, 1958, 1963), in a number of early studies on the relationship of creativity and age, examined individuals in the arts, sciences, and everyday life; he concluded that the greatest creative productivity occurred between the ages of 30 and 39, with a gradual decline in quality and quantity with increasing age. However, Dennis (1956a, 1956b, 1958, 1966) studied creative productivity between the ages of 20 and 80 by examining bibliographies of scholars and found that scholars were as productive in their 70s as in their 40s and were actually more productive in their 60s. Alpaugh and Birren (1977) found differences by age in divergent thinking, preferences for complexity, and transformations, suggesting that these may be explanations for the changes in creative contributions. In addition, they suggest that the Guilford Test of Creativity and the Barron-Welsh Art Scale may measure different aspects of creativity (the former measuring intellectual func-

Creativity in later life

tioning and creative problem solving, the latter measuring interest or motivation); thus creative productivity may be due to a decrease in one or more of these aspects of creativity.

There are numerous examples of creativity in older persons. McLeish (1976) has hundreds of examples of creative older persons who, just as Ulysses continued to make new voyages when he was advanced in years, continue to live creatively throughout life's journey.

Impact of arts on the elderly

Artistic endeavors have been shown to have a significant impact on older persons. Dawson and Baller (1972), in a study of the impact of oil painting on older persons (ages 65 to 89) and college students, found that the older persons exceeded the college students in measures of satisfaction and subjective ratings of performance; in a follow-up study of the older persons 11 years later 55 percent were still painting and 50 percent were involved in creative activities other than painting. Hospital Audiences, Inc. (1979) conducted an evaluation in 1976 of the impact of arts services (concerts and arts workshops) on 60 residents of skilled nursing facilities (SNFs), using a pre and post experimental research design. After 6 months of weekly concerts and twice weekly arts workshops, there was a significant increase in participation in formal activities by the residents in the treatment group; no significant change was found in the control group.

Older persons are generally an unrealized audience for the arts. The National Research Center on the Arts, Inc. (1975), as a result of a representative survey, classified an aggregate of 56 percent of the population 65 years of age or older as "cultural nonattenders" because during the preceding year only 5 percent had attended a live performance of ballet and/or modern dance, only 11 percent had attended a concert and/or opera performance, only 13 percent had attended live theater, and only 31 percent had been to an art museum. Johnson (1976), in a 1975 study of arts administrators (e.g., directors of art centers, managers of performing arts companies, and administrators of community programs) with 677 respondents from 49 states and the District of Columbia, found that:

1. Only 7 percent were directing their efforts to older persons, although 75 percent of the arts organizations were making efforts to build their audience.
2. Only 40 percent offered special rates to older persons, although 70 percent of those surveyed gave special ticket rates to students.
3. Arts administrators had difficulty orienting arts programming to older persons, with 60 percent perceiving the older audience as difficult to attract and 46 percent perceiving older persons as having more conservative tastes and being less willing to experiment with new art forms.
4. When the administrators did orient the programming toward older persons there was an emphasis on institutionalized older persons (be-

cause they were easier to reach) rather than the 95 percent of the elderly who live in the community.

5. When asked why they thought more older persons did not attend arts activities, administrators reported the major factors to be inadequate or inconvenient public transportation, reluctance to attend alone or go out at night, and ticket price or admission fee.

It may be concluded, based on the findings from the research on arts and the elderly, that:

1. Persons can and do live creatively throughout life.
2. Arts can have an immediate and long-term impact on older persons.
3. Older persons, as an unrealized audience for the arts, require systematic targeting of efforts and resources by arts administrators and programmers.

Arts programs for older persons are facilitated through systematic organization and management. This section will examine key components of arts programs—assessment, funding, staffing, site selection, programming, and evaluation.

ORGANIZATION AND MANAGEMENT OF ARTS PROGRAMS

An assessment must be made to determine the needs and interests of the community for arts programs. The success of the assessment will depend on the identification of available programs, determination of service gaps, and evaluation of needs and interests.

Assessment

IDENTIFICATION OF AVAILABLE PROGRAMS. Arts programs may already be available through a variety of community agencies. A systematic determination of available programs should be conducted in senior centers, nutrition sites, planned community housing, institutions, recreation centers, adult education programs, county extension programs, regional planning agencies (e.g., Area Agency on Aging), and colleges and universities. The types and quality of programs offered need to be identified at this early stage of the assessment process.

DETERMINATION OF SERVICE GAPS. Service gaps are determined by assessing approaches currently employed in arts programs. Service gaps may be uncovered by answering certain questions:

1. Are the programs intellectually accessible to older persons?
2. Are the programs age integrated or age segregated?
3. Are the programs offered in a variety of locations, or are they concentrated in a particular locale?
4. Are program costs shared by participants and agency or borne solely by the participants?
5. Will additional arts programs fill a need or interest of older persons for new or alternative experiences?

6. Will additional arts programs fill a community need or interest? The answers to these and similar questions will assist in the determination of service gaps.

EVALUATION OF NEEDS AND INTERESTS. The information compiled from the identification of available programs and determination of service gaps must now be evaluated. Analyses of needs and interests may result in the surfacing of specific needs and interests held by a large number of individuals or groups. An overwhelming consensus on needs and interests may emerge in some areas, whereas in other areas a divergence may be noticed. Meetings, workshops, and seminars involving older persons, administrators, practitioners, and the community at large should be called to rate and assign priorities to the needs and interests for eventual incorporation into a plan.

Funding

Arts programs may be funded from a variety of sources and may employ a number of strategies. This section will consider funding sources and strategies.

FUNDING SOURCES. Funding sources are found in both the public and private sectors. Public sector funding may include The National Endowment for the Arts, the Older Americans Act, Title XX of the Social Security Act, community development funds, and revenue sharing funds. Private funding includes community arts councils, United Way, and community service organizations.

The National Endowment for the Arts. The National Endowment for the Arts is an independent federal agency within the executive branch. It allocates fellowships to individual artists and grants to nonprofit arts organizations to be matched by funds from recipient arts organizations. The National Endowment has given grants to programs in the visual and performing arts, has funded technical assistance and consultation services through the National Council on the Aging's National Center on Arts and the Aging, and has encouraged its program directors to request and review grant proposals that include older persons.

The National Endowment for the Arts has a network of arts agencies in every state and trust territory (Appendix B). These arts agencies are part of the executive branch of state government and report to the governor. These state arts agencies also interact with community arts councils.

The Older Americans Act. The Older Americans Act (OAA) (Appendix F), first enacted in 1965, is not specifically mandated to fund arts programs for the aging, but its funds may be used for arts programs. OAA funds can come from the state office on aging (Appendix A) through a direct grant or through an Area Agency on Aging (AAA) to purchase services or make grants to senior centers, community action agencies, local government units, and other organizations.

Title XX of the Social Security Act. Title XX of the Social Security Act provides social services for all age groups to enable individuals to be as independent, self-sufficient, and economically self-supporting as possible. The state agencies responsible for social services (e.g., Department of Human Resources and Department of Public Welfare) administer the program and must develop an annual state plan specifying the age groups to be served and the types of services to be provided. The federal law and regulations dealing with social services do not directly refer to the arts, but the arts can support social services by helping clients achieve social service goals.

Community development funds. The federal department of Housing and Urban Development (HUD) administers community development funds through a local community development corporation. Local communities use these resources for architectural preservation, renovation, or construction of buildings. Art centers, theaters, and so on could qualify for such funding.

Revenue sharing funds. Revenue sharing funds are distributed by the federal government to local governments for community projects. Local governments have flexibility in use of funds, but public hearings must be held to determine local funding priorities. According to federal guidelines, supplying services to older persons is one of the ten areas of priority.

Community arts councils. Community arts councils are important local resources for funding at the city and county level. There are approximately 2,000 community arts councils in small, medium, and large cities and counties across the United States. These councils may have limited financial resources but can serve as a valuable resource for contacting local artists.

United Way. The United Way raises funds from local communities for local projects consistent with community priorities. Active personal involvement and participation in artistic pursuits is one of the United Way funding areas relevant to arts programs for the elderly.

Community service organizations. Community service organizations can be found in almost all areas. Fraternal organizations, unions, garden clubs, and other influential organizations can help provide financial resources and develop awareness of arts needs in the community.

FUNDING STRATEGIES. Two major issues facing arts programs are the development of multiple funding sources and long-term support. Funding strategies to address these issues will be discussed.

Multiple funding sources. A partnership should be formed between community arts resources and the state arts agency. A local arts council may have limited monetary resources, but it may know where the arts and artists are and which artists are interested in working with older persons. Local resources may be joined to develop a pilot program with funding sought from the state arts agency and The National Endowment for the Arts.

A partnership should likewise be developed between community arts resources and the local AAA and state office on aging. The area agency should be contacted to determine its funding and planning cycle so that a bid for support can be made. Funding requests may be presented to the advisory council of the AAA at public hearings, with groundwork being laid before the hearings in the form of constituent support and documentation from a needs analysis of the older population. Each AAA is required by law to submit an annual area plan to the state as a proposal for the upcoming program year. Any proposals for funding under Title III of the Older Americans Act require matching funds.

Matching grants encourage private, foundation, and corporate support for the arts. Matching grants may require a dollar for dollar match or only 10 percent local money to gain 90 percent outside support. An in-kind match of time, space, and other resources rather than money may also be allowed. The requirement of a match facilitates the development of multiple funding sources so that when federal or state funds are removed a substantial base of long-term support remains.

Long-term support. Community and local private funding are the most permanent and easiest to obtain for long-term support of arts programs for the elderly. Community and local long-term support may be in-kind (e.g., space for programs and instructional assistance from volunteers) and logistical (e.g., transportation), which may be donated more readily than money. Community arts councils, United Way, community service organizations, community colleges, the Chamber of Commerce, industries, and local foundations should all be evaluated for their potential support and funding either directly or through in-kind contributions.

Staffing

One of the most difficult tasks in the organization and management of an arts program for older persons is the selection and training of staff. This section discusses the process of selection and training of arts staff.

SELECTION. The first step in the selection of an arts staff is the identification of potential staff members. A letter containing a brief statement of the proposed program should be sent to local arts councils and art educators, local college and university arts personnel, state arts agencies, and national organizations (e.g., National Art Education Association, The Alliance for Art Education, the American Association for Retired Persons, and the National Center on Arts and the Aging of the National Council on the Aging). Arts agencies are a particularly valuable resource for staff identification because they are familiar with the qualifications and experience of artists in the local area, state, or region. Many arts agencies have newsletters and regular meetings that can serve as vehicles for communication. Artists themselves can spread the news by word-of-mouth that a program is being organized.

The selection of staff should be based on the needs of the program and the qualifications of the individual applicants. Community Programs in the Arts and Sciences (COMPAS) of St. Paul, Minnesota (COMPAS, 1976, p. 9) suggests some major qualifications:

1. A professional background in the arts
2. Demonstrated responsibility in previously held positions
3. Openness to new and different art forms as demonstrated through innovative work
4. Open-mindedness and adaptability in new circumstances
5. Ability to establish rapport with others
6. Interest in working with older persons

Prospective staff should be asked to provide resumes containing a record of

EXAMPLE 9-1

SAMPLE CONTRACT

The following is an understanding of our agreement.

You, the artist, will provide classes in _____ to senior citizens. These classes will take place in a twice weekly residency at the site to which you are assigned. You will be present at that location a minimum of _____ hours per week.

In concert with the classes, you will plan outings, field trips, and other special events germane to your art form.

Records will be kept for the purpose of documenting the total program, and at the end of the program year you will assist in the evaluation.

The period for which these services will be rendered will be from _____ _____ through _____ .

You will be paid at a rate of _____ per hour.

If the aforementioned stipulations are not adhered to, this contract may be declared null and void.

If you agree, please sign and return one copy.

_____	_____
Artist	Program director
_____	_____
Date	Date

From COMPAS: Artists and the aging, St. Paul, 1976, Community Programs in the Arts and Sciences, p. 10.

---

training and accomplishments; representative examples of their work (if possible); and recommendations from previous work sites, teachers, and other artists. They should be interviewed by the program administrator, who should pay particular attention to artistic dedication and openness to working with older persons.

The artists selected by the agency should have a contract specifying the responsibilities and the payment for their services (Example 9-1). The salary determination may be based on data gathered from the local school board, arts agency, and consultation with local artists.

TRAINING. Arts staff should be familiar with the aging process, a variety of art forms, and the arts program. An introduction to gerontology should include information on the biological, psychological, and social aspects of aging presented in an initial orientation and through in-service education sessions after staff have had some work experience with older persons. Hoffman (1980, p. 11) stresses the need for staff members who are unfamiliar with particular forms of art "to be guided to an understanding of music, drama, the visual arts, dance, and creative writing." Staff should understand the philosophy, goals, objectives, and organization of the arts program in an attempt to equip staff with an appreciation of the program's direction and constraints. Regular staff meetings on a weekly or bimonthly basis can serve as an opportunity for further training through problem solving and sharing successes and failures.

Site selection

A successful arts program with older persons depends not only on the competence of the arts staff but also on the sites selected for the programs. This section will examine some of the issues involved in site selection.

The first step in site selection for arts programs is the preparation of a comprehensive list of possible sites. Agencies working in the area can be of assistance in identifying programs for older persons currently operating in senior centers, planned community housing, institutions, and programs operated by schools, churches, and voluntary agencies.

Selection of sites from this comprehensive list should be based on the consideration of certain criteria. COMPAS (1976, pp. 14-15) mentions a number of criteria that should be considered.

GEOGRAPHICAL DISTRIBUTION. Consideration should be given to areas with a high density of older persons or sites available to the largest number of participants.

SOCIOECONOMIC DIVERSITY. The program should enable older persons of a variety of incomes and educational backgrounds to participate.

PHYSICAL STRUCTURE. The physical structure of the site should be considered from the standpoint of both the elderly and the arts staff. Accessibility issues for older persons to be considered include proximity to transportation, availability of wheelchair ramps and good walkways, and acceptable toilet facilities. The arts staff need facilities that may be programmed for the particular art forms under consideration.

SUITABILITY OF SITE TO PROGRAM. The site may have certain characteristics that make it unsuitable for arts programming. Existing arts programs may be well established so that a new program would simply be a duplication. The site may be open only a limited number of hours per week or the schedule may not permit the inclusion of another regular program.

INTEREST. Interest at sites is vital for program success. Persons familiar with the sites should be consulted to determine the extent of true interest. The assessment of true interest should consider certain factors mentioned by COMPAS (1976, pp. 12-13):

1. *Staff support at the site,* which may be expressed through staff willingness to encourage older persons to participate and to help the frail elderly get to arts programs
2. *Inclusion of artists in site staff meetings,* which serves to make site and arts staff aware of one another's problems
3. *Outreach by an area coordinator,* who would help locate and encourage new participants—an important indicator of the interest in program growth

4. *Informal talks at the site between artists and the elderly,* which foster the development of relationships, enable the sharing of goals and interests, and provide an opportunity for informal evaluation
5. *Publicity,* which involves assessing the commitment to publicize the program in a variety of site and community media

This section will discuss a number of arts programs and approaches to the delivery of these programs.

Programming

VISUAL ARTS. Arts and crafts programs are a popular form for presenting the visual arts to older persons in a variety of leisure service settings. The quality of these programs is frequently criticized because of the lack of trained staff or volunteers. This section will describe programs in ceramics, fabrics, sculpture, photography and filmmaking, and drawing and painting.

Ceramics. The Center for Arts and Humanities Programming for the Elderly at the University of South Carolina (Hoffman, 1980) used the Japanese ceramic technique of Raku to help motivate older persons to participate in arts programs. The center's potter, as a result of 3 months of curriculum experimentation, developed a series of three Raku workshops. Each participant produced two ceramic pieces (a coil pot or container and a thrown-slab bottle) during the first two sessions; during the third session the pieces were glazed and fired. The advantages of Raku are the speed with which it can be formed, decorated, and fired and the high percentage of success—all of which contribute to a feeling of competence (Hoffman, 1980, pp. 18-19).

Fabrics. Many older persons have produced fabric-oriented art through sewing, knitting, crocheting, needlepointing, quilting, and rug hooking. Older persons have recently become involved in making and marketing fabric items such as quilts, afghans, potholders, embroidered towels, pillowcases, macrame items, handmade doll clothes, and baby clothes (Example 9-2).

Fabric design (weaving) and decoration (batik) were introduced to older persons in a four-session workshop titled "Creative Fabric Design and Decoration," which was developed by the Center for Arts and Humanities Programming for Elderly at the University of South Carolina (Hoffman, 1980, p. 19).

Session 1. Participants build the frame loom, string the warp, and begin weaving. Background information on the weaving and batik processes is presented in lectures, slide presentations, and demonstrations.

Session 2. Participants continue their weaving activities during this session. All participants are encouraged to work on weaving between sessions 2 and 3.

Session 3. Participants remove finished weaving from the loom and wax out the batik design.

Session 4. Participants remove the wax from the batik after the dyeing, add wax, and dye a second and third time to finish the batik.

Sculpture. Sculpture for older persons can serve a number of objectives. It can provide the experience of working in three dimensions, especially important

EXAMPLE 9-2

PRAIRIE PEOPLES' HANDICRAFT MARKET, INC.

Sponsor: Prairie Peoples' Handicraft Market, Inc., Armour, South Dakota, 57313, (605) 724-2404.

Project director: Judy Winter, Chair, Board of Directors, Parkston, South Dakota, 57366, (605) 928-3937.

Dates/history: The market was organized in 1971 by a group of women interested in selling handicrafts. The organization has received grants in the past but for the most part is self-supporting. This is done by selling items placed in the store on a commission-only basis. No craft items are bought outright.

Role of sponsoring organization: Prairie People received advisory help in organizing the group from a South Dakota agency, South Central Community Action, which helps low-income people through government funding. They also arranged a small grant to initially aid the new organization financially.

Objectives: The objectives of the Prairie People are to: (1) provide a market for handicraft producers; (2) keep alive the knowledge of age-old crafts such as crocheting, quilting, knitting and ceramics; (3) aid the elderly and handicapped through the sale of their crafts; and (4) give the elderly and low-income people pride in their work.

Content: Prairie Peoples' Handicraft Market, Inc. was formed to become a permanent organization. It is incorporated in the state of South Dakota as a nonprofit organization and is tax-exempt. A gift shop is open six days a week to sell the handmade crafts. The majority of these crafts are made by senior citizens who also operate the business as clerks and administrative personnel. The project is unique in South Dakota. To present knowledge, there is not another craft producing and marketing organization like it in the state.

Participants: The organization was formed for anyone interested in producing and marketing their crafts, though the elderly and low-income people have been specifically encouraged to join. Several years ago, some native Americans participated. There are a few younger people involved in the group because of their keen interest in furthering the organization. The number of participants in the group over the years has varied from 28 to 150. They were recruited through advertising, word-of-mouth, and members.

From The arts, the humanities and older Americans: a catalogue of program profiles, 1981, published by The National Council on the Aging, Inc., pp. 5-6.

EXAMPLE 9-2,
cont'd

Sites: During its ten-year existence, the market has opened three stores in different locations. Two were closed due to poor locations and poor communications caused by a great distance from the main store in Armour. All three stores had separate managers supervised by the Board of Directors. The group annually rents a booth at the Sioux Empire Fair in Sioux Falls and the South Dakota State Fair in Huron. Bazaars are held several times a year at shopping malls in Mitchell, Parkston and Yankton, South Dakota.

Organizational structure: All staff are part-time and volunteer; only the bookkeeper receives some compensation. The organization's business is conducted by an 8-member board of directors through monthly meetings. The board chairman is responsible for taking care of business between meetings. The Armour store has a manager who runs the store and supervises the workers in it. No professional people are involved in the group. It is run exclusively by volunteers using on-the-job experience and common sense. The board of directors is made up of homemakers, a retired farmer, a former teacher and a minister's wife.

Operation: The only cost to participants is a yearly membership fee and the cost of his or her craft supplies.

Products: There are many beautiful handmade items in the store such as quilts, afghans, potholders, embroidered towels, pillowcases, macrame items, ceramics, magnetics, handmade doll clothes and baby clothes. Two cookbooks have been published: *Favorite Recipes of the Prairie People,* Books I and II.

Publicity: Advertising is done through local and area publications.

Evaluation: Evaluation of the business is done primarily through monthly and year-end financial and membership reports.

Funding: A $40,000 grant was received from the Campaign for Human Development in 1975 and a $2,000 grant was awarded by the Gannett Foundation in 1978.

Contact persons: Emma Lehrkamp, corresponding secretary, Delmont, South Dakota, 57330; or Judy Winter, Chair, Board of Directors, Parkston, South Dakota, 57366.

Thea Lorin Breite

Woodcarving is a group activity that may be engaged in by both men and women.

for many older persons who may not have had this experience. Social interaction may be provided while individuals are learning about materials and techniques. Another important channel for the expression of feelings about self may be opened, with a consequent impact on self-concept.

Hoffman (1980, pp. 20-21) outlines an eight-session workshop sequence on sculpture.

Sessions 1 and 2: Introduction to sculpture. The process of forming, decorating, and dressing a modeled puppet is used to communicate the concepts of mass, roundness, and positive and negative spaces.

Session 3: Clay modeling of people. The three basic handbuilding techniques are explored through clay modeling to teach modeling and art as communication.

Session 4: Plaster-relief casting into ceramic forms. The process of ceramic modeling provides experience in relief design and casting as a relief form is developed.

Sessions 5 and 6: Cardboard, paper, and wood construction. Woodworking tools, glues, and joining techniques that employ scraps of cardboard, paper, and wood are used to construct sculptured forms of differing complexity and size.

Sessions 7 and 8: Carving. Carving tools are used to produce a form from wood, stone, fire brick, salt blocks, and clay/plaster conglomerates.

This introduction to sculpture will not provide the depth for older persons who have previous experience or those who want to more fully explore any of the areas of modeling, casting, construction, and carving (Hoffman, 1980, p. 21).

Photography and filmmaking. Photography and filmmaking offer older persons a variety of experiences. Through the communicative, creative, and reproductive nature of photography and filmmaking, an older person may better understand self, put past and present in a proper perspective, and respond to the environment and its relation to self.

Hoffman (1980, pp. 21-22) suggests that an introductory filmmaking experience encompass 10 sessions during a 3- to 4-week period.

Session 1. The introduction to film and filmmaking should include a presentation of historically important films, various filmmaking experiences, and techniques of filmmaking. A description of subsequent workshop sessions should also be presented.

Session 2. A description of the stages in filmmaking includes the following stages: *conceptualization* (documentary and planned narrative, an introduction to the storyboard); *shooting* (the use of film, a definition and an explanation of terms such as *zoom* and *pan*); *editing* (relationship of editing to storyboarding, including the definitions of scenes, sequencing, and cutting); *sound* (synchronization, the concept of postdubbing of a soundtrack); *final phase* (explanation of advanced preparation needed before final laboratory printing can be attempted). The instructor should have the demonstrations and equipment ready and arranged to allow participants the opportunity to use the techniques explained in this session. Participants must be able to immediately use the techniques presented and be able to shoot films.

Session 3. Participants use the camera and develop technical expertise in areas such as storyboards and wide-angle and close-up shots with pan and zoom lenses.

Session 4. Footage shot by both individuals or small groups and the determination of shooting schedules are developed.

Sessions 5 through 8. Footage is reviewed, shooting and reshooting of scenes continues, and material is initially edited to conform to the storyboard.

Sessions 9 and 10. The final versions of films are shown, the films are analyzed, sound is synchronized, and arrangements are made for the final printing.

Two photography and filmmaking projects involving older persons have received national attention. Example 9-3 presents HISTOP: History-Sharing Through Our Photographs, an intergenerational sharing of family photographs. Example 9-4 describes a New Jersey filmmaking project.

Drawing and painting. Drawing and painting need to encompass both
Text continued on p. 208.

EXAMPLE 9-3

HISTOP: HISTORY-SHARING THROUGH OUR PHOTOGRAPHS

Sponsors: (for the original HISTOP) The Mature Minglers, Bloomfield Hills, Michigan; Royal Oak Senior Citizens Center, Royal Oak, Michigan; Way Elementary School, Bloomfield Hills, Michigan, and Jefferson Elementary School, Royal Oak, Michigan.

Project director: Nancy Rosen, 1910 Torquay, Royal Oak, Michigan, 48073.

Dates/history: HISTOP I took place in March and April of 1979 and involved two communities in Oakland County, Michigan. HISTOP II and HISTOP III were done by other Michigan communities in 1980. The year 1981 will see more programs initiated in Detroit, Flint and Ann Arbor. HISTOP can be done with a minimum of funds. All that is needed for the project to be continued is senior citizens, children and family photographs.

Role of sponsoring organizations: The senior citizens groups and schools that sponsored HISTOP I were involved in the project through notifying potential participants (children and seniors), providing staff (one teacher per school and one liaison from each senior center), publicizing HISTOP via flyers/newsletters, and advising the project director. HISTOP incorporates the senior centers' desire to create stimulating activities for their members which bring them in contact with the community.

Objectives: HISTOP was created to serve as an intergenerational sharing of history through the family photograph, and to teach both old and young the importance of photographs as historical documents. In China people retire as early as 55 years of age and often are placed in schools as roving historians, teaching local history from their own experiences. The creators of HISTOP felt this sort of activity was needed in American society, as many families are often separated due to our society's mobile nature.

Content: HISTOP I was a five-week program designed to give both seniors and children a way of learning and having a good time together. The culmination of HISTOP is the Sharing Sessions where the seniors share their lives with the children through photos and the children share theirs with the seniors through Photo Family Trees they have made in school. It is important that all participants are actively involved in the completion of their respective projects.

Participants: Initially, HISTOP was done with senior center members and children in public and private schools. HISTOP III recruited seniors through the Muskegon County Historical Museum. In 1981, HISTOP at the Detroit Historical Museum will use senior citizen volunteers (50% Black) and Detroit Girl Scouts. In the Lansing area, an Hispanic women's organization will sponsor HISTOP as a consciousness-raising vehicle for their children in the summer of 1981.

From The arts, the humanities and older Americans: a catalogue of program profiles, 1981, published by The National Council on the Aging, Inc., pp. 14-15.

EXAMPLE 9-3,
cont'd

Sites: HISTOP I utilized schools and senior centers belonging to the four sponsoring organizations as sites. Subsequent HISTOPs were and will be done in historical museums and other public buildings. All program space is donated, and in the case of HISTOP I represented matching funds in the grant.

Organizational structure: HISTOP I had a project director, photographer, two project consultants and an exhibit consultant. Only the photographer and one project consultant received grant money; the others contributed their services. Volunteers were given an orientation by the project director. Subsequent HISTOPs have been done with a minimum of personnel.

Operation: HISTOP is a simple, flexible project that can vary according to the needs and facilities of the sponsoring groups. There is no cost to the participants.

Products: Products have included: (1) the HISTOP traveling exhibit; (2) the Corbet Family Mystery, an exercise in the importance of labeling family photographs; (3) Photofile workshops, free photopreservation workshops; (4) "Mildred, Danielle and WWII," a 14-minute video documentary; and (5) the HISTOP manual, which will be available in June 1981.

Publicity: HISTOP has been the subject of many articles, both in local newspapers and state publications. An article on HISTOP will appear in *History News* in 1981 as a result of the American Association of State and Local History awarding a certificate of commendation to the project director. HISTOP has been featured on television in Detroit and Grand Rapids, and the project director has led radio programs on the project in Detroit and Lansing.

Dissemination/replication: Lectures on HISTOP have been part of seminars at the University of Michigan Institute of Gerontology and at Michigan State University. The HISTOP exhibit often serves as a stimulus for those who see it to initiate their own HISTOP programs.

Evaluation: The Michigan Council for the Humanities evaluator, a professor of history at Michigan State University, concluded his summary of HISTOP thus: "As an observer, I got the sense that the modest sum of state funds were well spent, in that they promoted intergenerational and intercultural understanding. It is marvelous that a project of this sort is now conceived as part of the public role of the humanities." The evaluations of other humanists and educators will appear as appendices to the HISTOP manual.

Funding: HISTOP I was done with a mini-grant ($1100) from the Michigan Council for the Humanities, most of it going to the photographer and exhibit construction. Subsequent HISTOPs have been done with no special funding.

Contact: Nancy Rosen, HISTOP, address given above.

EXAMPLE 9-4

NEW JERSEY FILMMAKING PROJECT

The purpose of the project was to encourage older people to begin communicating in the visual language of films—to explore the elderly's potential for learning in a highly technical field, and to provide them with an opportunity for self-expression by first heightening their awareness of the environment, and then training them to capture their unique views of it on film.

The New Jersey Institute for Film Art, in cooperation with the Bergen County Office on Aging, was given a grant in October 1969 by the state unit on aging to help this pilot effort get off the ground. The funds paid for film and the hiring of a professional staff. Companies in the cinematic equipment field made some contributions of cameras, film, processing and editing equipment. Students built a copying stand, a rear projection screen and a motorized device for making titles. A facility was furnished by the Board of Chosen Freeholders, County of Bergen, through the Bergen County Office on Aging. The New Jersey Institute for Film Art and the Bergen County Extension Service provided in-kind services.

Design of course

Classes met every Thursday from 9:30 A.M. to 3:30 P.M. for three ten-week periods. The methodology encompassed lectures and demonstrations on filmmaking equipment; individual and small group activities in filmmaking; class discussions of ideas and goals of specific film projects; individual and small group practice sessions on technology; film viewing; film discussion and film appreciation sessions including role studies of the director, cameraman, editor, etc.

From Sunderland, J.: Older Americans and the arts: a human equation, 1976, published by The National Council on the Aging, Inc., pp. 23-24.

technique and personal creativity. Traditionally drawing and painting classes for older persons run by leisure service personnel have focused on technique through numbered paintings, copying landscapes, and realistic portrayals of people. Drawing and painting must be extended beyond technique to include creative abilities, thus allowing older persons to give expression to their creative impulses.

Hoffman (1980, p. 23) discusses the components of an eight-session drawing and painting workshop series. Such a series should include a presentation on the major schools in an effort to show the multiplicity of acceptable expressions. Techniques should be introduced and demonstrated, materials should be examined for their possibilities (e.g., oil crayons, watercolors, char-

EXAMPLE 9-4,
cont'd

The professional staff and volunteers

The professional staff consisted of the project director (founder of the New Jersey Institute for Film Art, who was the Rutgers University Community Development Specialist for Bergen County and a member of the Bergen County Office on Aging Education Committee), the instructor (a professor of Fine Arts at Montclair State College), and the program coordinator (the executive secretary of the New Jersey Institute for Film Art). Volunteers were recruited and trained to assist the project coordinator in facilitating group formation and group process.

Students

Fourteen persons—average age 70—were recruited through newspaper releases and the Bergen County Office on Aging. Recruitment was difficult because enrollment in the course required a commitment to attend the weekly all-day session for 30 weeks. The group that eventually emerged was composed of men and women from various backgrounds—most of whom were strangers both to each other, and to the world of the camera.

By April 1970, when the project came to an end, several films had been completed and 14 film devotees had been born. Half the group's members are still engaged in film-making: all of them have expressed a desire to continue seeking an opportunity to work with 16 mm equipment and to share their new skills and enthusiasm with others.

The essential ingredients for a successful project are the commitment of students, and the dedication of an instructor who can give the group the confidence to change and grow in this new medium.

The Bergen County Office on Aging and the New Jersey Institute for Film Art are available as a resource for information and assistance to those interested in setting up such a program.

coal, tempera, and pastels), and approaches should be discussed to encourage creativity.

Drawing and painting can play a vital role in an institutional setting such as a nursing home. Example 9-5 presents the experiences of an artist-in-residence at a nursing home, and Example 9-6 describes the Palmcrest Senior Eye Gallery, a display area for drawings and paintings.

MUSIC. Leisure service specialists tend to provide rudimentary musical experiences for older persons because they accept the belief that musical talent must be developed early in life. All too often older persons are exposed to vocal groups that sing the old favorites or entertain others through performances of a kitchen band. These experiences do not increase older persons' understanding

Text continued on p. 215.

EXAMPLE 9-5

ARTIST-IN-RESIDENCE AT A NURSING HOME

The Nursing Home is a large (300 bed) medical care institution. Most of the residents are lower income, predominantly white with small minorities of Indian and Black. Most of the people whom I had contact were physically and/or mentally deteriorated. Many are confined to wheel chairs, or have parts of their bodies numbed by strokes, or have poor eyesight, or are senile and disoriented, incontinent, have tremors or multiple sclerosis.

I would say that it took five months to get the art program firmly started, to create the trust and rapport with individuals to get it across that doing drawing and painting is something viable for them, that it is worthwhile, fulfilling, and enjoyable. In the beginning I held art sessions, and few people came. What I think got things rolling was my going door to door, talking to individuals. A few started coming, others started observing; the program became more and more visible to residents and staff alike. Some residents were willing to try their hand the first time that they came; others needed time to observe what was going on. Almost everyone had to be talked into trying it. In the beginning, "I can't draw a straight line," "I can't see as well as I used to," and "My hand is crippled from my stroke" were common retorts. I worked hard at trying to convince people that they could still do some form of drawing despite their infirmities. It wasn't a matter of coddling their infirmities, but helping them use what they had. This was (and is) a hard battle to fight because the reason that most of the residents at the Nursing Home are there is to be treated for their infirmities. To the medical staff, for example, B. is first the woman on GHI with a colostomy problem and H. is the multiple sclerosis patient on JKL. I think the reason why many staff members have expressed surprise that I could do something with some of the residents, is because they saw residents as their infirmities, rather than for their potential and energy they still have.

In a place like the Nursing Home, I believe that in order to make a program go, everyone on the staff, from housekeeping to administration, should know what's going on. If people are informed, they aren't threatened or suspicious, and everyone's combined positive energy really helps. Having a good rapport with the staff was important. Administration, nursing, social service, activities, dietary, maintenance, physical therapy, pharmacy, and housekeeping all collaborated at some time to realize the program. When I first came to the Home there was an Activities Director who had obviously made up her mind before I even stepped into the Home, that the program wasn't going to work. Her negativity affected not only my program. When she was replaced in December by a woman who was behind what I was trying to do, my program took a real upward swing. While I never was an extension of the Activities Department, we were able to collaborate for both of our benefits. The Activities Program now helped me to get residents to the art sessions—prior to this I was wheeling everybody there myself (a

From COMPAS: Artists and the aging, St. Paul, 1976, Community Programs in the Arts and Sciences, pp. 49-53.

EXAMPLE 9-5,
cont'd

strenuous and time consuming task which cut into my preparation of material time). Also, the Activities Program collaborated on the art show opening party in January, on field trips, and in helping to get the bulletin boards up to be used as resident gallery space.

It took a while for me to find a workable form and schedule. I didn't know what or whose needs I was going to try to meet. Deciding to meet on Thursdays and Saturdays and whether or not to meet with the MNO residents (the most severely impaired patients) separately or with the rest of the nursing home residents, were elements of my involvement which took some time to evolve. I chose to come in on Saturdays because the home was much quieter, with less hustle and bustle. The only activity on weekends is church. So Saturday seemed a natural to me. I felt the residents were much more relaxed. After I had a regular group coming to the twice weekly art sessions, I did not have the time to meet with as many people individually. I had to draw the line on who it was I wanted to teach. There were a couple that I chose to meet with outside of the regular session, both of whom had very different needs from the main group of art session goers.

Theft of supplies was a problem at the nursing home. But it wasn't just art supplies that were sometimes missing from resident's rooms. The main bulk of supplies were locked up. I think the size of the Home made it more conducive for such things to happen.

The Nursing Home was my first experience in teaching adults. I learned that it takes a while to get people away from their conventional preconceptions of art, to have them accept their own artistic manifestations as valid, whether they touched on realism or not.

I liked it when my role as artist-in-residence extended beyond my role as teacher during the art session. The art exhibit, including the opening party in January, which also included entertainment and a couple of films that I showed to any residents who wanted to come, were ways of reaching more people than just those who chose to participate actively in drawing and painting. I used the bulletin boards not only to encourage the residents who produced art work, but also for those who might just gain enjoyment from viewing them. I also hoped that I was able to convey an atmosphere surrounding the art sessions which made it possible for residents who chose not to participate actively, to observe what was going on.

For those residents that I dealt with who had multiple sclerosis, I came upon some helpful resources. The Multiple Sclerosis Society was able to foot the bill for an easel for H. so he could paint with a mouth stick in bed. Also the Physical Therapy department at the University of Minnesota was very helpful in giving me an initial exposure to mouth sticks and their use.

Planning a field trip is quite an endeavor, especially when you're transporting people who are in wheelchairs. A bus with a lift must be hired. In this city, these buses are primarily used for school children and runs for senior citizens

Continued.

**EXAMPLE 9-5,
cont'd**

ARTIST-IN-RESIDENCE AT A NURSING HOME

must be arranged between school time use. The destination of a field trip must have certain facilities: wheelchair ramps, elevators, and bathroom stalls large enough for wheelchairs to be brought in. Escorts are another consideration. My experience is that for a dozen residents with six or seven in wheelchairs, five escorts are necessary. One of these escorts should be a nursing staff person. Also, expect to not have everyone go that says they are going. You never know who's going to go on a field trip until the bus is loaded and on its way. This might seem self-evident, but I don't think I comprehended what it took to get a field trip off before I did it. When dealing with an institution like the Home, special arrangements for meals and medication must be requested beforehand. Some residents must get an O.K. from their doctor in order to go outside the Home.

For the most part, our painting and drawing projects were intended as one session endeavors. I often did a series of sessions using the same media or techniques, or following a similar theme. For example: several sessions using brush and ink in various ways; or a landscape series, or a still life series. Sometimes I would have a session where it was much less structured, when each person had to choose what tools they wanted to use and what they wanted to draw or paint with. This was difficult for many, who basically wanted something to plug into. Some considered it too much work to have to make those kinds of decisions. But as time went on, this became easier and easier for more people. Otherwise, I would set specific materials and tools out beforehand.

Besides drawing from objects—plants, shells, kitchen utensils and shop tools, still lifes and leaves—I also used pictures from the public library picture file as a resource for ideas—butterflies, birds, animals—to demonstrate, through examples, artist's differences in styles. Besides using different *kinds* of paper as a source of inspiration for a drawing, different shaped and size paper can also spur the imagination. Other projects that worked out well were craypas resist drawings, and placing a section of a magazine picture on a piece of paper and having each person extend the photograph with a drawing.

I tried doing some collage, most of which I wasn't satisfied with (many were having difficulty with the scissors). The Valentines we made were basically collage and they worked out.

Drawing from life is hard for anyone, no matter what age. I saw it being frustrating for many, but I'm glad that I kept coming back to it, because relative ease developed and it enabled us to move on to other things.

Sharing each others' drawings became an important part of the art sessions. It wasn't a critique period, but rather a showing time, a group supportive, sharing time. Criticism was usually something that was between me and one other person. Often others would pick up on something that I was trying to get across to someone sitting across from them or next to them.

EXAMPLE 9-5,
cont'd

One thing that I resisted for quite a while was the concept of collaborating with a resident to accomplish a drawing. I was hung up on the idea that all their drawings had to be their personal, individual statements, that I didn't want to impose myself on someone else. But one day I observed something beautiful. A resident and her daughter came to art session together, and they worked on a drawing together. The resident would probably not have attempted it alone. It was a rewarding experience for them both. After this I discovered that my helping a resident start a drawing was just what they needed to get going. There's nothing quite as scary sometimes as putting the first mark on a clean piece of nice drawing paper. I didn't do this for everyone, but it worked well for some. There's a fine line between not allowing someone to make the creative decisions along the way of picture making (spoon-feeding), and actually collaborating in a spirit of support and mutual interest.

EXAMPLE 9-6

PALMCREST SENIOR EYE GALLERY

Sponsors: Palmcrest House Senior Residency, Palmcrest North Convalescent Hospital, and Palmcrest Adult Health Day Care, all which can be contacted at 3501 Cedar Avenue, Long Beach, California, 90807, (213) 595-4551 or -1731; and Palmcrest Medallion Convalescent Hospital, 3355 Pacific Place, Long Beach, California, 90806, (213) 595-4336. The Adult Health Day Care center is a nonprofit organization. The others are private corporations.

Project director: Dr. Julian F. Feingold, 3501 Cedar Avenue, Long Beach, California, 90807, (213) 595-4551.

Dates/history: The Senior Eye Gallery was opened on May 25, 1974. Since then, many professional artists have exhibited their works at the gallery, and the calendar of future artists who will be exhibiting is full through June 1982. The Gallery is a permanent part of the Palmcrest hospital program.

Role of sponsoring organization: The four hospitals contribute to the Gallery budget, and all four hospitals have art classes that showcase works in the annual ART 70 PLUS exhibit. ART 70 PLUS is guided by professional art instructors who teach the seniors four times a week.

From The arts, the humanities and older Americans: a catalogue of program profiles, 1981, published by The National Council on the Aging, Inc., pp. 37-38.

Continued.

EXAMPLE 9-6,
cont'd

PALMCREST SENIOR EYE GALLERY

Objectives: The Palmcrest's objectives are to provide an atmosphere of sensitive and purposeful living and to combine lifestyle and the arts in a positive way. The Senior Eye Gallery reflects these objectives. Many of the frail and at-risk patients in the institution cannot leave the facility. The Palmcrest complex brings art, music and the humanities to them through the Senior Eye Gallery. Gallery staff encourages the elderly to live long, full lives through recognizing the interdependence of physical, psychological, social and aesthetic needs.

Content: Several leading artists have exhibited at the Senior Eye Gallery; many offers are received each year from artists wanting to exhibit. Exhibits have included realists, expressionists, sculptors, fiber artists and photographers. The professional artists and their works have been an inspiration to the patients.

Participants: More than 5,000 people have visited the Senior Eye Gallery. This number does not reflect patient visitors whose average age is 85.

Sites: The Senior Eye Gallery is located in the Palmcrest House. It was built specifically as a 45 by 35-foot gallery and has museum lighting.

Organizational structure: The Gallery is guided by Dr. Julian F. Feingold and Richard E. Feingold. Ms. Betje Howell, art critic for the *Santa Monica Outlook* has suggested many artists and written many reviews of the artists. An art student acts as curator, and the recreation therapist assists the artists in arranging their works.

Operation: The Gallery is open Wednesday through Sunday from 2-4:00 P.M. Many visitors from the community attend the exhibit openings and visit the gallery during its operating hours. Each exhibiting artist is honored with a dinner in his/her name on opening night and a reception which includes invited community members. Hospital patients attend the dinners on a rotating basis. Luncheons are held in the gallery with the patients and residents to discuss the works of art. No commissions are taken from the sales of the artworks, and more than $75,000 worth of art has been sold. There is also no cost to the visitors. A catalog is printed on each artist and is mailed to more than 3,500 people.

Some of the elderly volunteer to help the Gallery by showing visitors gallery attractions. Many of the residents' families also volunteer. The Palmcrest recreation department, guided by the recreation therapist, works on Gallery programs.

Publicity: Many newspaper articles have been written about the Senior Eye Gallery, five television programs have featured it, and various college art departments have sent students and professors to visit it.

Evaluation: Some of the artists who have exhibited their works at the Gallery have donated artwork to the permanent Palmcrest collection. This has been an invaluable contribution to the Gallery and a statement of its success.

Funding: The Gallery budget is supported by the Palmcrest hospitals. Each exhibit costs approximately $3,500 for the mailing, bulletins, dinner and opening reception. There are five exhibits per year, bringing the total approximate budget figure to $17,500. The annual ART 70 PLUS exhibit costs $1,500. Artist/teachers are paid $9.50 per hour of instruction.

Contact person: Dr. Julian F. Feingold, address given above.

and appreciation of music and limit their potential for musical involvement.

Davidson (1980) presents a variety of recommendations for the establishment of a successful music program for older persons based on her research.

Assessment. The various music programs currently offered, available staff, equipment and materials, interests and capabilities of population to be served, and support by administrators and program personnel must be assessed.

Leadership. Enthusiastic and dedicated leadership is essential. Primary efforts should be directed toward the recruitment of retired music teachers and retired professional musicians. Recruitment can be undertaken through contacts with national, state, and local organizations, as well as through advertising in the local community.

Equipment and materials. A variety of equipment and materials should be available. Whenever possible, instrumental and choral music, as well as songbooks, should be in large print. A music library should be available and may include equipment and materials such as sound equipment, film and filmstrip projectors, cassettes, tapes, disc recordings, magazines, journals, and books. A publicity campaign can be organized to solicit donations of money and materials, especially through community and civic organizations.

Program. The music program should be comprehensive, catering to differing interests and abilities. Programs might include basic music theory and reading as a part of the instrumental, vocal, and choral curricula. These programs require regular scheduling and a progression in the course of study. Social events that include music should be scheduled (e.g., parties, dances, and trips to concerts). Ethnic and cultural music should be included as an integral component of major celebrations throughout the year.

Music therapy may be used as a therapeutic intervention with older persons. Palmer (1977) showed how the goals of improving physical and mental functioning could be accomplished in a program.

Improving physical functioning. Exercises that are painful for the post-stroke or arthritic older person may be made more enjoyable by having the older person pretend to play the maracas in a mariachi band or wave flags in a parade. Arthritic fingers may be exercised by clapping to lively songs. Marching to music helps develop security in walking. Kicking and stomping to a march or polka can provide an incentive for extension and flexion, improve circulation, and increase tolerance and strength in the lower extremities of nonambulatory older persons.

Improving mental functioning. A variety of techniques were used to improve mental functioning. The call and response technique in a sing-along session is particularly effective when songs of youth are used because this technique allows recall of words, remembrance of when the song was learned, sharing of events associated with the song, recollection of composers and titles of songs, and encouragement of social interaction. The procedure called "lining-out" involves having a leader sing a song line that is repeated by the group until the entire song is learned by rote. Older persons with higher functioning may

Thea Lorin Breite

Creative movement allows for individual expression using the elements of movement, rhythm, dramatics, and multisensory activities.

perform vocal solos for a chapel service, learn to play a new instrument, participate in a choir or band, or write new words to a borrowed melody.

The book by Schulberg (1981) is a particularly valuable resource for additional music therapy activities.

DANCE. There is a general consensus among professionals that creative dance techniques can be adapted for older persons, even though there may be individual differences in stamina, mobility, and balance (Hoffman, 1980, p. 26).

A very exciting model program of creative dance for older persons has been developed by The Dance Exchange of Washington, D.C. Dancers not only work with older persons but also train professional dancers to work with older persons. Example 9-7 is a description of The Dance Exchange program.

EXAMPLE 9-7

THE DANCE EXCHANGE

Sponsor: The Dance Exchange, P.O. Box 50308, Washington, D.C., 20004 (Washington Humanities and Arts Center, 420 7th St., N.W., Washington, D.C.), (202) 783-8900.

Artistic director: Liz Lerman, artistic director, Dance Exchange, same address as above.

Dates/history: The Senior Citizens Program started in 1975 when Liz Lerman began teaching dance classes at the Roosevelt Hotel for Senior Citizens in Washington, D.C. The program has expanded to three classes each week taught at three locations in the Washington area. In 1975, a performing troupe of senior citizens was formed and named "The Dancers of the Third Age." This company consists of eight elderly people who dance with members of The Dance Exchange Performance Company in formal performances in Washington, D.C. and occasionally on tour. Their most frequent performances are in senior centers, community centers and schools. They have participated in artists-in-schools programs in three counties and were recently invited to join the touring program of the Mid-Atlantic States Consortium. A training course for dancers interested in teaching movement to senior citizens was held in the fall of 1980.

The Senior Citizens Program is a vital part of The Dance Exchange. The classes and performances will continue as long as certain conditions continue to exist: (1) the interest of the older and young dancers; (2) booking of the group by sponsors; and (3) outside funding to support overhead costs (administrative salaries, rehearsal support for artistic personnel, travel expenses).

Role of the sponsoring organization: The Dance Exchange provides artistic and administrative support for this program. The senior citizen dancers reflect The Dance Exchange's belief that dance can belong to everyone and add to their life. Dance programs operated through The Dance Exchange are often intergenerational in emphasis, mixing young and old in an atmosphere of mutual sharing.

Objectives: Project objectives are to: (1) bring the joy of dancing to a segment of the population that has been largely ignored by the dance community; (2) provide young dancers an opportunity to broaden their skills as teachers and performers; (3) encourage older and younger people to interact, sharing attention and affection within the context of dance; (4) broaden the concept of what dance is and who dances; (5) provide choreographers and dancers with a rich source of inspiration for their work so that their dances will integrate the experiences of older people as well as of those their own age and younger.

From The arts, the humanities and older Americans: a catalogue of program profiles, 1981, published by The National Council on the Aging, Inc., pp.18-20.

Continued.

**EXAMPLE 9-7,
cont'd**

THE DANCE EXCHANGE

Content: Dance is used as a mechanism for expression of feelings and for supporting positive feelings about oneself and others. Participants are encouraged to do what movement they can; even those restricted to wheelchairs are able to join in the basic warmup exercises led by a dancer. The class structure is similar to any dance class, with adaptation in content made to suit the flexibility and energy of participants. The class usually ends with short improvisations performed by the group. Performances take place at informal recitals in which all Dance Exchange dancers may participate, at formal concerts given by The Dance Exchange Performance Company, and in a show called "Transformations," which is most frequently given at elementary schools. In this show, the elderly lead the children in exercises, improvisations, and dance stories, many of which are based on stories from their own lives. The older dancers in the Dancers of the Third Age rehearse together once a week with a company member, in addition to the weekly dance class open to all older people.

Participants: Project participants range in age from young professional dancers to the oldest senior performer who is 83. Performances have been given for a diverse audience, largely through school performances (kindergarten through college), senior centers and hospitals. There is a definite intergenerational emphasis to classes and performances. Approximately 150 performances have been given by the Dancers of the Third Age since the group's formation in 1976.

Sites: Continuing and one-time classes are generally given at senior centers or residences. Workshops for recreational directors and others interested in teaching movement to seniors have been given at universities, community centers, dance studios and a medical school. The sites have usually not been linked. In sites out of the Washington, D.C. area, the goal has been to inspire a program that can continue after The Dance Exchange personnel have finished their residency there.

Organizational structure: Artistic Director Liz Lerman leads the Roosevelt Hotel class and directs the Dancers of the Third Age and most major residencies involving the senior program. Other staff members are: two teachers; the manager for continuing classes who also acts as studio manager for The Dance Exchange; the company manager for all performances, residencies, and single bookings of classes and workshops; and a bookkeeper who is also a member of the professional company, performing with the Dancers of the Third Age. All personnel except the teachers are full-time and involved with other programs; the older performers are volunteers who are selected by Liz Lerman from senior classes.

Operation: Classes and workshops are usually one hour long. The older people at local class sites are not charged for participation; fees are covered

by the site conducting the event. Performances are sponsored by a wide
variety of organizations—schools, community centers, churches, universities,
artists-in-schools programs, hospitals, clubs—and are usually 35-60 minutes
in length. Performance fees are used to cover administrative costs,
transportation and artist fees.

Products: In 1980, the Dancers of the Third Age were filmed for television by
"P.M. Magazine" and by WETA-TV, which did a one-hour special called "The
Dance Exchange: Live from Children's Hospital." These video-tapes, plus a
documentary video-tape of the Roosevelt program, are used as instructive
material for other organizations interested in beginning a movement program
for the elderly. Ms. Lerman's M.A. thesis on her work with seniors, to be
completed in the summer of 1981, will also be available as instructive
material.

Publicity: Outside of the two television specials mentioned above the senior
program has been written up in over 20 newspapers and magazines, mostly
in the Washington, D.C. metropolitan area including the May 26, 1977 edition
of the *Washington Post* and *Senior Citizen News,* December 1977, a
publication of the National Council for Senior Citizens.

Dissemination/replication: The Dance Exchange has led workshops in the
eastern United States and Canada on the subject of teaching movement to
senior citizens. The possibility of helping senior programs in Florida and Ohio
is being explored to develop a relationship between local dance artists and
the senior citizens in their community. The role of The Dance Exchange
would be as instructor and guide in an initial residency period, followed by
communication with the artists, seniors, and sponsoring community centers.
The problems and experiences confronted in their unique situations would be
addressed in a follow-up period.

Evaluation: Evaluation reports are required by The National Endowment for
the Arts Expansion Arts program for every year the senior program is funded
by this agency. Some of the strongest aspects of this program are in its
ability to introduce dance to people of all ages and to involve them together
in a creative and enjoyable experience. This supportive atmosphere
contributes to changing restrictive ideas of what older people can do.

Funding: A total of $55,719 (plus $3,658 in in-kind contributions) has been
given to The Dance Exchange in grants and contributions used for the senior
program and for productions involving the older dancers. Of this sum,
$51,104 is from government sources (mostly The National Endowment for the
Arts Expansion Arts and D.C. Commission on the Arts and Humanities), $100
from foundations, $513 from corporate sources, and $4001 from individual
contributors.

Contact persons: Liz Lerman, artistic director, or Diane Hull, company
manager at The Dance Exchange.

Creative movement programs are increasingly being implemented in residential settings where older persons may need some assistance in expressing themselves and in monitoring their optimum level of physiological functioning. Creative movement sessions involve improvisation and multisensory activities, often with rhythmical or musical accompaniment, thus encouraging individual exploration of a variety of ways that the body may be used to express ideas and feelings. An excellent resource on expressive activities for older persons is the book by Caplow-Lindner, Harpaz, and Samberg (1979).

CREATIVE WRITING. Older persons who have little or no background in creative writing can be taught this creative medium. The development of creative writing techniques is a challenge for both teacher and older student. Poet-in-residence programs supported in recent years by The National Endowment for the Arts have enabled poets over an extended period to assist older persons to develop their creative writing skills (Example 9-8 is a description of a poet-in-residence's experiences). Taproot Workshops, Inc. is an agency that has operated writing workshops in senior centers and nursing homes (Example 9-9 is a description of some instructional techniques)

EXAMPLE 9-8

POET-IN-RESIDENCE

I think one of the most important things to remember, as a teacher coming into a poetry program working with older people, is to be flexible. During my first year, especially at the beginning, I was constantly trying to find connections to (and judging myself in terms of) my teaching experiences with younger people. This is a mistake not only because the goals of older people are different from those who are younger, but because the artist will miss much of what is unique about older people by trying to fit them into a preconceived notion of what a "student" should be. For example, during my first year people were extremely unwilling to do a "poetry class." For a variety of reasons, they didn't want any part of it. For many weeks I fought like crazy to get them to conform to my idea of what should be happening—i.e., as a self-respectable "teacher of poetry" I should teach a class. Finally, more in despair than anything else, I realized I needed to come at the situation from an entirely different perspective, and it was then I developed the idea for taping conversations (see below).

So flexibility and a willingness to listen to what the people are actually saying, are important. If they say they are too tired to write, for example, it may well be that they *mean* it and that that isn't an excuse: they aren't kids trying to play hooky from school! It's easy to be arrogant. In most cases the poet will have more energy, hear better, walk faster, speak more quickly,

From COMPAS: Artists and the aging, St. Paul, 1976, Community Programs in the Arts and Sciences, pp. 38-41.

EXAMPLE 9-8,
cont'd

than the old person being worked with. It's easy to be paternalistic and assume you, as an experienced poet, have all the answers. It wasn't until I quit assuming this that I began to get somewhere.

Taping conversations is a great thing to do with people who don't want to write poetry. People find it easy to talk about themselves (this has been my experience anyway) if they have a good listener. And the very people who may be hardest to organize into a class (because they are isolated from one another in a housing project or day-care situation) are the very people who are longing most to be able to speak. This kind of taping is similar to oral history projects, but (the way I did it anyway) was different from most oral history projects I know about. First, there was no specific kind of information—historical or otherwise—I was trying to elicit. My purpose was to let people find the thing they most wanted to talk about (which was usually the thing—whether a person, the past, a hobby, a dream, whatever— that occupied the center of their attention *now* and kept them going, functioning coherently). I was not interested in their perspective on history, but in the way they looked at themselves *now*. This is close to the kind of state, or type of attention, that can produce poetry; quite often people would become more excited and animated during these conversations than any other time that I had seen them. The second thing that I did was to type up these conversations and then go through them, pulling out the places where the quality of attention, language, and feeling was particularly intense. It was these places where conversation turned into poetry, and I typed these sections into poems without changing any of the language and using natural pauses in speaking as places for linebreaks.

My second year I worked with a class. I began by doing collaborative poems, out loud, where each person would contribute a line, and we put the poems on the blackboard. Something like this is important to get people past the shyness about writing poetry which seems to infect almost everyone.

After a fair amount of experimenting, I found the way of organizing the class that worked best for me was to spend the first half an hour or so discussing a poem by a contemporary poet, and then moving from that into writing poems. I brought in poets of all kinds. Some of their favorites were Whitman, Bly, Ignatow, Williams, Lawrence, and James Wright. They particularly liked poems that touched on some aspect of their experience. Bly's poems that center around images that come from farming or a farm landscape were particular favorites. This, of course, will vary with how much poetry the people being worked with have already read, and other obvious factors like ethnic background, region of the country, etc. We always xeroxed the poems after the first few classes because it was much easier to hold a discussion when the people had the poems before them.

I tried to choose poems that would lead into a particular writing assignment, which I gave them at about the halfway mark of class. I tried all kinds of assignments, some of which were based on poets in the schools kinds of

Continued.

EXAMPLE 9-8,
cont'd

POET-IN-RESIDENCE

ideas. The ones that people seemed most to enjoy were those which gave them a chance to go back into their own pasts, especially their childhoods. Sometimes this was a problem, because people would end up writing memoir rather than poetry.

After they finished writing, we would take a few minutes and each person would read his or her poem. Then I took them with me, typed them up, made copies for everyone in the class and handed them back the next week. This became an important thing, a concrete bit of evidence of the work they had been doing. This was important because poetry, unlike the visual arts and crafts, has no outward, concrete proof of itself except for words—and words are not unusual, are something used by everyone all the time. Typing the poems up was a constant reminder of what had come before, and of what could happen in the future.

One problem in class, after we got going, was the danger of it turning into more of a social occasion than one where poems got written. People wanted to sit around and talk about who had moved in yesterday, what was for lunch, etc. I found, though I was hesitant to do it for fear of being arrogant in the way I described at the outset, that it was perfectly all right for me to speak up and say what was (poetry!) on *my* mind. People expected this, in fact.

There are things I didn't try that would be interesting in a program like this: ask people to keep journals, work collectively to put together a booklet of poems, work more on revisions, do more reading than we had time for, go to poetry readings, etc. These ideas that I've listed are very basic pointers, specific suggestions that might help a poet coming to work for the first time, as a poet, with older people.

The other part of what I want to say, about my personal experiences and their value in working with older people, is much harder to talk about. It's hard to boil it down to a few helpful tips.

In some ways I don't really think I had any "ideas" about older people before I started this job. I simply hadn't thought about older people as a class or a group. I had known a few older people, relatives, and that was all. For the first time, like an anthropologist visiting a new culture, I had to look at people very different from myself—not only in age, but in living situation. Often times at first it seemed impossible, it was such a different world. One

EXAMPLE 9-8,
cont'd

of the greatest joys this program has brought me has been that—to a certain extent at least—I've been able to enter that world. As a person, and particularly as an artist, this has been an incredible experience. A real danger for a poet today is to end up writing basically for (and of) other people like oneself. The "poetry ghetto" is very real. The opportunity to work in a humane way and over a long period of time (for this reason the residency part of the program was really helpful) got me more out of that ghetto than any single experience of my life, except for the period I was in prison.

A direct offshoot of this is that I now have several new friends whom I never would have met if I hadn't worked in the program. The opportunity to really get to know older people who aren't constricted to the role of grandparents is invaluable.

It's hard for me to tell at this point, how my art has been influenced. I know I will write about the people and situations that have become so important to me over the last couple of years. But because my poems tend to lag behind my experience, I can't say yet what form this will take. But, for the first time, I've written a poem about one of the people I've worked with and who has become a friend. I'm happy about this and want to do more.

One of the important ways in which my perception of older people has changed, is in simply realizing what an age variety there is within the category of "senior citizen" or "older person." I've worked with people who vary in age as much as 40 years, and yet all of them are categorized as "older." Their needs differ tremendously from person to person. As with any minority that is lumped together by the rest of a culture of society, this is easy to forget.

And I've seen the incredible courage that becomes a daily occurrence for older people. The physical problems, financial problems, the loneliness, the fear: it has to be experienced to be believed, and this program gave me that rare opportunity to experience it. I've been able to see, firsthand, the strategies people devise in order to survive.

There is a great deal more I could say. And what I have said feels inadequate. Basically, I've been given the chance to work with and come to know people closely, who are virtually lost to the rest of this country, stuck away in nursing homes and old age towers. To think that I was actually paid money for having this opportunity is simply incredible!

EXAMPLE 9-9

WRITING WORKSHOPS FOR ELDERS

Laura Fox
Director
Taproot Workshops, Inc.
Setauket, N.Y.

We now run six ongoing writing workshops. We're in two nursing homes, two nutrition centers, and two community groups in Suffolk County, New York.

Beginnings

We start each workshop by telling people we believe you're richer inside when you're older. It takes a long time for a dialog to get started. We sit around and talk all day. After a while, they believe we're sincere and not like the social scientists with their tape recorders who want to get their oral histories. We tell them we're writers who have certain techniques. We explain that they have the material to write about and we can help them with the techniques.

After all of this conversation, when they least expect it, we shove a piece of paper and pencil at them and tell them to write down what they just told the group. They say they can't write. But we persist. We explain that making a work of art out of what they have to say is nothing high flown and fancy and inaccessible. It only means shaping the material a bit.

We consider ourselves a workshop, not a class. We don't in any formal way explain how to write a ballad or piece of free verse.

If people have a physical handicap so they literally cannot write, we use scribes. A good relationship can develop between the two. Other than that, we don't accept any excuses. We tell them we don't care how they spell or punctuate or that they don't write English very well. We can fix that.

After a year, we produced a fabulous magazine of workshop writings. A third of the copies went to senior centers and the others to libraries, schools, and so on. After that, we began getting requests for the writers to read their own things at different places. So we developed the Taproot Readers and went wherever we were asked on reading engagements. It generated tremendous helpful feedback for them. We're now reading frequently in elementary schools as well.

The next logical step is for them to develop some work for the theater.

We give them three short sentences with no endings. In most of our workshops, we have sheets made up with these sentences on them.

- The people on the deck of the ship saw . . .
- The lost child sat crying in the woods and he/she saw . . .
- The frightened woman finally slept and in her dream she saw . . .

From Education: an arts/aging answer, 1979, published by The National Council on the Aging, Inc., pp. 34-35.

Using two lists on the board, they complete those three sentences. They can use only the two words or go on for as long as they like. We emphasize again that there's no right or wrong way to do this. We get astonishing responses. The students know tone instinctively. They always choose appropriate words.

When we meet the second time, we reiterate what we did in the lesson before. This is very important, especially in nursing homes where people are often quite sedated. We read back to them a few of the sentences from the week before, always anonymously. Then we go into the new material. We try to get a discussion going. They always ask for more poetry reading. We talk about the poems and ask what the obvious things mean without getting into anything that might require a difficult interpretation.

We get to the second exercise and say that it's very much like the first one only it is going to result in a genuine poem. We get lists of animals and actions that animals do. On their worksheets they have a structure with two unfinished lines:

• With you . . .
• I am a . . .

We have them relax and think about somebody they are close to or have been close to, somebody who's important to them. They try to get the picture and feeling of that person in their minds. Then they complete the line with the way they feel or felt with that person using the lists of animals and actions.

If there's time we go ahead and do another stanza with the lines:

• Without you . . .
• I am . . .

Exercises

We begin with poetry regardless of what we're going to write. I use a blackboard and write big to overcome visual or auditory problems. I write "What is poetry?" on the board. Everybody throws out ideas. We stress at this point and throughout that there is no wrong answer. Whatever your idea is about poetry is a part of poetry.

We get them to give us the names of birds which we write on the board. If we're getting only typical perching birds, we ask about water birds or birds of prey. Then we ask for words that describe actions that birds do with an "ing" ending. So we get a list of words such as "soaring," "pecking," "nesting."

For people who want to work in writing with older people, the best way to start is to go to the congregate sites, centers, or nursing homes and spend a long time just talking with people. Be sure you gain the enthusiasm of regular professional staff first. You only have so much time, so you may as well get cooperation. Don't go in without their help. You may wind up taking people in wheelchairs out narrow doors to the bathroom every few minutes instead of conducting writing workshops. The staff must be willing to put some time and energy into the program and understand why you're doing it. They must see it's not just an activity to fill up the hours in the day and relieve them of regular duties.

When I begin reading modern poetry to older people, some protest that it's not poetry because it doesn't rhyme. But I don't think beginners can rhyme and stay with meaning so we use only modern poetry. As you read more to them, they begin to like it.

Continued.

**EXAMPLE 9-9,
cont'd**

WRITING WORKSHOPS FOR ELDERS

We read each one and thank the author graciously but never comment on any of them. We try to avoid any competition. The leader does all the reading at first.

Logistics

We go into each site once a week and stay varying amounts of time. We're usually at the nursing homes only 1½ to 2 hours. In the nutrition sites and centers, they will tolerate us for much longer periods of time.

We're beginning to bring in people from the outside community, people who live not too far from the nursing homes on their own. They stimulate the nursing home patients enormously, and the people from the outside feel they're helping us.

We encourage the patients to read. If it's possible, we set up a reading committee of volunteers to meet with them between our sessions and read to them informally. We leave books when it's possible.

We always try to go in any site with two people from the beginning—a teacher and a trainee. That way, when the teacher must leave, the trainee stays on and continues the workshop.

We have a booklet that explains our teaching method in detail. It contains many of the poems we read and the exercises we use.

THEATER ARTS. The theater can be exprienced by older persons by attendance at theatrical performances or direct involvement. Older persons may attend performances of professional theater companies, college or university performances, and community theater through special arrangements such as preview performances, dress rehearsals, ticket subsidy, or direct purchase. For older persons interested in having a direct involvement with the theater but not interested in acting, a variety of assignments are available (e.g., costume design and sewing, set design and construction, lighting, sound, ticket sales, and ushering). Various parts in a variety of productions (e.g., drama, comedy, children's theater, puppet theater, and pantomime) are all possible avenues of direct involvement. An excellent resource on dramatic activities is the book by Thurman and Piggins (1982).

An example of a successful and innovative theater program is Free Street Too (Example 9-10). This Chicago-based, professional repertory company has actresses and actors all over 65 years of age who were selected after demanding auditions. Richard Driscoll, the former manager of Free Street Too, characterized the mission of this unique program:

> Instead of compartmentalizing our work as arts for older people, we prefer to think of it as an experience that should be available to everyone. One of

Text continued on p. 229.

EXAMPLE 9-10

FREE STREET TOO

Sponsor: Free Street Theater, 620 W. Belmont Street, Chicago, Illinois, 60657, (312) 822-0460.

Artistic director: Patrick Henry, Free Street Too, same address as above.

Dates/history: Free Street Too evolved in January 1976 from a pilot project conducted by Free Street Theater, a theatrical organization dedicated to developing new and broader audiences for the performing arts. Since that beginning, Free Street Too has become a regular component of Free Street's ongoing program of outreach services.

Role of sponsoring organization: Free Street Theater is the parent organization and provides both administrative and financial support for Free Street Too.

Objectives: Free Street Too has one principal objective: to make the performing arts and the artistic experience accessible to the older person.

Content: Free Street Too is a performing ensemble of eight people whose ages range from 67 to 81. The performance material is a kind of docu-drama; the content is derived from the actual life experiences and current involvements of the performers. Free Street Too presents kaleidoscopic verbal tapestries dramatizing the broad range of action and emotion in human longevity. The evolution of Free Street Too was an intergenerational process involving 22 young professional performers and the artistic staff of Free Street Theater with approximately 15 older people who volunteered for a pilot experiment in intergenerational communication through the performing arts. The combined group met for five hours a day during a month-long period in January, 1976. The daily sessions included interviews, theater games, general discussions and, as time went on, rehearsals, for the script was being developed out of life experiences of the older people. The final script, "To Life!," toured to 35 communities in 17 states; over 150 performances have been given to more than 45,000 people who have gathered in convention halls, classrooms, nutrition centers, nursing facilities and public parks to share this celebration of living. Subsequent scripts have been developed through this same cross-generational collaboration; some are performed with younger cast members and others feature only the older cast. The Free Street Too company currently has four productions in its repertoire.

Sites: Free Street Too is a non-traditional theater in terms of program content and presentation. Like its parent organization, Free Street Theater, Free Street Too will travel anywhere to engage a new audience. Consequently, performance locations can be as diverse as public plazas and specialized conferences on gerontological subjects.

Operation: What began as an experiment has become a second lifetime for

From The arts, the humanities and older Americans: a catalogue of program profiles, 1981, published by The National Council on the Aging, Inc., pp. 16-17.

Continued.

**EXAMPLE 9-10,
cont'd**

FREE STREET TOO

the members of the Free Street Too company. Eight of the original volunteers
have remained with the organization for five years and four other company
members have been recruited over that time. These people no longer
volunteer. After the initial month, Free Street Too became a professional
theater company administered by the Free Street organization. All Free
Street activities are offered to the general public free of charge. There are
fees for the services rendered which must be assumed by the sponsoring
organization (or underwritten by earmarked grants).

Dissemination/replication: In addition to performance activities, Free Street
Too also conducts seminars and workshops which explore notions and
realities about creativity and the older person. Free Street Too has inspired
and encouraged several other groups around the country; however, the
general message is to generate creative opportunities rather than carbon
copy companies.

Free Street Too has been featured at two Arts and Aging conferences
convened by the National Council on the Aging's Center on Arts and Aging;
the 26th annual National Council on the Aging conference; and the first
Aging and Employment conference. Further, Free Street Too has conducted
two mini-residencies at the Institute of Gerontology, University of Michigan,
Ann Arbor, Michigan.

Publicity: Free Street Too has become a model program; its story has been
documented in countless newspaper articles. Individual company members
have been cited in various books dealing with retirement options: *What Do
You Want To Be When You Grow Old?* by Harris Dinstfrey and Joseph
Lederer and *Living Longer and Loving It* by Arthur and Deborah Geller as
well as the 1980 edition of *Dynamics of Acting.* The early rehearsal process
was filed by WBBM-TV (CBS Chicago) and become a one hour color
documentary.

Funding: Free Street Too is funded by a combination of grants and
contributions from both public and private agencies and corporations, as well
as earned income from sponsor fees. Dollar amounts vary from year to year.
The principal sources have been: The National Endowment for the Arts, the
Illinois Arts Council, the Department of Health, Education and Welfare
Region V, the Department of Labor, CETA (for one year only), the Illinois
Department of Aging, the Illinois Humanities Council, the Robert R.
McCormick Charitable Trust, the Mobile Oil Foundation, and Warner
Lambert/Entenmanns.

Contact person: Carrol Hoch, general manager at Free Street Theater.

Free Street Too's interests is addressing, through the art of theatre, the problems of growing old in America to audiences that have not yet grown old. We want to help make growing old very much part of a process in the mind, not something that occurs only to other people. (National Council on the Aging, 1979, p. 32)

Evaluation serves a number of very important purposes in the organization and management of an arts program. Needed publicity may be generated by the products of evaluation (e.g., newsletters, monographs, and presentations), serving as a valuable mechanism for reaching underserved individuals and groups in the community. Evaluation may provide detailed information useful for the development of new programs. Support documentation for new funding initiatives may be facilitated particularly from final evaluations.

Evaluation

Central to an effective evaluation of an arts program is an evaluation process. This evaluation process should include internal evaluation by participants and staff and external evaluation by consultants or outside experts. Internal and external evaluation will be examined in this section.

INTERNAL EVALUATION. Evaluation by participants is vital to the evaluation process. Hoffman (1980, p. 45) suggests a variety of informational categories that might be examined by participants in workshop sessions (Example 9-11).

Staff evaluations should be gathered from both program and administrative staff. Program staff should gather information on how often an individual attends; how many older participants are in each session; comments on staff successes and failures in areas such as projects, materials, scheduling, field trips, and other activities related to arts programs (COMPAS, 1976, p. 24). Administrative staff may want to gather information on increased elderly participation, elderly involvement in other arts programs, increased sensitivity of arts administrators to elderly needs (e.g., increased communication with institutions, more convenient scheduling of performances, and more complimentary tickets), increased requests for arts programs from institutions serving the elderly, and increased involvement of area artists with arts programs for older persons (COMPAS, 1976, p. 24). Record keeping by administrative staff should include information related to budget, supplies, materials, equipment, staff (e.g., orientation and training procedures and evaluations), and public relations (e.g., exhibits, newspaper articles, and television features).

EXTERNAL EVALUATION. External evaluation by consultants and outside experts should be conducted on a regular basis (semiannually or annually). Consultants or outside experts should meet with persons such as participants, staff, advisory council, representatives from the sponsoring agency, and others as needed or required. Particular attention should be paid to whether program goals and objectives are being met. Documentation generated by consultants and outside experts should be evaluated by participants, staff, advisory council, and representatives of the sponsoring agency for needed integration into the ongoing planning process.

EXAMPLE 9-11

EVALUATION GUIDE

Date _____ Meeting site _____

1. Amount of administrative control:

2. General atmosphere of session:

3. Sequence of events:

4. Length of sessions:

5. Length of presentations:

6. Amount of presented material:

7. Quality of visuals and/or handouts:

8. Quality of material presented:

9. Quality of discussion:

10. Table arrangement (use of physical facilities):

11. Workshop agenda (Was it followed?):

12. Time schedule (Was it followed?):

13. Audience makeup (Were proper people at meeting?):

14. Amount and success of utilization of volunteer and area offices for actual presentation to group:

15. Amount of input by volunteers during group sessions:

From Hoffman, D.: Pursuit of arts activities with older adults: an administrative and programmatic handbook, 1980, published by The National Council on the Aging, Inc., p. 45.

Research on arts and the elderly has examined the issues of creativity in later life and the impact of arts on older persons. Research on creativity in later life is contradictory. Some research shows decline in quality and quantity with increasing age. Other research shows no decline in creative productivity and gives, in fact, numerous examples of creativity among individual older persons, showing that life can be a continual creative journey. Research on the impact of arts on older persons has shown that creative activities are carried on by community elderly years after formal instruction and that arts programs significantly increase participation in formal activities by nursing home residents. Older persons are an unrealized audience for the arts because of their generally low level of attendance at dance performances, concerts, the theater, and museums, which may be attributed to the lack of targeting of efforts and resources by arts administrators and programmers.

    The systematic organization and management of arts programs for older persons should consider the key components of assessment, funding, staffing, site selection, programming, and evaluation. The needs and interests of the community for arts programs are determined through an assessment focusing on the identification of available programs, determination of service gaps, and evaluation of needs and interests for an eventual incorporation into a plan. Arts programs may be funded by a variety of public and private sources; strategies such as the use of multiple funding sources and of community and local private funding as a means of long-term support may be employed. Staffing involves the selection of staff (based on a process of identifying interested persons, matching persons to program needs, and applicant qualification) and training of staff through an initial orientation, in-service education sessions, and regular staff meetings. The selection of a site for arts programs involves the preparation of a comprehensive list of possible sites and the determination of a site based on appropriate criteria (e.g., geographical distribution, socioeconomic diversity, physical structure, suitability of site to program, and interest). Programming of the arts may involve program areas such as the visual arts (ceramics, fabrics, sculpture, photography and filmmaking, and drawing and painting), music, dance, creative writing, and theater arts. Because it serves the important purposes of publicity, new program development, and new funding initiatives, evaluation should be done internally by participants and staff and externally by consultants and outside experts.

SUMMARY

REFERENCES

Alpaugh, P., and Birren, J.: Variables affecting creative contributions across the adult life span. In Reigel, K., and Thomae, H., editors: Human development, Basel, Switzerland, 1977, Karger.

Caplow-Lindner, E., Harpaz, L., and Samberg, S.: Therapeutic dance/movement: expressive activities for older adults, New York, 1979, Human Sciences Press, Inc.

COMPAS: Artists and the aging, St. Paul, 1976, Community Programs in the Arts and Sciences.

Davidson, J.: Music and gerontology: a young endeavor, Music Educat. J. 66(9):26-31, 1980.

Dawson, A., and Baller, W.: Relationship between creative activity and the health of elderly persons, J. Psychol. 82:49-58, 1972.

Dennis, W.: Age and achievement: a critique, J. Gerontol. 11: 331-333, 1956a.

Dennis, W.: Age and productivity among scientists, Science 123: 724-725, 1956b.

Dennis, W.: The age decrement in outstanding scientific contributions: fact or artifact, Am. Psychol. 13:457-460, 1958.

Dennis, W.: Creative productivity between ages of 20 to 80, J. Gerontol. 21:1-8, 1966.

Hoffman, D.: Pursuit of arts activities with older adults: an administrative and programmatic handbook, Washington, D.C., 1980, National Council on the Aging.

Hospital Audiences, Inc.: Research: the impact of the arts on the frail elderly, HAI News, pp. 1, 5, Fall, 1979.

Johnson, A.: Older Americans: the unrealized audience for the arts, Madison, Wis., 1976, Center for Arts Administration.

Lehman, H.: Age and achievement, Princeton, N.J., 1953, Princeton University Press.

Lehman, H.: Reply to Dennis' critique of age and achievement, J. Gerontol. 11:333-337, 1956.

Lehman, H.: The influence of longevity upon curves showing man's creative production rate at successive age levels, J. Gerontol. 13:187-191, 1958.

Lehman, H.: Chronological age versus present-day contribution to medical progress, Gerontologist 3:71-75, 1963.

McLeish, J.: The Ulyssean adult: creativity in the middle and later years, Toronto, 1976, McGraw-Hill Ryerson, Ltd.

National Council on the Aging: Education: an arts/aging answer, Washington, D.C., 1979, National Council on the Aging.

National Council on the Aging: The arts, the humanities and older Americans: a catalogue of program profiles, Washington, D.C., 1981, National Council on the Aging.

National Research Center on the Arts, Inc.: Americans and the arts, New York, 1975, Associated Council for the Arts.

Palmer, M.: Music therapy in a comprehensive program of treatment and rehabilitation for the geriatric resident, J. Music Ther. 14:190-197, 1977.

Schulberg, C.: The music therapy sourcebook, New York, 1981, Human Sciences Press, Inc.

Sunderland, J.: Older Americans and the arts: a human equation, Washington, D.C., 1976, National Council on the Aging.

Thurman, A., and Piggins, C.: Drama activities with older adults: a handbook for leaders, New York, 1982, The Haworth Press.

SUGGESTED READINGS

Caplow-Lindner, E., Harpaz, L., and Samberg, S.: Therapeutic dance/movement: expressive activities for older adults, New York, 1979, Human Sciences Press, Inc.

Hoffman, D.: Pursuit of arts activities with older adults: an administrative and programmatic handbook, Washington, D.C., 1980, National Council on the Aging.

McLeish, J.: The Ulyssean adult: creativity in the middle and later years, Toronto, 1976, McGraw-Hill Ryerson, Ltd.

National Council on the Aging: The arts, the humanities and older Americans: a catalogue of program profiles, Washington, D.C., 1981, National Council on the Aging.

Schulberg, C.: The music therapy sourcebook, New York, 1981, Human Sciences Press, Inc.

Thurman, A., and Piggins, C.: Drama activities with older adults: a handbook for leaders, New York, 1982, The Haworth Press.

Education

Education has traditionally been oriented toward assisting young persons to acquire a trade or occupation rather than toward the lifelong process of learning for all persons. The age grading of education has not encouraged the formal educational participation of individuals making the transition from middle age to old age. Likewise, older persons have not sought out adult education opportunities because of the perception that adult education is totally for the acquisition of work skills rather than for education in options for leisure.

Education is increasingly being recognized as valuable to older persons. Preretirement education can assist with preparation for retirement and postretirement in a critical area such as leisure education. Education programs for older persons should reflect a variety of options for leisure education–oriented content areas and courses. This chapter will be concerned with preretirement education and adult education of the elderly, with specific emphasis on leisure education.

PRERETIREMENT EDUCATION

Retirement as a widespread phenomenon has been made possible by the modern, twentieth century industrial society. Crandall (1980, p. 342) identifies four factors that have made retirement available to a large number of individuals.

1. *There is an increased probability of people reaching old age.* The proportion of older people in the population and the increase in life expectancy began to rise early in the twentieth century (Woodruff and Birren, 1975). The major increase in life expectancy is a result of changes in life expectancy at birth, although there has been some increase in the life expectancy at age 65.
2. *Today's industrial society is able to support an increasingly large nonworking proportion of the population.* There is a need for fewer workers as a result of increased worker productivity and output (Atchley, 1977).

The need for a large adult labor force is diminished because fewer workers are needed for the production and distribution of goods, even for a growing number of individuals.

3. *There is little demand for the labor of older persons.* Demographic trends have resulted in an older population structure and, combined with the increased productivity of workers, have heightened the competition for jobs (Cowgill, 1974). In addition, because many occupations require new technical skills and higher education, older workers have tended to be concentrated in industries of slow growth and fewer jobs. This implies that the skills and knowledge of older workers are obsolete.

4. *Social security and pension plans are more available.* Social security, according to Munnell (1977, p. 63), has affected retirement in three ways: (1) benefits moderate the reduction in income that workers have when they retire, (2) the earnings test forces workers to cut back on work, and (3) employers and employees are conditioned to the idea that the age of 65 is the time to retire. Economic growth has provided an economic surplus that business and industry have diverted into pension plans.

This section will examine the subject of preretirement education. The topics to be discussed are the definition and statistics on retirement, the decision to retire, the impact of retirement, preretirement education programs, and preretirement leisure education programs.

Definition of retirement

Retirement may be viewed from a variety of perspectives. Two views to be examined are retirement as an event and retirement as a role.

RETIREMENT AS AN EVENT. Retirement as an event signifies the end of employment and the beginning of life without a job. This event is often marked with a retirement ceremony, including a testimonial dinner, a gift, and a review of past achievements.

RETIREMENT AS A ROLE. Retirement may be described as exchanging a work role for a leisure role (McPherson and Guppy, 1979). The individual may

TABLE 10-1   Labor force participation rate*

	Actual			Projected			
	1970	1975	1980	1985	1990	2000	2010
Males							
55-64	81.8	75.7	74.3	71.6	69.9	66.6	63.2
65+	26.9	21.7	19.9	18	16.8	13.8	10.8
Females							
55-64	42.5	41	41.9	42.2	42.3	43.3	43.9
65+	9.6	8.2	8.1	7.8	7.6	7.1	6.6

From Clark, R., and Spengler, J.: Aging **279-280**:6-13, 1978.
*Expressed in percentages.

become a leisure participant, a senior center participant, a volunteer, and so on. This role is usually flexible and allows for a wide range of individual choices and decisions (Davis and Teaff, 1980).

Retirement is now and will become more prevalent in American society during the next 30 years (Clark and Spengler, 1978). Labor force participation rates, both actual and projected, show a decline for both men and women 65 years of age and older (Table 10-1).

Statistics on retirement

There are many reasons why people retire. This section will examine these reasons under the headings of voluntary retirement and involuntary retirement.

The decision to retire

VOLUNTARY RETIREMENT. An *adequate retirement income* is an important reason for retirement. Pollman (1971) found that 47 percent of the individuals surveyed said the primary reason in their decision to retire was an adequate retirement income. Patton (1977) found that 71 percent said they would retire early if conditions were right, with one of the most generally expressed "right" conditions being adequate retirement income.

Poor health has been declining as a reason for retirement. Pollman (1971) found that only 24 percent claimed they retired because their health was poor. The fact that jobs are less physically demanding and safer may explain why poor health is no longer the primary reason for retirement (Atchley, 1980).

More *leisure* was an attractive retirement feature for 19 percent of those surveyed (Pollman, 1971). From 1951 to 1963 an increase from 3 percent to 17 percent was noted in the preference for leisure as a reason for retirement (Palmore, 1964). The reason for an attraction to leisure may be the declining importance of work and satisfaction with individual jobs (Ward, 1979).

Workers' attitudes toward retirement are factors in the retirement decision. Glamser (1976) found workers' attitudes to be related to an anticipated adequate retirement income, number of friends, and expected range of activities after retirement.

The *type of job* may create conditions favorable for retirement. Pollman (1971) found that 17 percent of skilled workers, compared with 33 percent of assembly line workers, gave poor health as a reason for retirement. Retirement because of an adequate income was given as a reason for retirement by 52 percent of skilled workers and 41 percent of assembly line workers. Certain types of jobs may cause health problems; economic and retirement benefits may be more substantial in some jobs than in others.

INVOLUNTARY RETIREMENT. An individual may retire involuntarily because of the *inability to find a job.* Jobs for the older worker are only available if he or she is willing to work for low pay or if there is a chronic labor shortage (Atchley, 1980). Hiring policies may discriminate against the older worker on the basis of physical or skill requirements.

Pressure from employers may be applied to force an employee to retire.

Techniques used to pressure an employee include changing an employee's working conditions, reclassifying the job, or suggesting a transfer.

Mandatory retirement policies may require retirement at a specific age. Table 10-2 presents data from a National Council on the Aging study (1975), which showed that retirement is more likely to be forced for men, blacks, and persons with lower incomes and poor education. Mandatory retirement has been supported by union and industry policies and public and private pensions.

Impact of retirement

The literature on retirement presents a contradictory picture of retirement's impact. Past literature has presented a generally gloomy picture of the impact of retirement on individuals, with retirees portrayed as living boring and meaningless lives in an ambiguous "roleless role" (Blau, 1973; Donahue, Orbach, and Pollak, 1960; Rosow, 1974). Recent literature on the impact of retirement presents a more positive view. This literature will be discussed under the headings of satisfaction, health, social participation, and income.

SATISFACTION. Studies support the notion that retirees are generally satisfied with retirement. Streib and Schneider (1971), in a longitudinal study that examined workers before and after retirement, found no significant change in life satisfaction following retirement. Patton (1977) found that 86 percent of the retirees interviewed were satisfied with their decision to retire; early retirees were more satisfied than those who retired at the mandatory retirement age. Kell and Patton (1978), in a study of college professors who retired early, found that 73 percent were very satisfied; 62 percent claimed that they were happier than before retirement.

TABLE 10-2   **Retirement by choice or by force***

	Retired by choice	Forced to retire	Not sure
Men	58	41	1
Women	66	32	2
Under $3,000	53	46	1
$3,000-$6,999	62	36	2
$7,000-$14,999	68	30	2
$15,000 and over	65	35	—
White	63	36	1
Black	43	50	7
Some high school or less	58	41	1
High school graduate, some college	67	30	3
College graduate	70	30	—
TOTAL	61	37	2

From The myth and reality of aging in America, 1975, published by The National Council on the Aging, Inc.
*Expressed in percentages.

HEALTH. It is a myth that retirement causes poor health. In their longitudinal study Streib and Schneider (1971) found that declines in health were associated with increasing age rather than with retirement. Haynes, McMichael, and Tyroler (1978), in a study of approximately 4,000 rubber workers before and after retirement, found that health status *before* retirement was the significant predictor of mortality within 5 years after retirement. In fact, Streib and Schneider (1971) and Atchley (1976) report that mental and physical health improves after retirement because of the removal of the strain of work.

SOCIAL PARTICIPATION. Retirement has little impact on social participation. Streib and Schneider (1971) found that retirement had little effect in areas such as friendships, church attendance, seeing children and grandchildren, and voluntary association and community activity participation.

INCOME. Income is a significant factor affecting adjustment to retirement. Atchley (1975) found that financial problems were the primary reason for 40 percent of those who have retirement adjustment difficulties. Chatfield (1977) found the life satisfaction scores of the recently retired to be significantly lower than the scores of the nonretirees but found no differences in the life satisfaction scores of those retired 1 or more years; part of the score discrepancy was accounted for by income—the recently retired had lower incomes, whereas those who had been retired for more than 1 year had found ways to supplement their incomes.

Preretirement education programs

Preretirement education programs may facilitate an easier transition from worker to retiree by teaching people what to expect in retirement, to understand options open to them, and how to realistically select options. Subjects pertinent to preretirement education programs are history, prevalence, benefits, and planning and conducting programs.

HISTORY. The growth of preretirement education programs parallels the growth of industrial private pension programs. Many companies had well-established programs before 1950, in which they primarily conducted individual interviews to explain the pension benefits. Beginning in the 1950s, however, program content expanded into areas such as housing, health, family life, and leisure (Hunter, 1968).

Group discussion programs began in 1948 at the University of Michigan and in 1951 at the University of Chicago (Blank, 1982). These pioneering programs were an impetus for the development of programs in a variety of settings. Hunter (1968, p. 17), after a review of preretirement education programs, concluded that the programs sponsored by industries and unions failed "to reflect the growth of programs which were being sponsored by universities and colleges, public schools, libraries, the various branches of military service, governmental agencies at both the federal and state levels, YM-YWCA's and church organizations."

PREVALENCE. Preretirement education programs are not widespread. Mulanaphy (1978), in a survey of 2,210 institutions of higher education, found that only 4 percent had formalized preretirement education programs. O'Meara (1977), in a study of 800 companies, found that only 15 percent provide a comprehensive information and personal counseling program. The reasons why corporations do not offer preretirement education programs include the lack of qualified staff to develop and present the programs, not wanting to interfere in the private lives of employees, and budget constraints (Hodges, 1982). Preretirement education programs are carried out primarily by progressive employers, employee interest groups, and nonprofit organizations (Manion, 1974).

Most individuals do not plan for retirement (Monk, 1971; Rowe, 1972). Ninety-seven percent of workers would like to plan for retirement but only 28 percent actually do so (Kalt and Kohn, 1975; Kasschau, 1974). The National Council on the Aging (1981), in a Harris and Associates poll, found that only 10 percent of the population between 55 and 64 years old have participated in a preretirement education program.

BENEFITS. Preretirement education programs have benefits for both employers and employees. The benefits for employers include improved employee relations and morale, improved productivity, and the fulfilling of a social responsibility (Research and Forecasts, 1979). Green, Pyron, Manion, and Winklevoss (1969) found that employees were better adjusted, had reduced resistance to retirement, and had increased morale and work performance. Employees who participate feel very positive about the programs and believe that they have benefitted (Glamser, 1981; Glamser and DeJong, 1975; Rowe, 1973).

PLANNING AND CONDUCTING PRERETIREMENT EDUCATION PROGRAMS. This section examines a number of important aspects involved in the planning and conducting of preretirement education programs.

Sponsorship. Critical issues must be addressed when considering the sponsorship of a preretirement education program. What is the commitment of the sponsor (Kalt and Kohn, 1975)? What is to be the content and delivery style (Reich, 1977)? What is to be the scope of the program (Siegel and Rives, 1978)? Will older persons be comfortable with the type of sponsorship (Hunter, 1980)?

A variety of groups and organizations may sponsor preretirement education programs. Labor unions, industry, churches, YMCAs and YWCAs, libraries, government agencies, universities, and public schools have a history of sponsorship. Hunter[*] (1980, pp. 10-11) presents a number of reasons why public education should have the primary responsibility:

1. There is a growing recognition of public education's responsibility for continuing education.
2. Public education is in a better position to command financial support.
3. Personnel in public education have the skills to conduct programs and to develop new techniques and materials.
4. Public education can encourage the support and involvement of other community agencies (e.g., public health departments, libraries, and employment services).

[*]Modified from Hunter, W.: Preretirement education leader's manual, Ann Arbor, Mich., 1980, The University of Michigan, pp. 10-11.

5. Public education would be able to encourage older persons to view the community's resources as an avenue for retirement adjustment.

Promotion. Preretirement education programs may be promoted through various groups. Labor unions and industry can encourage the participation of older employees through the payment of all or part of the costs. Organizations such as churches, fraternal groups, libraries, and YMCAs and YWCAs, may promote programs through bulletins, newsletters, and pamphlets.

The mutual support and cooperation of community groups may help to overcome resistance. The tone of promotional materials and presentations should convey a positive image of the aging process. Enrollment may be encouraged through the creation of a supportive atmosphere in which questions are encouraged and honestly answered.

Eligibility. Preretirement education programs should be open to all persons who are interested. Pressure should not be exerted by those promoting the program. However, it is recommended that husband and wife attend the program together.

The age at which persons are allowed to attend should remain flexible, because there are differing opinions concerning the age at which one should begin preretirement education. Ward (1979, p. 225) suggests that a person could begin in a program at age 45 because financial and leisure planning need to start early. However, Knowles (1977) cautions against starting a program before persons are ready to absorb and act on the type of information presented.

Group composition and size. An important factor to consider when determining the composition of a preretirement education group is the predominant socioeconomic status of the group. Programs conducted by universities report that discussion of issues is facilitated when nonprofessional and professional employees are separated. On the other hand, a number of union programs encourage a mix of blue-collar and white-collar workers (Reich, 1977).

The size of the group for a group-oriented preretirement education program should not exceed 30 people, with the ideal number ranging from 15 to 30 persons (Reich, 1977). Groups larger than 30 do not allow individuals to interact and raise questions; groups of six to eight persons sometimes have difficulty maintaining an acceptable level of group interaction (Hunter, 1980).

Place and time of meeting. The meeting place should be comfortable and accessible. Table and chair arrangement should allow for ease of conversation, with the names of the participants printed on place cards rather than on name badges (Hunter, 1980). Physical environmental considerations of ventilation, lighting, heating, rest rooms, telephone, coat racks, electrical outlets, and elevators should be evaluated. Parking facilities should be accessible and well lighted.

Programs may be offered during the day or in the evening. The decision as to time of meeting should be based, whenever possible, on a consensus of the group. Evening meetings may allow more spouses to attend but may discourage others because of night driving or the fear of being out after dark.

Delivery process. The delivery process used in preretirement education programs may vary. Brenner and Linnell (1976) classified preretirement education programs into three approaches:

1. *The information-media approach* focuses on a variety of topics supported by printed materials, audiovisual media, guides for leaders, and informal group discussions.
2. *The group counseling approach* focuses on the psychological, social, and interpersonal aspects of the retirement process.
3. *The lecture-discussion approach* focuses on topics related to retirement by means of lectures, guest speakers, films, and group discussions.

The lecture-discussion approach is recommended and is being used by those in the forefront of preretirement education. It combines the sharing of information through a variety of communication techniques while allowing for group interaction and interchange.

Leadership. Leadership for preretirement education programs has been drawn from industry personnel, union leaders, clergy, librarians, adult educators, recreation personnel, and others (Hunter, 1980). Leaders should have basic information about aging and the retirement process, fundamental group facilitation and discussion skills, and knowledge of program content areas.

Information related to program content areas may be provided by resource persons. For example, physical and mental health issues may be addressed by a physician or nurse and psychologist or psychiatrist; legal and financial issues may be addressed by lawyers, accountants, and social security personnel. Resource persons should be knowledgeable not only about the subject but also about available community programs and services for the retired. The leader should inform the resource person in advance about the topic to be discussed and techniques for planning and guiding the discussion.

Content. The content of preretirement education programs has not been standardized. Brenner and Linnell (1976), in their study of retirees, found the topics in order of greatest interest to be finances, health, housing, social/personal aspects of retirement, and use of leisure time. Topics, however, may vary according to the time available for the program, expertise of the leadership, and the sponsor of the program (Reich, 1977).

Programs have included a variety of content areas. The Duke University Preretirement Model (Elmore, 1977) includes the following session content areas:

1. Introduction: the challenge of later maturity
2. Social Security and Medicare
3. Retirement budget
4. Finances
5. Legal problems
6. Physical and mental health problems
7. Changing family relations
8. Choosing a residence
9. Creative use of leisure
10. Ways to increase income after retirement

The University of Michigan Preretirement Education program (Hunter, 1980) contains the following session content areas:

1. Orientation
2. Work and retirement
3. Physical health
4. Mental health
5. Retirement income
6. Financial planning
7. Employment
8. Consumer information
9. Housing and living arrangements
10. Social relationships
11. Legal concerns
12. Leisure time
13. Widowhood
14. Death and dying
15. Sexuality and aging
16. Summary session

An examination of the two programs reveals an emerging consensus on important content areas. Health, income, housing, social and family relationships, and leisure are common topics of the two programs. However, it is suggested that, when initiating a program, members of a preretirement education group be given an opportunity to identify problems and concerns, giving assurances that these will be recognized in the discussion of the appropriate content areas.

Evaluation. Evaluations should be conducted for each session content area and for the overall program. Leaders will find that an evaluation of a session will allow for immediate changes, and the evaluation of the overall program will facilitate major long-range modifications. Example 10-1 is a session evaluation form, and Example 10-2 is an overall program evaluation form.

EXAMPLE 10-1

SESSION EVALUATION FORM

1. Topic of this session _____

2. Do you feel this session supplied you with answers to your questions or concerns? _____ Yes _____ No

3. What did you like about the session?

4. What did you dislike about the session?

5. What specific suggestions would you make for improvement?

6. If there was a special guest or speaker, how did you feel about his or her presentation? _____ I liked it _____ I didn't like it

   Why?

7. How did you feel about the coffee break?

8. Do you plan to attend the next session? _____ Yes _____ No

(You do not need to sign your name.)

From Hunter, W.: Preretirement education leader's manual, Ann Arbor, Mich., 1980, Institute of Gerontology, The University of Michigan. Reproduced by permission of the Institute of Gerontology at The University of Michigan.

EXAMPLE 10-2

PROGRAM EVALUATION FORM

The purpose of this worksheet is to help the leader organize participants' observations of the manner in which he or she conducted the meetings, techniques used and results achieved, and, also, to help organize observations of the manner in which the members of the group participated in the discussion, and the changes that took place from one meeting to another.

What to observe   **Your evaluation**

I. Preparation for the meeting
    1. Were the people seated so they could talk to each other easily?
    2. Was the comfort of members considered from the standpoint of lighting, acoustics, temperature, distracting noise, stairs and bathroom facilities?
    3. Had the leader prepared for the meetings?
       a. Knew something about members.
       b. Had objectives clearly in mind.
       c. Was able to clearly state objectives.
       d. Had a discussion plan in mind.

II. Opening the meeting
    1. What was done to welcome members?
    2. Were members introduced to each other and were they encouraged to learn each other's names? How?
    3. What about the length and content of the introduction?
    4. Did it create interest and anticipation?
    5. Did the leader give members the opportunity to express expectations and interests?

III. Developing discussion
    1. What techniques did the leader use to develop discussion?
    2. Did the leader succeed or fail to stimulate discussion? Why?
    3. How did the leader behave toward members?
       a. Friendly or reserved.
       b. Domineering or democratic.
       c. Rejecting or accepting.
       d. Humorous or serious.
       e. Calm or nervous or insecure.
       f. Understanding or lacking in understanding.
       g. Willing to listen or did all the talking.
       h. Appeared to like members or didn't like them.
       i. Respected members or showed disrespect.
       j. Talked down to group.

From Hunter, W.: Preretirement education leader's manual, Ann Arbor, Mich., 1980, Institute of Gerontology, The University of Michigan. Reproduced by permission of the Institute of Gerontology at The University of Michigan.

**EXAMPLE 10-2,
cont'd**

What to observe

Your evaluation

IV. Quantity of discussion
  1. How many preretirees were at the meeting? _____
  2. How many different preretirees took part in the discussion? _____

V. Quality of discussion
  1. Did the discussion flow back and forth within the group? _____
  2. Was the discussion primarily between leader and individual members? _____
  3. How did the members react to the leader? _____
  4. How did members react to each other? _____
  5. Did some member(s) monopolize the discussion? _____
  6. What did you observe about the non-talkers? _____
  7. Do you think the members learned anything from the discussion? _____
  8. Were members satisfied with their part in the meeting? _____
  9. Did any of the members initiate discussion on their own? _____
  10. Did members of the group discipline each other? _____
  11. Did the members stay on the topic? _____
  12. Did the members seem relaxed? _____

VI. Closing the meeting
  1. Did the leader summarize the meeting? _____
  2. Did the leader prepare members for the next meeting? _____
  3. Did the members appear eager to come to the next meeting? _____
  4. What was done to create anticipation for the succeeding meetings? _____

VII. General observations
  A. From the standpoint of the leadership:
    1. What were the weak points of this meeting? _____
    2. What do you think were the strong points? _____
    3. What improvements would you suggest making at the next meetings? _____
    4. Did the leader appear to learn anything from results of previous meetings? _____
  B. From the standpoint of member participation:
    1. What were the weak points of this meeting? _____
    2. What were the strong points? _____
    3. How would you improve member participation at the next meeting? _____
    4. Was participation at this meeting different from participation in previous meetings? _____

VIII. Physical facilities and arrangements
  1. Did everything appear in readiness for the meeting? _____

Continued.

EXAMPLE 10-2,
cont'd

PROGRAM EVALUATION FORM

What to observe   **Your evaluation**

    2. What type of seating arrangement was em-
       ployed?

    3. What was done, if anything, to increase the
       physical comfort of the group members?

    4. Was lighting adequate for purposes of the
       meeting?

    5. Was the room temperature satisfactory?

    6. Were there any distractions during the meet-
       ing?

    7. Was the meeting room easy for the members
       to locate?

    8. Did the older people have any difficulty enter-
       ing or leaving the building?

    9. Was the room decor pleasing?

    10. Were drinking and toilet facilities easily ac-
        cessible?

IX. Social arrangements

    1. What procedures were used to welcome the
       group members?

    2. What was done to acquaint participants with
       each other?

    3. Did the participants wear name badges? How
       legible were the badges?

    4. What was done to encourage socialization
       among the participants?

    5. What evidence was there that the members
       were becoming acquainted?

    6. Were some participants more reluctant than
       others to become acquainted?

X. Program materials

    1. What types of materials were employed? (List
       the different kinds of materials and evaluate
       the use of each of them.)
       a.

       b.

       c.

       d.

       e.

    2. What methods were used relative to the vari-
       ous kinds of materials?

    3. What evidence was there during the meeting
       that the participants were interested in the ma-
       terials?

    4. What evidence was there that the materials
       provoked discussion?

    5. What other kinds of materials could have been
       used effectively during the meeting?

The purpose of preretirement leisure education programs is to facilitate an "individual's transition from a work to a leisure role" (Weiner, 1982, p. 368). This section will examine a number of topics related to the carrying out of this purpose—the importance of preretirement leisure education, delivery format, leadership, programming, and evaluation.

Preretirement leisure education programs

IMPORTANCE OF PRERETIREMENT LEISURE EDUCATION. The importance of preretirement leisure education was well summarized by the 1971 White House Conference on Aging (1973, p. 53):

> Society should adopt a policy of preparation for retirement, leisure and education for life off the job. The private and public sectors should adopt and expand programs to prepare persons to understand and benefit from the changes produced by retirement. Programs should be developed with government at all levels, education systems, religious institutions, recreation departments, business and labor to provide opportunities for the acquisition of the necessary attitudes, skills and knowledge to assure successful living. Retirement and leisure-time planning begin with the early years and continue through life.

The subject of leisure is vitally important to persons approaching retirement. Leisure attitudes and patterns of participation are significant predictors of retirement life satisfaction (Darnley, 1975; McPherson and Guppy, 1979).

DELIVERY FORMAT. Preretirement leisure education programs may be delivered either as a part of an existing preretirement education program or as an independent program. Each format has advantages and disadvantages (Weiner, 1982, pp. 376-377).

An existing preretirement education program has the advantage of attracting a larger audience because of the diversity of program content (e.g., finances, health, and housing), but this diversity may also be a disadvantage because leisure may not be given necessary time and attention by specially trained staff.

An independent program has the advantage of devoting the time and attention to leisure by a leisure specialist, but a disadvantage of such a format is the small audience that may be attracted by such a specific topic.

The planner of a preretirement leisure education program should evaluate the advantages and disadvantages of the two formats, taking into consideration the possibilities of being the resource person for the session or sessions on leisure in an existing program, developing a follow-up independent program for those persons who have completed the program with a diverse content, or of being the overall coordinator or primary staff person for a diverse content program to ensure adequate coverage of leisure, as well as the other content topics.

LEADERSHIP. Leaders should have competence in leisure education. Specific knowledge of how leisure interacts with the psychosocial aspects of aging, resulting in a leisure life-style particular to an individual retiree, is also a requirement.

PROGRAMMING. The preretirement leisure programming process is designed to assist the preretiree to plan for leisure in retirement. This process employs certain steps.

Assessment of current leisure life-style. The assessment of current leisure life-style involves an analysis of the importance of leisure in a preretiree's overall pattern of living. Exercises have been developed by a number of authors to assess and clarify the value of leisure in a person's life-style.

Personal Resources Inventory. The Personal Resources Inventory (Lynch, 1975) has two sections.

PERSONAL ASSETS. Responses may be listed under six categories:
"Things I do well"
"Things that make me feel fully alive or happy to be me"
"Things I would like to try at least once"
"Things I might start doing again"
"Things I would enjoy doing for others"
"Things I would like to do for my community"

PERSONAL LIABILITIES. Responses may be listed under four categories:
"Things that I would like to learn about or learn to do"
"Things I should stop wasting time on"
"Relationships that I could develop and enjoy more"
"Things that I could do for myself—for my own growth, health, satisfaction"

"Twenty Things I Love to Do." "Twenty Things I Love to Do" (Simon, Howe, and Kirschenbaum, 1972) is an exercise that allows a person to list and examine activities from a variety of dimensions. Group members should fill out the worksheet individually (Example 10-3), and at the completion of the exercise participants share what they learned with one other person and then with the group. In addition to the codes listed at the bottom of the form in Example 10-3, Simon* (1974, pp. 7-10) suggests additional codes that might be used:

1. Put the number 52 by those activities that you would want to do at least once each week for the rest of your life.
2. Frittering your time on nonproductive pursuits may be frowned upon. If any of your favorites are frittering (your time away), mark them F.
3. Developing skill in any pursuit is a challenge. Indicate areas with DS wherever you want to improve yourself.
4. Exercise is essential for physical as well as mental health. An E can mark those activities that involve exercise.
5. Some of your likes may involve the possibility of physical or psychological danger. Mark them CR for calculated risk.
6. Some activities help us grow intellectually and emotionally. Indicate SI for self-improvement.
7. Too often we don't spend the time we want to on things we like. Put an MO by these for more often.
8. Which of these activities are a source of relaxation? Mark those R.
9. Sometimes enthusiasm for one of your activities can be so strong that you want to spread and share it with others. Mark these S.

*For information about current Values Realization materials and a schedule of nationwide training workshops, contact Sidney B. Simon, Old Mountain Rd., Hadley, MA 01035.

EXAMPLE 10-3

TWENTY THINGS I LOVE TO DO

	1	2	3	4	5	6
1.						
2.						
3.						
4.						
5.						
6.						
7.						
8.						
9.						
10.						
11.						
12.						
13.						
14.						
15.						
16.						
17.						
18.						
19.						
20.						

1—Put letter "A" after activities you like to do alone, "P" after those you enjoy doing with people, and "AP" by those you enjoy doing either alone or with people.

2—Put a dollar sign after all the activities that cost at least $4 or more each time you do them.

3—Put "N5" after those activities you would not have had on your list five years ago.

4—Put "PL" next to the activities that need planning. (Use your personal definition of planning.)

5—After each activity indicate when was the last time you did it (month or year).

6—Put a check beside those things your friends usually initiate.

From Simon, S., Howe, L., and Kirschenbaum, H.: Values clarification: a handbook of practical strategies for teachers and students, New York, 1972, Hart Publishing Co., Inc., pp. 30-34. (For information about current Values Realization materials and a schedule of nationwide training workshops, contact Sidney B. Simon, Old Mountain Rd., Hadley, MA 01035.)

10. If you live to be 100 and are in good health, which of these activities do you think you will still enjoy? Write 100 by these.
11. Write the letters FY next to those items that you think will not appear on your list five years from now.

Slice of Life. The purpose of the Slice of Life exercise (Simon, 1974) is to allow a person to determine the present pattern of daily living and the time available for leisure. In this exercise each person draws a large circle representing a day, then divides the circle into four quarters (using dotted lines), each quarter representing 6 hours, and finally divides the quarters into segments to represent the following typical day:

1. Hours sleeping
2. Hours at work on the job
3. Hours spend on work that is taken home
4. Hours spend with friends away from work place
5. Hours with family, including mealtimes
6. Hours doing household chores
7. Hours of free time

The processing should focus on the use of free time, with group members discussing how free time is spent.

Days of Delight. Days of Delight (Simon, 1974) is a fantasy exercise whose purpose is to help individuals organize and use their time ideally to meet their needs. Participants construct an ideal 48-hour period, including what they will be doing, who they will be with, where they will be, and any other pertinent details. Processing in the group will focus on a comparison of actual days with ideal days in terms of components (e.g., work, sleep, eating, and exercise), feelings, and how the ideal days might be incorporated into current and future life-style.

Guided fantasy. The guided fantasy exercise is designed to enable participants to experience leisure as a "state of mind." Individual participants get comfortable, close their eyes, and practice relaxation techniques such as breathing and exhaling slowly. Once the participants are relaxed, they are then guided toward the perfect leisure fantasy (Example 10-4 illustrates leadership techniques). Processing the fantasy should involve the encouragement of group members to share their individual experiences, focusing on sights, sounds, smells, tastes, and so on, and closing with a discussion of some of the differences between their fantasies and their real lives.

Retirement leisure decision making. Once the assessment of an individual's current leisure life-style has been completed, the program leader should encourage participants to engage in retirement leisure decision making. The purpose of such decision making is to design retirement leisure goals. Participants may be assisted in this process of decision making through a series of exercises.

Barriers to leisure. The purpose of the barriers to leisure exercise is to help participants anticipate some of the barriers to leisure. As a group, the participants list real or perceived barriers and constraints that may inhibit leisure. The

EXAMPLE 10-4

GUIDED FANTASY EXERCISE

The following outline is a guide to use in leading a guided fantasy experience. It is only meant as an aid and should not be read word for word.

I. *Relaxation phase:* Participants must feel relaxed to fully gain something from the experience.
   A. Find a comfortable position, either in your chairs or on the floor. (Pause)
   B. It is most helpful if you close your eyes and allow yourself to get in the experience in a total way. (Pause)
   C. Be aware of your surroundings. Know the building you are in, the room you are in, and the people around you.
   D. Let everything go! Let the outside sounds drift by and begin to focus on *yourself.* (Pause)
   E. Begin to focus on your breathing. Be aware of inhalation and exhalation of breath. Watch your cycle of breath go in and out, in and out. (Pause)
   F. Be aware of your body. Feel the contact of your body with the chair or floor. Feel where the tension in your body is. Feel the tenseness and release it—let it go. (Pause)
   G. Continue to be aware of your breathing. Follow it in and out, inhale and exhale. (Pause)

II. *Fantasy phase:* Slowly move into assisting the participants to move into their respective fantasies. Do not plant specific ideas in their fantasies, but give them plenty of free space to roam.
   A. Begin to move into the place you want to be in your fantasy. (Pause)
   B. Be aware of the surroundings in this place. What does it look like there? (Pause)
   C. What does it *feel* like to be in this place? (Pause)
   D. Are you with other people or alone? (Pause)
   E. What does it *feel* like to be with these people or to be alone? (Pause)
   F. Be aware of the smells, sights, and sounds at this place. What are they like? (Pause)
   G. Begin to be aware of your breathing once again. Inhale and exhale, in and out. (Pause)
   H. Slowly and at your relaxed pace, begin to pull out of your fantasy and return to the group.
   I. Take your time; do not hurry! Slowly open your eyes and pull back with us!

Used with permission of the Leisure Exploration Service, Student Recreation Center, Southern Illinois University, Carbondale, Illinois.

group will also collectively list steps to take to reduce or overcome these barriers. The group leader should be particularly sensitive to the barriers of attitude, finances, health, living arrangement, and social relationships that are important for leisure adjustment and that Manion (1974) has identified as important areas to be addressed in the retirement planning process.

Autobiographical leisure presentations. Autobiographical leisure presentations are designed to allow retired persons who have adjusted well to retirement to relate their experiences in arriving at leisure decisions. The presenters and group members should be allowed to engage in interchanges—experience has shown that this type of activity is one of the most effective techniques for eliciting group discussion (Hunter, 1980).

Field trips. Observations of programs and services for older persons such as those provided by voluntary associations, senior centers, and planned community housing provide opportunities for firsthand exposure to leisure service settings. Participants should be oriented to the programs and services before the field trips. Time should be allowed for the processing of observations and questions by the group.

Steps in decision making. the purpose of this activity is to provide participants with a systematic approach to decision making. Steps in the decision making process are:

1. Select a decision to be made.
2. Determine the purpose of that decision.
3. Collect information relative to the decision.
4. Examine the alternatives to the decision.
5. Determine whether anyone is influencing the decision.
6. Make either a final or tentative decision.
7. Examine feelings related to accomplishing the goal.

Participants are then given the opportunity to use these steps (Example 10-5 is a worksheet) in the leisure decision making process.

Evaluation. The preretirement leisure education program should be evaluated, including the strengths and weaknesses of the program materials. The evaluation form presented in Example 10-2 is equally as applicable to a preretirement leisure education program as to a general preretirement education program. Participants should fill out individually the evaluation questionnaire and return it to the program leader.

ADULT EDUCATION OF THE ELDERLY

Adult education programs for the elderly have emerged in recent years because of the research confirming that older persons can learn and that the learning process can be carried out in effective ways (Eklund, 1969; Vermilye, 1976). Programs of education designated as older adult education, continuing education, lifelong learning, and life-cycle learning have emphasized the transmitting of content on a variety of topics. This section will discuss the topics of elderly

EXAMPLE 10-5

LEISURE DECISION MAKING PROCESS

Select decision _____

Purpose of decision _____
_____

What information did you collect? _____
_____

How was the information relevant to your decision? _____
_____
_____

Did you consider any alternatives and the outcomes for the alternatives?
_____
_____

Did anyone influence this decision? _____
_____

Was your decision final or tentative? _____
_____
_____

How did you feel about accomplishing your goal? _____
_____
_____

Used with permission of the Leisure Exploration Service, Student Recreation Center, Southern
Illinois University, Carbondale, Illinois.

participation in adult education, structuring adult education for the elderly, and
elderly adult education as a leisure service.

Older persons tend to be underrepresented in formal adult education activities.
Participation rates, reasons for participation, and reasons for low participation
will be examined.

**Elderly
participation in
adult education**

  PARTICIPATION RATES. The participation rates of older persons in adult
education classes are very low. Table 10-3 presents data from a Harris and
Associates study that shows an almost constant participation decline by age
category. Only 2 percent of all persons over 65 are enrolled in some type of
course. This low participation rate is confirmed in a study by Heisel, Darkenwald, and Anderson (1981), which shows that less than 3 percent of those over
the age of 60 take part in organized education.

  It has been suggested that the statistics reported on the participation of
older persons in organized education understate their involvement in *learning*.
Hiemstra (1976) has noted that many older persons undertake self-directed

learning projects that total an average of 324 hours annually. Lack of participation should not therefore be considered the same as lack of learning.

REASONS FOR PARTICIPATION. Older persons participate in education for various reasons. The National Council on the Aging (1975), in a Harris and Associates study, presented information concerning the reasons why older persons participate in education. An examination of Table 10-4 shows that the primary reasons for educational participation *for all ages* was to expand "knowledge about some field or hobby," but for the young the primary reason was to acquire job skills. Older persons were more interested in taking courses to make good use of time and to be with others.

REASONS FOR LOW PARTICIPATION. A number of reasons may be given for the low participation by older persons in formal adult education activities. These reasons may be grouped into what Spencer (1980) calls barriers.

Informational barriers. Informational barriers produce an inadequate awareness of available educational resources. Older persons often lack knowl-

TABLE 10-3 **Participation in education by age categories***

Ages	Enrolled
18-24	34
25-39	15
40-54	5
55-64	5
65+	2
TOTAL PUBLIC	13

From The myth and reality of aging in America, 1975, published by The National Council on the Aging, Inc., p. 100.
*Given in percentages.

TABLE 10-4 **Reasons for participation in education by age categories***

Reasons	Public 18-24 (34%)	Public 25-39 (15%)	Public 40-54 (5%)	Public 55-64 (5%)	Public 65+ (2%)
To expand your general knowledge about some field or hobby	72	67	85	80	76
To acquire job skills	60	60	14	24	6
To make good use of your time	34	20	14	49	39
To be with other people	23	8	—	44	28
Other	6	12	3	—	2

From The myth and reality of aging in America, 1975, published by The National Council on the Aging, Inc., p. 108.
*Given in percentages.

edge of local learning opportunities and, as Peterson (1981, p. 245) points out, the consequences are that "people are likely to attend courses only in an institution that they have previously visited and thus view as accessible."

Situational barriers. Factors such as poor health, lack of transportation, and competing demands on time (Graney and Hays, 1976; Goodrow, 1975; National Council on the Aging, 1975) are significant situational barriers.

Institutional barriers. Institutional barriers include adult education program components that often discourage participation. Barriers that have a negative impact on enrollment are costly program fees (Graney and Hays, 1976; National Council on the Aging, 1975), strict requirements for attendance, the red tape involved in class registration (Goodrow, 1975), and class scheduling inconvenient for the elderly (night classes) (Hiemstra, 1975).

Attitudinal barriers. Negative stereotypes depicting the elderly as unable to learn are often accepted and internalized by older persons; this results in a reluctance to enter an educational setting. Internalized negative stereotypes are expressed by older persons who say they are too old to learn (Graney and Hays, 1976; Goodrow, 1975; National Council on the Aging, 1975), they lack past educational achievements reflected in poor grades, and they dislike tests (Goodrow, 1975).

Proper structuring of adult education for the elderly may help to overcome attitudinal as well as the other barriers.

The structure of adult education for the elderly must reflect the needs of older persons. This section will examine a number of considerations in offering adult education for the elderly.

Structuring adult education for the elderly

RECRUITMENT. The recruitment of older persons for adult education should involve the appropriate constituencies. This involvement may take the form of establishment of an advisory committee consisting of agency personnel and older persons to develop effective outreach and recruitment techniques. A variety of techniques of outreach and recruitment may be employed such as sending out informational letters and course application forms to senior centers and other facilities, follow-up letters and phone calls in response to all inquiries, and visits by the instructor or planner to meet with groups of older persons and program personnel. These techniques allow the offering of personalized outreach to older persons and agency personnel, thus providing opportunities to discuss the purpose, content, and value of programs or classes.

REQUIREMENTS TO ENTER AND CREDIT. The requirements to enter should avoid excessive paperwork and registration red tape and should provide options for taking the course noncredit or for credit. Crandall (1980, p. 492) states that the requirements to enter should be "motivation, interest, basic reading skills, and willingness to learn." The option of taking college or university classes noncredit helps alleviate some of the concerns an older learner might have about strict attendance requirements, studying, grades, and tests (Goodrow, 1975). If credit is desired, then the older person should be informed of skill requirements, course requirements, and necessary steps for degree completion.

FINANCING. Adult education programs and classes should be offered to the elderly at a nominal cost or free of charge. Long and Rossing (1979) found that 27 states had state legislation or policies allowing tuition reduction or waivers for older persons. Tuition reduction or waivers provide a motivator for older adult participation and may decrease the low participation rate.

SCHEDULING. Adult education programs and courses should be scheduled to meet in a 2- to 3-hour block of time and during the day rather than in the evening. Scheduling for longer but less frequent periods should help alleviate transportation problems. Meeting during the day will relieve the fear of going out at night, as well as facilitate the use of public transportation (Goodrow, 1975).

CLASS SETTING. Class settings should be in convenient locations and in environments conducive to learning. Senior centers, housing sites, and nursing homes provide convenient locations, enhance ease of mobility, and avoid transportation problems. The class setting should be in an environment with comfortable seating that can be moved to increase social interaction, with excellent acoustics and lighting and controllable air conditioning and heat.

INSTRUCTOR SELECTION. Instructor selection is one of the most important components in the process of structuring adult education for the elderly. Previous teaching experience with older persons or special interest in adult education are important criteria in the instructor selection process (Stuen, Spencer, and Raines, 1982, p. 27). Potential instructors should be contacted on an individual basis, the class or program described, and interest ascertained before the position is offered. Written communication specifying the instructor's obligations, the goals of the class or program, and a class outline should not be overlooked.

TEACHING TECHNIQUES. The instructor should have a knowledge of principles regarding older adult learning and teaching techniques for older adults. Stuen, Spencer, and Raines (1982, p. 43) list the principles of older adult learning:

1. Older adults learn differently from children and resent being treated in a childlike manner. Older adults want to be self-respecting and, consequently, want to be responsible for their actions.
2. Older adults want the learning situation to make use of their life experience. It should have direct application to the unique aspects of their own personal situations.
3. Older adults want problem-centered learning that represents "real world" attitudes and values. Realistic examples help adults to apply learning to their own problems and needs.
4. Older adults learn when there is a need to know. Personal motivation and readiness exist when what is to be learned is important for learners.
5. Older adults learn when facts, ideas, or concepts relate to already known information. This form of association, building on what is previously known, helps to promote long-term learning.

6. Older adults learn through self-activity. Learning is a personal process that requires the involvement of adults in self-planned or initiated experiences.
7. Older adults learn best by doing. The "learn by doing" concept helps older adults to gain self-confidence and task mastery. The involvement of different senses in learning adds reinforcement.
8. Older adults learn in a continuing and continual process. Through participation in lifelong learning, older adults who are "never too old to learn," structure their learning around what is of greatest importance to them.

Stuen, Spencer, and Raines* also present teaching techniques for older adults, adapted from Okun (1977, pp. 139-155):

RATE OF PRESENTATION OF INFORMATION

1. Present new information at a fairly slow rate.
2. Let the older adult learner proceed at his or her own rate whenever feasible.
3. Provide the older adult learner with ample time to respond to questions.
4. Present a limited amount of material in any single presentation to prevent "swamping" effects.

ORGANIZATION OF INFORMATION

1. Present new information in a highly organized fashion.
2. Use section headings, handouts, summaries, and so on so that the adult learner can get a "handle" on the material.
3. If memory processes are taxed in a learning project, encourage the adult learner to use retrieval plans.
4. To prevent confusion, avoid introduction of irrelevant information.
5. If visual displays are used, employ simple stimuli.

PRESENTATION OF INFORMATION

1. Use auditory mode of presentation when presenting discrete bits of information to be used immediately.
2. Use visual mode when presenting textual materials to capitalize on opportunity for review during reading.

MEANINGFULNESS OF MATERIAL

1. Present information that is meaningful to the adult learner.
2. Assess cognitive structure of the adult learner to ensure that material is introduced at the appropriate level.
3. Use examples, illustrations, and so on that are concrete.
4. Take advantage of the experience that the adult learner possesses.
5. Relate new information to what the adult learner already knows.

---

*Modified from Stuen, C., Spencer, B., and Raines, M.: Seniors teaching seniors: a manual for training older adult teachers, New York, 1982, Brookdale Institute on Aging and Human Development, pp. 28-30.

DEGREE OF LEARNING

1. Provide ample opportunity for the older adult learner to "overlearn" material before moving on to new material.
2. Remove time constraints from instructional and evaluation process.

TRANSFER EFFECTS

1. As an initial step in learning, identify and eliminate inappropriate responses that may "compete" with appropriate responses.
2. Organize instructional units so that potentially interfering materials are spaced far away from each other.
3. Stress differences between concepts before similarities.
4. Make instructional sequence parallel hierarchy of knowledge in any given area.
5. Instructional procedures should be premised on knowledge of the conditions required for a type of learning based on task analysis.
6. Introduce a variety of techniques for solving problems.

FEEDBACK EFFECTS

1. Develop learning sets that maximize opportunity for positive transfer effects (i.e., learning to learn effects).
2. Provide verbal feedback concerning correctness of responses after each component of the task is completed.
3. *Do not* assume that initially poor performance on a novel, complex task is indicative of low aptitude.

CLIMATE

1. Establish a supportive climate.
2. Engage the older adult learner in information-oriented, collaborative evaluation.
3. Encourage the older adult learner to take educated guesses.

EVALUATION. Evaluation should be an integral part of any program. Participants should be informed of the importance of evaluation, because it is through evaluation that one determines the extent to which the program achieved its objectives. Participants should also be informed that the completion of all evaluation procedures will help improve future programs through a better understanding of participant needs. If evaluation instruments are used, they should be printed in large type and have directions that are succinct. To ensure that participants fully understand the questions on the evaluation instrument, the facilitator could circulate among the participants, giving individual assistance when necessary, while attempting to remain as unobtrusive as possible. If necessary, the evaluator could read each question or passage aloud, instructing each participant to take time on each question.

Adult education as a leisure service for older persons has a philosophy support-ive of the two developmental challenges of the later years, as put forward by Moody (1978). The first developmental challenge for older persons is to live their lives as fully functioning adults in society's mainstream and to avoid disengage-ment by engaging in meaningful activity and life experiences. The second de-velopmental challenge is to facilitate self-actualization through a process of "transcendence of the past, transcendence of previous social roles and tran-scendence of a limited definition of the self," (Moody, 1978, p. 44) resulting in new personal meaning and growth. This section will examine the learning needs and interests of older persons and adult education delivery systems that have a leisure focus.

Elderly adult education as a leisure service

LEARNING NEEDS. Howard Y. McClusky (1974) has aptly set forth five categories of learning needs that most older persons experience. Each of these five categories of needs will be examined from the perspective of need satisfac-tion through leisure.

Coping needs. Coping needs relate to the maintenance of adequate physical, psychological, and social well-being. This need category includes ed-ucational competencies in exercise and social interaction to enable individuals to better cope with physical, psychological, and social changes.

Influence needs. Influence needs include the needs of individuals to con-trol and shape the quality of life as social change agents. Education in this category focuses on the process of leisure decision making for the individual and for society to assure quality of life for all.

Expressive needs. Expressive needs relate to the satisfaction derived from activities of an intrinsic value that have been unexpressed or underex-pressed in earlier years. Learning to write poetry, to weave, to woodcarve, or to make films are examples of expressive need satisfaction through leisure.

Contribution needs. Contribution needs are concerned with older per-sons giving to others because of a desire to be helpful. These needs may be satisfied through volunteering in a variety of settings.

Transcendence needs. Transcendence needs are expressed in the desire for continued growth and self-fulfillment. Leisure education enables older per-sons to transcend earlier stages or levels of development, moving toward higher levels of leisure literacy.

LEARNING INTERESTS. Adult education as a leisure service for older per-sons must offer programs and courses to specifically meet the interests of con-sumers. Hendrickson and Barnes (1967) found that the most frequently men-tioned learning interests were in the areas of religion, problems of aging, physi-cal fitness, leisure activities, the arts, public affairs, and practical affairs. Sarvis (1973) found that older persons were most interested in arts, crafts, consumer protection, foreign languages, and the senior power movement. A review of the findings of these two studies shows that older persons have a strong interest in leisure services such as physical fitness, the arts, crafts, and the general area of

TABLE 10-5 **Reasons for joining Duke Institute for Learning in Retirement**

Reason	No. of times given*
Intellectual stimulation and growth	59
Association with peers of similar interests	53
Desire to acquire new knowledge, skills, in subjects for which formerly no time	21
Opportunity to use skills	12
Interest in discussion groups or specific courses	11
Service to the community	9
To learn more about retirement	5
For enjoyment	4
Want association with a university	2

From Lefstein, L., and O'Barr, J.: Continuing education and the older learner: a program development model based on Duke University's Institute for Learning in Retirement, Center Reports on Advances in Research, Duke University Center for the Study of Aging and Human Development 3(1):5-6, 1979.
*Some gave more than one reason.

TABLE 10-6 **Areas of special interest within Duke Institute for Learning in Retirement**

Area of interest	No. of times given
Literature	51
Current events, economics, politics	31
Music	24
History	24
Philosophy and religion	20
Travel	19
Editing and writing	15
Community service and activities	10
Languages	10
Photography	9
Art	15
Concerns of aging and retirement—health, nutrition	13
Ecology, wildlife, and environment	7
Drama	6
Human relations, discussion groups	6
Swimming	7
Science: botany, biology	6
Movies, TV production	4
Money management	3
Communications, semantics	3
Genealogy, historic preservation	2
Dancing	2
Social work	4
Psychic research	2
Statistics	1

From Lefstein, L., and O'Barr, J.: Continuing education and the older learner: a program development model based on Duke University's Institute for Learning in Retirement, Center Reports on Advances in Research, Duke University Center for the Study of Aging and Human Development 3(1):5-6, 1979.

leisure activities. Interest in public affairs, consumer protection, and the senior power movement can be channeled into volunteer service activities in a variety of leisure service settings.

ADULT EDUCATION DELIVERY SYSTEMS. Adult education for older persons, in an effort to overcome participation barriers and meet the needs of older persons, has developed a variety of delivery systems. The strategies of outreach, linkage, and accessible environments have enabled educators to work with groups and organizations such as colleges and universities, senior centers, institutions, and libraries.

Colleges and universities. Colleges and universities have been slow in responding to the educational needs of older persons. Studies have shown that less than 3 percent of those over 60 are enrolled in institutions of higher education, although as many as 50 percent want to continue their education (Heisel, Darkenwald, and Anderson, 1981; Shepherd, 1980). Two programs enabling older persons to continue their education are the Duke Institute for Learning in Retirement and Elderhostel.

Duke Institute for Learning in Retirement. The Duke Institute for Learning in Retirement (DILR) was founded in 1977 at Duke University in Durham, North Carolina. The curriculum was based on a learning exchange/peer teaching model in which members would function as both teachers and students in an atmosphere encouraging active participation of the older learner who had life experiences and skills to share. A conscious decision was made to place the program on a university campus to attract the independent older learner and "to acknowledge the intellectual abilities of the participants and allow the share use of libraries, classrooms, and other university facilities" (Lefstein and O'Barr, 1979, p. 2). Table 10-5 presents reasons given by older consumers for joining DILR, Table 10-6 illustrates the areas of special interest, and Table 10-7 displays course offerings for 1977 through 1979. An examination of Tables 10-6 and 10-7 reveals that the areas of interest and the course offerings are a mixture of academic and leisure-oriented subjects. Information on DILR may be obtained by writing to the Institute for Learning in Retirement.

Elderhostel. Elderhostel is a rapidly expanding national educational program that enables persons 60 and over to use the facilities of colleges and universities. Programs usually take place in the summer and are organized into 1-week units that combine course work designed for the elderhostelers with dormitory living and a variety of leisure opportunities.

The Elderhostel concept originated with David Bianco, director of Residential Life at the University of New Hampshire, and Marty Knowlton, a well-known social activist, philosopher, and educator who had just finished a 4-year walking tour of Europe. Beginning in 1975 with courses at five New Hampshire colleges serving 200 pioneering hostelers, Elderhostel has become a national program of more than 400 institutions in all 50 states and six provinces in Canada. It serves more than 35,000 older people.

An array of liberal arts and science courses that explore various aspects of the human experience are offered. In general the courses do not presuppose

TABLE 10-7   **Duke Institute for Learning in Retirement course offerings (1977-1979)**

Course title	Session offered*					
Great Decisions	1	2	3			6
Writing for Publication	1	2				
Drugs	1					
James Joyce	1	2				
What's Happening to Ourselves	1	2				
Comparative Religions	1		3			
China	1					
Socratic Circle	1					
Opera	1		3			
Archives Workshop	1					
Sculpture Workshop	1					
Swimming Can Be Fun!		2	3	4	5	6
Nature & Function of County Government	1					
Energy		2				
Points of View: Short Story Discussion		2	3		5	6
Mobility Maintenance		2				
Trip Through the Light Fantastic			3			
Crisis in American Institutions			3		5	6
Introduction to General Semantics			3		5	
Current Events Workshop			3		5	6
Pottery Workshop			3			
Water Color			3			
Cardiopulmonary Resuscitation			3			
Writers' Workshop			3		5	
Nutrition				4		
Poetry				4		
Discovering the Past				4		
Writing Nostalgia				4		
Cuba				4		
Medicine & Society				4		
New Deal				4		
Being Human				4		
Othello and Otello				4		
Conversational French					5	6
Issues in Humanistic Medicine					5	
The Long Search: A Study in Religions					5	

From Lefstein, L., and O'Barr, J.: Continuing education and the older learner: a program development model based on Duke Universty's Institute for Learning in Retirement, Center Reports on Advances in Research, Duke University Center for the Study of Aging and Human Development 3(1):5-6, 1979.
*1, Fall, 1977; 2, Winter, 1978; 3, Spring, 1978; 4, Elderhostel, 1978; 5, Fall, 1978; 6, Spring, 1979.

TABLE 10-7 **Duke Institute for Learning in Retirement course offerings (1977-1979)—cont'd**

Course title	Session offered
In Search of Reality	5
Art History, Oil & Water Colors	6
Chemistry and Societal Problems	6
Dublin: The Early Abbey Theater, 1900-1925	6
Globetrotting	6
The Joseph Saga	6
Enjoying Music	6
Photography: Its Social, Economic & Artistic Impact	6
Physical Education	6
TV Production	6
Words, Words, Words	6

previous knowledge of the subject; require no homework or examinations; and are offered at a modest cost that includes fees, room, board, and leisure opportunities. Participating adults are not lectured to but allowed to engage in discussion in groups limited to 30 or 40 adults. Courses are offered at large, urban, public universities and at small, rural, private liberal arts colleges. Choosing an Elderhostel is usually guided by the two considerations of location and courses offered. Elderhostel institutions are committed to encouraging the "hosteling" part of the Elderhostel—that is, to make it as easy as possible for participants to travel from campus to campus and to integrate an Elderhostel into a longer trip to visit family or to see a new part of the country. For more information write to Elderhostel (see Appendix C).

Senior centers. An increasing number of active, healthy older persons who are retired and living in the community turn to the senior center as a source of meaningful leisure. Likewise, an increasing number of older persons who have professional skills or expertise want to enhance their self-worth and self-esteem through teaching and service roles. This section will examine two programs involving colleges and universities and linkages with senior centers. One addresses the leisure education needs of senior center participants; the other addresses teaching and service roles of senior center participants.

Developing Adult Resources Through Education. Developing Adult Resources Through Education (DARE), a cooperative effort of Huron College in Huron, South Dakota and the Huron Area Senior Center, was designed to meet the adult education needs and interests of older persons in that rural area (Price, 1980). More than 300 people 60 years of age and older participated in a wide variety of courses—Poetry and Creative Writing, Senior Surfers (swimming), Relaxation Exercises/Learn to Manage Stress, Armchair Travelogues, Senior Drama and Expression, Film Festival, Health Topics Series, and First Aid.

Courses are offered by Huron College instructors at the senior center, thus allowing senior center participants to continue their other involvements and take courses in a familiar and nonthreatening environment.

A 20-member advisory board composed primarily of older persons has been cited as the key to the success of DARE (Price, 1980, p. 426). Courses have been designed to reach the goals of knowledge, social interaction, and personal fulfillment. Instructors have appreciated the opportunity to work with older students who have an ability and eagerness to learn. Had the courses been taught at Huron College, enrollments would have been drastically reduced. The success of DARE has resulted in expansion of classes to rural satellite centers.

Seniors Teaching Seniors. The Seniors Teaching Seniors (STS) program at Columbia University in New York City was designed to strengthen senior centers by training selected center members to become teachers, organizers, and leaders of education programs for older persons. The specific objectives of the program, according to Stuen, Spencer, and Raines,[*] were:

1. To recruit and select 30 elderly from among the senior centers in New York City who would enhance their leadership and teaching role among their elderly peers through training
2. To enlist the cooperation of major senior centers and negotiate their assurance that the trainees would be assigned program responsibilities on graduation
3. To design an 8-week training program for the 30 selected elderly based on an understanding of teaching methods and learning patterns of older people, group techniques and skills, substantive teaching areas, and course support needs
4. To conduct two 8-week training sessions with at least 15 older adults in each
5. To involve major university departments through provision of teaching faculty
6. To provide follow-up and consultation to participants and involved senior centers on completion of the course
7. To involve university graduate students in the planning, implementation, and evaluation of this program

An evaluation of the program showed that 92.5 percent of those older persons who registered for the program successfully completed it, and 82 percent of the graduating class succeeded in attaining a teaching position within 4 to 5 months. More than 80 percent of the members desired a continuation of the program at a later date (Kaye, Monk, and Stuen, 1982).

Institutions. Adult education programs have been adapted to meet the needs of the physically and mentally impaired institutionalized older person. These programs must be "flexible, non-threatening, self-enhancing, personalized" (Wass and West, 1977, p. 415). Reduced visual and auditory acuity can be compensated for by using large visual aids, by pacing presentations to allow time for processing and interpreting of visual and auditory stimuli, and by using

---

[*]Modified from Stuen, C., Spencer, B., and Raines, M.: Seniors teaching seniors: a manual for training older adult teachers, New York, 1982, Brookdale Institute on Aging and Human Development, pp. 11-12.

Thomas O. Byerts

These institutionalized older persons eagerly await their late afternoon
adult education course.

a variety of sensory modalities in instruction (e.g., hearing the instructor, touching an object, and seeing a visual representation). Lewis (1979) gives two examples of successful education programs for institutionalized older persons.

Lakeside Place Nursing Home. Lakeside Place Nursing Home in northern
Kentucky established a cooperative agreement with Northern Kentucky University. Preliminary to the establishment of a program, resident needs and interests were assessed with the assistance of nursing home staff, and ways of
adapting the presentations of instructors to meet the needs of residents were
determined. Classes were taught in the evening for 1 hour per week for 13
consecutive weeks and covered topics such as "The Arts of Africa," "Tips on
Grandparenting," and "Coping with the Future." Each instructor brought materials that residents placed in portfolios.

Evaluation of the program stressed the importance of a number of implementation strategies. Staff cooperation was vital to program success, particularly the cooperation of nursing staff, who assisted with transportation,
arranged clinic appointments, and so on. Scheduling classes in the evenings
were preferred by both instructors and residents. The awarding of one college
credit hour to each resident who completed at least 10 courses was a highly
valued form of recognition.

Philadelphia Geriatric Center. The Philadelphia Geriatric Center (PGC),
having a predominately Jewish resident population, collaborated with Gratz

College, the oldest Hebraic college in the western hemisphere, to develop a course sensitive to the religious and cultural backgrounds of PGC residents. The PGC Residents' Council cosponsored the courses, assuming responsibility for registration, note taking during classes, and dissemination of these notes after they were typed in large print. Students were charged a registration fee of $1 to help with the cost of class note reproduction, paper, pencils, handouts, student folders, and refreshments. A graduation ceremony complete with certificates was held to which members of the board of directors of PGC and Gratz and relatives of graduating students were invited. The success of the program may be measured by the number of students completing the course (50 residents) and by the number of times the series was offered (twice).

Libraries. Libraries provide both individual and group adult education services to older persons. Individual services may include books by mail and print magnifiers for the visually impaired. Group services may be provided to settings such as senior centers, planned community housing, and institutions.

An example of a library providing services for older persons is the Adriance Memorial Library of Poughkeepsie, New York. The program began in 1953; the library now serves more than 3,000 older people in private homes, senior centers, residential housing units, nursing and boarding homes, and hospitals (Odescalchi, 1979). The older person who is living at home may require frequent visits from the library-owned station wagon, especially if the person is an avid reader. Individuals in senior centers, nursing and boarding homes, and hospitals are supplied with bimonthly or monthly rotating book collections placed on a special "library shelf" in the recreation room of each facility. These collections include nonfiction, fiction, mystery, romance, westerns, travel, and cookbooks—all in regular and large print. In addition, magazines, musical and spoken records, phonographs, films, and framed art prints are supplied to persons in both individual and group living situations. Materials are delivered directly to nonambulatory persons in their rooms or at their bedsides. A variety of other programs are offered by the library such as sing-along programs, craft and hobby classes, essay contests, talent shows, and weekly movie programs. Outreach efforts by a library may thus serve to transform the isolated older person into a participating member of the community.

SUMMARY

Education has recently accepted the view that learning is a lifelong process for all persons and the challenge of preretirement education and adult education for the elderly. Leisure education is a critical element in the retirement preparation process and an important content area of adult education courses.

Retirement has become a more widespread phenomenon in the twentieth century because of increased life expectancy, increased worker productivity, little demand for the labor of older persons, and availability of social security and pension plans. Retirement may be viewed as an event signifying the end of employment or as a role involving the exchange of the work role for the leisure role. The decision to retire may be voluntary, based on the availability of adequate retirement income, the desire for more leisure, and a more positive attitude toward retirement; or the decision may be involuntary because of the inability to find a job, pressure from employers, and mandatory retirement policies. Recent literature on the impact of retirement shows that retirees are generally satisfied with retirement, that retirement does not cause poor health, and that retirement has little impact on social participation. However, lower income may be a significant factor affecting adjustment to retirement.

Preretirement education programs may facilitate the transition from worker to retiree. Such education programs have a long history, beginning with the efforts of business and industry to explain their pension plans and later followed by the expansion of content and sponsorship. These programs are not widespread in institutions of higher education or in business and industry; the result is that most individuals do not plan for retirement. Preretirement education programs have been shown to benefit both employers and employees in improved productivity, morale, and reduced resistance to retirement.

Planning and conducting preretirement education programs involve a variety of considerations. Preretirement education programs may be sponsored by business, industry, government agencies, colleges and universities, and community agencies. Promotion should convey a positive image of aging to gain community support and cooperation and thus help to overcome resistance. Eligibility for program participation should be based on interest and flexible age criteria. The impact on group discussion of the mixing of social classes and professional with nonprofessional employees should be considered when determining group composition. Group sizes of 15 to 30 people allow for group interaction and the raising of questions. The meeting place should be comfortable and accessible. Group consensus should be used whenever possible to determine the meeting time, whether this be during the day or in the evening. The delivery process that emphasizes the lecture-discussion approach is recommended because it allows for group interaction and interchange as the focus of information sharing. Leaders for preretirement education programs may be drawn from a variety of business, service, and professional groups, provided that the leaders have the necessary knowledge and skills. There seems to be an emerging consensus that the content of preretirement education programs should address the topics of health, income, housing, social and family relationships, and leisure. Evaluations should be conducted for each session and for the overall program.

Preretirement leisure education programs are important because of the significance of leisure attitudes and patterns for life satisfaction after retirement. These programs may be delivered through an existing preretirement education program or as an independent program. Leaders of such programs should have competence in leisure education and knowledge of the psychosocial aspects of aging and leisure. The preretirement leisure programming process should focus on the assessment of current leisure life-style, retirement leisure decision making, and an evaluation of the strengths and weaknesses of the program.

Adult education programs for the elderly have emerged in recent years and have emphasized a variety of topics, including leisure-oriented subjects. Studies of elderly participation in adult education show that the participation rates of older persons in adult education classes tend to be very low—from 2 to 3 percent of all people over 65 years of age. Reasons for participation of older persons include an interest in taking courses to make good use of time and to be with others. Reasons for low participation are the presence of informational barriers (inadequate awareness of educational resources and learning opportunities), situational barriers (poor health, lack of transportation, and competing demands on time), institutional barriers (costly program fees, attendance requirements, class registration red tape, and poor class scheduling), and attitudinal barriers that depict older persons as unable to learn.

Structuring adult education for the elderly should reflect the needs of older persons. Recruitment should use an advisory committee for outreach, informational letters, phone calls, and visitation with older persons and agency personnel to discuss the purpose, content, and value of programs and classes. The requirements to enter should avoid excessive paperwork and red tape and should provide options for taking a course for noncredit or for credit. Financing should enable programs and classes to be offered at a nominal cost or free of charge. Scheduling should be in a 2- to 3-hour block of time and during the day rather than in the evening. Programs and classes should be held in convenient locations and in environments conducive to learning. Whenever possible, instructors selected should have previous teaching experience with older persons or a special interest in adult education. Teaching should be based on sound principles of older adult learning and teaching techniques appropriate for older adults. Evaluation should be an integral part of every program, with adequate personnel available to assist with the evaluation process.

Adult education as a leisure service for older persons should respond to the learning needs and interests of older persons. It should be provided through delivery systems employing strategies such as outreach, linkage, and accessible environments. Five categories of learning needs may be satisfied through leisure: coping needs (exercise and social interaction), influence needs (leisure decision making), expressive needs (poetry, weaving, and woodcarving), contribution needs (volunteering), and transcendence needs (leisure education). Studies of the learning interests of older persons show a strong interest in leisure services such as physical fitness, the arts, crafts, and the general area of leisure activities. Examples of adult education delivery systems with a leisure focus are programs offered by colleges and universities, senior centers, institutions, and libraries.

REFERENCES

Atchley, R.: Adjustment to loss of job at retirement, Int. J. Aging Hum. Dev. **6:**17-27, 1975.

Atchley, R.: The sociology of retirement, New York, 1976, Schenkman Publishing Co., Inc.

Atchley, R.: The social forces in later life: an introduction to social gerontology, ed. 3, Belmont, Calif., 1980, Wadsworth Publishing Co.

Blank, R.: A changing worklife and retirement pattern: an historical perspective. In Morrison, M., editor: Economics of aging: the future of retirement, New York, 1982, Van Nostrand Reinhold Co.

Blau, Z.: Old age in a changing society, New York, 1973, New Viewpoints.

Brenner, H., and Linnell, R.: Preretirement planning programs, CUPA J. **27:**77-89, 1976.

Chatfield, W.: Economic and sociological factors influencing life satisfaction of the aged, J. Gerontol. **32:**593-599, 1977.

Clark, R., and Spengler, J.: Population aging in the twenty-first century, Aging **279-280:**6-13, 1978.

Cowgill, D.: Aging and modernization: a revision of the theory. In Gubrium, J., editor: Late life: communities and environmental policies, Springfield, Ill., 1974, Charles C Thomas, Publisher.

Crandall, R.: Gerontology: a behavioral approach, Reading, Mass., 1980, Addison-Wesley Publishing Co.

Darnley, F.: Adjustment to retirement: integrity or despair, Fam. Coordinator **24:**217-226, 1975.

Davis, N., and Teaff, J.: Facilitating role continuity of the elderly through leisure programming, Ther. Recreation J. **14:**32-36, 1980.

Donahue, W., Orbach, H., and Pollak, O.: Retirement: the emerging social pattern. In Tibbitts, C., editor: Handbook of social gerontology: societal aspects of aging, Chicago, 1960, University of Chicago Press.

Eklund, L.: Aging and the field of education. In Riley, M., Riley, J., and Johnson, M., editors: Aging and society, vol. 2, Aging and the professions, New York, 1969, Russell Sage Foundation.

Elmore, A.: Manual for coordinators of preretirement planning programs, Durham, N.C., 1977, Duke University Center for the Study of Aging and Human Development.

Glamser, F.: Determinants of a positive attitude toward retirement, J. Gerontol. **31:**104-107, 1976.

Glamser, F.: The impact of preretirement programs on the retirement experience, J. Gerontol. **36:**244-251, 1981.

Glamser, F., and DeJong, G.: The efficacy of preretirement preparation programs for industrial workers, J. Gerontol. **30:**595-600, 1975.

Goodrow, B.: Limiting factors in reducing participation in older adult learning opportunities, Gerontologist **15:**418-422, 1975.

Graney, M., and Hays, W.: Senior students: higher education after age 62, Educ. Gerontol. **1:**343-359, 1976.

Green, M., Pyron, H., Manion, V., and Wink=levoss, H.: Preretirement counseling, retirement adjustment and the older employee, Eugene, Ore., 1969, University of Oregon Press.

Haynes, S., McMichael, A., and Tyroler, H.: Survival after early and normal retirement, J. Gerontol. **33:**269-278, 1978.

Heisel, M., Darkenwald, G., and Anderson, R.: Educational participation behavior of adults 60 and older, Educ. Gerontol. **6:**227-240, 1981.

Hendrickson, A., and Barnes, R.: Educational needs of older people, Adult Leadership **16:**2-4, 32, 1967.

Hiemstra, R.: The older adult and learning, Lincoln, Neb., 1975, University of Nebraska.

Heimstra, R.: The older adults' learning projects, Educ. Gerontol. **1:**331-341, 1976.

Hodges, P.: Preretirement training: a business perspective, Generations pp. 27-29, Summer, 1982.

Hunter, W.: Preretirement education for hourly workers, Ann Arbor, Mich., 1968, The University of Michigan.

Hunter, W.: Preretirement education leader's manual, Ann Arbor, Mich., 1980, The University of Michigan.

Kalt, N., and Kohn, M.: Preretirement counseling: characteristics of programs and preferences of retirees, Gerontologist **15:**179-181, 1975.

Kasschau, P.: Reevaluating the need for retirement preparation programs, Industr. Gerontol. **1:**42-59, 1974.

Kaye, L., Monk, A., and Stuen, C.: The efficacy of a self help leadership training program for older adults, Paper presented at the annual scientific meeting of the Gerontological Society of America, Boston, November 19-23, 1982.

Kell, D., and Patton, C.: Reaction to induced early retirement, Gerontologist **18:**173-178, 1978.

Knowles, M.: The modern practice of adult education, New York, 1977, Association Press.

Lefstein, L., and O'Barr, J.: Continuing education and the older learner: a program development model based on Duke University's Institute for Learning in Retirement, Center Reports on Advances in Research, Duke University Center for the Study of Aging and Human Development 3(1), 1979.

Lewis, K.: Education for the institutionalized aged, Aging **299-300:**25-28, 1979.

Long, H., and Rossing, B.: Tuition waiver plans for older Americans in post-secondary public education institutions, Educ. Gerontol. **4:**161-174, 1979.

Lynch, J.: A fresh look at yourself: your most important resource. In Manion, V., editor: Plan now for your retirement: free to do, free to be, Eugene, Ore., 1975, Retirement Services, Inc.

Manion, V.: Issues and trends in preretirement education, Ind. Gerontol. **1:**28-36, 1974.

McClusky, H.: Education for aging: the scope of the field and perspectives for the future. In Grabowski, S., and Mason, W., editors: Learning for aging, Washington, D.C., 1974, Adult Education Association.

McPherson, B., and Guppy, N.: Preretirement life style and the degree of planning for retirement, J. Gerontol. **34:**254-263, 1979.

Monk, A.: Factors in the preparation for retirement by middle-aged adults, Gerontologist **11:**348-351, 1971.

Moody, H.: Education and the life cycle: a philosophy of aging. In Sherron, R., and Lumsden, D., editors: Introduction to educational gerontology, Washington, D.C., 1978, Hemisphere Publishing Corp.

Mulanaphy, J.: Retirement preparation in higher education, New York, 1978, Teachers Insurance Annuity Association.

Munnell, A.: The future of social security, Washington, D.C., 1977, The Brookings Institute.

National Council on the Aging: The myth and reality of aging in America, Washington, D.C., 1975, National Council on the Aging.

National Council on the Aging: Aging in the eighties: America in transition, Washington, 1981, National Council on the Aging.

Odescalchi, E.: Library extension services for older adults, Cath. Library World **50:**290-291, 1979.

Okun, M.: Implications of gero-psychological research for the instruction of older adults, Adult Educ. **27:**139-155, 1977.

O'Meara, J.: Retirement: reward or rejection? New York, 1977, The Conference Board, Inc.

Palmore, E.: Retirement patterns among aged men: findings of the 1963 survey of the aged, Social Security Bull. **27:**3-10, 1964.

Patton, C.: Early retirement in academia: making the decision, Gerontologist **17:**347-354, 1977.

Peterson, D.: Participation in education by older people, Educ. Gerontol. **7:**245-256, 1981.

Pollman, A.: Early retirement: a comparison of poor health to other retirement factors, J. Gerontol. **26:**41-45, 1971.

Price, W.: Developing the resources of the rural elderly through education, Educ. Gerontol. **5:**423-427, 1980.

Reich, M.: Group preretirement education programs: whither the proliferation? Industr. Gerontol. **4:**29-43, 1977.

Research and Forecasts: Retirement preparation: growing corporate involvement, New York, 1979, Corporate Committee for Retirement Planning.

Rosow, I.: Socialization to old age, Berkeley, Calif., 1974, University of California Press.

Rowe, A.: The retirement of academic scientists, J. Gerontol. **27:**113-118, 1972.

Sarvis, R.: Educational needs of the elderly: their relationship to educational institutions, Washington, D.C., 1973, U.S. Department of Health, Education, and Welfare.

Shepherd, N.: The response of higher education to older adults: a federal perspective, Alt. Higher Educ. **5:**7-17, 1980.

Siegel, S., and Rives, J.: Characteristics of existing and planned preretirement planning programs, Aging Work **1:**93-100, 1978.

Simon, S.: Meeting yourself halfway, Niles, Ill., 1974, Argus Communications.

Simon, S., Howe, L., and Kirschenbaum, H.: Values clarification: a handbook of practical strategies for teachers and students, New York, 1972, Hart Publishing Co., Inc.

Spencer, B.: Overcoming the age bias of continuing education. In Darkenwald, G., and Larson, G., editors: Reaching hard-to-reach adults, San Francisco, 1980, Jossey-Bass, Inc., Publishers.

Streib, G., and Schneider, C.: Retirement in American society, Ithaca, N.Y., 1971, Cornell University Press.

Stuen, C., Spencer, B., and Raines, M.: Seniors teaching seniors: a manual for training older adult teachers, New York, 1982, Brookdale Institute on Aging and Human Development.

Vermilye, D., editor: Lifelong learners: a new clientele for higher education, San Francisco, 1976, Jossey-Bass, Inc., Publishers.

Ward, R.: The aging experience: an introduction to social gerontology, New York, 1979, J.B. Lippincott Co.

Wass, H., and West, C.: A humanistic approach to education of older persons, Educ. Gerontol. **2:**407-416, 1977.

Weiner, A.: Pre-retirement education: assisting in the transition from a work to a leisure role. In Teague, M., MacNeil, R., and Hitzhusen, G., editors: Perspective on leisure and aging in a changing society, Columbia, Mo., 1982, The University of Missouri.

White House Conference on Aging: Toward a national policy on aging, vol. 2, Washington, D.C., 1973, U.S. Government Printing Office.

Woodruff, D., and Birren, J.: Aging: scientific perspectives and social issues, New York, 1975, D. Van Nostrand Co.

SUGGESTED READINGS

Atchley, R.: The sociology of retirement, New York, 1976, Schenkman Publishing Co., Inc.

Elmore, A.: Manual for coordinators of preretirement planning programs, Durham, N.C., 1977, Duke University Center for the Study of Aging and Human Development.

Hunter, W.: Preretirement education leader's manual, Ann Arbor, Mich., 1980, The University of Michigan.

Siegel, S., and Rives, J.: Characteristics of existing and planned preretirement planning programs, Aging Work **1:**93-100, 1978.

Vermilye, D., editor: Lifelong learners: a new clientele for higher education, San Francisco, 1976, Jossey-Bass, Inc., Publishers.

Weiner, A.: Pre-retirement education: assisting in the transition from a work to a leisure role. In Teague, M., MacNeil, R., and Hitzhusen, G., editors: Perspective on leisure and aging in a changing society, Columbia, Mo., 1982, The University of Missouri.

11

Outdoor recreation

There is a great need to acknowledge the importance of outdoor recreation for older persons and to dispel the myths about the capacity of older persons to participate in outdoor recreation. Quality of life can be enhanced through the provision of outdoor recreation opportunities that allow the older person "to achieve that special understanding of one's place in nature" (Tedrick, 1983, p. 12). A growing number of older persons are participating in vigorous and challenging outdoor recreation such as outdoor adventure programs (Ewert, 1983). This chapter will consider a number of research issues related to the outdoor recreation participation of older persons, followed by program and management issues concerning outdoor environments, travel, horticulture, and adventure programming.

OUTDOOR RECREATION PARTICIPATION OF OLDER PERSONS

The literature concerning the outdoor recreation of older persons is not extensive. Research studies have been mainly directed toward an examination of outdoor recreation participation. This section will consider outdoor recreation participation of older persons, focusing on participation rates, participation preference rates, obstacles to participation, and conclusions and implications.

Participation rates

Studies on the participation rates of older persons in outdoor recreation reveal differing participation according to activity. McAvoy (1979), in a study of 540 people 65 years of age and older residing in Minnesota, found the most frequently identified outdoor recreation activities (listed among the top five most frequently participated in) were gardening (49.4 percent), driving for pleasure (32.4 percent), and walking (30.7 percent). Strain and Chappell (1982), in a study of 80 rural Canadian elderly, found the participation rate (at least once a year) in activities in which more than half of the respondents participated were walking/hiking (94 percent), visiting a park/picnicking (75 percent), and gardening (72 percent). On the other hand, the frequency of participation in these three activities was quite high: walking/hiking (56 percent participated daily), visiting a park/picnicking (40 percent participated monthly), and gardening (56 percent participated daily).

Participation preference rates

There are differences between participation rates and participation preference rates of certain outdoor recreation activities. McAvoy (1979) found the outdoor activities most frequently named as one of the top five preferred activities to be gardening (53.2 percent), walking for pleasure (45.4 percent), driving for pleasure (33.7 percent), and sightseeing (33.1 percent). Thus gardening, walking for pleasure, and driving for pleasure had both high participation rates and high participation preference rates. Strain and Chappell (1982) found that the respondents would like to increase participation in walking/hiking (41 percent) and visiting a park/picnicking (49 percent). Thus walking/hiking and visiting a park/picnicking had both high simple participation rates and high participation preference rates.

Obstacles to participation

Older persons frequently encounter obstacles to participation in outdoor recreation activities. McAvoy (1979) found the outdoor recreation activities in which at least 10 percent encountered obstacles to participation to be sightseeing (25.4 percent), walking for pleasure (22.8 percent), fishing (17.2 percent), gardening (16.5 percent), and driving for pleasure (16.3 percent). The predominant problem with all of these activities was lack of physical ability. Strain and Chappell (1982) found the most frequent obstacle to be lack of facilities (36 percent of all reasons given), followed by lack of time (17 percent), lack of companionship (15 percent), poor health (14 percent), and inadequate transportation (4 percent).

Conclusions and implications

Based on a review of the research on outdoor recreation participation rates, participation preference rates, and obstacles to participation among older persons, it may be concluded that:

1. Older persons participate in and prefer outdoor recreation opportunities such as walking, hiking, visiting, and picnicking in pleasant parks and outdoor areas; travel or sightseeing; and gardening.
2. Obstacles to participation encountered by older persons include lack of physical ability; lack of facilities, time, and companionship; poor health; and inadequate transportation.

Leisure services with the elderly should offer a variety of outdoor recreation opportunities that help to overcome these obstacles. Outdoor recreation opportunities for older persons to be examined in the following sections are program and management issues concerning outdoor environments, travel, horticulture, and adventure programming.

The environment has an impact on older persons through what Crandall (1980, p. 276) calls the "people effect" and the "thing effect." The "people effect" is the influence persons have on other persons in the environmental setting. The "thing effect" is the influence that things in the physical environmental setting have on persons. People and things can influence both the behavior and the physical well-being of older persons (Lawton and Nahemow, 1973).

OUTDOOR ENVIRONMENTS

It may be necessary to provide prosthetic, supportive, or compensatory environments for older persons to enhance functioning. These environments should allow older persons to function at their maximum level without being overly protective or creating anxiety and stress (Lawton and Nahemow, 1973). This can be achieved through provision of opportunities for stimulation, mobility, safety, social interaction, privacy, and comfort (Crandall, 1980, pp. 281-286). Two planned outdoor environments to be examined are parks and camps.

Parks often serve as a major outdoor recreation resource for older persons, particularly for inner city elderly. Inner city residents, because of their reduced mobility, declining health, fixed incomes, and limited family ties, have fewer outdoor recreation options. As a consequence, the park may become a major source of associations and inexpensive recreation, and its design should therefore reflect the needs of the population served.

Parks

Byerts and Teaff (1975), in a case study analyzing MacArthur Park in Los Angeles—an inner city park used predominantly by the elderly, found the reasons for park use to be (in order of frequency) to "get away" from home, exercise, relate to nature, see and meet friends, and because there was "nothing else to do." Some of the frequently mentioned assets of the park were the open landscape of trees and shrubs, park wildlife, the lake, outdoor air, and having the company of interesting people. Problems cited by park users were the presence of winos, panhandlers, gambling, and crime; inadequate park services; dirty lake water; desire for more flowers and shrubbery; poor toilet facilities; and the need for the restoration of facilities for outdoor gas cooking. However, users were willing to tolerate the problems rather than attempt to make changes and risk disrupting current use or "designing out" people who were undesirable.

The researchers concluded that in spite of the problems MacArthur Park was a successful, well-used park with areas in differing landscape arrangements for individual relaxation and introspection and for small and large groups. It is a successful leisure space because of the population density and composition of the surrounding neighborhood, urban transportation, and parking availability. However, improvements could be made for security, increased options, revitalization of facilities, and comfort.

Byerts and Teaff's study closed with design recommendations based on the research findings and conclusions. These recommendations are presented in the list below as examples of design directives suitable for implementation of a more "socially connected" park environment and are categorized under the headings of overall park environment, park furniture design, park furniture organization, and park shelter*:

OVERALL PARK ENVIRONMENT

1. Should contain a variety of settings with focal points of social interaction and "connectedness," which are important features to the well-being of high concentrations of older people—the primary users
2. Should clearly afford safety from criminals and hazards and be "barrier free" by design
3. Should incorporate areas for a wide range of functions, from vigorous recreation activities to solitude
4. Should relate to the natural amenities of the site and offer private and public settings usable at different times of the day and under different weather conditions
5. Should be organized so that the various settings are located in reasonable walking distances for most people
6. Should relate to the surrounding community and its urban design

PARK FURNITURE

1. Should be comfortable (especially for people who spend long periods sitting), attractive, and easy to get into and out of
2. Should in some cases be portable to allow for adjustment to the users' desires, group sizes, and weather conditions
3. Should accommodate individuals and small groups and define spaces through its arrangement

ORGANIZATION OF PARK FURNITURE

1. Should relate to various group sizes to encourage a wide range of private and public social interaction and activity, especially among and between the generations
2. Should encourage the formation of informal recreation and gaming groups, with attention given to the role of the observer and the new visitor
3. Should be oriented to the movement patterns, structures, activities, and natural amenities of the park
4. Should be interspersed within and among activity areas and facilities to allow for appropriate rest and observation locations with views that encourage circulation and understanding of the overall park plan

PARK SHELTER

1. Should serve as a focal point for informal social groupings, promote interaction between and among generations, and permit a choice between structured and spontaneous activity

*Modified from Byerts, T., and Teaff, J.: Parks Recreat. **10**:64-66, 1975.

Thomas O. Byerts

MacArthur Park serves as the "living room" for older persons from the surrounding inner city neighborhood. The linear arrangement of park benches requires older persons to sit on the edge of the bench to talk.

2. Should be situated according to natural park assets, circulation patterns, and activity areas to promote user identity and interaction
3. Should provide a flexible or portable enclosed space on occasion and be equipped to accommodate a wide range of activities for both individuals and groups
4. Should reflect the historical and cultural backgrounds of the park users in the park's theme and spatial configuration
5. Should provide protection from extremes of weather
6. Should contain or have nearby toilets, a snack bar, storage, and other commonly needed facilities
7. Should be safe, durable, one level, surveillable, and relatively easy to maintain

Camps

Camps for older persons exist throughout the United States. They are supported by a number of groups under the umbrella organization Vacations for Aging and Senior Citizens Association (VASCA). Benefits, types, management and programming, and examples of camps for older persons will be presented.

    BENEFITS. The benefits of camping for older persons have been described in glowing terms in promotional literature, but little research is available on the topic. Tedrick (1983, p. 12), in the evaluation process of an ongoing program, has asked participants to rate the benefits of the outdoor experience; the most important perceived benefits have been "the opportunity to get away from everyday surroundings, the enjoyment of being with others, and the chance to develop a new appreciation for the outdoors." Other important benefits cited were good food and opportunities to hike and swim.

TYPES. Camps may be categorized according to the degree of convenience provided for older campers. Camping may occur at an organized camp site with comfortable cabins or a lodge, modern kitchen facilities, and other conveniences or it may occur in more rustic settings that have campgrounds for tents and for cooking over an open fire. Deciding on the type of camping will depend on program goals, clientele, and available facilities.

MANAGEMENT AND PROGRAMMING. The successful camp and camping program depend on quality managing and programming. Topics to be considered are marketing, funding, facilities, health and safety, staff, program, and evaluation.

Marketing. An essential element in a marketing strategy is determining the target population. Possible organizations to be targeted include senior centers, municipal park and recreation departments, planned community housing sites, retirement communities, and institutions. The targeting of a specific population allows personal contact with older persons and agency personnel to explain the program. Targeting also allows the use of specific media rather than relying on mass advertising.

Funding. Every older person should have the opportunity to experience the joys of nature, no matter what the economic background. Special rates or subsidies should be sought as a means of reducing expenses. Service organizations might be asked to sponsor an older person who may not be able to afford the costs. Whenever possible, transportation to and from the site should be included in the overall price.

Facilities. Facilities need to be reviewed when considering a camp for older persons. Ford* recommends the following design considerations when evaluating a site:

SLEEPING QUARTERS

1. Should be well insulated and heated
2. Should provide hot and cold running water
3. Should have toilet facilities near each sleeping room
4. Should include comfortable beds (if bunk beds, only use bottom bunk)
5. Should provide chair near bed
6. Should maximize privacy, with rooms for two, three, or four being ideal
7. Should have sufficient storage space
8. Should include a comfortable living room in the sleeping quarter area

*Modified from Ford, P.: Camping Magazine **50:**13, 1978.

TOILETS
1. Should be indoors if at all possible
2. Should contain grab bars on either side of the toilet
3. Should be well marked and have a night-light
4. Should provide an air freshener device, particularly if a pit toilet

SHOWERS
1. Should be individual if possible
2. Should provide nonslip flooring
3. Should include a bench or chair near shower as a place for sitting or depositing clothes and other items

TERRAIN
1. Should be level around main camp buildings
2. Should contain wide, smooth walking trails
3. Should provide a variety of plant life and interesting topography
4. Should include various levels of trails for hiking (i.e., easy, medium, and difficult)
5. Should have natural formations (e.g., river, lake, stream, cliffs, and so on) in short and easy walking distance

Mobility problems may be expected with older persons. Facilities should be examined for entry and exit barriers. Buildings should be free of steps or should contain ramps.

Health and safety. A health form should be received from all participants. The form should contain information about use of medications, emergency contact person or persons, and health precautions. A waiver should be included on the health form, stating that the older person assumes responsibility for his or her actions.

A health and safety program should include the following considerations[*]:

1. A camp nurse should talk to each camper on arrival to explain medical assistance procedures and to check that each health form is in order.
2. Staff should know the emergency procedures in case of a medical emergency.
3. Arrangements should be made in case there is a need for emergency transportation.
4. Each hiking group away from camp should take a first aid kit and have a staff member with a current Standard Red Cross First Aid Card.

Staff. Staff should include regular camp staff and older campers. Including participants in the management, programming, and leadership provides an ideal opportunity for age integration of young staff with older participants. This assumption of responsibilities can enable the ratio of staff to camper to be lower than the American Camping Association (ACA) recommendation of one staff member to every eight campers (Ford, 1978).

Program. An essential component of the program is a sound rationale to

---

[*]Modified from Ford, P.: Camping Magazine **50:**14, 1978.

provide direction for the programming process. Tedrick* lists a number of objectives of the Institute for Creative Outdoor Living at Brockport, New York, which may also serve as a rationale for a camp program:

1. To enjoy the fellowship of others in a nonthreatening setting (i.e., comfort and convenience)
2. To incorporate participant planning in the design of the program
3. To offer a range of activities for those with varying degrees of fitness
4. To offer educational experiences in the outdoors and to develop new skills and appreciations
5. To assist the educational experience by enabling older persons to share skills learned throughout life

A camping program may be implemented based on these objectives. The following are implementation strategies for each.

Fellowship in a nonthreatening setting. Programs should be in comfortable and convenient facilities and settings. Program scheduling should be sensitive to weather (e.g., avoiding vigorous activities during the heat of the day), distances (e.g., providing most of the activities on site), and safety (e.g., inspecting areas and facilities for mobility hazards).

Participant involvement in program planning. Participants should be involved in decisions related to the planning of the program. Involvement should be early in the planning process, focusing on issues such as site selection, travel to and from the site, activities, meals, cleanup, and contingency planning in case there are problems with weather, equipment, illness, and so on.

Range of activities according to degree of fitness. An array of activities should be planned with varying degrees of structure and opportunities for self-selection (e.g., the more active nature walks and the more sedentary nature crafts).

Educational experiences to develop new skills and appreciations. The natural environment should be used as a learning setting. Programs such as nature walks, bird-watching, fishing, nature crafts, and ecology should be maximized. Staff or older volunteers should have knowledge of the subjects and be able to initiate discussions and answer questions.

Enable older persons to share skills. Staff should be sensitive to the skills available among the older campers. These skills may be used to supplement programs already planned or to provide new programs.

Evaluation. All elements of the management and programming process (marketing, funding, facilities, health and safety, staff, and program) should be evaluated. Written evaluations from all participants, as well as an evaluation by the planning committee, will provide diversity of information.

EXAMPLES. The Institute for Creative Outdoor Living (Tedrick, 1983) is a joint effort of the State University of New York at Brockport's Department of Recreation and Leisure Studies and the Division of Continuing Education. The Institute sponsors a series of overnight camping experiences in the university's 500-acre, outdoor learning laboratory, which has facilities such as a lodge,

*Modified from Tedrick, R.: Camping Magazine **55**:11, March, 1983.

modern kitchen, swimming pool, and boating area. Staff consist of college professors and students who volunteer their time, thus helping to keep the registration fee to a minimum. Older persons have been recruited from local senior centers and nutrition sites; the number of participants averages 20. The program seeks a balance between structured and unstructured activities such as bird-watching expeditions, nature walks, weaving, fishing, swimming, bocci, an evening campfire, and group singing. Evaluations have shown that the participants approve of the balance of structured and unstructured activities. Marketing of the experience as an outdoor "institute" helped to overcome the image of camping in the minds of the older persons as one of mosquitoes, tents, and poor food.

The Vacation Lodge for Older Adults, a part of the Episcopal Camp and Conference Center, is located on a 650-acre site in Ivoryton, Connecticut (about 100 miles from New York City between New Haven and New London). Funding is provided by an endowment, support from sponsoring parishes and organizations, and fees (kept as low as possible); scholarships are provided for campers with low and moderate incomes. Facilities include three winterized buildings containing individually heated single and double bedrooms (with accommodations for 85 men and women in each session), a kitchen, a dining hall, three recreation halls (each with a stone fireplace), a chapel, and a craft shop. Outdoor facilities consist of a shuffleboard court in a courtyard; a croquet court in a shady area; tennis courts; screened porches and sundecks overlooking wooded grounds; and a waterfront on a mile-long lake for swimming, paddleboating, rowing, and boatrides in a six-passenger launch. Prospective campers must be in good health and on a regular diet (no special diets are provided). A physician's checkup is recommended but not required. Staff members are especially screened for their emotional maturity, experience, and variety of program skills. The program is especially tailored to meet the needs of individuals 50 to 85 years of age and includes activities such as swimming, fishing, boating, tennis, dance, drama, singing, crafts, and group discussions. Campers are encouraged to take a leadership role in flag raising, table setting, and bell ringing; participation is optional.

TRAVEL

Opportunities to travel are important if older persons are going to be socially integrated into society. Travel can expand the social world of older persons; lack of travel can force disengagement and social isolation. This section will consider the importance of travel, modes of travel, and leisure travel.

Importance

Travel is important to the life satisfaction of older persons. Cutler (1972, 1975) found that 58 percent of those older persons with some type of personal transportation had high life satisfaction scores, whereas only 37 percent without personal transportation had high scores. Cutler (1972), in a longitudinal study, found that 54 percent of older persons deprived of transportation during the study had a decrease in life satisfaction scores, whereas only 36 percent of those who had transportation had a decrease in life satisfaction scores. Cutler (1972) further found that even after socioeconomic status and health were accounted for transportation was still the most important factor in determining life satisfaction scores.

Modes

There are several modes of travel available to older persons. This section will examine three modes of travel (automobile, mass transit, and walking), destinations associated with different modes, and satisfaction with these modes.

AUTOMOBILE. The automobile is an important mode of travel for older persons. The Federal Highway Administration (1973), in a study that did not include walking, found the automobile to be the dominant mode of travel for all ages (Table 11-1), with the majority of all trips for those 65 years of age or older involving the older person as the driver. Many more trips are made by those who drive automobiles than those who are passengers. Carp (1972a) found that 3 percent of older persons acting as passengers could count on daily rides, 50 percent could count on weekly rides, and 87 percent could count on occasionally being offered a ride. Carp (1974) found frequency of trips to be associated with car ownership, good health, and distance from the center city.

MASS TRANSIT. Mass transit is another kind of travel opportunity available to older persons. An examination of Table 11-1 shows that trips made by public mass transit are a small portion of trips made by persons 65 years of age or older. Lawton (1980), in a review of a number of studies, concluded that only in New York is mass transit the dominant mode of travel. Carp (1974) found use of mass transit to be highly associated with nearness to a bus stop, good health, and living in the center city.

TABLE 11-1   **Percentage distribution of trips**

Age	Automobile		Public transit	Other
	Driver	Passenger		
21-25	62	29	4	5
26-29	68	23	4	5
30-39	70	19	3	8
40-49	66	21	4	9
50-59	62	25	4	9
60-64	58	26	8	8
65-69	58	29	6	7
70+	50	41	5	4

From Federal Highway Administration: Mode of transportation and personal characteristics of tripmakers, Nationwide Personal Transportation Study, Report No. 9, Washington, D.C., 1973, U.S. Department of Transportation.

WALKING. Walking for pleasure was found by Nahemow and Kogan (1971) to account for 20 percent of the trips of older New York residents. Eckmann (1974), in a study of pedestrian behavior in two cities, found that 32 percent of older persons were walking for pleasure, in contrast to 21 percent of persons of all ages; 34 percent walked for enjoyment, and 39 percent walked for "exercise," even though other modes of transportation were available. Carp (1974) found walking to be done mostly by older persons in good health, by men, and by those living in the center city. Among center city residents, 50 percent of the elderly walked everyday, whereas 50 percent in the suburbs never walked.

DESTINATIONS. Lawton (1980, p. 151), after reviewing a number of travel studies, concluded that the automobile is used most often for visiting children, visiting relatives, and attending entertainment and organizational functions. Mass transit is used most frequently to attain health care and to shop for items other than groceries. Walking is most frequently used to visit friends, shop for groceries, and attend religious services.

SATISFACTION. Satisfaction differs with the various modes of travel. Carp (1972a) found that most older persons preferred private automobiles to mass transit because of convenience, speed, and sociability; drawbacks of automobile travel are scarce rides and feeling indebted to or not trusting the driver. Cutler (1975) found that many older persons did not like mass transit because of the crowds or the sense of being rushed.

Leisure travel

Travel may not only be a supportive resource linking older persons with life's necessities; it may also be a life enriching resource. Leisure travel as a life enriching resource for older persons will be examined from the perspectives of its prevalence, modes, and programming.

PREVALENCE. Leisure travel is quite prevalent among older persons but does not equal the rates of other age groups (Gordon, Gaitz, and Scott, 1976). Carp (1972b) and Friedsam and Martin (1973) found that more than half of the older persons surveyed in two Texas communities had taken at least one long trip during the previous year, most often with their spouses, and combining sightseeing with visits to relatives. Friedsam and Martin (1973, p. 207) found that older blacks traveled almost as much as older whites but usually not as far.

Leisure travel is related to income. Friedsam and Martin (1973) found that only a third of those with annual incomes of $2,000 reported taking a trip, whereas two thirds of those with incomes above $4,000 reported a trip. Szinovacz (1982, p. 150) found that 78 percent of women retirees mentioned travel as one of the "things they would like to do but could not afford."

MODES. Modes of leisure travel by older persons are quite varied. Some of the more common modes are automobile, bus, recreational vehicle, rail, plane, and cruise ship.

Automobile. The automobile is the most common mode of leisure travel by older persons, as reported by Carp (1972b) and Friedsam and Martin (1973) in their studies of older Texas travelers. Automobile travel by older persons has been facilitated by motel chains such as Days Inn of America, Inc., who developed a September Days Club for persons 55 and older, entitling them to motel, food, and other discounts. Another resource facilitating leisure travel is the Golden Age passport, a carload permit allowing persons 62 or older to enter national forests and certain national parks at a reduced rate of charge.

Bus. The bus is an important means of leisure travel for older persons, particularly for the less affluent and for those who have had to give up their automobiles. Friedsam and Martin (1973) found that older blacks engaged in leisure travel more often by bus. Bus travel passes enable older persons to visit a variety of leisure attractions in a large area in a short period. Bus tours for older persons are economical means of leisure travel, particularly for organizations, centers, and groups of older persons.

Recreational vehicle. Older persons are increasingly using recreational vehicles for travel (Born, 1976a; Guinn, 1980). The users live in self-contained travel trailers, truck campers, and motor homes (Born, 1976b). These recreational vehicles are often parked in popular winter tourist areas such as the Lower Rio Grande Valley of Texas (Guinn, 1980) and the Lower Colorado River basin (Born, 1976b). Born (1976b) estimates that there are about 8 million retirees living in recreational vehicles. Successful accommodation of these older persons requires the provision of a wide range of facilities to meet their varying economic backgrounds (Born, 1976a).

Rail. Rail passenger service, as a means of fast, comfortable travel, has been improving in recent years. Special interest groups are chartering trains with increasing frequency because of "the special atmosphere and camaraderie that is traditionally associated with group excursions by train" (Chubb and Chubb, 1981, p. 558). Amtrak offers a variety of tours to different parts of the country, as well as individual tickets, many specially priced by travel region or time of the year.

Plane. Deregulation of air travel has resulted in increased competition among the airlines and has reduced air fares as a consequence. New customers have been attracted to air travel, including "elderly widows . . . and retired couples starting out to explore another region or a different continent" (Chubb and Chubb, 1981, p. 193).

Cruise ships. Cruise ships offer opportunities for limited or extended trips on inland, coastal, and ocean waterways. River boats such as the *Mississippi Queen* and the *Delta Queen* travel the Ohio and Mississippi Rivers. Coastal cruises focus on a particular coastal area and usually last for part of a day. Ocean cruises of one or more weeks concentrate on traveling to places such as the Caribbean, the west coast of Mexico, or the Mediterranean. On-board cruise ship facilities such as restaurants, bars, casinos, ballrooms, shops, swimming pools, saunas, shuffleboard, and jogging tracks provide a variety of leisure choices for all age groups. The cruise package is quite economical because lodging, food, entertainment, sightseeing, and other options are usually included in the initial cost, making this an especially attractive mode of leisure travel.

PROGRAMMING. Programming for successful leisure travel should be an important part of leisure services for older persons. Aspects of this programming to be considered are components of travel, selection of a tour, and health concerns of travel.

Components of travel. Travel and travel destinations should be evaluated with care. The making of an appropriate choice requires the consideration of a number of essential components of the travel process. Beverley (1975, pp. 171-172), summarizing the work of Ruth Lana (travel consultant of the National Association of Retired Teachers/American Association of Retired Persons), lists six components of the travel process.

Transportation. The basic mode of transportation, whether bus, train, plane, or ship, is only one of the considerations when planning for travel. Thought should be given to planning transportation from place of residence to depot, station, airport, or dock and back to place of residence.

Accommodations. Accommodations need to be planned from time of leaving place of residence until return. Because many travel packages are priced based on double occupancy of a room, consideration should also be given as to whether the older person has a need for a single room and whether the need warrants the added cost.

Meals. Meals should be planned based on an assessment of individual needs, the cost, and the travel package. Individual needs may dictate a special diet, which requires specific planning. It may be cheaper to purchase meals individually rather than as a part of a travel package, especially if there are dietary constraints. Very often, however, meals can be purchased as a part of a travel package and are cheaper than if purchased individually, particularly when foreign travel is involved.

Sightseeing. Sightseeing is an integral part of the travel experience. Each day's schedule, however, should be realistic, allowing time for breaks, meals, shopping, and free time.

Step-by-step management. The management of the travel process requires attention to certain step-by-step details. Reservations need to be made and confirmed, itineraries need to be planned, luggage collected and dispatched, and so on. Management of these travel details may be an individual's responsibility or the responsibility of a tour director.

Necessary arrangements before leaving. Necessary arrangements before leaving include routine matters such as stopping mail and paper delivery and obtaining passports and visas. Planning well in advance will enable such details to fall into place.

Selection of a tour. Traveling with a group has a number of distinct advantages for both the first-time traveler and the veteran traveler, particularly in foreign travel. Group travel provides the services of a professional to integrate all of the necessary components of the travel experience and is usually offered at lower costs. It provides personnel to solve problems and make adjustments as needed in transportation, accommodations, meals, and sightseeing. The older traveler should be aware of the different forms of group tours that are available when selecting a tour (Beverley, 1975, pp. 172, 174).

1. The fully escorted and all-inclusive tour has an escort available at all times to manage all details and has few additional costs.
2. The fully escorted but not all-inclusive tour usually provides fewer group activities such as meals and shows but does have a full-time escort.
3. The hosted tour provides transportation and accommodations but no escort. Instead, an agent or employee of the wholesale tour operator is available to handle the details of arrival and departure; hear complaints; answer questions; and give advice on restaurants, shopping, sightseeing, and so on.
4. The throwaway package includes economy air fare and other elements such as some accommodations and meals. The cost is often less than an individually backed economy air fare; thus it allows the traveler certain accommodations and meals, but the traveler is allowed or even required to plan other elements not included in the land portion of the package.

The older traveler should be advised to examine in detail what a tour includes before making a decision and paying a deposit. A list of the names, locations, and classes of hotels should be provided along with number of meals, form of land transportation, tipping expectations and procedures, and so on.

Health concerns of travel. The older traveler should take certain health precautions and make certain health preparations before traveling. He or she should match the travel to physical ability and health status before making the decision about a particular travel plan, examining in particular the number of travel days, pacing of the days (e.g., length of day, breaks, and free time), and days free of scheduled activities. Health preparations should include having prescription slips with the generic name of medications and not just the brand names, booster immunizations, insurance cards and/or funds to cover a medical emergency, a list of precautions concerning particular countries, and the names of physicians in an area or country.

HORTICULTURE

Many older persons have throughout their lives been involved in yardwork, gardening, care of flowers and plants, and other types of horticultural activities. These activities have a great potential for continuing contacts with nature and the outdoors. In addition, these activities can be integrated into a rehabilitation program. Gardening and horticultural therapy will be examined in this section.

Gardening

Gardening may take place outdoors or indoors. Program participants may engage in outdoor gardening by landscaping, maintaining window boxes and planters, and using individual or group garden plots. In the months when outdoor gardening may be prohibited or to maintain program continuity indoor gardening may be engaged in with house plants, hydroponics, and a greenhouse.

The following program and management suggestions will assist in starting a gardening effort:

1. Good soil is a necessity for program success.
2. Seeds, seedlings, cuttings, and store-bought plants are all possibilities for starting a program. Donations or discounts may be sought from seed houses, garden centers, and nurseries to avoid undue expense.
3. Older persons should be involved in ordering equipment and supplies, making planting and cultivating decisions, and obtaining staff understanding and cooperation.
4. Participants should learn about plants and the process of planting, nurturing, and reaping through formal instruction and through the sharing of helpful hints and gardening tips.
5. Every opportunity should be provided for gardening both as an individual pursuit and as a group experience motivated through the sharing of seedlings and cuttings and gardening awards and prizes.

Horticulture as therapy uses "plant materials to provide a sense of responsibility and a feeling of accomplishment and self-worth" (Van Zandt and Grace, 1981, p. 51). The goals of horticultural therapy, according to Van Zandt and Grace (1981, p. 51), are:

Horticultural therapy

1. To rehabilitate the geriatric resident suffering from a social, psychological, physiological, or any other disorder
2. To maintain and improve the geriatric resident's social, psychological, physiological well-being so as to make their retirement more full and enjoyable

Four areas of human functioning can be maintained or improved*:

1. *Intellectual* competence may be maintained or improved through the learning of new skills and techniques (e.g., drying flowers).
2. *Social* activities may be set up to encourage social interaction through the completion of a group project requiring teamwork and the working toward a common goal.
3. *Emotional* growth and development may be enhanced through horticultural activities that promote creativity, self-esteem, self-confidence, and venting of aggression.
4. *Physical* activity of an older person may be maintained by horticultural activity. Gross and fine motor control and coordination may also be improved (e.g., through watering and trimming plants).

The provision of horticulture as therapy for older persons requires the consideration of five major elements when establishing a program of treatment†:

1. *Understanding the need for treatment:* To assess the need for treatment, the older person must be assessed. Medical history should be gathered,

---

*Modified from Van Zandt, K., and Grace, J.: HortTherapy **1**:52, 1981.
†Modified from Moore, S.: HortTherapy **1**:56-57, 1981.

EXAMPLE 11-1

HORTICULTURAL THERAPY CASE

Mr. A.B. was admitted to the Nursing Home Care Unit of a Veterans Administration Hospital. He was admitted by a son who felt that he was no longer able to care for Mr. A.B. Admissions records indicated that Mr. A.B. was 63 years old, was suffering from acute osteoarthritis in his left wrist and elbow. His son indicated that he was becoming "senile," and had become more and more withdrawn following the death of his wife several years ago.

During a joint meeting with the staff, Mr. A.B. agreed to the following goals:

Ultimate goal: To return to self-care in the community

Immediate goals:

1. Receive standard medication for arthritis
2. Involvement in Advanced Reality Orientation class to deal with his "senility," or confusion
3. Assignment to horticultural therapy for improved socialization, exercise for arthritis of wrist and elbow

Prior to his attending the assignment in horticultural therapy, the therapist in charge established the following tasks for Mr. A.B.:

1. Assigned for one hour in morning to work with greenhouse group pinching chrysanthemums. The analysis indicated that reaching across the bench should force full flexion of the left elbow. Pinching flower buds should force full rotation of wrist. Group interaction should be supportive and force some immediate social contacts.
2. Assigned for one hour in afternoon to work in a craft group. The analysis indicated that the group has primarily a social function. It has proven beneficial for increasing social ability. Crafts should help with fine motor development, especially in wrists.

Mr. A.B. did well in the morning group. He exhibited some confusion about his role in the group, but little confusion about physically completing the task. He understood the concept of work, and was willing to bear the resulting pain caused by the arthritis because it was necessary to produce a good crop of chrysanthemums.

He did not do well in the afternoon group. After several days of withdrawing farther from his peers and the staff, he finally exploded with the statement, "I don't want to sit around like an old woman!" As a result, the therapist made the following change in his plan:

Amend task 2 to read:

2. Reassignment to yard care group for one hour every afternoon—the analysis indicates that client responds better to productive activity.

Mr. A.B. seemed to find it dehumanizing that he was given a task that he perceived to be an affront to his masculinity. His response was not untypical of an older male client placed in an activity completely contrary to his life style.

From Moore, S.: HortTherapy **1:**55-59, 1981.

and a social history should be elicited from family and friends for information on life-style.

2. *Assessing the type of treatment needed:* The determination of the type of treatment required necessitates the involvement of the treatment team, which should consist of a variety of disciplines.

3. *Treatment delivery:* Delivery is concerned with the planning and implementing of an activity or activities designed to meet certain treatment goals.

4. *Evaluating effectiveness of treatment delivered:* The delivery of the treatment must meet the goals set for the older person. Evaluation of the treatment must take place on a continual basis to determine the effectiveness of established goals.

5. *Adjusting treatment to meet population needs:* It is necessary to continually evaluate and make adjustments in the program, even when the established goals have been accomplished. Goals and tasks will change as the needs of the older person change.

An illustration of a program of treatment is provided in Example 11-1.

The programming and management of a new horticultural therapy service in an institutional setting is not unlike the development of a gardening program mentioned in the previous section. However, some adaptations may be necessary such as the use of a lighted greenhouse-on-wheels to conduct bedside sessions and the use of older independent and semiindependent volunteers from the institution to help with horticulture classes and other activities (e.g., working in the greenhouse, flower and garden shows, maintaining landscape and garden plots, and publishing a newsletter).

An illustration of a horticultural program in an institutional setting is that of John Knox Village (Example 11-2).

EXAMPLE 11-2

JOHN KNOX VILLAGE HORTICULTURAL THERAPY PROGRAM

Project location: Lees Summit, Missouri

Funding: John Knox Village supports and funds the Horticultural Therapy Program.

Target population: People over 55 years of age.

Program goals: To maintain or rehabilitate the geriatric patient suffering from a social, psychological, physiological, or any other disorder.

Program operation (overview): The average client enters the health or medical facility and probably comes in contact with the activity director first. The activity director evaluates this person and gives the horticultural therapist his recommendations as to their suitability for horticultural therapy.

From the National Council for Therapy and Rehabilitation Through Horticulture: Innovative horticultural therapy programs, Alexandria, Va., 1978, National Council for Therapy and Rehabilitation Through Horticulture, pp. 18-19.

Continued.

EXAMPLE 11-2,
cont'd

The horticultural therapist then visits this person and makes the final decision whether this person attends horticultural therapy. Each therapy-activity is designed specifically for that patient's needs. Reality Orientation is used in the horticultural therapy session depending upon the patient's level of awareness.

Med Center Horticultural Therapy—We deal mainly with patients who are confused and suffer from emotional or psychological disorders. We also deal with patients suffering from physical handicaps in the Med Center.

Health Center Horticultural Therapy—Residents in the Health Center are generally more alert and oriented. Many of the residents are just below the level of self-care. The therapy group is very large and a therapeutic atmosphere is hard to achieve.

We use a fluorescent light greenhouse to conduct our therapy in the Med Center. The patients in horticultural therapy are responsible for taking care of their plants. We also hope to have a garden plot in which the patients can grow their own vegetables and flowers. Horticulture is also taught throughout the village. We combine the science of horticulture with crafts through horticulture. Trips to local greenhouses are conducted every month for the village residents.

Project operation (innovative aspects): This is the only horticultural therapy program in a life care retirement village. We deal with a variety of patients ranging from physically handicapped to the extremely psychotic. The job as a horticultural therapist also enters into the lives of the residents living in apartments, homes and cottages. The horticulture class members have a garden project in which all class members work and harvest the vegetables. Reality Orientation is an integral part of all Hort-Therapy conducted in the health facilities.

Disadvantages:
1. Budgetary problems
2. Limited greenhouse working area
3. Too large patient/therapist ratio
4. No raised flower beds or pathways for wheelchair patients

Advantages:
1. Even though small we do have a Lord and Burnham lean-to greenhouse and a garden area.
2. High patient interest.
3. Resident volunteers helping get patients out to activities.
4. Many people in Health Center are ambulatory and able to work outside in flower beds.

Special project research:
1. Health Center patients have developed a wildflower garden outside.
2. Greenhouse on wheels (4 tiered gro-lite flora cart used in Med Center). Plants are grown where residents can watch their progress and are responsible for taking care of their respective plants.
3. Residents in horticulture classes in the village have a common garden where they are growing their own vegetables and flowers. It requires group cooperation and socialization.

For more information: Horticulture Therapist, John Knox Village, Murray and O'Brien Roads, Lees Summit, Mo., 64063

Adventure programming, experiential education, stress-challenge, and *risk recreation* are all terms used to describe the outward bound process. Since the advent of the Outward Bound School at Aberdovey, Wales, in 1941 (Hogan, 1966), outward bound–oriented and adapted programs have expanded to 32 schools in 17 nations (Miner, 1966). Wichmann (1976) identified 250 outward bound adapted programs, and Andrew (1977) reported an additional 10 programs. Although efforts have been made to adapt the outward bound process to a variety of settings and groups, older persons have generally been excluded (Ewert, 1983, p. 64). The history, principles, process, and a program example with older persons will be examined in this section.

ADVENTURE PROGRAMMING

Outward bound was developed and implemented by Kurt Hahn and Lawrence Holt at the first Outward Bound School in Aberdovey, Wales, in 1941 (Hogan, 1966) to train seamen to survive under stress. The impetus for the school was the discovery during the early days of World War II that a large number of young English seamen died with little struggle when forced to abandon ship, whereas the older, more experienced seamen were able to survive. The school was established to teach sailing, physical training, map and compass techniques, expedition-at-sea skills, and rescue techniques while developing self-confidence and generating feelings of sensitivity and responsibility for others.

History

Adventure programming today is based on five basic principles that serve as the foundation for the implementation of the programming process. Pieh (1974), in a report to the First North American Conference on Outdoor Pursuits in Higher Education, stated five basic principles:

Principles and process

1. *Encouraging personal growth* is the keystone or primary principle. The meeting with other persons provides the impetus for renewal and self-creation.
2. *Developing interpersonal relationships* is necessary for the overall success of adventure programming. Extensive and intensive relationships develop the capacity for sensitivity and empathy.
3. *Developing the ability to deal with stress* is important. Handling stress in a way conducive to learning is difficult, particularly when fear is involved. Sharing fear in the context of support and follow-up is necessary if the impact of an experience is to be sustained.
4. *Developing a capacity to prevail* is necessary. The goal is to prevail, not just endure, and involves the pacing of self, living economically and efficiently, and relying on one's natural resources. Fatigue is to be avoided because it results in unproductiveness, staleness, and the possibility of accidents.
5. *Developing a spiritual attitude* involves the recognition that worship is a force that goes beyond time and place and permeates all of a person's

existence. Adventure programming can allow for spiritual illumination.

The adventure programming process involves tasks that develop problem-solving skills in a physical and social environment and impells the participant to master the tasks and to thus reorganize the meaning and direction of life's experiences. Each component of the process will be examined.

PROBLEM-SOLVING TASKS. Activities such as the teams course, caving, climbing, and rappelling, because they are generally unfamiliar, pose problems that must be overcome both individually and cooperatively. The participant may choose to fail to complete the task or to strive for completion.

PHYSICAL ENVIRONMENT. The outdoors is used as a unique physical environment that provides an element of contrast. This contrast is seen as a help to enable the participant to generalize the experience and apply it to a familiar environment.

SOCIAL ENVIRONMENT. The social environment is the group. The group promotes individual decision making while taking into consideration the welfare and wishes of the group. The group thus enhances cooperation and social interaction.

MASTERING THE TASKS. The activities are arranged to make mastery probable but not simple. The participant finds the solving of concrete, reasonable, and manageable tasks to be rewarding.

MEANING AND DIRECTION OF LIFE'S EXPERIENCES. The participant feels good about self and those who have assisted in the mastery of tasks. The more positive perception of self and others makes the participant better equipped and more likely to engage in subsequent problem solving.

Value

Research has documented the value of adventure programming. Changes in self-concept (Heaps and Thorstenson, 1974; Thorstenson and Heaps, 1973), self-esteem (Gold, 1978; Rathus, Siegel, and Justice, 1973), self-image (Clifford and Clifford, 1967), self-actualization (Lambert, Segger, Staley, Spencer, and Nelson, 1978), and feelings of competence (Krajick, 1978) have been reported in the literature. Research on the value of adventure programming with older persons is sorely needed.

Program example

Adventure programming with older persons has been conducted in a series of Elderhostels at Touch of Nature Environmental Center at Southern Illinois University at Carbondale. Activities and an evaluation will be presented.

ACTIVITIES. Activities were designed to be consistent with the principles and process of adventure programming previously discussed. The activities to be examined are the teams course, rockcraft, map and compass, canoeing, caving, Tyrolean traverse, and solo.

Teams course. On the teams course the older participants are faced with various obstacles designed to challenge them physically and mentally, individually and collectively.

Spaceship. The group of older persons is told that the earth is going to explode in 5 minutes. The only means of escape is to climb aboard a spaceship (represented by a 2- by 2-foot wooden box placed on the ground), which will take off to safety once the entire group is aboard. Each older person must climb aboard the spaceship in such a way that the entire body is within the perimeter of the box. The group must decide on a satisfactory method of boarding through conversing and proposing solutions. The solution involves group discussion, physical contacts, and total participation.

Pipe. The pipe is 30 feet long and 18 inches in diameter, lies horizontally on the ground, and is covered with earth. Individuals are asked to crawl through the pipe. The challenge is primarily mental—little strength and endurance are required to overcome this obstacle. However, the mental challenge is great for some. Those possessing any degree of claustrophobia must overcome or at least postpone their fears long enough to complete the task. Another challenge is also presented if the participants wish to try to admit one person from each end of the pipe, necessitating persons crawling through and climbing over one another to pass through and exit at opposite ends of the pipe. No one is forced to engage in this exercise, but most older participants create a self-imposed discipline to succeed.

Electric corral. A length of rope placed approximately 4 feet from the ground is made into a square (corral) between four trees. The group is "corralled" into this area and must try to cross over without touching the rope to avoid being captured by "giants." There is an imaginary electric current running through the rope and from the rope to the ground. If the rope is touched, the imaginary current will "detach" whatever body part is touched, causing that individual to lose the use of that body part when helping the rest of the group over the rope. The group must plan a method for getting the last person across the rope, using their resources wisely.

This obstacle, as the others, requires communication, assessment of resources, and team work. There are many solutions for the successful completion of the task. Some solutions may not be the best, but any solution is considered to be a good solution.

Spool. A steel cable spool is placed approximately 5½ feet from the ground, suspended from a pipe, and lashed to two trees. The pipe thus becomes the axle of this revolving spool. The group's challenge is to cross over this revolving spool and land feet first on the other side. Because the spool spins easily, it is not possible for one person to cross it alone—a group effort is required to complete this task. An additional challenge is for one person to have "an allergic reaction to wood" and as a consequence is not able to touch the spool while going over. Many different methods can be used to get older persons across, but as more and more cross the spool fewer are left to help on the other side. Eventually, one older person will be left; the group must plan a method to help this person over. The spool is not a difficult challenge, but a group effort is needed to successfully overcome the obstacle.

Trust fall. The trust fall requires a telephone pole embedded in the

Thea Lorin Breite

An Elderhostel member falls back into the waiting arms of group members
in a trust fall.

ground, with 4 feet remaining above ground. Each older person takes a turn
standing on top of the pole with his or her back facing the group. The rest of the
group members are divided evenly into two groups that face each other, and
each person joins hands and elbows with the person opposite, making a square
with their arms. On signal the person on top of the pole falls back into the
waiting arms of the group. The person falling backwards from the top of the
pole has to trust that the rest of the group will execute a catch; the group
members have to trust that the person falling will fall correctly (body erect,
hands and arms straight and clutched to the side of the body). If properly
executed, the trust fall builds group confidence and cooperation and allows
each group member to be responsible and so share in the success or failure.

Thea Lorin Breite

Rock climbing and rappelling develop trust between the climber or rappeller and the belayer.

Rockcraft. The rockcraft activity has two components. The first is rock-climbing, or *ascending* a bluff face, with the climber equipped with safety gear (proper shoes and helmet), ropes, and a locking carabiner (an aluminum device that attaches the harness to the rope). The second component is rappelling, or *descending* a bluff face, using ropes and other safety gear such as a helmet, gloves, locking carabiner, and figure-eight descender ring.

The site chosen for climbing and rappelling is a bluff about 90-feet high. One rappelling and one climbing site is rigged. The older participants are given thorough instructions on the proper use of the gear, ropes, and verbal communication (a very important element of climbing or rappelling). The climber or rappeller must rely on his or her belayer, the person at the top of the bluff who protects the climber or rappeller. The rope connected to the climber or rappeller is anchored through a rope system tied to the belayer, and, as the older person ascends or descends, the belayer regulates the slack of the rope and supports the climber or rappeller in the event of a fall.

When climbing and rappelling the older person must have complete faith in the belayer and believe that the gear and the instructions are reliable. Most older persons trying to climb or rappell for the first time experience some degree of fear but have managed to postpone, control, or overcome their fear to complete the exercise. This activity leads to self-evaluation and self-discovery and fosters a one-to-one relationship in which respect and friendship are created.

Map and compass. Topographical maps of the area are distributed to each group. The groups are taught how to interpret contour lines and distances and how to locate items found in the legend.

After a brief introduction to the mechanics of the compass, the members of the group take compass bearings on nearby objects until everyone is familiar with the procedures. The participants then orient their maps and take a compass bearing on several map locations. Once familiar with their map and compass, they pack up their gear and prepare to go on a hike.

Map and compass skills enable the participants to become more self-sufficient in the outdoors. As the program progresses, older persons become more self-reliant and better able to cope with the environment.

Canoeing. The groups are shown how to place a canoe in the water, how to enter the canoe, the positions of the bowman and the sternman, and the particular function of each. Further instruction in paddling techniques and strokes are also given. Everyone is issued a paddle and a life jacket, grouped into pairs, and then given the opportunity to canoe.

Caving. After a drive and a short hike the group reaches the cave entrance. Nestled in the underbrush is an opening about 2 feet in diameter. Each older person enters the cave by crawling downward and begins the quarter-mile journey in total darkness and 50-degree temperature. The passageway is extremely narrow and often requires the cavers to crawl on hands and knees in a combination of dirt, water, and mud. They often encounter bats, salamanders, and a variety of insects. Midway through the cave the group enters a large room that allows the entire group to assemble and stand upright, and at this point the instructor asks the group to extinguish the lamps and sit quietly in total darkness for a few minutes. In this darkness many different feelings are expressed. The cavers then crawl back to the opening of the cave and climb out into the more familiar environment.

The cave presents an excursion into a totally new environment for most older persons. A group typically demonstrates a great amount of apprehension before entering a cave. The apprehension is gradually overcome as the caving expedition continues.

Tyrolean traverse. Hiking to a 60-foot bluff, the group is exposed to a Tyrolean traverse. Rope is attached to a tree at the top of one bluff using a bowline-in-a-coil knot, and the rope is then stretched taut across the 60-foot gorge t ` another tree, again using a bowline-in-a-coil knot. To cross the gorge the participants, wearing slings and attaching carabiners, must hook into the rope and step off the top of the bluff. Trusting the rope to hold them, they "zip" across the gorge to the other side of the bluff. There they unlock their carabiners and step away to safety.

The bluff is very steep, and at first the older participants are very apprehensive. The feeling of flying through the air and the fear of falling also

Thea Lorin Breite

Caving is often a new experience, requiring older persons to overcome apprehension and anxiety.

create feelings of stress. After completion, however, the older participants express feelings of relief, personal accomplishment, and joy.

Solo. Each individual is assigned a small plot of land that will comprise the living area for the rest of the evening and the next morning. The solo sites are spaced far enough apart that the participants have a maximum amount of privacy. Each individual has only the bare essentials to get through the night. Periodically, the instructors make a safety check as a safety measure.

The solo is designed to be a time for reflection and introspection. It also provides the older individual with an opportunity for self-assessment. The reactions to this experience are varied—some older persons are fearful, others are joyous, and many are both.

EVALUATION. Evaluation by a group of Elderhostel participants elicited a variety of reactions (Klueter, 1982, pp. 96, 97, 102-103):

"I've found I have few physical fears, and still have years to look forward to after seeing a 74 year old complete this week. My reason for coming was that there was everything I'd never done before."

"I have done a lot of things I did not think I would be either able to do, or willing to do, which makes me feel more comfortable about handling the physical world. You pointed out my dependence on guidance and support in these areas. I feel I have been daring, something I never was ever in childhood."

"I have been on three Elderhostel programs and enjoyed them fully. I was not disappointed in coming here. The course was much more rigorous than I had anticipated, but I was able to survive and the learning of new adventures was great. I especially enjoyed the people and then the program of rappelling, climbing, camping, etc. was outstanding."

"The reason I came on this trip is because I am always looking for 'an adventure' and something different—not just a cruise or bus trip or bird watching. I did not come primarily to challenge myself because I knew when I come on a project I am going to do everything—at least try everything that is on the schedule."

SUMMARY   Older persons have the capacity to participate in a variety of outdoor recreation activities. Research indicates that older persons participate in and prefer walking, hiking, visiting, and picnicking in pleasant parks and outdoor areas; travel and sightseeing; and gardening. Obstacles to participation in outdoor recreation activities by older persons are lack of physical ability; lack of facilities, time, and companionship; poor health; and lack of transportation.

Outdoor environments such as parks and camps can have an impact on older persons through the influence that persons can have on other persons in the environmental setting and through the influence that things in the physical environmental setting can have. Parks serve as a major outdoor recreation resource for older persons because of the opportunities to get away from home, to exercise, to relate to nature, and to see and meet people; such parks should reflect in their design the needs of older persons through the provision of differing landscape arrangements and facilities that help to socially connect older persons. Camps for older persons provide benefits such as the opportunity to get away from the everyday surroundings to be with others and to develop a new appreciation for the outdoors. The successful camp and camping program should have:

1. A marketing strategy that is targeted to a specific population or populations of older persons
2. Funding resources to allow special rates or subsidies

3. Facilities adequate for the comfort, privacy, safety, and mobility needs of older persons

4. A health and safety form containing information on medications, health precautions, and emergency contact persons

5. A staff that integrates the regular staff with the older campers in management, programming, and leadership responsibilities

6. A program that is implemented in comfortable and convenient facilities and settings, that allows for participant involvement in planning, that provides a range of activities according to the degree of fitness among the older campers, that uses the outdoor environment as a learning setting, and that enables older persons to share skills

7. An evaluation of all elements of the management and programming process through written evaluation and consultation with a planning committee

Travel is an important resource for the social integration of older persons into society. Such a resource has been shown to have an impact on life satisfaction. Of the several modes of travel available to older persons, the automobile is the dominant mode and is used most often for visiting children, visiting relatives, and attending entertainment and organizational functions; it is also the most preferred form of travel because of the convenience, speed, and sociability that it provides. Mass transit is the dominant mode of transportation only among New York City elderly; it is used most frequently to attain health care and to shop for items other than groceries. It is not generally liked by older persons because of the crowds and the sense of being rushed. Walking is done mainly for pleasure and exercise, although it is frequently done to visit friends, shop for groceries, and attend religious services. Leisure travel, a life enriching resource for older persons, is quite prevalent among older persons but does not equal the rates of other age groups because of the generally lower incomes of older persons. The automobile is the most common mode of leisure travel for older persons, although buses, recreational vehicles, trains, planes, and cruise ships are other important resources. Programming for successful involvement in leisure travel should alert the older person to the important components of travel (transportation, accommodations, meals, sightseeing, step-by-step management details, and the necessary arrangements before leaving), the process of selecting a tour (advantages and forms of group tours), and health concerns of travel (health precautions and preparations).

Horticultural activities have a great potential for enabling older persons to maintain contacts with nature and may be integrated into a rehabilitation program for older persons. Gardening may be engaged in outdoors through landscaping, maintaining window boxes and planters, and using individual or group garden plots or indoors with houseplants, hydroponics, or a greenhouse. Horticultural therapy is concerned with the rehabilitation and maintenance of older persons in four areas of human functioning (intellectual, social, emotional, physical) and uses a combination of individualized treatment, adapted equipment, and volunteers.

Adventure programming for older persons is a relatively new adaptation of the outward bound process. Originally designed to train seamen in World War II to survive under stress, adventure programming today is based on five principles: developing the ability to deal with stress, developing a capacity to prevail, encouraging personal growth, developing interpersonal relationships, and developing a spiritual attitude. The process is designed to pose tasks that require problem-solving skills in a physical and social environment and that compel the participant to master the tasks and reorganize the meaning and direction of life's experiences. Research on the value of adventure programming with older persons is sorely needed; research on other populations has shown changes in self-concept, feelings of competence, self-esteem, self-image, and self-actualization. Activities that may be used in adventure programming with older persons include the teams course, climbing and rappelling, map and compass, canoeing, caving, Tyrolean traverse, and solo. Evaluation by a group of Elderhostel participants has shown heightened feelings of physical competence, ability to survive, and the joy of adventure.

REFERENCES

Andrew, S.: An evaluation of two stress-challenge programs for delinquent youth, Unpublished masters thesis, 1977, Southern Illinois University at Carbondale.

Atchley, R.: The social forces in later life, ed. 2, Belmont, Calif., 1977, Wadsworth Publishing Co., Inc.

Beverley, E.V.: The retiree's vacation dilemma—what to do with more time but less money, Geriatrics 30:171-172, 174, 176, 181, 1975.

Born, T.: Variables associated with the winter camping location of elderly recreational vehicle owners in Southwestern Arizona, J. Gerontol. 31:346-351, 1976a.

Born, T.: Elderly RV campers along the Lower Colorado River: a preliminary typology, J. Leisure Res. 8:256-262, 1976b.

Byerts, T., and Teaff, J.: Social research as a design tool, Parks Recreat. 10:34-36, 62-66, 1975.

Carp, F.: Retired people as automobile passengers, Gerontologist 12:66-72, 1972a.

Carp, F.: The mobility of older slum-dwellers, Gerontologist 12:57-65, 1972b.

Carp, F.: Transportation and the older person, Final report, Administration on Aging Grant AA-4-70-087, Washington, D.C., 1974, Administration on Aging.

Chubb, M., and Chubb, H.: One third of our time? New York, 1981, John Wiley & Sons, Inc.

Clifford, E., and Clifford, M.: Self-concepts before and after survival training, Br. J. Soc. Clin. Psychol. 6:241-248, 1967.

Crandall, R.: Gerontology: a behavioral approach, Reading, Mass., 1980, Addison-Wesley Publishing Co., Inc.

Cutler, S.: The availability of personal transportation, residential location, and life satisfaction among the aged, J. Gerontol. 27:383-389, 1972.

Cutler, S.: Transportation and changes in life satisfaction, Gerontologist 15:155-159, 1975.

Eckmann, A.: The behavior and perception of elderly pedestrians and appropriate accommodations, Washington, D.C., 1974, Institute of Public Administration.

Ewert, A.: Adventure programming for the older adult, J. Phys. Educ. Recreat. Dance 54(3):64-66, 1983.

Federal Highway Administration: Mode of transportation and personal characteristics of tripmakers, Nationwide Personal Transportation Study, Report No. 9, Washington, D.C., 1973, U.S. Department of Transportation.

Ford, P.: Senior camping, Camping Magazine 50:12-14, 1978.

Friedsam, H., and Martin, C.: Travel by older people as a use of leisure, Gerontologist 13:204-207, 1973.

Gold, M.: Scholastic experience, self-esteem, and delinquent behavior: a theory for alternative schools, Crime Delinquency 24:290-308, 1978.

Gordon, C., Gaitz, C., and Scott, J.: Leisure and lives: personal expressivity across the life span. In Binstock, R., and Shanas, E., editors: Handbook of aging and the social sciences, New York, 1976, Van Nostrand Reinhold Co.

Guinn, R.: Elderly recreational vehicle tourists: life satisfaction correlates of leisure satisfaction, J. Leisure Res. 12:198-204, 1980.

Heaps, R., and Thorstenson, C.: Self-concept changes immediately and one year after survival training, Ther. Recreat. J. 8:61-63, 1974.

Hogan, J.: The establishment of the first Outward Bound School at Aberdovey Merionethshire. In Rohrs, H., and Behrens, T., editors: Kurt Hahn, London, 1966, Routledge & Kegan Paul.

Klueter, K.: Analysis of morale of two Elderhostel groups participating in a seven-day environmental stress-challege program at Touch of Nature, Unpublished masters thesis, 1982, Southern Illinois University at Carbondale.

Krajick, K.: Three weeks in the woods, Corrections Magazine 10:36-47, 1978.

Lambert, M., Segger, J., Staley, J., Spencer, B., and Nelson, D.: Reported self-concepts and self-actualization value changes as a function of academic classes with wilderness experience, Percept. Mot. Skills 46:1035-1040, 1978.

Lawton, M.P.: Environment and aging, Monterey, Calif., 1980, Brooks/Cole Publishing Co.

Lawton, M.P., and Nahemow, L.: Ecology and the aging process. In Eisdorfer, C., and Lawton, M.P., editors: The psychology of adult development and aging, Washington, D.C., 1973, American Psychological Association.

McAvoy, L.: The leisure preferences, problems, and needs of the elderly, J. Leisure Res. 11:40-47, 1979.

Miner, J.: Outward bound in the U.S.A. In Rohrs, H., and Behrens, T., editors: Kurt Hahn, London, 1966, Routledge & Kegan Paul.

Moore, S.: Horticultural therapy and the aging client, HortTherapy 1:55-59, 1981.

Nahemow, L., and Kogan, L.: Reduced fare for the elderly, New York, 1971, Mayor's Office for the Aging.

The National Council for Therapy and Rehabilitation Through Horticulture: Innovative horticultural therapy programs, Alexandria, Va., 1978, National Council for Therapy and Rehabilitation Through Horticulture.

Pieh, R.: The Janus report. In Smathers, K., editor: The proceedings of the first North American Conference on Outdoor Pursuits in Higher Education, Boone, N.C., 1974, Appalachian State University.

Rathus, S., Siegel, L., and Justice, M.: Delinquent attitudes and self-esteem, Adolescence 8:265-276, 1973.

Strain, L., and Chappell, N.: Outdoor recreation and the rural elderly: participation, problems and needs, Ther. Recreat. J. 16:42-48, 1982.

Szinovacz, M.: Retirement plans and retirement adjustment. In Szinovacz, M., editor: Women's retirement, Beverly Hills, Calif., 1982, Sage Publications, Inc.

Tedrick, R.: Senior "institutes," Camping Magazine 55:10-12, March, 1983.

Thorstenson, C., and Heaps, R.: Outdoor survival and its implications for rehabilitation, Ther. Recreat. J. 7:31-33, 1973.

Van Zandt, K., and Grace, J.: The role of horticultural therapy in a retirement community, HortTherapy 1:49-54, 1981.

Wichmann, T.: Affective role expectation for delinquent youth in environmental stress-challenge programs, Unpublished masters thesis, 1976, Southern Illinois University at Carbondale.

SUGGESTED READINGS

Beverley, E.V.: The retiree's vacation dilemma—what to do with more time but less money, Geriatrics **30:**171-172, 174, 176, 181, 1975.

Byerts, T., and Teaff, J.: Social research as a design tool, Parks Recreat. **10:**34-36, 62-66, 1975.

Ewert, A.: Adventure programming for the older adult, J. Phys. Educ. Recreat. Dance **54**(3):64-66, 1983.

Ford, P.: Senior camping, Camping Magazine, **50:**12-14, 1978.

Moore, S.: Horticultural therapy and the aging client, HortTherapy **1:**55-59, 1981.

Tedrick, R.: Senior "institutes," Camping Magazine **55:**10-12, March, 1983.

Van Zandt, K., and Grace, J.: The role of horticultural therapy in a retirement community, HortTherapy **1:**49-54, 1981.

PART FOUR
The future elderly and leisure services

Planning future leisure services with the elderly requires the examination of what the elderly will be like. Older persons of the future will be different because of differing individual histories and contexts that have shaped their lives. Leisure services of the future must therefore be shaped by the nature of the older persons to be served, as well as by the contexts in which those services are delivered. Part Four will consider Elderly in the Future Society (Chapter 12) and Planning for Future Leisure Services (Chapter 13).

12

Elderly in the future society

Forecasting of the characteristics of the future elderly must take place if leisure services and policies are to be rationally planned. This chapter will examine the concept of social forecasting, characteristics of future elderly, emerging life-style changes, and the future leisure environment of the elderly.

Social forecasting of the future elderly is vital if choices are to be made and if the future is to be shaped, not simply responded to. Such forecasting is "based on extrapolation from current trends" in an attempt "to rationally and self-consciously set policies affecting future generations" (Ward, 1979, p. 505). The resulting predictions should be based on the best available information, with such predictions being balanced to avoid extreme optimism or pessimism.

SOCIAL FORECASTING

Older persons will become a larger and more influential element in the future society. Characteristics of the future elderly to be examined are number and percentage, dependency ratio, life expectancy, health, socioeconomic status, minority group status, residential concentration, living arrangements, political power and activism, retirement, and leisure.

CHARACTER-ISTICS OF FUTURE ELDERLY

The number and percentage of older persons in the United States are expected to increase. Table 12-1 presents the numerical and percentage increases in the

Number and percentage

total elderly populations from 1900 to 1980 and the projections for the next 40 years. It should be noted that the projected increase between 1990 and 2010 will be quite small because of the low birthrates during the depression years and World War II; but between 2010 and 2020 a net increase of about 9 million older persons is projected because of the retirement of the post-World War II baby boom, resulting in approximately 15.5 percent of the population being 65 years of age or older.

The proportion of the population 75 years of age or older is also increasing. Those 75 or older in 1930 comprised 29 percent of those over age 65, in 1950 they comprised 31 percent, in 1979 they comprised 37 percent, and by the year 2000 they are expected to comprise 45 percent of the population over 65 years of age (Leaf, 1982). Such a high proportion of the older population over 75 years of age should increase the needs for income maintenance programs and health care among the elderly. However, it is important to note that any changes in future birthrates and life expectancy could alter the number and percentage of older persons projected for the future.

Dependency ratio   Demographers such as Easterlin (1976) have projected a major increase in the birthrate during the 1980s, which could have a significant impact on dependency ratios. These increased birthrate projections are important because by

TABLE 12-1   **Number and percentage of older persons in the United States**

Year	Number of persons age 65+ (thousands)	Percent of total population	Percent of increase from preceding decade
1900	3,099	4.1	—
1910	3,986	4.3	28.6
1920	4,929	4.7	23.7
1930	6,705	5.4	36.0
1940	9,031	6.8	34.7
1950	12,397	8.2	37.3
1960	16,675	9.2	34.5
1970	20,087	9.8	20.4
1980	25,544	11.3	27.1
Projections:			
1990	29,824	12.2	16.7
2000	31,822	12.2	6.7
2010	34,837	12.7	9.5
2020	45,102	15.5	29.5

From U.S. Bureau of the Census: Demographic aspects of aging and the older population in the United States, Current Population Reports, Series P-23, Pub. No. 59, Washington, D.C., 1976, U.S. Government Printing Office; U.S. Bureau of the Census: Projections on the population of the United States: 1977 to 2050, Current Population Reports, Series P-25, Pub. No. 704, Washington, D.C., 1977, U.S. Government Printing Office; and U.S. Bureau of the Census: Statistical abstracts of the United States, Washington, D.C., 1981, U.S. Government Printing Office.

reducing the proportion of the nonworking-age population to the working-age population, the ratio of the dependent (nonworking) to the independent (working) is reduced. Sheppard and Rix (1977) have concluded that between 1975 and 2010 the working-age population will have a projected increase of about 38 percent, whereas the old-age dependent population will have a projected increase of only 19 percent. Even with the projected increase after 2010 (see Table 12-1), older persons will not be as burdensome because of the reduced pressure to support children and adolescents with financial and other resources.

Life expectancy is predicted to increase in the coming decades. According to Hayflick (1977), longevity is extended by the elimination of the major causes of death and by increases in life span. Advances in disease control should increase the life expectancy by 5 to 10 years by the year 2000, according to the consensus of a panel of biological and medical specialists (Neugarten and Havighurst, 1977).

Life expectancy

Improved health status for older persons *cannot* automatically be assumed because of the expectation that the average life expectancy will increase during the next 20 years. An increase in the "quantity" of life through increases in survival rates does not necessarily mean improvements in the "quality" of life. The extension of life may produce increasingly "larger numbers of ill and disabled persons of advanced age . . . with medical services keeping these persons alive while keeping them neither healthy nor happy" (Neugarten, 1982, pp. 33-34). On the other hand, future older persons should experience "improved levels of health because poverty is diminishing over the life cycles of successive generations, because educational levels are rising, and because there will be more effective forms of public health and improved systems of health care . . . a principal goal of public and private effort should be to make the later years of life vigorous, healthy, and satisfying, instead of merely adding years to life" (Pegels, 1981, p. 3).

Health

The socioeconomic status of the future elderly will improve—that is, "they will be better educated, with higher occupational status and income than present older people" (Ward, 1979, p. 506). The ranks of older persons will reflect in future years greater amounts of education and the consequent higher occupational status because of the expansion of opportnities for formal education that began in the 1920s and accelerated after World War II (Lammers, 1983). The income status should improve in coming decades because more and more workers will be receiving private pensions that will be supplemented by Social Security benefits. However, solvency of pension plans and Social Security will continue to be problematical because of the growing numbers of older persons and the increasing life expectancy of individual retirees (Hess and Markson, 1980).

Socioeconomic status

Minority group status

The percentage of European-born elderly should decline (Uhlenberg, 1977), whereas the percentage of black and Hispanic elderly should continue to increase. The greater life expectancy of older blacks and Hispanics should account for the increase in these minority groups and may also be another factor contributing to the growth of the future elderly population (Lammers, 1983).

Residential concentration

The residences of older persons will continue to be concentrated largely in metropolitan areas, partially in the older sections of center cities (Ward, 1979). However, the number of older persons residing in the suburbs should increase as World War II veterans, who helped to establish the suburbs, grow older. Moving within the home state to smaller communities should become more common because the cost of living is lower and the distance from friends and family would not be greatly increased (Lammers, 1983).

Older persons will continue to migrate to the sunbelt. Planned retirement communities will continue to be concentrated in the sunbelt states, although they will become more prevalent in metropolitan areas of the northern United States (Ward, 1979).

Living arrangements

A substantial majority of older persons will continue to live in an independent household, most often in older, single-family dwellings that they own (Lammers, 1983). There are also indications that the number of elderly living alone is increasing (U.S. Bureau of the Census, 1980).

Political power and activism

The political power of the elderly is expected to grow because of increases in voting participation (largely because of increases in education) and because of changes in the voting-age population. The projected increase in the voting-age population is displayed in Table 12-2, which shows changes in the voting-age population from 1900 to 2030. Persons 65 years of age or older are projected to be 24.2 percent of the 18 and older population in 2020, accounting for almost

TABLE 12-2   **Changes in voting-age population, 1900-2030***

Age	1900	1940	1970	2030 (projection)
18-44	70.1	61.6	54.1	46.3
45-64	23.1	28.6	31.1	29.5
65+	6.8	9.8	14.8	24.2
TOTAL	100	100	100	100

From U.S. Bureau of the Census: Historical statistics of the United States: colonial times to 1970 (Bicentennial edition), Washington, D.C., 1975, U.S. Government Printing Office; and U.S. Bureau of the Census: Projections on the population of the United States: 1977 to 2050, Current Population Reports, Series P-25, Pub. No. 704, Washington, D.C., 1977, U.S. Government Printing Office.
*Expressed in percentages.

one quarter of eligible voters. On the other hand, the 45 to 64 age group is projected to remain unchanged between 1970 and 2030, whereas the 18 to 44 age group is projected to decrease from 54.1 percent to 46.3 percent of the voting-age population.

Greater political activism is projected among future elderly because of their greater numbers, increased education, greater affluence, and longer history of activism (Cutler, 1977; Neugarten, 1974; Peterson, Powell, and Robertson, 1976; Verba and Nie, 1972). The effectiveness and extent of this activism may be lessened as the status of the elderly as a deprived minority declines (Hess and Markson, 1980; Ward, 1979).

Retirement

The retirement of larger percentages of the labor force will continue, as well as the trend toward retirement before age 65 (Atchley, 1980; Hess and Markson, 1980). The better-educated and better-paid workers will be less attached to work as an end in itself and will view the retirement years as an opportunity and not a loss (Hess and Markson, 1980). However, the federal government's encouragement of later retirement by the denial of substantial Social Security benefits before age 68 or age 70 could have a great impact on future retirement.

Leisure

The higher socioeconomic status of the future elderly (reflected in better education, higher occupational status, and more income) should result in more involvement in educational and community organizations, increased cultural interests, more widespread travel, and greater interests for women outside of the home. A greater variety of leisure life-styles are expected to emerge, with perhaps more interest in and emphasis on service roles (Havighurst, 1975).

EMERGING LIFE-STYLE CHANGES

One of the most controversial views of the future of society has been termed by Daniel Bell (1973) the *postindustrial society.* Bell predicted that there would be an increase in the number and preeminence of the technical and professional occupations, with a consequent shift from the production of goods to the provision of services, resulting in an economy that is increasingly based on services. Bell also highlighted the emerging contention in society between those who are dedicated to work, saving, and delayed gratification and those who favor a deemphasis of material considerations, personal liberation through the immediate gratification of desires, and a personal form of functioning based on satisfying social experiences and human relationships. Bell's contentions are supported by Trist (1976), who sees the postindustrial society as moving from an endurance of life's events to a greater capacity for joy, from an emphasis on achievement to a focus on self-actualization, from control of self to an expression of self, and from independence to interdependence. This section will examine what the impact of these emerging changes will have on the life-styles of the future elderly as reflected in changes in work and leisure.

Work

Flexible, alternative work patterns are being proposed. The effort to propose alternative work patterns is manifested through the formation of a National Council of Alternative Work Patterns, based in Washington, D.C.; national and international conferences on innovative work patterns (Miller, 1978); and a growing number of studies on alternative work scheduling (Katzell, Beinstock, and Faerstein, 1977; Nollen and Martin, 1978). The introduction of alternative work patterns is directed toward increasing worker productivity, improving the quality of work life, and providing greater work flexibility. There are a number of ways to provide flexible, alternative work patterns.

COMPRESSED WORKWEEK. The compressed workweek, involving the completion of 40 hours of work in 4 rather than 5 days, has been shown to reduce absenteeism and increase morale (Katzell, Beinstock, and Faerstein, 1977). It is most advantageous for younger, single workers who prefer longer weekends (McConnell, 1980). Research (Balch, 1974) indicates that a 4-day, 40-hour workweek may not be suited to the older worker because of the stress and consequent fatigue. Balch (1974) suggests that older workers should be reassigned to the less fatiguing jobs and should be allowed more frequent rest periods or flexible scheduling.

FLEXIBLE SCHEDULING. Flexible scheduling, often referred to as "flexitime," does not decrease the number of hours to be worked in a given day but does provide freedom for workers to set their own hours as long as they are on the job during certain core hours in the middle of the day. Flexitime is advantageous to workers because it allows time to take care of personal responsibilities during the workday. It does, however, have the disadvantage of often requiring a time clock on the work site (Miller, 1978). Flexitime is beneficial to older workers who may want a more flexible work schedule to break the monotonous nine-to-five workday, to visit the physician, and so on. It may also enable the older worker to continue in the labor force for a longer time, especially when used in conjunction with part-time work or job sharing.

PART-TIME WORK. Part-time work, or 1 to 34 hours of work per week (Hedges and Gallogly, 1977), is advantageous to the employer because it facilitates the balancing of the work force with the work load, promotes greater flexibility in operations, and enables higher productivity for boring and tedious jobs (Nollen and Martin, 1978). Part-time work is advantageous to the older

TABLE 12-3   **Percentage of employed persons voluntarily working part time (May, 1977)**

Age	Men	Women
16-19	50.4	55.9
20-24	10.8	16.8
25-54	1.5	18.6
55-64	2.8	19.4
65+	39.3	54.3

From Deuterman, W., and Brown, S.: Monthly Labor Rev. **102**(6):3-10, 1978.

worker because it is generally less strenuous, results in a smaller reduction in Social Security benefits, and allows for the greater pursuit of nonwork interests. Table 12-3 shows that of the workers 65 years of age or older employed in 1977, almost 40 percent of working men and more than 50 percent of working women were voluntarily employed part-time. Jacobsohn (cited in Sheppard, 1978), in a study of British factory workers, found that 55 percent of respondents, when asked whether they preferred full-time work to retirement, stated that they favored retirement; but only 21 percent selected retirement when asked if they preferred retirement to part-time or occasional employment.

JOB SHARING. Job sharing, or two individuals sharing permanent part-time work, is advantageous to both the employer and the older worker. The employer has the advantage of having an employee pool of people not traditionally available for full-time work (e.g., mothers and older workers). It makes available a number of job applicants with a wide range of skills and allows valued employees to be retained because of the team approach to work. Job sharing is good for the older worker's attitude because it does not have the connotation of part-time work—it is a shared, full-time position that may be scheduled to divide the workday, workweek, or month.

The development of flexible, alternative work patterns such as the compressed workweek, flexible scheduling, part-time work, and job sharing reflects the growing need for more work options through the life span and the appreciation of the changes in work capacity and needs with age. The introduction of work flexibility also recognizes the contributions that the skills and experience of older workers can make to employers as the supply of younger workers decreases.

Leisure

An examination of flexible, alternative work patterns also requires the consideration of the relationships among education, work, and leisure through the life cycle. American society has adopted a "linear life plan" that begins with a period of education, followed by work, then followed by a period of leisure that has been called "retirement." Since 1900 the percentage of work activities for men has declined from 66.6 percent to 58.4 percent; time by men devoted to education has increased by 12 percent; and the percentage of a man's total life span in retirement has increased from 6.5 percent to 16.8 percent—an increase of 150 percent (Best, 1978). Although the average workweek has declined from approximately 60 hours to 39 hours (Morrison, 1982), allowing for steady increases in leisure, a growing percentage of this leisure has been concentrated in old age. Fig. 12-1 depicts a linear life plan with its periods of schooling, work, and leisure and a cyclical life plan with nonwork time redistributed to allow for periods of education and leisure. This redistribution of education and leisure through the life cycle may be accomplished through the mechanisms of periodic sabbaticals and phased retirement.

PERIODIC SABBATICALS. Periodic sabbaticals, allowing yearlong interruptions of work for the purpose of education and leisure, are just beginning. The

French have a system of taxation of employers to provide leaves of absence for the purpose of education and training; a fund would be set up to enable workers to draw out money at various intervals to take sabbatical leaves (McConnell, 1980). Rehr, a French consultant, has proposed to integrate educational loans, disability funds, Social Security, and pensions into a "lifelong drawing fund" (Best, 1978). A less comprehensive plan has been suggested for the United States by Jules Sugerman, a former Civil Service Commissioner, who proposed the reallocation of Social Security to allow for three 1-year sabbaticals at 10-year intervals throughout the work career, with the expectation that workers would continue employment beyond the normal age of retirement in exchange for the salaries paid through Social Security (Herzog, 1978).

Periodic sabbaticals have advantages for workers. Such a plan allows retraining and reduces the possibility of work skills becoming obsolete. Increased employment for young and old are also provided through the temporary withdrawal of workers from the labor force. Finally, worker "burnout" may be reduced through regular opportunities for a change of pace.

PHASED RETIREMENT. Phased retirement allows older workers to reduce the number of days worked while receiving a partial pension. Swedish pension laws were changed in 1976 to allow workers to receive 65 percent of preretirement income if they worked at least 17 hours per week (McConnell, 1980). Selective Early Partial Retirement, a plan developed by General Research Corporation of Santa Barbara, California, enables employees 55 years of age or older who have at least 5 years of service to reduce their workdays to 100 per year, with pay and all but some benefits prorated according to the number of days worked per year (McConnell, 1980).

■ ■ ■

The cyclical life plan, rather than the linear life plan, thus allows for interruptions during the work years through the provision of opportunities for personal enrichment such as periodic sabbaticals and phased retirement. The recognition of and the beginning efforts to implement aspects of the cyclical life plan are important in the context of future leisure options for young and old through life.

THE FUTURE LEISURE ENVIRONMENT OF THE ELDERLY

The future leisure environment of the elderly will be built on the foundation of increasing societal respect for old age. The minority group status of the aged is changing because the number of foreign-born older persons is declining, resulting in more older persons who have not had to face the adjustments brought about by immigration and urbanization of past elderly. An increased social status has been assisted by the growing prosperity of older persons resulting from gains in educational and occupational status. The "young old" (ages 55-75) are now challenging the image of the incapacitated older person and are working toward more positive images of aging and the aged through various forms of activism on their own behalf.

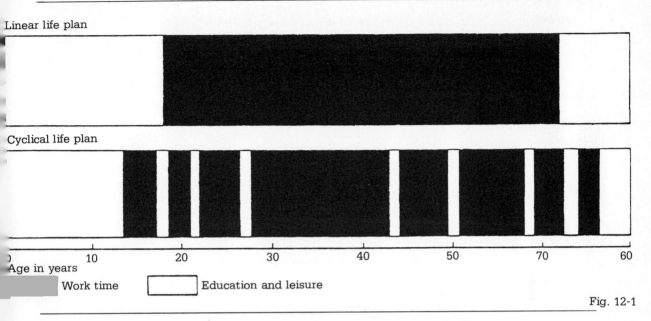

Linear life plan

Cyclical life plan

Age in years

10   20   30   40   50   70   60

Work time   Education and leisure

Fig. 12-1

Fig. 12-1. Alternative lifetime patterns. Linear life plan (the way life is now organized): An extended period of nonwork at the beginning of life is followed by a solid period of work years and then another period of nonwork. Under this plan, most increases in nonwork are taken in the form of reduced workweeks and more time for education during youth and leisure during old age. Such expansion reduces the compressions of work into the midyears of life but maintains the linear progression from school to work to retirement. Cyclical life plan (the way life may be organized in the future): Nonwork time is redistributed through the middle years of life to allow extended periods of leisure or education in midlife.

From Best, F.: Futurist **12**(1):5-6, 1978, published by the World Future Society, Washington, D.C.

The development of the future leisure environment of the elderly is being assisted by efforts to view retirement as a valid life-style built around this respected and prized commodity called leisure. The transition from worker to retired leisure participant is becoming less traumatic because of the challenges to societal definitions of what are age-appropriate or age-possible leisure options. Leisure may indeed become the dominant option for all persons as the needs for food, shelter, and health are being satisfied, resulting in higher-order needs becoming a more possible and probable option for all (Maslow, 1954). Making leisure a dominant societal option not only for the elderly but for all members of society requires that learning about leisure be a lifelong process. As Weiner (1982, p. 23) states, "If begun early and continued throughout life the leisure education process can help individuals prepare for leisure throughout their lives and especially in retirement where leisure and its use is of paramount importance."

SUMMARY

Social forecasting of the characteristics of future elderly is an attempt to make predictions based on currently emerging trends. Forecasting must take place if future leisure services and policies are to be rationally planned.

The elderly in the future society will become a larger and more influential element. The number and percentage of persons 65 years of age or older in the United States is expected to increase between the years 2010 and 2020 to approximately 15.5 percent of the population; however, by the year 2000 the proportion of the population 75 years of age or older is expected to comprise 45 percent of the population over 65 years of age, thus increasing the need for income maintenance and health care programs. A projected major increase in the birthrate during the 1980s should help in the next century to reduce the dependency ratio (the ratio of the nonworking to the working). As a result of advances in disease control, the life expectancy by the year 2000 is predicted to increase 5 to 10 years. Future older persons should experience improved levels of health because of diminished poverty, better education, and more effective health care; however, there may be an increasing number of ill and disabled older persons of advanced age kept alive by medical services. The socioeconomic status of future older persons should improve because of the expansion of opportunities for formal education, resulting in higher occupational status and income. The percentage of black and Hispanic elderly should increase because of increasing life expectancy; however, the percentage of European-born elderly should decline. Older persons will continue to be concentrated largely in metropolitan areas, with increases projected in the number of older suburban elderly, elderly living in sunbelt retirement communities, and elderly in smaller communities. A substantial majority of older persons will continue to live in independent households; in older, single-family dwellings that they own; and by themselves in growing numbers. The political power and activism of older persons is expected to increase because of their greater numbers, increasing percentage of the voting-age population, better education, greater affluence, and longer history of activism. The trend toward retirement before age 65 will continue, with the better-educated and better-paid workers less attached to work as an end in itself. A greater variety of leisure life-styles is expected to emerge and will be reflected in more involvement in educational and community organizations, increased cultural interests, more widespread travel, greater interests of women outside the home, and more emphasis on service roles.

Emerging life-style changes in the postindustrial society will have an impact on the future elderly in the form of changes in work and leisure. Flexible, alternative work patterns such as the compressed workweek, flexible scheduling, part-time work, and job sharing are directed toward improving worker productivity and the quality of work life and providing greater work flexibility, while reflecting changes in work capacity and needs with age. A cyclical life plan, with nonwork time redistributed to allow for periods of education and leisure through the life cycle, may be accomplished with periodic sabbaticals and phased retirement, thus allowing for interruptions during the work years and breaking up the current "linear life plan" of education, work, and retirement.

The future leisure environment of the elderly will be built on the foundation of growing societal respect for old age because of changes in the minority group status of older persons, increased social status based on growing prosperity, and challenges to the image of the elderly as incapacitated. The development of the future leisure environment of the elderly is being assisted by efforts to view retirement as a valid life-style built on leisure freed from societal definitions of what are age-appropriate or age-possible leisure options. Leisure may thus become a dominant societal option not only for the elderly but also for all members of society, provided there is a focus on leisure education through life.

REFERENCES

Atchley, R.: The social forces in later life: an introduction to social gerontology, ed. 3, Belmont, Calif., 1980, Wadsworth Publishing Co.

Balch, B.: The four-day week and the older workers, Personnel J. **53:**894-896, 1974.

Bell, D.: The coming of post-industrial society, New York, 1973, Basic Books, Inc., Publishers.

Best, F.: Recycling people: work-sharing through flexible life scheduling, Futurist **12**(1):5-6, 1978.

Cutler, N.: Demographic, socio-psychological, and political factors in the politics of aging: a foundation for research in "political gerontology," Am. Political Sci. Rev. **71:**1011-1025, 1977.

Deuterman, W., and Brown, S.: Voluntary part-time workers: a growing part of the labor force, Monthly Labor Rev. **102**(6):3-10, 1978.

Easterlin, R.: The conflict between aspirations and resources, Population Dev. Rev. **2:**417-426, 1976.

Havighurst, R.: The future aged: the use of time and money. In Neugarten, B., editor: Aging in the year 2000: a look at the future, Gerontologist **15**(1-Part II):10-15, 1975.

Hayflick, L.: Perspectives on human longevity. In Neugarten, B., and Havighurst, R., editors: Extending the human life span: social policy and social ethics, Washington, D.C., 1977, U.S. Government Printing Office.

Hedges, J., and Gallogly, S.: Full and part time: a review of definitions, Monthly Labor Rev. **101**(3):21-28, 1977.

Herzog, B., editor: Aging and income: programs and perspectives for the elderly, New York, 1978, Human Sciences Press, Inc.

Hess, B., and Markson, E.: Aging and old age: an introduction to social gerontology, New York, 1980, Macmillan Publishing Co., Inc.

Katzell, R., Beinstock, P., and Faerstein, P.: A guide to worker productivity experiments in the United States: 1971-75, New York, 1977, New York University Press.

Lammers, W.: Public policy and the elderly, Washington, D.C., 1983, CQ Press.

Leaf, A.: Long-lived populations and extreme old age, Am. Geriatr. Soc. **30:**485-487, 1982.

Maslow, A.: Motivation and personality, New York, 1954, Harper & Row, Publishers, Inc.

McConnell, S.: Alternative work patterns for an aging work force. In Ragan, P., editor: Work and retirement: policy issues, Los Angeles, 1980, The University of Southern California Press.

Miller, J.: Innovations in working patterns, Washington, D.C., 1978, Published jointly by the Communications Workers of America and the German Marshall Fund of the United States.

Morrison, M.: Flexibility in retirement: U.S. and international experience. In Morrison, M., editor: Economics of aging: the future of retirement, New York, 1982, Van Nostrand Reinhold Co.

Neugarten, B.: Age groups in American society and the rise of the young-old, Ann. Am. Acad. Political Soc. Sci. **415:**187-198, 1974.

Neugarten, B.: Older people: a profile. In Neugarten, B., editor: Age or need? Beverly Hills, Calif., 1982, Sage Publications, Inc.

Neugarten, B., and Havighurst, R., editors: Extending the human life span: social policy and social ethics, Washington, D.C., 1977, U.S. Government Printing Office.

Nollen, S., and Martin, V.: Alternative work schedules, parts 2 and 3, New York, 1978, American Management Association.

Pegels, C.: Health care and the elderly, Rockville, Md., 1981, Aspen Systems Corp.

Peterson, D., Powell, C., and Robertson, L.: Aging in America: toward the year 2000, Gerontologist **16:**264-270, 1976.

Sheppard, H.: Research and development strategy on employment related problems of older workers, Washington, D.C., 1978, Final report to American Institutes for Research.

Sheppard, H., and Rix, S.: The graying of working America: the coming crisis in retirement-age policy, New York, 1977, The Free Press.

Trist, E.: Toward a postindustrial culture. In Dubin, R., editor: Handbook of work, organization, and society, Chicago, 1976, Rand McNally & Co.

Uhlenberg, P.: Changing structure of the older population of the USA during the twentieth century, Gerontologist **17:**197-202, 1977.

U.S. Bureau of the Census: Historical statistics of the United States: colonial times to 1970 (Bicentennial edition), Washington, D.C., 1975, U.S. Government Printing Office.

U.S. Bureau of the Census: Demographic aspects of aging and

the older population in the United States, Current Population Reports, Series P-23, Pub. No. 59, Washington, D.C., 1976, U.S. Government Printing Office.

U.S. Bureau of the Census: Projections on the population of the United States: 1977 to 2050, Current Population Reports, Series P-25, Pub. No. 704, Washington, D.C., 1977, U.S. Government Printing Office.

U.S. Bureau of the Census: Annual survey of housing, Washington, D.C., 1980, U.S. Government Printing Office.

U.S. Bureau of the Census: Statistical abstracts of the United States, Washington, D.C., 1981, U.S. Government Printing Office.

Verba, S., and Nie, N.: Participation in America, New York, 1972, Harper & Row, Publishers, Inc.

Ward, R.: The aging experience: an introduction to social gerontology, New York, 1979, J.B. Lippincott Co.

Weiner, A.: Leisure education for retirement, Lifelong Learning: 6(2):14-15, 23, 1982.

SUGGESTED READINGS

Best, F.: Recycling people: work-sharing through flexible life scheduling, Futurist 12(1):5-6, 1978.

Lammers, W.: Public policy and the elderly, Washington, D.C., 1983, CQ Press.

McConnell, S.: Alternative work patterns for an aging work force. In Ragan, P., editor: Work and retirement: policy issues, Los Angeles, 1980, The University of Southern California Press.

Morrison, M.: Flexibility in retirement: U.S. and international experience. In Morrison, M., editor: Economics of aging: the future of retirement, New York, 1982, Van Nostrand Reinhold Co.

Neugarten, B.: Older people: a profile. In Neugarten, B., editor: Age or need? Beverly Hills, Calif., 1982, Sage Publications, Inc.

Peterson, D., Powell, C., and Robertson, L.: Aging in America: toward the year 2000, Gerontologist 16:264-270, 1976.

Planning for future leisure services

Leisure can become a dominant option for all future elderly only if there is planning for future leisure services. This chapter will consider the subject of planning for future leisure services through an examination of planning orientations, future leisure service settings, meeting future leisure service needs, and a leisure and aging public policy.

PLANNING ORIENTATIONS

Future leisure services with the elderly must be based on informed and rational approaches to the planning process. Informed and rational decision making requires an understanding of planning orientations such as the rational comprehensive approach, interest group competition, minimal intervention, and social experimentation.

Rational comprehensive approach

The rational comprehensive approach to planning advocates a highly rational and centralized form of planning in which governments gather information to make comprehensive assessments and analyses (Lakoff, 1976, p. 652). Governments will as a consequence provide planning guidance that will define the priorities and goals based on analysis of technical information, assessment of the constraints, and the detailed determination of the objectives and procedures necessary to reach the most important goals.

This approach to planning of services for older persons implies a centralized policy based on accurate, technical, and comprehensive information translated into carefully developed objectives. Advocates of this strategy call attention to the deficiencies in the current planning approach, based as it is on crisis planning, stop-gap responses, lack of objectives, and fragmented programs.

Interest group competition

Interest group competition is a form of planning in which interest groups compete in the political arena for the necessary resources (Ward, 1979, p. 515). Goverment's role in this form of planning is simply to act as the arbiter among the competing factions and forces and to serve as a forum for consensus building.

Interest group competition tends to place the elderly at a disadvantage, although the elderly may assume more of a political activist role in the future. Other competing social groups will continue to make demands for the limited resources, resulting in conflict between the increasing demands for services and the decreasing capacity of service providers to respond to the demands.

Minimal intervention

Minimal intervention as a planning orientation encourages flexible services to allow for adaptation to personal situations and to provide a variety of individual options (Ward, 1979, pp. 516-517). This form of intervention seeks to be minimally disruptive of the individual's usual functioning (Kahn, 1975, p. 29).

Planners of services to older persons would seek to make the necessary services available should there be a need. The danger in such a planning approach, however, is not to intervene and thus be perceived as neglecting older persons.

Social experimentation

Social experimentation allows the introduction of a variety of services on an experimental basis to encourage the consideration and evaluation of a variety of service delivery approaches before embarking on nationwide efforts (Lakoff, 1976, p. 654). Older persons can profit from social experimentation as long as there is an assessment of both the impact of the implementation and the impact of services provided (Estes and Freeman, 1976).

Conclusion

Planning for future leisure services with the elderly should thus be based on a rational and informed approach that is sensitive to both the short-term and long-term consequences of those services, that is cognizant of the needs of other social groups and seeks to avoid interest group competition, that is minimally disruptive of the older person's usual functioning while still retaining a commitment to intervention, and that is based on an assessment of a variety of leisure service experiments. It is hoped that the planning for future leisure services will be more coordinated and less piecemeal, more cooperative and less competitive.

The growth of the older population, both in absolute numbers and as a percentage of the total population, will result in a substantial increase in the need for and use of leisure services in a variety of emerging settings. This section explores emerging settings that will have an impact on the delivery of future leisure services.

FUTURE LEISURE SERVICE SETTINGS

There are indications that the growth in the number of nursing home beds will level out in the future as a result of increasing demand for home health care and adult daycare (Pegels, 1981, p. 17). Home health care and adult daycare, as alternative forms of caring for the frail elderly, will be examined.

Expanded community-based services

HOME HEALTH CARE. Home health care has become a valuable resource in many communities. The professional care, along with the social support of family and friends, provides a valuable and viable alternative for those older persons for whom institutionalization is not necessary or inappropriate. This section will consider home health care from the perspectives of definition, objectives, categories of service, funding, and cost-effectiveness; will present an example of a home health care service; and will discuss implications for future leisure services.

Definition. The Council of Home Health Agencies and Community Health Services (1974) defined home health care as ''an array of health care services provided to individuals and families in their places of residence or in ambulatory care settings for purposes of preventing disease and promoting, maintaining or restoring health, or minimizing the effects of illness and disability.'' For example, an older person who is functionally disabled may need assistance with activities of daily living (ADL) such as dressing, bathing, and moving around the house. Home health care services extend an older person's functioning ability, allowing that person to continue to live in and be a part of the community.

Objectives. The objectives of home health care are listed by Pegels (1981, p. 51):

1. To furnish comprehensive medical, nursing, social work, and related care to patients in their homes, whose needs can be satisfactorily met in this milieu
2. To furnish ''better'' care in the home for selected types of patients than would be possible in the institutions
3. To furnish comprehensive care at lower cost than the institutional setting by using the home for treatment
4. To shorten the hospital stay or prevent the hospitalization or rehospitalization of selected patients
5. To improve utilization of existing facilities and reduce demand for more beds by releasing hospital beds for those who need them
6. To expedite recovery, prevent or postpone disability, and maintain personal dignity by restoring patients to normal family living and useful functional activity

It is hoped that home health care can "through coordinated planning, evaluation and follow-up procedures, provide for medical, nursing, social, and related services to selected persons . . . with a view toward shortening the length of hospital stay, speeding recovery, or preventing inappropriate institutionalization" (U.S. Senate, Special Committee on Aging, 1972, p. 25).

Categories of service. Home health care, providing an array of services to meet the needs of older persons, can be grouped into three categories (U.S. Senate, Special Committee on Aging, 1972).

Intensive or skilled services. Intensive or skilled services are ordered by the physician, are delivered under the supervision of a nurse, and usually involve a complex grouping of services. Examples of services that could be included in a complex grouping of services would be regular visits by physicians and nurses and less frequent visits by personnel providing services such as physical therapy, occupational therapy, nutrition, pharmacy, medical supplies, transportation, and other diagnostic and therapeutic services. The provision of such an array of services requires a high level of coordination because of the number of services and the modification of care plans for a long period.

Personal care or intermediate services. Personal care or intermediate services can be provided in conjunction with or independent of skilled care and are given to persons who suffer from chronic illness or a temporary disability related to a chronic illness or an acute illness. These persons are usually medically stable but do need assistance with ADL.

Chore or basic services. Chore or basic services can be provided in conjunction with or independent of skilled or intermediate care and are given to help maintain older persons at home who cannot care for themselves or their personal environment. The homemaker-home health aide is trained to care for both the older person and his or her environment and performs tasks such as cleaning, preparing food, doing laundry, bathing, checking pulse rate, assisting with medications, and performing simple exercises. Heavy housecleaning and home maintenance (e.g., painting and carpentry) are not a part of homemaker-home health aides' functions and must be done by someone specially hired or who volunteers.

Funding. There are five basic ways of funding home health care (Gelfand and Olsen, 1980).

Client fees. Client fees are the most common way of paying for home health care. Agencies providing the service may have a fixed fee for service, a sliding fee scale, or simply no charge at all. According to the Administration on Aging (1977), proprietary agencies are the most likely to charge a fixed fee, voluntary agencies are the most likely to have a sliding fee scale, and public agencies are the most likely to have no charge.

Medicare. Medicare may provide home health care when both the client and the agency meet the necessary eligibility standards. Eligibility narrowly defines in-home services to exclude ADL.

Medicaid. Medicaid, unlike Medicare, is available to fund home health care only for those who meet the strict income requirements. In 1970 home health care became a required service and could be provided by the same agencies that are eligible for Medicare.

Title XX of the Social Security Act. Title XX funds are given to individual home health care agencies to provide certain services to eligible clients. Like Medicaid, an older person must have limited income to be eligible. Unlike Medicare and Medicaid, services are not based on reimbursement on a service-by-service basis but on the amount of money available to the agency to provide the service.

Title III of the Older Americans Act. Title III provides funding for home health care through the local Area Agency on Aging (AAA), with the only eligibility requirement being a client age 60 or older. The service is limited, however, by the funding allocations to both public and private agencies.

Cost-effectiveness. The subject of cost-effectiveness of home health care has been a hotly debated issue because of efforts to contain the rising costs of health care while preserving the overall quality of services to older persons. A U.S. Senate, Special Committee on Aging (1972) report showed that almost half of the older persons receiving home health care services would have required hospitalization if the services had not been available. After 15 years of studying long-term care, using the testimony of hundreds of health professionals and consumers, the U.S. Senate Subcommittee on Long-Term Care (1974) concluded that convincing evidence supports the fact that costly placement in a nursing home may not only be postponed but may possibly be prevented through the use of home health care.

Example of a home health care service. In 1973 St. Vincent's Hospital in New York City developed a hospital-based home health care service for abandoned, homebound, and isolated older persons living in the areas surrounding the hospital (Chelsea and Greenwich Village) (Brickner, Janeski, Rich, Duque, Starita, LaRocco, Flannery, and Werlin, 1976). The hospital used the team approach, with the team consisting of physician, nurse, social worker, and in certain cases a homemaker. During the program's first 4 years, more than 3,500 home visits were made to 466 individuals with an average age of 80. Two thirds were women, and two thirds lived alone. Clients not only had physical and mental problems but financial and housing difficulties and were socially isolated. The program was supported by private philanthropical agency grants, some money from the New York City Department of Health, and $50,000 per year by the hospital. To prevent a client from not requesting or accepting care there was no charge for it. The cost of care was about $105 per visit (1975 dollars), with an estimated savings of $150,000 in hospital and $340,000 in nursing home costs during its first year of operation—about half the cost of institutionalization. Many older persons were thus able to lead independent lives while remaining in their homes and receiving care from a diversified health care team.

Implications for future leisure services. Home health care is expected to remain a small component of community-based services for older persons, but it will continue to grow because 95 percent of older persons live in the community, and 80 percent of those in the community have some level of impairment (Pegels, 1981). There is indeed a great potential demand for home health care.

Leisure services, currently considered to be *desirable* services that may be obtained through community support programs, should be upgraded to the category of *essential* home health care services that are currently eligible for insurance coverage (home health aide-homemaker, medical supplies and equipment, nursing, nutrition, occupational therapy, physical therapy, speech pathology, and social work). Leisure services, it may be argued, are essential to help the homebound overcome social isolation and maintain community integration—essential ingredients for the maintenance and enhancement of physical and mental health. Home health care agencies and the National Council of Homemaker-Home Health Aides should be approached with specific suggestions concerning the inclusion of leisure services in the home health care system.

ADULT DAYCARE. One of the newer resources provided for older persons is adult daycare. This section will consider the history, definition, services, funding, and cost-effectiveness of daycare and implications for future leisure services.

History. Adult daycare began in England during the 1940s with the establishment of outpatient centers in psychiatric hospitals, later extended in the 1950s to include geriatric patients (Gelfand and Olsen, 1980). Crowley Road Hospital in Oxford, England, became the model adult daycare program for elderly patients with illnesses and physical disabilities (Lorenze, Hamill, and Oliver, 1974).

The first geriatric adult daycare program in the United States was established in 1947 by the Menninger Clinic in Topeka, Kansas (Gelfand and Olsen, 1980). A similar program was begun in 1949 at Yale University (McCuan, 1973).

Definition. The National Institute of Adult Daycare, a program of the National Council on the Aging (NCOA), developed the following definition of adult daycare (National Institute of Adult Daycare, 1979):

> Adult daycare is a generic term for a variety of programs, each providing a gamut of services. These services range from social and health related to the provision of active rehabilitation and physical and mental health care. Various terminology is applied: daycare, day treatment, day health services, psychiatric day treatment, therapeutic center, day hospital. It is coordinated with, and relates to, other agencies and services such as senior centers, in home services, and institutional and hospital care. It is an innovative way to organize and blend the more traditional health and social services for disabled older persons.

This definition acknowledges the wide range of services that may be included in an adult daycare program.

Services. Adult daycare centers may offer a wide range of services in a structured program and environment. The range of services could include medical and nursing care, social work, counseling, physical therapy, occupational therapy, therapeutic recreation, education, personal care, and transportation. Programs are structured, with clients being scheduled for a certain number of days per week in activities conducted to meet the goals of the client's individual care plan. The environment tends to be intimate, with adult daycare centers using a high staff-to-client ratio in a setting that serves an average of 15 to 25 clients.

The wide range of services that may be included in an adult daycare program has resulted in a major controversy concerning the priority of particular services provided under the headings of social components and health components. Trager (1976, p. 16) has summarized the difficulties of viewing the social and health components as separate and distinct and thus which is more important:

> The development of centers which set policies and objectives in the context of treatment and physical restoration may tend to exclude those in need of some, but not all of these services. For those who are considered candidates for supervision and socialization, there may be a tendency to ignore essential health related services. Facilities which are treatment oriented may also tend to take on institutional characteristics and to make a "patient" of the participant—an aspect of institutional care which often is counterproductive in terms of the objectives of treatment. On the other hand, major emphasis on a supervision-socialization policy excludes consideration of restoration and rehabilitation possibilities which may appear to be relatively limited but are of great importance to the participant and such facilities might take on the characteristics of current institutions which are "holding facilities" and ignore essential health needs.

The solution to this controversy may be the provision of a variety of community-based adult daycare centers, offering the services needed by the population of potential clients in an area while meeting the requirements of funding sources.

Funding. Adult daycare services may be funded from a variety of sources. Services are typically funded through Titles XIX and XX of the Social Security Act, the Older Americans Act (OAA), revenue sharing, United Way, and direct payments by participants. Title XIX of the Social Security Act (Medicaid) allows reimbursements for adult daycare centers conducted by hospitals and "clinics under state laws," with reimbursable services being medical, nursing, diagnostic, physical therapy, speech therapy, occupational therapy, inhalation therapy, therapeutic recreation, pharmaceutical, dental, social work, dietary, optometric, self-care, and transportation (Gelfand and Olsen, 1980). Adult daycare centers without the extensive medical services required under Title XIX may also be funded under Title XX of the Social Security Act; however, funding is based on the annual population statistics for each state, is limited, and is not always available to meet the rising costs (Gelfand and Olsen, 1980). Most centers face a continuous battle for survival because of the necessity of seeking a variety of funding sources, the lack of Medicare funding, and the debate over the cost-effectiveness of the service.

Cost-effectiveness. Studies vary in their assessment of the cost-effectiveness of adult daycare services, particularly when comparing adult daycare to institutional care. Weissert (1978) found adult daycare to be less costly than nursing home care, leading to the conclusion that adult daycare should be expanded. On the other hand, Grimaldi (1979) questioned Weissert's conclusions concerning costs because adult daycare centers do not generally provide all the necessary medical services nor do such centers include the cost of family or friends helping to maintain the older person at home. Adult daycare services may not necessarily be less costly if all costs of care are considered.

Cost should be examined in the light of total benefits. Holmes and Hudson (1975) propose that a cost-benefit analysis should consider the totality of benefits of daycare. Adult daycare services may be evaluated based on Kaplan's (1976) assumptions, as phrased by Gelfand and Olsen (1980, p. 202) in the form of questions:

1. Do daycare centers enable impaired elderly to maintain residence in the community?
2. Do daycare services improve or maintain their participants' level of physical or emotional functioning?
3. Do the centers increase the participants' independence on basic activities of daily living?
4. Do daycare services prevent or postpone institutionalization of participants?
5. Do daycare services improve or maintain the participants' interpersonal relationships with family and friends?
6. Do daycare services assist individual participants in reestablishing their desired lifestyle or increase their life satisfaction?
7. Do daycare services offer supports for family members involved in the care of an elderly individual?

Implications for future leisure services. Future adult daycare leisure services can make an impact on the quality of life for older persons and their families. Gelfand and Olsen (1980, p. 235) project that leisure services in adult daycare centers will be adapted to meet the needs of an older population with "more diverse experiences and higher educational levels" through the provision of more creative arts and education programming. Gelfand and Olsen (1980, pp. 191, 235) further project that adult daycare services will be expanded to 24-hour service delivery systems, thus allowing families respite and the opportunity to engage in leisure, take vacations, and so on. If projections are correct, employment opportunities for full- and part-time leisure service specialists in adult daycare should be expanding in the future as adult daycare continues to provide services with both social and health components.

Increased establishment of hospices

The hospice is an alternative to the traditional hospital care of terminally ill older persons. This section will examine hospice care from the perspectives of history, definition, importance, services, funding, and cost-effectiveness; will present examples; and will examine implications for future leisure services.

HISTORY. The hospice program of care for the terminally ill has its origin in the work of Cicely Saunders who in 1967 developed the St. Christopher's Hospice in Syndeham, England (DuBois, 1980). The first hospice in the United States was founded in New Haven, Connecticut, in 1971 under the leadership of Yale University (Lammers, 1983). By the late 1970s 59 hospices had been developed and more than 20 more were being developed (Cohen, 1979).

DEFINITION. The term *hospice,* a place of rest for pilgrims and travelers, reflects the concept that a hospice is to be a place with staff who have skills found in a hospital and who provide the hospitality and warmth found in a home. Hospice care is explained by the General Accounting Office (1979, p. 1):

> It is generally agreed that the hospice concept in the United States is a program of care in which an organized interdisciplinary team systematically provides palliative care (relief of pain) and supportive services to patients dying from terminal illness. The team also assists the patient's family in making the necessary adjustments to the patient's illness and death. The program's objective is to make the patient's remaining days as comfortable and meaningful as possible and to help the family cope with the stress.

The hospice concept is thus concerned with caring for the dying person and with providing support to the family.

IMPORTANCE. Hospice care is receiving more public attention because the public has recognized the importance of providing for the needs of the terminally ill and their families. Acute care hospitals, although they have the latest medical equipment, often do not have persons with the training, time, and commitment to work with the dying. Older persons are prime candidates for hospice care; terminally ill cancer patients constitute the majority of hospice patients, and 60 percent of such patients are 65 years of age or older (General Accounting Office, 1979, p. 18).

SERVICES. Services for the terminally ill are provided by an interdisciplinary staff. The physician is an essential member of the interdisciplinary team and has the primary responsibility for evaluating and prescribing the necessary medications for pain, nausea, vomiting, and so on. Nursing staff are responsible for conveying to the physician any changes in the patient's condition so that adjustments may be made in the care plan; they are also responsible for providing understanding and compassion and for attending to an individual's preferences. Social workers help to develop open communication with the families, marshalling patient and family resources for the necessary support of both patient and family. Clergy and other church-related personnel provide spiritual care through ecumenical services and through their expressions of love and concern. Volunteers, after being carefully screened and provided with extensive orientation, may be assigned to particular tasks with individual patients or groups or patients, thus helping to serve as a visible sign of community interest, support, and involvement.

FUNDING. The delivery of hospice care requires the development of funding sources. Efforts have been made to include hospice care as one of the services to be funded by Medicare. Support has come from federal grants, United Way, AAA, health maintenance organizations, and voluntary contributions. Funding should be provided not only for the development of new facilities and programs but also for the recruitment and training of personnel for this very demanding work.

COST-EFFECTIVENESS. Hospice care is a potential means of reducing the health costs of older persons. Hospital and nursing home care for older persons who are terminally ill constitutes a major portion of health costs. However, the actual determination of cost-effectiveness must not only consider the variations in actual cost from hospice to hospice but also the capital construction cost (General Accounting Office, 1979).

EXAMPLES OF HOSPICES. St. Christopher's Hospice in England is a 54-bed inpatient facility serving the needs of the total patient and family of terminally ill through attention to physical, interpersonal, and spiritual needs. The goal of St. Christopher's is "to recognise the interest and importance of the individual who must be helped to live until he dies and who, as he does so in his own way, will find his 'own' death with quietness and acceptance" (Saunders, 1966, p. 74). Although major attention is given to inpatient care, the value of home care must also be recognized; 10 to 15 percent of patients are discharged home for periods before death to provide the opportunity for patient and family to have a period of limited and temporary normalcy (Pegels, 1981, p. 199).

Hospice, Inc. of New Haven, Connecticut, using St. Christopher's Hospice as a model, provides both a home care and inpatient facility for the terminally ill with an interdisciplinary staff of physicians, nurses, volunteers, and consultants (clinical pharmacologist, psychiatrist, radiologist, and physical therapist). The philosophy of Hospice, Inc. is that the patient should be maintained as long as possible in the home, and as a consequence all staff are on call 24 hours a day through answering and paging services to provide medical and nursing consultation, family counseling, and pain consultation (Pegels, 1981, p. 200).

IMPLICATIONS FOR FUTURE LEISURE SERVICES. Care of the terminally ill older person receiving hospice care can be improved through the provision of leisure services. Philosophies of hospice care in England and the United States stress the importance of relieving physical pain and mental anguish while facilitating opportunities to enjoy life until death—all philosophical positions that may be implemented through the programming of quality leisure services. The recruitment and training of leisure service personnel for full-time, part-time, and consultation services with hospice care agencies should stress both the demands and the satisfactions of this area of service and provide special course work in death and dying and experience in working in hospice care settings. Professional leisure service organizations should support regulatory provisions that attempt to assure quality hospice care and organizational accountability for new facilities and services.

MEETING FUTURE LEISURE SERVICE NEEDS

Meeting future leisure service needs of the elderly will require the consideration of new concepts and theories, research, training, information dissemination, and advocacy. This section will examine these critical issues.

New concepts and theories about leisure and the aging process need to be developed. The traditional concept of retirement as an identity crisis is being replaced by the concept that giving up the work role and assuming the leisure role does not have to be traumatic nor demoralizing (Atchley, 1971). Disengagement and activity theories are being examined in the light of age stratification and developmental processes, resulting in leisure and aging being considered in the broader frameworks of the whole life cycle.

New concepts and theories

The leisure service specialist can assist with the development of new concepts and theories concerning leisure and aging. Retirees who have been successful in making the transition from the work role to the leisure role should be asked to share their experiences in preretirement education leisure life-style awareness forums to help overcome the myths surrounding retirement. Lifelong leisure education in a life cycle developmental framework should be offered as programs or courses in community park and recreation departments, park districts, voluntary agencies, industrial settings, rehabilitation settings, colleges and universities, health and fitness centers, and so on. The tailoring of lifelong leisure educaton to meet the developmental challenges of each stage of the life cycle will result in an increased understanding of leisure through the life cycle and could help to expand the conceptual and theoretical basis for future leisure services.

Leisure and aging research must be expanded. Governmental agencies such as the National Institute on Aging (NIA), National Institute of Mental Health (NIMH), the Administration on Aging (AOA), and the Veterans' Administration need to develop research priorities that include leisure and aging. Private foundations such as NRTA-AARP Andrus Foundation provide considerable flexibility in their research guidelines and are willing to entertain proposals that have both theoretical and practical implications. Leisure researchers and leisure service providers need to reach a consensus on leisure and aging research priorities and to present these priorities to governmental research agencies and foundations.

Research

A consensus of leisure and aging research priorities can emerge through a variety of strategies. Students engaged in internship and fieldwork in leisure service settings for the elderly could in the process of submitting reports to their professors share the observations they have made concerning critical research concerns and issues. Research and leisure and aging classes at colleges and universities could survey agencies and settings to determine the most important research concerns of leisure service providers in settings for the elderly. State, regional, and national forums under the auspices of the American Alliance for Health, Physical Education, Recreation, and Dance (AAHPERD) and the National Recreation and Park Association (NRPA) can serve to develop a research consensus of their respective memberships on a variety of leisure and aging concerns and to convey this consensus to research funding agencies.

Training

Training of leisure service specialists in aging must be increased. Occupational Forecasting, Inc. has projected that leisure service specialists (described as a "geriatric social technician") should be firmly established by 1990, having a job demand of 610,000 persons with a starting salary of $15,000 and a midrange salary of $22,000 (Changing Times, 1983, p. 30). To qualify for these positions in leisure services with the elderly, undergraduate and graduate students should not only take courses in leisure services but also in social gerontology, psychology of aging, and health and rehabilitation of the aged. If an interdisciplinary certificate in gerontology is offered at the college or university, the completion of the requirements for such a certificate is recommended for leisure service specialists because the courses previously mentioned may often be applied toward the certificate. Continuing education opportunities are available through the local AAA, activity director's association, state association on aging, and national organizations (e.g., National Council on the Aging and Gerontological Society). Particular mention should be made of the University of Maryland's "Leisure and Aging Management School"; it is a pioneering national effort to bring practitioners and educators together for concentrated course work in leisure and aging and interdisciplinary content in gerontology.

Information dissemination

Mechanisms for information dissemination at the local, state, and national levels need to be explored. City, county, and regional activity directors' associations may be formed to share program ideas and problem-solving strategies. Leisure service specialists can serve as advisory council members for the local AAA, using this opportunity to share program information with the network of senior center and nutrition sites. State recreation society journals should be approached to publish articles on leisure and aging topics; the possibility of publishing letters to the editor or columns directed toward sharing the latest leisure and aging information should be explored. Regional therapeutic recreation symposia should have programmatic and research sessions on leisure and aging scheduled on an annual basis at each of the symposia. The Leisure Research Symposium held annually at the NRPA convention is an ideal forum for sharing the latest leisure and aging research, and that research may in turn be submitted for publication in leisure journals (e.g., *Journal of Leisure Research, Leisure Sciences,* and *Therapeutic Recreation Journal*) or gerontological publications (e.g., *Journal of Gerontology* and *The Gerontologist*).

Advocacy

A leisure services with the elderly national advocacy strategy needs to be implemented. National organizations representing leisure service specialists have been involved in training and information dissemination; particularly notable efforts are those of the aging committees of the AAHPERD and the NRPA. However, there is not a coordinated national advocacy strategy between AAHPERD and NRPA, nor is there a strategy that involves major aging research and service organizations such as the Gerontological Society, the National

Council on the Aging, and the National Retired Teachers Association-American Association of Retired Persons. The barriers among national professional organizations must be overcome if comprehensive service, research, and policy efforts are to be implemented to meet the needs of older persons.

Planning for future leisure services with the elderly will require that an even greater future effort be directed toward the articulation of a leisure and aging public policy based on the best available information gathered from service providers, researchers, and policy specialists. This section will present a number of efforts at articulating such a leisure and aging public policy.

LEISURE AND AGING PUBLIC POLICY

In the Older Americans Act of 1965 the United States supports the right of older persons to leisure. Under Title I, Section 101 of the Older Americans Act, the right of older persons to the "pursuit of meaningful activity within the widest range of civic, cultural, and recreational opportunities" is stated as objective 7.

Right to leisure

The guarantee of an adequate leisure income is a prerequisite for a leisure-oriented retirement. The Older Americans Act of 1965, Title I, Section 101, objective 1 states that older persons of the United States are entitled to "an adequate income in retirement in accordance with the American standard of living." A leisure-oriented retirement thus requires more than a subsistence level of income.

Guarantee of adequate leisure income

The guarantee of choice and change in pursuit of leisure has not been formally stated in current legislation; however, in congressional hearings the subject of altering the existing linear progression of education, work, and retirement that characterizes the lives of so many persons in contemporary society has been discussed (see Chapter 12). The leisure period of life could be changed from the current period of retirement to other periods in the life span through means such as "guaranteed minimum vacations, extended vacations as a reward for long service, and layoffs for workers in reverse order of seniority with supplemental unemployment benefits" (Fritz, 1980, p. 20).

Guarantee of choice and change in pursuit of leisure

Support of guaranteed adequate leisure education through the life cycle has been the subject of national and international policy conferences. The 1971 White House Conference on Aging expressed its support of life cycle leisure education in two statements:

Guarantee of adequate leisure education through the life cycle

> Emphasis should be given at every level of education to implement and expand the expressed educational objective of "worthy use of leisure."

Education must be directed toward an acceptance of the dignity and
worth of non-work pursuits as well as development of leisure skills and
appreciation. (White House Conference on Aging, 1973, p. 7)

Society should adopt a policy of preparation for retirement, leisure, and
education for life off the job. The private and public sectors should adopt
and expand programs to prepare persons to understand and benefit from
the changes produced by retirement. Programs should be developed with
government at all levels, educational systems, religious institutions,
recreation departments, business and labor to provide opportunities for
the acquisition of the necessary attitudes, skills and knowledge to assure
successful living. Retirement and leisure time planning begins with the
early years and continues through life. (White House Conference on Aging,
1973, p. 53)

The 1982 United Nations World Assembly on Aging made two very significant
recommendations concerning life span leisure education:

In many instances, the knowledge explosion is resulting in information
obsolescence with, in turn, implications of social obsolescence. These
changes suggest that the educational structures of society must be
expanded to respond to the educational needs of an entire life-span. Such
an approach to education would suggest the need for continuous adult
education, including preparation for aging and the creative use of time.
(National Council on the Aging, Inc., 1982b, pp. 80-81)

In accordance with the concept of lifelong education promulgated by the
United Nations Educational, Scientific and Cultural Organization
(UNESCO), informal, community-based and recreation-oriented programs
for the aging should be promoted in order to help them develop a sense of
self-reliance and community responsibility. Such programs should enjoy
the support of national governments and international organizations.
(National Council on the Aging, Inc., 1982b, p. 82)

**Guarantee of
leisure services
provided by
professionally
educated staff**

A public policy statement in support of qualified leisure service specialists has
been made by the 1971 White House Conference on Aging when it stated that
"training and research agencies, including university programs which relate to
recreation and leisure, should be encouraged to concern themselves with the
needs of older persons as an integral part of their training curriculum" (White
House Conference on Aging, 1973, p. 54). Support of curriculum standards was
provided by the 1981 North American Regional Technical Meeting on Aging
when it stated, in the section on education, recreation, leisure, and cultural
activities, that "suitable standards of training must be established and developed for service providers by national governments and/or local providers"
(National Council on the Aging, Inc., 1982a, p. 144).

The articulation of concise, integrated, and realistic public policy statements on leisure and aging is a challenge for the future. Service providers,
researchers, and policy specialists in the area of leisure and aging need to take
up the challenge of such a task if leisure services with the elderly are to gain
and retain their rightful position among the services offered to and with older
persons.

SUMMARY

Planning for future leisure services with the elderly requires an understanding of various planning orientations. The rational comprehensive approach to planning is a centralized form of planning in which governments gather information, define goals and priorities, assess constraints, and determine objectives. Interest group competition is a planning orientation in which interest groups compete in the political arena for the necessary resources, while government acts as an arbiter among competing factions and serves as a consensus builder. Minimal intervention encourages adaptation to personal situations through the provision of flexible services and individual options minimally disruptive to the individual's usual functioning. Social experimentation fosters the consideration and evaluation on an experimental basis of a variety of service delivery approaches before embarking on nationwide efforts.

Future leisure services with the elderly are expected to be expanded into the community as a result of developments in home health care and adult daycare for the frail elderly. Home health care provides a variety of services to individuals and families in their places of residence or in ambulatory care settings to shorten hospitalization, speed recovery, and prevent inappropriate or unnecessary institutionalization. Home health care can be separated into the categories of intensive or skilled services, personal care or intermediate services, and chore or basic services, with funding for these services provided by client fees, Medicare, Medicaid, Title XX of the Social Security Act, and Title III of the Older Americans Act. Home health care has been shown to be cost-effective because it helps prevent or postpone unnecessary hospitalization and costly placement in nursing homes. Leisure services in home health care should be upgraded to an essential service because of the assistance that leisure services can provide in helping to maintain and enhance physical and mental health through overcoming social isolation and maintaining community integration. Adult daycare, beginning in England in the 1940s, is a generic term for a variety of programs providing a range of health and social services in the contexts of restoration-rehabilitation and supervision-socialization. Adult daycare services are typically funded through Title XIX and XX of the Social Security Act, the Older Americans Act (OAA), revenue sharing, United Way, and direct payments by participants; most daycare services face a continuous battle for funding because of the lack of Medicare funding and the debate over the cost-effectiveness of the service when compared with institutional care. Future adult daycare should be expanding to include more educational and creative arts programming and 24-hour service delivery systems to allow families respite and leisure opportunities.

The hospice, as an alternative to traditional hospital care of the terminally ill older person, is expected to increase in number and in the future include leisure services as an element of care. The hospice began in England in the late 1960s and was brought to the United States in the early 1970s. The hospice is a program of care directed toward the relief of pain and the provision of support for the family, with services provided by an interdisciplinary team consisting of physicians, nurses, social workers, clergy, volunteers, and other medical and social service personnel. Funding for hospice care has come from federal grants, United Way, Area Agency on Aging, health maintenance organizations, and voluntary contributions. Hospice care has the potential to be cost-effective through the reduction of health costs, but the actual determination of cost-effectiveness should consider variations in actual cost from hospice to hospice and capital construction costs.

Meeting future leisure service needs of the elderly offers many challenges. New concepts and theories about leisure and aging need to be developed to replace traditional concepts of retirement as an identity crisis and disengagement and activity theories. Leisure and aging research must be expanded through the development of a consensus concerning leisure and aging research priorities and the presentation of these priorities to governmental research agencies and foundations. Training of leisure service specialists to work with the elderly must be increased. A leisure and aging information system needs to be developed to meet the needs of practitioners, researchers, and policymakers. A leisure services with the elderly advocacy strategy needs to be implemented involving a coordinated effort of national organizations in leisure and recreation and aging research and service organizations.

Planning for future leisure services with the elderly will require the articulation of a concise, integrated, and realistic public policy on leisure and aging. Efforts at articulating such a leisure and aging public policy have been directed toward the establishment of the older person's right to leisure, guarantee of an adequate leisure income, guarantee of choice and change in pursuit of leisure, guarantee of adequate leisure education through the life cycle, and guarantee of leisure services provided by a professionally educated staff.

REFERENCES

Administration on Aging: Human resources issues in the field of aging: homemaker-home health aide services, Washington, D.C., 1977, U.S. Government Printing Office.

Atchley, R.: Retirement and leisure participation: continuity or crisis? Gerontologist **11**:13-17, 1971.

Brickner, P., Janeski, J., Rich, G., Duque, T., Starita, L., LaRocco, R., Flannery, T., and Werlin, S.: Home maintenance for the homebound aged, Gerontologist **16**:25-29, 1976.

Changing Times: Get the jump on tomorrow's jobs, Changing Times **37**(8):26-31, 1983.

Cohen, K.: Hospice: prescription for terminal care, Rockville, Md., 1979, Aspen Systems Corp.

Council of Home Health Agencies and Community Health Services: Proposed model for the delivery of home health services, New York, 1974, National League for Nursing.

DuBois, P.: The hospice way of death: Port Washington, New York, 1980, Human Sciences Press, Inc.

Estes, C., and Freeman, H.: Strategies of design and research for intervention. In Binstock, R., and Shanas, E., editors: Handbook of aging and the social sciences, New York, 1976, Van Nostrand Reinhold Co.

Fritz, D.: Changing work and retirement patterns: the role of government. In Ragan, P., editor: Work and retirement: policy issues, Los Angeles, 1980, The University of Southern California Press.

Gelfand, D., and Olsen, J.: The aging network: programs and services, New York, 1980, Springer Publishing Co., Inc.

General Accounting Office: Hospice care: a growing concept in the United States, Washington, D.C., 1979, Comptroller General of the United States.

Grimaldi, P.: The costs of adult day care and nursing home care: a dissenting view, Inquiry **16**:162-165, 1979.

Holmes, D., and Hudson, E.: Evaluation report of the Mosholu-Montefiore day care center for the elderly in the northwest Bronx, New York, 1975, Community Research Applications.

Kahn, R.: The mental health system and the future aged. In Neugarten, B., editor: Aging in the year 2000: a look at the future, Gerontologist **15**(1-Part II):24-31, 1975.

Kaplan, J.: Goals of day care. In Pfeiffer, E., editor: Day care for older adults, Durham, N.C., 1976, Duke University Center for the Study of Aging and Human Development.

Lakoff, S.: The future of social intervention. In Binstock, R., and Shanas, E., editors: Handbook of aging and the social sciences, New York, 1976, Van Nostrand Reinhold Co.

Lammers, W.: Public policy and the elderly, Washington, D.C., 1983, CQ Press.

Lorenze, E., Hamill, C., and Oliver, R.: The day hospital: an alternative to institutional care, J. Am. Geriatr. Soc. **22**:316-320, 1974.

McCuan, E.: An evaluation of a geriatric day care center as a parallel service to institutional care, Baltimore, 1973, Levindale Geriatric Research Center.

National Council on the Aging: Aging in North America: projections and policies, Washington, D.C., 1982a, National Council on the Aging.

National Council on the Aging: Aging in all nations, Washington, D.C., 1982b, National Council on the Aging.

National Institute of Adult Daycare: Operating procedures, Washington, D.C., 1979, National Council on the Aging.

Pegels, C.: Health care and the elderly, Rockville, Md., 1981, Aspen Systems Corp.

Saunders, C.: Terminal patient care, Geriatrics **21**:70, 74, 1966.

Trager, B.: Adult day facilities for treatment, health care and related services, Washington, D.C., 1976, U.S. Government Printing Office.

U.S. Senate, Special Committee on Aging: Home health services in the United States, Washington, D.C., 1972, U.S. Government Printing Office.

U.S. Senate Subcommittee on Long-Term Care: Nursing home care in the U.S.: failure in public policy, Introductory report, Washington, D.C., 1974, U.S. Government Printing Office.

Ward, R.: The aging experience: an introduction to social gerontology, New York, 1979, J.B. Lippincott Co.

Weissert, W.: Costs of adult day care: a comparison to nursing homes, Inquiry **15**:10-19, 1978.

White House Conference on Aging: Toward a national policy on aging, vol. 2, Washington, D.C., 1973, U.S. Government Printing Office.

SUGGESTED READINGS

DuBois, P.: The hospice way of death: Port Washington, New York, 1980, Human Sciences Press, Inc.

Gelfand, D., and Olsen, J.: The aging network: programs and services, New York, 1980, Springer Publishing Co., Inc.

Lakoff, S.: The future of social intervention. In Binstock, R., and Shanas, E., editors: Handbook of aging and the social sciences, New York, 1976, Van Nostrand Reinhold Co.

Lammers, W.: Public policy and the elderly, Washington, D.C., 1983, CQ Press.

National Council on the Aging: Aging in North America: projections and policies, Washington, D.C., 1982a, National Council on the Aging.

National Council on the Aging: Aging in all nations, Washington, D.C., 1982b, National Council on the Aging.

Pegels, C.: Health care and the elderly, Rockville, Md., 1981, Aspen Systems Corp.

White House Conference on Aging: Toward a national policy on aging, vol. 2, Washington, D.C., 1973, U.S. Government Printing Office.

APPENDIXES

State agencies on aging

Alabama
Commission on Aging
740 Madison Avenue
Montgomery, AL 36130

Alaska
Office on Aging
Department of Health and
   Social Services
Pouch H-OIC
Juneau, AK 99811

American Samoa
Territorial Aging Program
Government of American Samoa
Office of the Governor
Pago Pago, American Samoa

Arizona
Bureau on Aging
Department of Economic Security
1400 W. Washington, P.O. Box 6123
Phoenix, AZ 85015

Arkansas
Office on Aging
Department of Human Services
1200 Westpark Drive
Little Rock, AK 72204

California
Department of Aging
918 J Street
Sacramento, CA 95814

Colorado
Division of Services for the Aging
Department of Social Services
1575 Sherman Street
Denver, CO 80203

Connecticut
Department on Aging
90 Washington Street, Room 312
Hartford, CT 06115

Delaware
Division of Aging
Department of Health and Social
   Services
Newcastle, DE 19720

District of Columbia
Office on Aging
Executive Office of the Mayor
1012 14th Street, N.W.
Suite 1106
Washington, DC 10005

Florida
Program Office of Aging & Adult
   Services
Department of Health & Rehabilita-
   tion Services
1323 Winewood Boulevard
Tallahassee, FL 32301

Georgia
Office of Aging
Department of Human Resources
618 Ponce De Leon Avenue, N.E.
Atlanta, GA 30308

Guam
Office of Aging
Social Service Administration
Government of Guam
P.O. Box 2816
Agana, Guam 96910

Hawaii
Executive Office on Aging
Office of the Governor
State of Hawaii
1149 Bethel Street, Room 307
Honolulu, HI 96813

Idaho
Idaho Office on Aging
Statehouse
Boise, ID 83720

Illinois
Department on Aging
Monadnock Building, Room 731
53 W. Jackson Boulevard
Chicago, IL 60604

Indiana
Commission on Aging and Aged
Graphic Arts Building
215 N. Senate Avenue
Indianapolis, IN 46202

Iowa
Commission on Aging
415 W. 10th Street
Jewett Building
Des Moines, IA 50319

Kansas
Kansas Department on Aging
610 W. 10th Street
Topeka, KS 66612

Kentucky
Center for Aging Services
Department for Human Resources
403 Wapping Street
Frankfort, KY 40601

Louisiana
Bureau of Aging Services
Division of Human Resources
Health & Human Resources
   Administration
P.O. Box 44282, Capitol Station
Baton Rouge, LA 70804

Maine
Bureau of Maine's Elderly
   Community Services Unit
Department of Human Services
State House
Augusta, ME 04333

Maryland
Office on Aging
State Office Building
301 W. Preston Street
Baltimore, MD 21201

Massachusetts
Department of Elder Affairs
110 Tremont Street—Fifth Floor
Boston, MA 02108

Michigan
Office of Services to the Aging
300 E. Michigan Avenue
P.O. Box 20036
Lansing, MI 48909

Minnesota
Governor's Citizens Council on
   Aging
Suite 204, Metro Square Building
Seventh and Robert Streets
St. Paul, MN 55101

Mississippi
Council on Aging
P.O. Box 5136, Fondren Station
510 George Street
Jackson, MS 39216

Missouri
Office of Aging
Division of Special Services
Department of Social Services
Broadway State Office Building
P.O. Box 570
Jefferson City, MO 65101

Montana
Aging Services Bureau
Department of Social & Rehabilita-
   tion Services
P.O. Box 4210
Helena, MT 59601

Nebraska
Commission on Aging
P.O. Box 95044
301 Centennial Mall, S.
Lincoln, NB 68509

Nevada
Division of Aging
Department of Human Resources
505 E. King Street
Kinkead Building, Room 101
Carson City, NV 89710

New Hampshire
Council on Aging
P.O. Box 786
14 Depot Street
Concord, NH 03001

New Jersey
Division on Aging
Department of Community Affairs
P.O. Box 1768
363 W. State Street
Trenton, NJ 08625

New Mexico
Commission on Aging
Pera Building, Room 515
Santa Fe, NM 87501

New York
Office for the Aging
New York State Executive Depart-
   ment
Empire State Plaza, Agency Build-
   ing No. 2
Albany, NY 12223

North Carolina
North Carolina Division of Aging
Department of Human Resources
Administration Building
708 Hillsborough Street
Suite 200
Raleigh, NC 27603

North Dakota
Aging Services
Social Services Board of North
   Dakota
State Capitol Building
Bismarck, ND 58505

Ohio
Ohio Commission on Aging
50 W. Broad Street—Ninth Floor
Columbus, OH 43215

Oklahoma
Special Unit on Aging
Department of Institutions
Social & Rehabilitative Services
P.O. Box 25352
Oklahoma City, OK 73125

Oregon
Office of Elderly Affairs
Human Resources Department
772 Commercial Street, S.E.
Salem, OR 97310

Pennsylvania
Office for the Aging
Department of Public Welfare
Health & Welfare Building
Room 511, P.O. Box 2675
Seventh and Forster Streets
Harrisburg, PA 17120

Puerto Rico
Gericulture Commission
Department of Social Services
P.O. Box 11697
Sancture, PR 00908

Rhode Island
Department of Elderly Affairs
79 Washington Street
Providence, RI 02903

South Carolina
Commission on Aging
915 Main Street
Columbia, SC 29201

South Dakota
Office on Aging
Department of Social Services
State Office Building
Illinois Street
Pierre, SD 57501

Tennessee
Commission on Aging
Room 102, S & P Building
306 Gay Street
Nashville, TN 37201

Texas
Governor's Committee on Aging
Office of the Governor
P.O. Box 12786
Capitol Station
Austin, TX 78711

Trust Territory of the Pacific
Office of Aging
Community Development Division
Government of the Trust Territory
  of the Pacific Islands
Saipan, Mariana Islands 96950

Utah
Division on Aging
Department of Social Services
150 W. N. Temple, Room 315
Box 2500
Salt Lake City, UT 84102

Vermont
Office on Aging
Agency of Human Services
Waterbury Office Complex
State Office Building
Montpelier, VT 05602

Virginia
Office on Aging
830 E. Main Street
Suite 950
Richmond, VA 23219

Virgin Islands
Commission on Aging
P.O. Box 539, Charlotte Amalie
St. Thomas, VI 00801

Washington
Office on Aging
Department of Social & Health
  Services
OB-43G
Olympia, WA 98504

West Virginia
Commission on Aging
State Capitol
Charleston, WV 25305

Wisconsin
Division on Aging
Department of Health & Social
  Services
One W. Wilson Street, Room 700
Madison, WI 53702

Wyoming
Aging Services
Department of Health & Social
  Services
Division of Public Assistance &
  Social Services
Hathaway Building, Room 372
Cheyenne, WY 82002

State arts agencies

Alabama
Executive Director
Alabama State Council on the Arts
   & Humanities
Gallagher House
114 N. Hull Street
Montgomery, AL 36130

Alaska
Director
Alaska State Council on the Arts
619 Warehouse Avenue
Anchorage, AK 99501

American Samoa
Chairman
American Samoa Arts Council
Office of the Governor
P.O. Box 1540
Pago Pago, American Samoa
   96799

Arizona
Executive Director
Arizona Commission on the Arts
   and Humanities
6330 N. Seventh Street
Phoenix, AZ 85024

Arkansas
Executive Director
The Office of Arkansas State Arts
   and Humanities
Continental Building, Suite 500
Main and Markham Streets
Little Rock, AR 72201

California
Director
California Arts Council
2022 J Street
Sacramento, CA 95814

Colorado
Executive Director
The Colorado Council on the Arts
   and Humanities
Grant-Humphreys Mansion
770 Pennsylvania Street
Denver, CO 80203

Connecticut
Executive Director
Connecticut Commission on the
   Arts
340 Capitol Avenue
Hartford, CT 06106

Delaware
Executive Director
Delaware State Arts Council
Wilmington State Office Building
Ninth and French Streets
Wilmington, DE 19801

District of Columbia
Executive Director
D.C. Commission on the Arts and
   Humanities
1012 14th Street, N.W., Suite 1200
Washington, DC 20005

Florida
Fine Arts Administrator
Fine Arts Council of Florida
Division of Cultural Affairs
Department of State
The Capitol
Tallahassee, FL 32304

Georgia
Executive Director
Georgia Council for the Arts and
   Humanities
225 Peachtree Street, N.E.
Suite 1610
Atlanta, GA 30303

Guam
Chairman
Insular Arts Council of Guam
Office of the Governor
P.O. Box 2950
Agana, Guam 96910

Hawaii
Executive Director
Hawaii State Foundation on Cul-
   ture and the Arts
250 S. King Street, Room 310
Honolulu, HI 96813

Idaho
Executive Director
Idaho Commission on the Arts and
   Humanities
c/o Statehouse
Boise, ID 83720

Illinois
Executive Director
Illinois Arts Council
111 N. Wabash Avenue, Room 700
Chicago, IL 60602

Indiana
Executive Director
Indiana Arts Commission
Union Title Building
155 E. Market, Suite 614
Indianapolis, IN 46204

Iowa
Executive Director
Iowa State Arts Council
State Capitol Building
Des Moines, IA 50319

Kansas
Executive Director
Kansas Arts Commission
509A Kansas Avenue
Topeka, KS 66603

Kentucky
Executive Director
Kentucky Arts Commission
302 Wilkinson Street
Frankfort, KY 40601

Louisiana
Executive Director
Louisiana State Arts Council
Division of the Arts
Old State Capitol
Baton Rouge, LA 70801

Maine
Executive Director
Maine State Commission on the
    Arts and Humanities
State House
Augusta, ME 04330

Maryland
Director
Maryland Arts Council
15 W. Mulberry
Baltimore, MD 21201

Massachusetts
Executive Director
Massachusetts Council on the
    Arts and Humanities
One Ashburton Place
Boston, MA 02108

Michigan
Director
Michigan Council for the Arts
Executive Plaza
1200 Sixth Avenue
Detroit, MI 48226

Minnesota
Executive Director
Minnesota State Arts Board
314 Clifton Avenue, S.
Minneapolis, MN 55403

Mississippi
Executive Director
Mississippi Arts Commission
301 N. Lamar Street
P.O. Box 1341
Jackson, MS 39205

Missouri
Deputy Director
Missouri State Council on the Arts
Raeder Place
727 N. First Street
St. Louis, MO 63102

Montana
Executive Director
Montana Arts Council
235 E. Pine
Missoula, MT 59801

Nebraska
Executive Director
Nebraska Arts Council
8448 W. Center Road
Omaha, NB 68124

Nevada
Executive Director
Nevada State Council on the Arts
Building D, Suite 134
4600 Kietzke
Reno, NV 89502

New Hampshire
Executive Director
New Hampshire Commission on
    the Arts
Phoenix Hall, 40 N. Main Street
Concord, NH 03301

New Jersey
Executive Director
New Jersey State Council on the
    Arts
109 W. State Street
Trenton, NJ 08608

New Mexico
Executive Director
The New Mexico Arts Commission
113 Lincoln Avenue
Santa Fe, NM 87501

New York
Executive Director
New York State Council on the
    Arts
80 Centre Street
New York, NY 10013

North Carolina
Executive Director
North Carolina Arts Council
North Carolina Department of
    Cultural Resources
Raleigh, NC 27611

North Dakota
Executive Director
North Dakota Council on the Arts
    and Humanities
North Dakota State University
309D Minard Hall
Fargo, ND 58102

Ohio
Director
Ohio Arts Council
50 W. Broad Street, Suite 3600
Columbus, OH 43215

Oklahoma
Executive Director
Oklahoma Arts and Humanities
    Council
Jim Thorpe Building
2101 N. Lincoln Boulevard
Oklahoma City, OK 73105

Oregon
Executive Director
Oregon Arts Commission
835 Summer Street, N.E.
Salem, OR 97301

Pennsylvania
Executive Director
Commonwealth of Pennsylvania
    Council on the Arts
3 Shore Drive Office Center
2001 N. Front Street
Harrisburg, PA 17102

Puerto Rico
Executive Director
Institute of Puerto Rican Culture
Apartado Postal 4184
San Juan, Puerto Rico 00905

Rhode Island
Executive Director
Rhode Island State Council on the
    Arts
334 Westminster Mall
Providence, RI 02903

South Carolina
Executive Director
South Carolina Arts Commission
1800 Gervais Street
Columbia, SC 29201

South Dakota
Executive Director
South Dakota State Fine Arts
  Council
108 W. 11th Street
Sioux Falls, SD 57102

Tennessee
Executive Director
Tennessee Arts Commission
222 Capitol Hill Building
Nashville, TN 37219

Texas
Executive Director
Texas Commission on the Arts and
  Humanities
P.O. Box 13406, Capitol Station
Austin, TX 78711

Utah
Director
Utah State Division of Fine Arts
617 E. S. Temple Street
Salt Lake City, UT 84102

Vermont
Executive Director
Vermont Council on the Arts
136 State Street
Montpelier, VT 05602

Virginia
Executive Director
Virginia Commission of the Arts
  and Humanities
400 E. Grace Street, First Floor
Richmond, VA 23219

Virgin Islands
Executive Director
Virgin Islands Council on the Arts
Caravelle Arcade
Christiansted, St. Croix
U.S. Virgin Islands 00820

Washington
Executive Director
Washington State Arts Commission
1151 Black Lake Boulevard
Olympia, WA 98504

West Virginia
Executive Director
West Virginia Arts and Human-
  ities Commission
Science and Culture Center
Capital Complex
Charleston, WV, 25305

Wisconsin
Executive Director
Wisconsin Arts Board
123 W. Washington Avenue
Madison, WI 53702

Wyoming
Executive Director
Wyoming Council on the Arts
200 W. 25th Street
Cheyenne, WY 82002

National organizations pertaining to the elderly

American Academy of Geriatric
  Dentistry
2 N. Riverside Plaza
Chicago, IL 60603

American Association for Geriatric
  Psychiatry
230 N. Michigan Avenue, Suite
  2400
Chicago, IL 60601

American Association of Homes for
  the Aging
1050 17th Street, N.W., Suite 770
Washington, DC 20036

American Association of Retired
  Persons-National Retired
  Teachers Association
1901 K Street, N.W.
Washington, DC 20006

American College of Nursing Home
  Administrators
4650 East-West Highway
Washington, DC 20014

American Geriatrics Society
10 Columbus Circle
New York, NY 10019

American Nurses Association, Inc.
Council of Nursing Home Nurses
Division on Gerontological Nursing
  Practice
2420 Pershing Road
Kansas City, MO 64108

American Nursing Home
  Association
1200 15th Street, N.W.
Washington, DC 20005

American Psychiatric Association
Council on Aging
1700 18th Street, N.W.
Washington, DC 20009

American Psychological Associa-
  tion
Division of Adult Development and
  Aging
1200 17th Street, N.W.
Washington, DC 20036

American Public Health Association
Section on Gerontological Health
1015 18th Street, N.W.
Washington, DC 20036

Asian and Pacific Coalition on
  Aging
1851 S.W. Moreland Avenue
Los Angeles, CA 90006

Asociacion Nacional pro Personas
  Mayores
(National Association for Spanish
  Speaking Elderly)
1730 W. Olympic Boulevard, Suite
  401
Los Angeles, CA 90015

Association for Gerontology in
  Higher Education
1835 K Street, N.W.
Washington, DC 20006

Association for Humanistic Gerontology
1711 Solano Avenue
Berkeley, CA 94707

Canadian Association on Gerontol-
  ogy/Association Canadienne de
  Gerontologie
722 16th Avenue, N.E.
Calgary, Alberta T2E 6V7

Elderhostel
100 Boylston Street
Suite 200
Boston, MA 02116

Gerontological Society of America
1835 K Street, N.W., Suite 305
Washington, DC 20006

Gray Panthers
3700 Chestnut Street
Philadelphia, PA 19104

International Center for Social
  Gerontology
425 13th Street, N.W., Suite 840
Washington, DC 20004

International Federation on Aging
1909 K Street, N.W.
Washington, DC 20006

International Senior Citizens
  Association, Inc.
11753 Wilshire Boulevard
Los Angeles, CA 90025

National Association of Area
  Agencies on Aging
1828 L Street, N.W., Suite 404
Washington, DC 20036

National Association of Mature
  People
918 16th Street, N.W.
Washington, DC 20006

National Association of Retired
  Federal Employees
1533 New Hampshire Avenue,
  N.W.
Washington, DC 20036

National Association of State Units
  on Aging
1828 L Street, N.W., Suite 505
Washington, DC 20036

National Caucus of the Black Aged
1424 K Street, N.W., Suite 500
Washington, DC 20005

National Citizens' Coalition for
  Nursing Home Reform
1424 16th Street, N.W., Suite 204
Washington, DC 20036

National Committee on Careers for
  Older Americans
1414 22nd Street, N.W., Room 602
Washington, DC 20037

National Council on the Aging
600 Maryland Avenue, S.W., West
  Wing 100
Washington, DC 20024

National Council of Senior Citizens
1511 K Street, N.W.
Washington, DC 20005

National Geriatric Society
212 W. Wisconsin Avenue
Milwaukee, WI 53203

National Indian Council on Aging,
  Inc.
P.O. Box 2088
Alburquerque, NM 87103

National Institute of Senior Centers
600 Maryland Avenue, S.W., West
  Wing 100
Washington, DC 20024

National Interfaith Coalition on
  Aging
P.O. Box 1904
Athens, GA 30603

National Voluntary Organization
  for Independent Living for the
  Aging (NVOILA)
600 Maryland Avenue, S.W., West
  Wing 100
Washington, DC 20024

Retired Officers Association
1625 I Street, N.W.
Washington, DC 20006

Retired Professionals Action Group
200 P Street, N.W., Suite 711
Washington, DC 20001

Southern Gerontological Society
Gerontology Center, Georgia State
  University
Atlanta, GA 30303

Urban Elderly Coalition
1828 L Street, N.W.
Washington, DC 20036

Western Gerontological Society
785 Market Street, Room 1114
San Francisco, CA 94114

Periodicals on aging

Activities, Adaptation and Aging
The Haworth Press, Inc.
28 E. 22nd Street
New York, NY 10010

Aged Care and Services Review
The Haworth Press, Inc.
28 E. 22nd Street
New York, NY 10010

Ageing International
International Federation on Aging
1909 K Street, N.W.
Washington, DC 20049

Ageing and Society
Cambridge University Press
32 E. 57th Street
New York, NY 10022

Aging
U.S. Government Printing Office
Washington, DC 20402

Aging and Work
National Council on the Aging, Inc.
600 Maryland Avenue, S.W., West
    Wing 100
Washington, DC 20024

Clinical Gerontologist
The Haworth Press, Inc.
28 E. 22nd Street
New York, NY 10010

Concern in Care of the Aging
American Association of Homes for
    the Aging
1050 17th Street, N.W., Suite 770
Washington, DC 20036

Educational Gerontology
Hemisphere Publishing Corp.
1025 Vermont Avenue, N.W.
Washington, DC 20005

Geriatric Nursing
American Journal of Nursing Co.
555 W. 57th Street
New York, NY 10019

Geriatrics
Harcourt Brace Jovanovich, Inc.
One E. First Street
Duluth, MN 55802

Gerontologist
Gerontological Society
1835 K Street, N.W.
Washington, DC 20006

Gerontology and Geriatrics
    Education
University of Texas Press
P.O. Box 7819
Austin, TX 78712

International Journal of Aging and
    Human Development
Baywood Publishing Co., Inc.
43 Central Drive
Farmingdale, NY 11735

International Social Security
    Review
International Social Security
    Association
Case Postale 1, CH-1211
Geneva 22, Switzerland

Journal of the American Geriatrics
    Society
W.B. Saunders Co.
W. Washington Square
Philadelphia, PA 19105

Journal of Applied Gerontology
University of South Florida
P.O. Box 3183
Tampa, FL 33620

Journal of Geriatric Psychiatry
International Universities Press,
  Inc.
315 Fifth Avenue
New York, NY 10016

Journal of Gerontological Nursing
Charles B. Slack Publications
Thorofare, NJ 08086

Journal of Gerontological Social
  Work
The Haworth Press, Inc.
28 E. 22nd Street
New York, NY 10010

Journal of Gerontology
Gerontological Society
1835 K Street, N.W.
Washington, DC 20006

Journal of Housing for the Elderly
The Haworth Press, Inc.
28 E. 22nd Street
New York, NY 10010

Journal of Long-Term Care
  Administration
The American College of Nursing
  Home Administrators
4650 East-West Highway, P.O.
  Box 5890
Washington, DC 20014

Journal of Nutrition for the Elderly
The Haworth Press, Inc.
28 E. 22nd Street
New York, NY 10010

Lifelong Learning
Adult Education Association of the
  U.S.A.
1201 16th Street, N.W., Suite 301
Washington, DC 20036

Modern Maturity
American Association of Retired
  Persons
1901 K Street, N.W.
Washington, DC 20026

Modern Nursing Homes
American Nursing Home
  Association
1200 15th Street, N.W.
Washington, DC 20005

Nursing Homes
American Nursing Home
  Association
1200 15th Street, N.W.
Washington, DC 20005

Omega, Journal of Death and
  Dying
Baywood Publishing Co., Inc.
43 Central Drive
Farmingdale, NY 11735

Physical and Occupational Therapy
  in Geriatrics
The Haworth Press, Inc.
28 E. 22nd Street
New York, NY 10010

Research on Aging
Sage Publications
275 S. Beverly Drive
Beverly Hills, CA 90212

Retirement Life
National Association of Retired
  Federal Employees
1533 New Hampshire Avenue, N.W.
Washington, DC 20036

Senior Citizens News
National Council of Senior Citizens
1511 K Street, N.W.
Washington, DC 20005

Social Security Bulletin
U.S. Government Printing Office
Washington, DC 20402

Social Work in Health Care
The Haworth Press, Inc.
28 E. 22nd Street
New York, NY 10010

Programmatic resources

BOOKS AND PERIODICALS

Exercise

American Alliance for Health, Physical Education, Recreation, and Dance and North Country Community College: A national directory of physical fitness programs for older adults, Saranac Lake, N.Y., 1981, North Country Community College.

Casper, U.: Joy and comfort through stretching and relaxing for those who are unable to exercise, New York, 1982, The Seabury Press, Inc.

Corbin, D., and Metal-Corbin, J.: Reach for it: a handbook of exercise and dance activities for older adults, Dubuque, Iowa, 1983, Eddie Bowers Publishing Co.

Couey, R.: Lifelong fitness and fulfillment for senior adults, Nashville, Tenn., 1980, Broadman Press.

deVries, H., and Hales, D.: Fitness after fifty, New York, 1982, Charles Scribner's Sons.

Frankel, L., and Richard, B.: Be alive as long as you live: the older person's complete guide to exercise for joyful living, New York, 1980, Lippincott & Crowell.

Garnet, E.: Chair exercise manual: an audio-assisted program of body dynamics, Princeton, N.J., 1982, Princeton Book Co., Publishers, (268-page manual and four audio cassette tapes).

Juengling, P.: Yoga for the over-60, Perspect. Aging 6(6):15-18, 1977.

Leslie, D., and McLure, J.: Exercise for the elderly, Des Moines, Iowa, 1975, Iowa Commission on Aging.

Creative arts

Bright, R.: Music in geriatric care, Melville, N.Y., 1980, Belwin-Mills Publications.

Bright, R.: Practical planning in music therapy for the aged, New York, 1981, Musicgraphics.

Burger, I.: Creative drama for senior adults, Wilton, Conn., 1980, Morehouse-Barlow Co., Inc.

Caplow-Lindner, E., Harpaz, L., and Sandberg, S.: Therapeutic dance/movement: expressive activities for older adults, New York, 1979, Human Sciences Press.

Cornish, R., and Kase, R., editors: Senior adult theatre, University Park, Pa., 1981, Penn State Press.

Curley, J.: Leading poetry writing groups in a nursing home activities program, Phys. Occup. Ther. Geriatr. 1(4):23-34, 1982.

Gold, S.: Educating the new leisure class: teaching humanities to the elderly, Lifelong Learning 6(1):16-17, 26, 1982.

Kartman, L.: The use of music as a program tool with regressed geriatric patients, J. Gerontol. Nurs. 3(4):38-42, 1977.

Koch, K.: I never told anybody: teaching poetry writing in a nursing home, New York, 1977, Random House, Inc.

Lerman, L.: Teaching dance to senior adults, Springfield, Ill., 1984, Charles C Thomas, Publisher.

Reiner, A.: Ethnic music in music therapy: a program for Jewish geriatric residents, Long Term Care Health Serv. Admin. Q. 3:301-306, 1979.

Rissell, W.: Craftwork the handicapped elderly can make and sell, Springfield, Ill., 1981, Charles C Thomas, Publisher.

Schulberg, C.: The music therapy sourcebook: a collection of activities categorized and analyzed, New York, 1981, Human Sciences Press.

Shapiro, E.: Guidelines for a creative newspaper written by and for residents of homes for aged, Int. J. Aging Hum. Dev. 5:365-368, 1974.

Telander, M., Quinlan, F., and Verson, K.: Acting up! An innovative approach to creative drama for older adults, Chicago, 1982, Coach House Press.

Thurman, A., and Piggins, C.: Drama activities with older adults, New York, 1982, The Haworth Press.

Weiss, J.: Expressive therapy with elders and the disabled: touching the heart of life, New York, 1984, The Haworth Press.

Zeiger, B.: Life review in art therapy with the aged, A. J. Art Ther. 15:47-50, 1976.

Education

Gentile, L., and McMillan, M.: Reading: a means of renewal for the aged, Educ. Gerontol. **4**:215-222, 1979.

Harvey, R., and Dutton, D.: Reading interests of older adults, Educ. Gerontol. **4**:209-214, 1979.

Horacek, B., and Francke, S.: Senior citizen celebration days: a university-based education program, Educ. Gerontol. **3**:61-69, 1978.

Marks, C.: Learning in the sun: a winter retreat, Educ. Gerontol. **4**:143-145, 1979.

Okun, M., editor: Programs for older adults, San Francisco, 1982, Jossey-Bass, Inc., Publishers.

Peterson, D.: Facilitating education for older learners, San Francisco, 1983, Jossey-Bass, Inc., Publishers.

Sprouse, B., and Brown, K.: Developing community-based learning centers for older adults, Madison, Wis., 1981, Faye McBeath Institute on Aging and Adult Life (University of Wisconsin-Madison, 7239 Social Science Building, 1180 Observatory Drive, Madison, Wis., 53706).

Outdoor recreation

Bultena, G., and Field, D., and Renninger, R.: Interpretation for retired national parkgoers, Trends **15**(2):30-33, 1978.

Dickinson, P.: Travel and retirement: Edens abroad, New York, 1983, E.P. Dutton, Inc.

Ong, H., and Coleman, M.: For adventure, seniors go camping, Parks Recreat. **13**(4):44-47, 1978.

Rogolsky, E.: Camping? At my age! Perspect. Aging **9**(3):18-20, 1980.

Weintz, C., and Weintz, W.: The discount guide for travelers over 55, New York, 1983, E.P. Dutton, Inc.

FILMS AND SLIDE PRESENTATIONS
General

Priory: The Only Home I've Got. 16 mm and ¾-inch videocassette/29 min/color/1978. Producer: Anne Wheeler. Director: Mark Dologoy (National Film Board of Canada). Distributed in the U.S. by Phoenix Films, Inc., 470 Park Avenue S., New York, NY 10016, (212) 684-5910. Sale: $435 film, $305 video. Rental: $40.

Residents are shown enjoying swimming at a natatorium and experiencing a day of Christmas shopping at a department store. Intergenerational interactions are shown when a group of junior high students come to help wrap the Christmas presents. It is a very positive and upbeat presentation showing the importance of leisure in the lives of institutionalized older persons.

Together We Can Plan and Do. ¾-inch videocassette/33½ min/color/1978. Producer: Ruth Davidow, R.N., assistant professor, University of California School of Nursing, San Francisco (partially financed by Long-Term Gerontological Nursing Project, DHEW Division of Nursing Grant No. 1-D23-NU-00101-01). Distributed by Life and Living Films Center, 1207 De Haro, San Francisco, CA 94143, (415) 666-4694 or (415) 282-9318. Sale: $375. Rental: $35.

The objective of the film is to emphasize that everyone has important input in planning and participating in the care of the resident in the nursing home. A systemized plan is presented for persons in each role, working together to provide better care. The second objective is to present the rehabilitation concept of making the most of what one has left after an illness, in spite of disabilities brought about by disease. The film also illustrates that patients know what they need.

Exercise

Grow Older, Feel Younger. 16 mm/10 min/color/1976. Sale: $50. Pianist Victor Borge offers an amusing talk on the merits of exercise for older persons.

Active People Over 60. 16 mm/20 min/color/1976. Sale: $125. Mr. Borge and several physicians stress the importance of exercise for the body, particularly for the heart. A basic exercise program is also presented.

Basic Exercises for People Over 60: Parts 1 to 3. Slides/15 min each/color/1977. Sale: $35 each. Exercise routines for mild, moderate, and advanced categories are illustrated, with older persons providing visual examples.

Producer: National Association for Human Development, 1750 Pennsylvania Avenue, N.W., Washington, DC 20006, (202) 393-1881. The entire exercise package emphasizes flexibility, strength, and endurance. Explanation is suitable for older persons to conduct their own exercise sessions without guidance, as well as for the more trained volunteer, physical therapist, occupational therapist, or therapeutic recreation specialist.

Health, Fitness, and Leisure for a Quality Life. 16 mm/20 min/color/1979. Distributed by American Alliance for Health, Physical Education, Recreation, and Dance, 1900 Association Drive, Reston, VA 22091, (703) 456-3400. Sale: $350. Rental: $18 (applicable to purchase price).

Older persons are shown engaged in a variety of vigorous and not so vigorous activities. The myths surrounding fitness and the older person are dispelled.

Senior Olympics. 16 mm/9 min/color/1980. Producer: Ron Litrell Productions. Distributed by Jewish Community Centers Association, 11001 Schuetz Road, St. Louis, MO 63141, (314) 432-5700. Available on free loan basis, subject to change.

The first senior olympics in the state of Missouri are shown. Scenes of competition, as well as background information on planning and community organization efforts, are presented. It should be of interest to both senior center participants and to planners of senior olympics. It was selected for showing at the 1981 White House Conference on Aging Film Showcase and has won awards.

Tai Chi: A Creative Life Force. ¾-inch videocassette/27 min/color/1980. Producer: Ruth Davidow, R.N., assistant professor, University of California School of Nursing, San Francisco. Distributed by Life and Living Films Center, 1207 De Haro Street, San Francisco, CA 94107, (415) 666-4694 or 282-9318. Sale: $375. Rental: $35.

The majority of the presentation shows residents of an intermediate nursing care facility as they are led in performing graceful, slow-moving exercises that they visualize in their minds and then allow their bodies to carry out. The philosophy of Tai Chi permeates the presentation.

Thoughts on the Run. 16 mm and ½-inch or ¾-inch videocassette/9 min/color/1979. Producer: Sports Productions, Inc. Distributed by MTI Teleprograms, Inc., 3710 Commercial Avenue, Northbrook, IL 60062, (800) 323-5343 (in Illinois, Alaska, and Hawaii call collect, (312) 291-9400). Sale: $220 film, $200 video. Rental: $45 per week (applicable to purchase price).

   Older runners, as well as runners of other age groups, are shown enjoying their running. It should be used with additional follow-up information because there is no mention of precautions or the importance of medical or other supervision.

Creative arts

Close Harmony. 16 mm/30 min/color/1980. Distributed by Learning Corporation of America, 1350 Avenue of the Americas, New York, NY 10019, (212) 397-0330. Sale: $450. Rental: $40.

   The story is told of an intergenerational chorus of older persons from a senior center and fourth and fifth grade students. It provides the incentive to think of activities that can bring young and old together and helps dispel myths and stereotypes about the elderly.

Sunshine's on the Way. 16 mm/47 min (full version), 30 min (edited version)/color/1982. Distributed by Learning Corporation of America, 1350 Avenue of the Americas, New York, NY 10019, (212) 397-0330. Sale: $625 (full), $450 (edited). Rental: $50 (full), $40 (edited).

   The psychological rehabilitation of TP, an elderly jazz trombone player who has suffered a stroke and recently moved into a nursing home, is portrayed. TP is encouraged to take up the trombone again, and he leads the nursing home band to excellence. TP is enabled, through the support of a 15-year-old nurse's aide, to pursue his lifelong interest in music. The film helps to dispel myths often held by the young.

The Women of Hodson. 16 mm and ¾-inch videocassette/30 min/color/1980. Producer: Josephine Hayes Dean. Distributed by Filmmaker Library, Inc., 133 E. 58th Street, Suite 730 A, New York, NY 10022, (212) 355-6545. Sale: $425 (16 mm), $375 (video). Rental: $50 (16 mm), no rental available for video.

   Nine women in the Bronx at the Hodson Senior Center are shown learning to dramatize memories through skits actually presented before an audience. The women use drama to underline the common experience of older persons. Rehearsals, warmups, interviews, and shots of performances are included. It conveys the message that drama is an activity that challenges the imagination, requires teamwork, and results in the reward of being in the spotlight.

Education

Group Programs Involving the Older Adult. Slide/tape (130 slides, 15 min audiocassette)/color/1980. Distributed by Bi-Folkal Productions, Inc., Route 1, Rainbow Farm, Blue Mounds, WI 53517, (618) 437-8146. Sale: $85.

   These programs use music and visuals to expand the viewers' vision of the many ways that older persons can have stimulating, multisensory, "hands-on" learning and social experiences. Examples of programs are information (e.g., food preparation), interests (e.g., travel), history (e.g., oral history tapes), and reminiscence (e.g., cars).

Retirement—The Best is Yet to Be. Slide-tape/color/five 12 min sections/1979. Distributed by Iconographic Productions, Ltd., 1776 Broadway, New York, NY 10019, (212) 581-3140. Sale: $295 for five presentations with cassette, leader's guide, and scripts.

   Comments of upbeat, actively retired persons spotlight learning, volunteering, working, and being alone. The slides, coupled with the open-ended discussion questions in the leader's guide, present the preretirement planning process.

Outdoor recreation

Ruth Stout's Garden. 16 mm/23 min/color/1975. Producer: Arthur Mokin Productions, Inc., 17 W. 60th Street, New York, NY 10023, (212) 757-4868. Sale: $390. Rental: $40 (first day). Study guide included.

   The film consists of a blend of Ruth's reminiscences about her life and description of the development of her garden. The viewer is moved from a contemplation of aging to gardening and ecology. It is the winner of the 1976 Cine Golden Eagle Award, the Red Ribbon, American Film Festival and the Chris Statuette Award, Columbia Film Festival.

RECORDS
Dance

Dances Without Partners. 12-inch LP/33 ⅓ RPM. Distributed by Educational Activities, Inc., P.O. Box 392, Freeport, NY 11520.
   Easy group dances feature the individual.

Folk Dances for All Ages. 12-inch LP/33 ⅓ RPM. Distributed by RCA Records, 1133 Avenue of the Americas, New York, NY 10003.
   It includes dances such as the Norwegian Mountain March and the schottische.

Folk Dances of the World. 12-inch LP/33 ⅓ RPM. Distributed by Hoctor Dance Records, Inc., P.O. Box 38, Waldwick, NJ 07463.
   Dances of Israel, Yugoslavia, Greece, Poland, Sweden, Turkey, Mexico, Hungary, Ireland, and Italy are presented. Instructions are also included.

Singing Square Dances. 12-inch LP/33 ⅓ RPM. Distributed by Bowmar Records, Inc., 622 Rodier Drive, Glendale, CA 91201.
   This is a three-album set with a "singing" caller. Verbal instructions are presented before each dance.

Square Dances. 12-inch LP/33 ⅓ RPM. Distributed by Folkways Records, 701 Seventh Avenue, New York, NY 10036. No. 2001.
   Calls to both Western and Eastern dances are included.

Exercise

Keys to Life. 12-inch LP/33 ⅓ RPM. Distributed by Melody House Publishing Co., 819 N.W. 92nd Street, Oklahoma City, OK 73114.

Thirty exercises to be done from a sitting position are presented to enhance muscle strength, fitness, and coordination. Instructions are slow and given along with the music.

Light N' Lively. 12-inch LP/33 ⅓ RPM. Distributed by Melody House Publishing Co., 819 N.W. 92nd Street, Oklahoma City, OK 73114.

This record is a program of exercise to music for older persons. The program begins with warmup activities and leads to activities that are not only challenging physically but also mentally. The routines are presented so that all can participate.

The Magic of Movement. 12-inch LP/33 ⅓ RPM. Distributed by Melody House Publishing Co., 819 N.W. 92nd Street, Oklahoma City, OK 73114.

This is an album of activities for those with limited movement—all activities are done from a sitting position. Music enhances the exercises, motivates, and makes movement more precise. Verbal instructions are included for each activity.

Music

Memory Lane. 12-inch LP/33 ⅓ RPM. Distributed by Melody House Publishing Co., 819 N.W. 92nd Street, Oklahoma City, OK 73114.

Sing along with old favorites.

Rhythm Band Time. 12-inch LP/33 ⅓ RPM. Distributed by Melody House Publishing Co., 819 N.W. 92nd Street, Oklahoma City OK 73114.

Basic music for rhythm instruments are presented initially but a progression is allowed as the program moves from slow, basic tempos to faster speeds.

Summary of Older Americans Act of 1978

The Older Americans Act (OAA) has been amended eight times (in 1967, 1969, 1972, 1973, 1974, 1975, 1977, and 1978) since its passage as Public Law 89-73 on July 14, 1965. The OAA has had a major influence on programs for older persons in the United States. Each of the titles of the OAA will be summarized.

Title I: Objectives

The 10 objectives of the OAA as passed in 1965 stressed the importance of an adequate income; the best possible physical and mental health; suitable housing; full restorative services for those who require institutional care; opportunity for nondiscriminatory employment; retirement in health, honor, and dignity; pursuit of meaningful activity within the widest range of civic, cultural, and recreational opportunities; efficient community services readily available when needed; immediate benefit from proven research knowledge; and freedom, independence, and the free exercise of individual initiative. In 1973 the target population was changed to individuals 60 years of age or older from the original target population of individuals over the age of 65. In 1978 the importance of a choice among a variety of community-subsidized living arrangements was stressed.

Title II: Administration on aging

The Administration on Aging (AoA), directed by the commissioner of aging appointed by the president of the United States and confirmed by the Senate, is charged with carrying out the provision of the OAA. The responsibilities of of the AoA include planning, setting policies, gathering statistics, and coordinating efforts on behalf of the elderly at federal and local levels. The 1973 amendments authorized the Federal Council on the Aging to provide the president with advice concerning the elderly; the 1978 amendments expanded the responsibilities of the Federal Council on Aging to the conducting of evaluative studies with emphasis on the number of minority and low-income participants.

Title III: Grants for state and community programs in aging

Title III is the most important component of the OAA because it outlines the agencies and services at the state and local levels. Each state is to have an agency designated by the governor with the major responsibility for providing services to the aging (see Appendix A), and Area Agencies on Aging (AAAs) responsible for developing a 3-year service plan to be submitted to the state. Services to be provided include social services (e.g., health care, homemaker services, transportation, tax counseling, housing assistance, residential repairs, and ombudsman services) and nutrition programs that serve one hot meal 5 days a week at designated congregate meal sites and that provide home-delivered meals.

Title IV: Training, research, and discretionary projects and programs

Training and research efforts of local and state governments, as well as private and public organizations, have included short-term training and the establishment of university multidisciplinary centers on aging. Efforts have been especially directed at training individuals to work with minority, rural home-bound, blind, and disabled elderly. Demonstration projects have been authorized to reduce energy costs, to provide legal services, and to upgrade long-term care.

Title V: Community service employment for older persons

Title V is directed toward the development of special employment programs for the elderly and the removal of age discrimination at the work place. This title stresses the coordination of projects already underway in various federal, state, and private agencies and the delineation of the role of contracting groups relative to the provision of community service employment.

Title VI: Grants for Indian tribes

Grant funds for Indian tribes to develop social and nutrition services were authorized. These funds were to be provided if Title III programs were not currently providing adequate services.

Index

t indicates a table.